Impossible Dreams

A Red Sox Collection

Also by Glenn Stout (and Richard A. Johnson)

Yankees Century: One Hundred Years of New York
   Yankees Baseball

Red Sox Century: One Hundred Years of Red Sox Baseball

Ted Williams: A Portrait in Words and Pictures

DiMaggio: An Illustrated Life

Jackie Robinson: Between the Baselines

Edited by Glenn Stout

The Best American Sports Writing 1991–present
   (series editor for annual volumes)

The Best American Sports Writing of the Century
   (with David Halberstam)

Chasing Tiger: The Tiger Woods Reader

Top of the Heap: A Yankees Collection

Impossible Dreams

A Red Sox Collection

Glenn Stout, Editor

Houghton Mifflin Company
Boston · New York 2003

Library of Congress Cataloging-in-Publication Data

Impossible dreams : a Red Sox collection / Glenn
Stout, editor.
p.   cm.
Includes index.
ISBN 0-618-30398-7
1. Boston Red Sox (Baseball team) — Miscellanea.
I. Stout, Glenn, 1958–
GV875.B62I66 2003
796.357'64'0974461 — dc21   2002191265

Printed in the United States of America

Book design by Robert Overholtzer

QUM 10 9 8 7 6 5 4 3 2 1

Credit lines and permissions appear at the end of the book.

To "the Knights of the Keyboard,"
the men and women who have written
about the Red Sox, and to all the readers
who make that task worthwhile

ACKNOWLEDGMENTS

A book like this isn't created overnight but is built over time. My thanks first go to the authors represented herein. My gratitude also goes to all my friends who have supported me as I work on these projects and to those who alerted me to material that I may never have found otherwise. They include Richard A. Johnson, the late Doc Kountze, Joe Farara, Howard Bryant, John Dorsey, Al Lizotte, Scott Bortzfield, Mike Hourihan, and the late William Gavin. Thank you to Steve Buckley, Jeff Horrigan, Tony Massarotti, Bill Littlefield, Michael Silverman, Gordon Edes, and Dan Shaughnessy, who suggested items for inclusion in this volume. The collections of the Sports Museum of New England, the Boston Public Library, the Lamont Library of Harvard University, and the library of the National Baseball Hall of Fame are invaluable, for they are responsible for the preservation of the words in this book. My editor, Susan Canavan, continues to let me do the books I choose to do, and Jaquelin Pelzer, Gracie Doyle, Larry Cooper, and Barbara Jatkola of Houghton Mifflin always make my work easier. Siobhan and Saorla show incredible patience each time I disappear into the basement for hours, and Sappho always barks when the FedEx truck pulls up.

CONTENTS

PART II: YAWKEY'S WAY

PART III: THE TRYOUT

INTRODUCTION

For much of their history, the Boston Red Sox have been a team caught between the promise of dreams impossible to reach and reality often too harsh to bear. As Sox fans know too well, they are a team whose early potential, with six pennants and five world championships in their first 18 seasons, has not been fulfilled in more recent history, which is to say since 1918. They have gone from a dynasty to a dynasty-always-in-waiting. And more so than any other team in sports, perhaps, writing about the Red Sox has alternately explored and exploited this gulf, often to excess.

Since 1967, when the Red Sox improbably won the pennant, sparking interest in the moribund franchise for a new generation, and particularly since 1986, when — well you *know* what happened then — the Sox have become favorites of baseball's literary intelligentsia. That peculiarly local phenomenon created a new species of writer, one who, upon reaching success in one field, suddenly decides that what he or she really wants to do is write Red Sox–inspired baseball romance.

That has its place, I suppose, but not here. Just as the drought of championships is not the whole story of this team, such overtly literary work is not necessarily the best or most memorable writing about the team.

I became aware of this some 20 years ago when I first discovered the old newspapers and microfilm collections held at the Boston Public Library, beginning an exploration that has continued to this day. I think the best writing and reporting about the Red Sox have come primarily from the writers who have played a role in what may well be the oldest and best tradition of baseball writing in the country.

One can make the argument that it was in Boston that the baseball writer was bred and that here the genre has flourished and taken on significance that exists in few other places. The Red Sox have inevitably been a part of that, for they have often provided the writer with near-perfect subject matter — loss — for loss is, inherently, more interesting than victory. Winning simply requires an interesting way to tell the score, but loss demands more of a writer. After all, the reader already knows, and likely detests, the ending. The writer must, therefore, provide a reason to read on, to revisit the pain, and somehow, from that experience, to rise above the intractable result and look forward.

The best writing in any genre transcends both the moment and the game, and that is no less the case here. Apart from a few stories selected for their historicity, such as Arthur McPherson's account of how the team came to be named the Red Sox, I have selected stories that move me the way any fine writing does — with its ability to take me away from *here* to over *there*.

New York might boast that it was there that Henry Chadwick became the first "baseball writer," plying his trade for the last half of the nineteenth century for the *New York Times*, the *Brooklyn Daily Eagle*, and the *New York Sun*, but it was in Boston that the genre came of age. One can, in fact, trace the history of baseball writing in Boston back to just after the Civil War. A weekly newspaper known as the *New England Baseballist*, one of the earliest baseball periodicals, was published in Boston in 1868. At a time when the Boston Common often had to be cleared of cows before the ball could be put in play, it charted the games and activities of some of the first organized teams in the history of the game — such forgotten nines as the Tremonts and Twin Oaks. And when baseball's first professional team, the Red Stockings, relocated to Boston in 1870, baseball began elbowing its way into the daily newspapers of the city, which celebrated its early stars like no place else.

The Red Stockings eventually evolved into the Boston team of the National League and in the 1890s became one of the most powerful teams in the league. But it was not until the American League was created in 1901 and an AL team was placed in Boston that Boston baseball writing truly began to flourish. Sparked by early newspaper wars and inspired by a team made up primarily of stars signed away from the NL club, the Boston Americans, as they were popularly known, immediately seized the imagination of the city.

Although it was possible to attend a game for only 25 cents, few working-class fans could afford to attend the late-afternoon contests, except on weekends. Then it was left to the newspapers to provide a fan his or her daily fix of information. Writing about the game became almost as important as the game itself, for it was through the newspapers that most fans came to know their team. That is no less true today. Even though the games are all available on television and discussed *ad nauseam* on radio, the writers still provide the context and character of what has happened. For more than a century, Boston's baseball writers have framed and determined the course of the debates as they have tried to answer the age-old question "What's the matter with the Red Sox?"

Tim Murnane of the *Boston Globe,* a former National League player, was one of the first of these local observers. He cut his journalistic teeth covering the NL team and at the turn of the century was the most respected reporter in the game. Like most other Boston baseball cranks, he soon began following the AL team almost exclusively. Other journalistic pioneers, such as Walter S. Barnes of the *Boston American* and Frederic P. O'Connell and Paul Shannon of the *Boston Post,* joined him.

Their task was clear-cut. In essence, it was up to them to re-create the game, to deliver to each reader the experience that just took place at the ballpark. With a flair and style no longer in vogue, they often did a far more thorough job of reporting the actual events than their counterparts do today. One can virtually re-create every game from the newspapers of one hundred years ago. Today, that responsibility lies elsewhere, as the "why" of the result has replaced the nuts and bolts of "how."

Boston, one of the few two-newspaper cities remaining today, has always been journalistically competitive. For the first half of the 1900s, as many as eight daily newspapers grappled for readers, plus an equal number from the other major cities of the region. Yet baseball writing in Boston has never been the sole province of the newspaper reporter, or even of Boston writers alone. Boston was also the birthplace of *Baseball Magazine,* the first successful baseball monthly. Magazine reportage and, more recently, work from Internet venues have continued to enrich and influence the way Red Sox fans view their team. In addition, the Red Sox have always been seen as a ready subject by writers from elsewhere. I believe this multitude of voices has lifted the Red Sox from a regional phenomenon, with all its inherent parochialism, to one with national, even international, appeal.

From the time I was a kid and before I was even aware of it, I collected writing about baseball as others collected baseball cards. Soon after arriving in Boston more than 20 years ago, I discovered the musty marbled halls of the Boston Public Library and its accompanying collections. It was there, in microfilm and old books, that I began to uncover the great, still evolving tradition of baseball writing in this city. I soon became as familiar with writers such as Murnane, O'Connell, Harold Kaese, Dave Egan, and Bill Cunningham as fans are today with Peter Gammons, Dan Shaughnessy, and Tony Massarotti. While at work on a variety of writing projects — a biography of Ted Williams, hundreds of articles and columns on Red Sox history and more contemporary events, even as series editor of *The Best American Sports Writing* — I began to uncover, page by page, this incredible legacy.

I'm not much of a note taker — I find the copy machine to be the technological peak of our civilization — so much of what I found was able to make its way into my basement. A few years ago, looking at the piles of paper that threatened to consume me, I realized that my basement had taken on the characteristics of a sort of verbal baseball mine, one I was determined to quarry someday for a book such as this one. In recent months I have become a sort of miner, digging through those cartons of material. *Impossible Dreams* is the result of that labor, as I've sifted through tens of thousands of pages, chipping away the coal and brushing away the dust to reveal diamonds.

The work I have selected to appear in *Impossible Dreams* is the best baseball writing on the Red Sox that best tells the story of the team. In the end, the result is a sort of a source book of more than a century of Red Sox baseball. It includes not only reportage, features, and columns but also occasional contributions from players and documents from other sources.

Most of the material in this book will, I think, be new to most readers, either never before encountered or perhaps read once years ago and forgotten. I suspect many readers will be delighted to find some old friends here they haven't heard from for a while, such as *Boston Globe* columnist Ray Fitzgerald and the *Herald*'s Tim Horgan. Readers also will find classic tales that haven't been collected before, such as Peter Gammons's story on the unforgettable game six of the 1975 World Series, and George Frazier's extraordinary front-page account of Opening Day, 1973, titled, "Tibialibus Rubris XV, Eboracum Novum V." Frazier wrote the story entirely in Latin but fortunately provided a translation "in case anyone's Latin is rusty," revealing the title in English as the rather pedestrian "Red Sox 15, New York 5." I also think readers will find it useful to read the work of writers they have only heard of, such as the controversial "Colonel" Dave Egan of the *Boston Record,* and to read of seminal events, such as the sad and cynical "tryout" of Jackie Robinson and two other Negro Leaguers in 1945. Although a few selections in *Impossible Dreams* are well known, I have chosen not to reprint stories with which the reader is likely already too familiar. John Updike's classic "Hub Fans Bid Kid Adieu," though unquestionably a classic, has been so widely reprinted that I saw no need to include it again here. With a few exceptions, I have also chosen to focus on writing more immediate to the event at hand rather than reports written years later. And I have chosen not to use excerpts from the many books that have been written about the Red Sox, for the fact that something is printed between hard covers doesn't necessarily make it better in quality.

It is, of course, impossible to include everything — everyone's favorite writer, favorite Red Sox moment, and favorite story — or to cover every event. It is, in short, as impossible to create a perfect book as it is to create a perfect team.

Both are *Impossible Dreams.* But I believe this book, like the Red Sox franchise itself, demonstrates that the pursuit of a dream is not without value in itself. In fact, it may just be why Red Sox fans care about the team at all.

GLENN STOUT
October 2002

EDITOR'S NOTE: In order to preserve the authors' original intent and the historical value of the selections, the items selected for *Impossible Dreams: A Red Sox Collection* are reprinted as they originally appeared. Readers may notice occasional archaic spellings, word usages, and styles.

PART I

GLORY DAYS

From the moment of their birth in 1901, the team that would become the Red Sox was one of the most potent teams in the American League. They were known as the Boston Americans then, and their formula for success was simple: the new team raided the powerhouse Boston Nationals of their best players, such as Irish American player-manager Jimmy Collins, and signed St. Louis pitcher Cy Young, already a baseball legend with nearly 300 wins to his credit.

The Boston Americans were an immediate success, as local fans flocked to the brand-new Huntington Avenue Grounds to see their heroes. The Royal Rooters, led by Boston bartender Nuf Ced McGreevey, became the most celebrated and vociferous group of fans in the history of baseball.

The new team won the inaugural World Series in 1903 over the Pittsburgh Pirates and followed that with world championships in 1912, 1915, 1916, and 1918. They also produced an unending stream of stars whose talents were matched only by their colorful personalities. In addition to Collins and Young, early heroes included Harry Hooper, Duffy Lewis, "Smoky" Joe Wood, and a left-handed pitcher turned outfielder named Babe Ruth.

Spurred by the success of the team on the field, baseball coverage flourished in Boston more than any other place. Paced by Tim

Murnane, Paul Shannon, Walter Barnes, and Mel Webb, Boston's early baseball writers were pioneers. With as many as nine daily newspapers vying for readers, the writers covering the Red Sox scrambled to get an edge on the competition. While scribes in other cities did little more than tell how the runs were scored, the Boston press corps went further. They were among the first to use "Notes" columns and run features and profiles not only on the players but also on fans and front office personnel. They created the template for baseball coverage that was soon imitated all over the country.

Boston was the center of the baseball world, and the Red Sox were its best representative. As one writer smugly and accurately noted after the 1918 World Series, "Boston has yet to lose a World Series."

Those were the days.

RING LARDNER

ODDITIES OF BLEACHER "BUGS"

Listen to Some of the Funny Mistakes
the "Fans" Make

from *The Boston American*, July 23, 1911

If reporters of baseball didn't have to sit up in the press box they would probably like their jobs better. Not that said box is such a dull place, with all the repartee of the scribes, operators and "critics." But it would be much more fun to listen to, and take part in, the conversations in the bleachers, where the real "bugs" sit.

Time was when we liked nothing better than to pay our two bits, rush for a point of vantage back of first or third base or out in the neighborhood of right or left field, invest a nickel in a sack of peanuts, another nickel in a score card, and then settle down to try to prove, by our comments and shouts, that we knew more about baseball than anyone around us.

That was when we spoke of "inshoots" and "outs" and "drops" and "outdrops"; wondered who that was hitting in place of So-and-So and thought ball players were just a little bit better than other people, because they wouldn't pay any attention to us if we drummed up nerve enough to speak to them outside the park.

It was before we knew that there's no such thing as an inshoot, that "outs," "drops" and "outdrops" are merely "curve balls"; before we could identify a substitute batter or a new pitcher by just glancing for an instant at his left ear, or his walk, or noting the way his hair was brushed in the back; before we were absolutely positive that the players are just common human beings and that some of them are really no better than ourselves.

But it was lots more joy in those days. There may be a certain kind of pleasure in brushing majestically past the pass-gate man, strutting along the rear aisle of the stand in the hope that some one will know you are a baseball writer, speaking to a player or two and getting answered, finding your own particle seat in the press box and proceeding to enlighten the absent public regarding the important events on the field, in your own, bright, breezy style. But what fun is all that compared with scraping up the necessary quarter, or half dollar, and knowing you are going to SEE a game, not report it?

The man who is on intimate terms with the ball players, who calls at their hotel and takes them out in his machine, goes to the station with them to see them off, gets letters from them occasionally, and knows they are just people, isn't the real "fan" or "bug," even if he does have to pay to get into the park.

The real article is the man who knows most of the players by sight, as they appear on the field, but wouldn't know more than one or two of them if he saw them on the street, struggles hard to keep an accurate score and makes a mistake on every other play, or doesn't attempt to score at all, disputes every statement made by his neighbors in the bleachers whether he knows anything about said statement or not, heaps imprecations on the umpire and the manager, thinks something is a bonehead play when it really is good, clever baseball, talks fluently about Mathewson's "inshoot," believes that Hank O'Day has it in for the home team and is purposely making bad decisions, and says, "Bransfield is going to bat for Moore" when Walsh is sent in to hit for Chalmers.

He doesn't know it all, but he's happy. He is perfectly satisfied when the folks around him believe what he says, and sometimes he almost gets to believing it himself. He's having a thoroughly enjoyable afternoon, if his team wins. If it doesn't, he knows just why and can tell his wife, his brother or his pal, that evening, how the tables could have been turned if only Manager Tenney had used a little judgment.

His imagination is a wonderful thing. Without it he would be unable to make any sort of an impression on his fellows. He must talk unhesitantly, as if he had all the facts, and never stammer or back up when his assertions are questioned.

Pat Moran is catching for the Phillies. Everybody knows Pat. He is getting a chance to work because President Lynch has set down

Charley Dooin for a "bad ride." A tall foul is hit. Pat gets under it but makes a square muff.

"He's a rotten catcher," says a nearby fan.

"He's a mighty good catcher when he's right," replies our friend.

"Why isn't he right?" queries the nearby one, sarcastically. "He's had time enough to get in shape, hasn't he?"

"No ball player can keep in shape and drink the way Pat does," is the come-back. "I was down town last night and I saw the whole Philadelphia bunch. Pat was certainly pouring in the strong stuff. He's a regular reservoir."

This remark is greeted with silence because no one has nerve enough to come out with a positive denial of the tale. As a matter of fact, Pat never touches the "strong stuff," and if he bunched all his annual drinking into one night, he'd still be thirsty. But that doesn't make any difference with our friend. He has scored a point by seeming to know why Pat dropped the foul ball.

Charley Herzog is on first base. He starts for second with the pitch. Kaiser, at bat, takes a healthy swing and fouls one over the third base seats. Charley crosses second, but is called back.

Our friend is in a rage.

"He had it stole," he roars, "and that bonehead Kaiser went and spoiled it by fouling off that ball. It was a bad ball, too. They must have chloroformed Tenney when they handed him that guy."

If you'd tell the angered one that Kaiser and Herzog were trying to work the hit and run, and that Kaiser would have been "called" if he hadn't swung, you would be laughed at or treated with contemptuous silence. It never happens, on a hit-and-run play, where the pitch is fouled, that some one doesn't say "He had it stole," and storm at the batter.

The Rustlers are at bat in the last half of the ninth. The score is 5 to 3 against them. Jones singles, and Spratt, batting for Mattern, sends a double to right. "Buster" Brown, coaching at third, makes Jones stop there. There is a pretty good chance for him to beat Schulte's throw to the plate. There is also a small chance that Schulte's throw will beat him. Coacher Brown's act raises a storm of protest.

"You BONEHEAD. He could have walked in. Get somebody out there that knows something."

And just because Brown DOES know something, he has held Jones at third. What he knows is that a 5 to 4 defeat is just as bad as a 5 to 3 beating, that Jones's run isn't worth six cents if Spratt doesn't score, too, and that Jones's run is almost sure to be scored if Spratt's, the needed one, is.

Sweney fans, Tenney fouls out and Hoffman takes Herzog's long fly. The fan goes home convinced that "Buster" Brown has an ivory dome. If he stopped to think, he would realize that Jones's record of runs scored was the only thing that possibly could be affected by the act of Mr. Brown, and that there was just a chance that Schulte's throw would have hastened the end.

The argument that Schulte might have thrown wild and thus allowed Spratt also to score doesn't hold water, for good outfielders aren't taking any chances of overthrowing in cases like that. They are just getting the ball back into the diamond, so that some one can prevent liberties on the bases.

Here's one that actually did happen. It was at the Detroit game on the Huntington Avenue grounds on the twelfth day of June. With one out, Nunamaker singled through Bush. Hall sent a grounder to O'Leary, who tried to nail the catcher at second, but was too late. Hooper popped a fly which Bush gathered in.

Gardner hit a slow one over second. O'Leary picked up the ball, but saw that he had no chance to throw out Gardner. He bluffed to peg to Delehanty, who was playing first, and then uncorked a throw to Moriarty. Nunamaker had reached third and wandered a few feet toward home. He tried desperately to get back, but it was too late, and Moriarty tagged him for the third out.

Almost simultaneously the following storms broke from two real fans:

"Well, what do you think of that stone-covered, blankety-blank Irish Donovan letting him get caught like that?"

"Well, that fat-headed bum of a Dutch Engle. Who told him he could coach?"

Bill Carrigan was the coacher, and Bill has no strings attached to Mr. Nunamaker's feet. Nor had he done anything to deserve being called a stone-covered Irish Donovan or a bum of a Dutch Engle.

However, Bill and "Buster" Brown and Pat Moran and all of them are still alive and happy, and the fans are even happier. They go out there to have a good time and they have it. Things are often done which don't please them at all — things that would be done differently if they were in charge. But, believe us, they wouldn't have half as much fun if they were in charge, or if they got in through the pass gate.

Few Boston fans realize that humorist and short story writer Ring Lardner once worked the baseball beat for the Boston American *before finding lasting fame as a columnist in Chicago and New York. While most of Lardner's reportage in Boston was rather ordinary, on occasion Lardner couldn't resist unleashing his eye and wit on the scene that surrounded him.*

Boston, even then, was a town where baseball mattered. Lardner took obvious delight in the atmosphere and never-ending cast of characters that included fellow scribes, fans (known as cranks), sporting men, and ballplayers.

ANONYMOUS

....

RIVAL BASEBALL NINE FOR BOSTON

"Chutes" Leased for the American League
and 25-Cent Games. Hugh Jennings Manager

from *The Boston Post*, January 18, 1901

A club in the American League, the Ban Johnson organization, and 25-cent baseball for Boston is assured. Yesterday the Boston Elevated Company, the owners of the Chutes grounds on Huntington avenue, executed a lease of them for five years to "Connie" Mack of the Philadelphia club, who represented the league in the transaction.

This means that of a certainty Boston will have two teams and possibly three, in case Messrs. Irwin and Hart, the lessees of Charles River Park, succeed in having the new American Association include the city in their circuit.

Lawyer E. J. Moore of School Street, who cited an attorney for Mr. Mack in securing the lease, did not feel free yesterday to divulge the names of the Boston parties back of the proposed club, but that their financial standing is satisfactory is evident from the readiness which the Boston Elevated people showed in granting the lease. In response to a query of a certain bank in the West to which reference was given of the one principally interested in the new club, the reply in substance was that a draft for $200,000 would be honored.

Jennings Manager

Hugh Jennings, the Brooklyn first baseman, and known as one of the brainiest leaders in baseball, is to manage the team. A short time ago it was stated that Jennings had signed a contract to coach Cornell for three years, and was to give up playing to study law, but the statement that he has been secured to manage the Boston club is founded upon excellent authority.

As to the make-up of the rest of the team, it is probable that one of the cities in last year's American League circuit will lose its franchise, and the players will be transferred to Boston.

The negotiations for the lease of the Huntington avenue grounds have been pending for five days, since "Connie" Mack's arrival in town. It will be remembered that Mr. Somers, the owner of the Cleveland Baseball Club, visited Boston a short time ago and conferred with Mr. B. D. Hyde, the president of the Massachusetts Athletic Association, with a view of securing Charles River Park.

Being satisfied that the lease given to Messrs. Irwin and Hart was absolute, Mr. Somers began prospecting for another location. Either the American League men did not care to deal with the lessees of the Charles River Park or else no satisfactory arrangement could be made with them.

Grand Stand Plans Ready

That no time is to be wasted in getting things in order is apparent from the fact that Mack, accompanied by Hugh Duffy called at the building commissioners' office yesterday forenoon with plans for the grand stand to be erected in the proposed park. As the exact location of the stand had not been determined the plans were not filed, but this matter will be attended to within a few days. The grand stand is to be similar to the structure in the baseball park at Philadelphia.

President Ban Johnson and Charles Somers are on their way East and they intend a visit to Baltimore, Washington, Philadelphia and Boston, with a view of arranging the details of the respective clubs to be launched in those cities. Upon their arrival in Boston plans for the laying out of the park will be made, and then the operations will at once begin.

Expect to Lose at First

It can be stated upon the authority of one who was concerned in securing the lease that the American League Boston club is prepared to lose money the first year, and that if 30 per cent of their money is returned this will fully meet with their expectations. The admission charged will be 25 cents, and grand stand seats will be a quarter extra.

Connie Mack's Statement
Seven Cities, Besides Boston, Pledged to the American League

EAST BROOKFIELD, JAN. 17 — Connie Mack, manager of the Philadelphia American League baseball team, and representing Ban Johnson and C. W. Somers, left his home here tonight for New York and Philadelphia. He announced that he had leased the grounds on Huntington avenue in Boston, heretofore used by Chutes Company, from the Boston Elevated Railroad Company.

Mr. Mack said the American League had seven other cities pledged, Milwaukee, Detroit, Chicago, Cleveland, Washington, Baltimore and Philadelphia. They have had Indianapolis, Buffalo and Boston under consideration, and as a result of the leasing of the grounds in Boston, that city will be included in the circuit.

He said the Boston team will have strong backing, but refused to give the names of those interested.

They didn't have any players, an owner, a name, or even a place to play, but the headline "Rival Baseball Nine for Boston" finally confirmed the rumors that had been swirling around town for weeks. In 1901 Ban Johnson was determined to make his American League the equal of the National League and decided to go head-to-head with his more established rival in a number of cities, including Boston. Johnson crony and Philadelphia owner Connie Mack, a Massachusetts native, was dispatched to Boston to grease the skids — er, find a place for the new team to play. He did, securing a lease on a large piece of property on Huntington Avenue, just across the railroad tracks from the South End Grounds, the home of Boston's National League team. Opening Day of a new era in Boston baseball was only three months away.

W. S. BARNES, JR.

AMERICANS' FIRST GAME

Bostons Blanked the Virginians.
A Perfect Fielding Exhibition.

from *The Boston Journal,* April 6, 1901

CHARLOTTESVILLE, VA., APRIL 5 — The Boston Americans lined up for their first game today after a very stiff morning practice, and they made the Virginia University team look like novices by blanking them while they themselves ran up a big score.

In justice to the University of Virginia nine it should be emphasized that Cracraft, their substitute pitcher, was so wild that he put his team out of the game right from the start. He had no less than five bases on balls and as many wild pitches in three innings. Peese and Hansborough, two more substitutes, finished the game, and the Bostons did very little against them, Hansborough, a left-hander, shutting them out without a hit in the last two innings.

Capt. Collins gave his "colt" pitchers a trial. Kane, Connor and Mitchell, each pitched three innings. All Virginia's hits were made against Kane, but the Whitman pitcher was evidently holding back. All three pitchers showed fair form and control, but it would be folly to form conclusions on anything shown today.

The Bostons gave a perfect fielding exhibition. Ferris and Parent did some remarkably fast fielding on the skin diamond. Capt. Collins was very much pleased with the clever work of his second baseman, and seems convinced that he will fit into his infield in good shape as soon as he gets used to his new position.

Jones, Hemphill and Criger did the best batting for Boston, and Woodward used his stick with excellent effort against Kane. The fielding of Steptoe and Stearns for Virginia was worthy of commendation.

It was expected that big "Jack" McLean would be given a chance to show his mettle, but Capt. Collins evidently thought he had been working hard enough. Stahl was the only regular to lay off, and he officiated as umpire. Schreckengost caught the last five innings, and it was plain that his arm was not in shape.

The next game with Virginia is scheduled for next Thursday, when Carter, the most successful of their pitchers, will probably be in the box. Pennsylvania plays Virginia here tomorrow.

COLLINS'S MEN LOSE

10,000 Baltimoreans Cheer Wildly
Floral Emblems and Base Hits Plenty

from *The Boston Journal,* April 27, 1901

Baltimore's Joy

Great Crowd Sees Heavy Batting and Brilliant Fielding — Parade Before the Game

BALTIMORE, MD., APRIL 26 — After two vexatious disappointments the Baltimore base ball "fans" had a chance to celebrate the opening of the American League season this afternoon under clear skies and a broiling sun. It was an ideal day for the national game, and 10,000 people gave the "Orioles" a send off and waxed enthusiastic, while their favorites trounced the Boston Americans by a vigorous use of the bat. There was no time in the game when the local "fans" were a bit uneasy. It was a good game to advertise the "Orioles with their own people, but could hardly be claimed as such to anyone else."

The Parade Before

To help along the local enthusiasm a parade of ball players, club and city officials, trades unions and rooters, all in carriages, followed a band through the principal streets. The procession started from the Eutaw House at 1 o'clock, and reached the new and attractive base ball park about 2:20. Everywhere along the line the greatest interest was manifested, and Baltimore showed plainly that she is ready for base ball again. One barge, carrying a load of youngsters in white base ball uniforms, flaunted a placard which read thus: "Farewell, National; Welcome, American League."

President Ban Johnson came over to Baltimore with President Somers of the Boston club, and threw out the first ball when Umpire Cantillion started the game. There were presentations of bouquets and floral designs a plenty, and Capt. Collins, among others, was presented with an elaborate piece with the words, "Welcome, Boston," handsomely designed with carnations.

McGinnity in the Box

McGinnity, the "Iron man," was selected to go into the box, and though he has been sick with malaria, he allowed the Bostons only three hits up to the eighth inning, when he appeared to weaken. He served up his old choice assortment of deliveries, and it was "all off" before the game was well under way. Kellum, the ex-Indianapolis southpaw, was in the box for Boston, and he was bumped hard at the start and near the finish. The length of some of those opening hits was amazing, and it did not matter much how deeply the outfielders played, the batsmen found room enough beyond them. It recalled the lively ball of brotherhood days. There was not a hit made in the first six innings, and there were seven of them that did not count for extra bases. Three of them were triples and the rest doubles. In fact the Baltimores made only three singles in the game.

The Heavy Hitters

McGraw, Donlin, Keister, Jackson and Criger did the best hitting of the game. In the finish big "Jack" McLean was sent up to the plate to bat for Kellum, and as he walked up the crowd took in his size at once, and soon everyone was shouting, "Whoa, whoa," in anticipation that the ball would suffer. He did not wait for a real good one, but just threw his bat at a ball on the outside, and it sailed up against the right field fence. It was good for two bases, and thus the big fellow had the laugh on his good-natured tormentors. "Jimmy" Collins hit very hard, but not in the best of luck.

Fine Work in the Outfield

The contest was marked by some very brilliant fielding, especially by the outer guards, who were kept constantly upon the jump. "Tommy" Dowd and "Chick" Stahl made several great catches after long runs and Parent showed up well at short. Criger caught a beautiful game. For Baltimore McGraw made a wonderful catch of Dowd's foul fly in the third inning. The surprise of the game was young Jackson, whom McGraw signed from the lots about Philadelphia. They say that "Mac" did not know the lad's first name before the game, but now he is the "fans'" "white-haired boy." He made one brilliant catch close in and kept in the running in batting sending in runs with both his hits.

The Early Innings

The Bostons went out in quick order in the first inning, but not so the "Orioles." McGraw banged a double against the right field fence and "Mike" Donlin made Stahl and Hemphill leg it for a three-bagger almost to the club house at right centre. Williams drew a base on balls and Keister whacked the ball so hard to right that Williams scored from first, and three runs were in with no one out. It was a two-bagger. Seymour struck out and the next two men were easy.

In the second inning, with one down, Freeman and Parent drew passes to first, but Ferris and Criger could not help things along. Donlin opened the third inning with another terrific three-bagger and the ball Williams hit seemed to have the same ticket, but "Chick" Stahl got under it by splendid running and great judgment. It served a purpose, however, as Donlin walked home.

Capt. Collins opened the hitting and the run-getting for the Bostons by lining a beautiful two-bagger to left with one out in the fourth inning. Robinson's throw to second, with no one covering the bag, put "Jimmy" on third, and Freeman's pretty single to left brought him home. Parent flied out to Jackson and "Buck" died at second in an attempt to steal.

With one out in the fifth, McGraw hit for two bases, but Criger made a monkey of him when he tried to steal third. Donlin, who drew his base, was run down between first and second.

The Game Won

With Williams out in the sixth, Keister hit to second for three bases, and "Si" Seymour was given his base. "Si" stole and Keister came home on the throw. Jackson drove the ball to left for a double, scoring Seymour. The next two men went out, leaving Jackson at third.

Louis Criger put the Bostons in the game again in the eighth inning by leading off with a fine double to right. Kellum scratched a hit toward third and Dowd singled just over Keister's head, scoring Criger. Hemphill drew his base on balls, filling the bases. "Chick" Stahl cut loose at the first ball and fouled out to Robinson. Collins made a gallant attempt to clear the bases with a terrific liner to left, but Donlin got in front of it. Kellum scored. Freeman, too, tried to do business, but Seymour played deep and it was all off.

The "Orioles" clinched the game in the eighth. Keister opened with a base hit and Seymour followed with a safe bunt. Jackson made himself solid with a single, Keister coming home. A base on balls by Foutz filled the bases, and "Jimmy" Collins's failure to stop Robinson's grounder let two more runs in. McGinnity bunted, but forced Robinson at second. McGraw forced McGinnity and Foutz scored. Donlin fouled out to Hemphill.

Boston's Final Spurt

With one out in the ninth the Bostons made a spurt and added three runs to their tally sheet. A wild throw by Williams gave Ferris his base, and Criger put him on third with a fine drive to right centre. McLean was sent up to bat for Kellum amid the murmurs of wonder at his size. He made good with a two-bagger against the right-field fence, and Ferris came home. Criger followed him in on Keister's fumble of Dowd's grounder. Hemphill's fly brought McLean across the plate. Stahl closed the game with a grounder to Keister.

Notes

Today the Baltimoreans gave their sixth opening to base ball after being out of the game each time. They say they are in it to stay this time.

Cantillion hustled the game along and it would have rivaled the National League game had it not been for the numerous presentations of flowers.

The University of Pennsylvania team saw the game in uniform. They came to Baltimore under a misunderstanding to play the University of Maryland nine.

"Cy" Young is likely to do the pitching for Boston tomorrow, and Howell will probably do the same for Baltimore.

*   *   *

Barnes, along with Tim Murnane, was one of Boston's foremost baseball reporters during the Red Sox's first few seasons. His initial reports on the team are perhaps the most detailed of any Boston reporter's. At a time when most newspapers barely reported spring training happenings, Barnes accompanied the team to their initial spring training camp held in Hot Springs, Arkansas.

BOSTON AMERICANS ARE THE CHAMPIONS OF THE WORLD

Win the Series 5 to 3. Outhit and Outfield
Pirates. Victorious in Last Four Games.
Billy Dineen is the Star in the Final.
Pirates Get Four Hits and a Shutout.
Hats off to the World's champions.

from *The Boston Post,* October 14, 1903

By defeating the National league champions from Pittsburg at the Huntington-av grounds yesterday, the Boston Americans made it five victories out of eight games played, which gives them a clear title to the highest honor ever achieved in baseball.

The closing play of the series was a thrilling climax to the greatest sporting event ever known in this country.

From one end of the country to the other eager ears were alert for the tick of the telegraph instrument that would announce the victor.

The crowd rushed onto the field and the leaders grabbed Dineen, Collins, Parent, Stahl and Ferris, hoisting them on their shoulders and carried them to the stand.

All of the players were surrounded by a cheering band of baseball enthusiasts the bunch of loyal rooters being conspicuous and cheered, and jabbed and cheered again and again. Everyone in the crowd seemed anxious to secure one of the victorious players as a human souvenir.

The defeated team was entirely overlooked, the gallant Phillippi never lost head or heart and offered his hand in congratulation to Capt. Collins as they were passing.

For fully 15 minutes after the game was over the crowd remained to extend all-round congratulations.

Crowd Knew Baseball

The crowd was small owing to the weather conditions, but a more thoroughly representative baseball gathering was never pressed into one ball park.

For there were present the old-time professional player, who had brought championships to Boston; the college player and the genuine amateur, the coming player; the "fan," and the man who enjoys all honest sport, and quite a number of women; all were there, and while there was nothing but praise for Pittsburg all were forced to admit that the American league had the "joker" in the Boston club.

It was a grand game and a glorious finish.

No man of good judgment, after witnessing both champions at work through a summer's campaign, had picked either team for a sure winner. Pittsburg looked strong when Boston looked only fairly so. The close of the series, however, has forced all fair minded critics to award the palm for greatness to Collins' boys, for they outfielded, outbatted, outpitched and outnerved the Pirates, and won the series strictly on the merits of clean and clever baseball. They wound up with a shutout, Dineen's second, and won both of these games by the same score.

From the time that Beaumont went out on strikes at the opening, until Wagner was disposed of in like manner at the close yesterday, the contending ball players were as serious as they could be. There was no by-play, no mixing up. Every man was bent on doing his best, and everyone knew that the least slip up might turn the tide of battle. This was particularly noticeable until Boston scored the first run of the game. This meant a great deal to the boys, for, strangely enough, the club to make the first run has in every case come out a winner in the series and the players are peculiarly superstitious.

The players had heard the wildcat stories of how the series had been fixed. It was the same old story, started by thoughtless people and cold-blooded enemies of the national game. It was an insult to the sport, and as far from the truth as Deer island is from the north pole.

To win the game and have a fighting chance tomorrow, Cap.

Clarke sent in, for the fifth time, Phillippi, his greatest pitcher. The young man had won every game credited to the league champions, and he was willing to make the effort of his life in an attempt to stop the American champions.

Fred Clarke figured that if he could win yesterday Boston would lose some of its confidence, and Brever would be sent in for the last game with Phillippi still in harness and able to help out.

The Pittsburg men had confidence in Phillippi, and were bent on mischief.

Capt. Collins, however, knew that Billy Dineen had the nerve for a grueling contest, and Willie was anxious to show what he could do. Uncle Cy Young was kept ready for an emergency, however.

Dineen went through the game with the index finger of his pitching hand in bad shape, the skin having peeled off. Cy Young and Farrell worked constantly back of the stand during the last four innings, and Cy was ready to go in if Dineen gave out.

Duke Farrell would come through the alley from back of the grand stand, and take a mental note of Dineen's work, and then go back to continue the warming up process with Cy.

When he came to look in the ninth inning the Syracuse boy was still cutting loose, and Farrell remarked: "Bill will stay all right; now watch him burn them over." The tip was a good one, and Farrell chuckled as each fast one went smash into Criger's big mitt.

Never were ball players more bent on winning a game, and the spectators will have a story to tell about the most important game ever played and won since the sport was introduced at the Elysian fields of Hoboken in 1845.

Capt. Collins decided to play the game if it were possible to play. "I don't care if there isn't 10 people at the grounds," said the captain. "We have as good a chance as Pittsburg, and the sooner the series is over the better for us."

A dark day and damp grounds gave Boston a shade the better of it, as Dineen is fond of lowering clouds, and the flying Pirates enjoy a bright sunshine.

When the teams lined up for practice, they found about 150 royal rooters occupying chairs on the field in front of the grand stand, and with them was the Letter Carriers' band ready to play Tessie and other popular selections.

The practice work was slow, owing to the damp grounds. The game was enlivened by music, and that familiar mascot tune of "Tessie," with Charley Waldron leading.

The Boston players could fully appreciate the meaning of this tune, for it was a solace and comfort to them when the wild children of the Monongahela and Allegheny were howling like wolves to shake their nerves and stop the downfall of the league champions. "Tessie" will evermore stand well with the admirers of the American league, and the royal rooters who took such a prominent part in landing Boston a winner.

How the Game Was Won

The game was called by Hank O'Day behind the bat. Beaumont was the first man to face Dineen and he was fanned to the delight of the crowd. "Dineen must be right to dispose of that boy so easily," said a lone Pittsburg man in the front row. Clarke lined the ball to left but it never reached the turf for Freddie Parent dashed back and made a flying leap forking the ball out of the air with one hand. It was one of the finest catches ever made on the grounds. The applause had the true ring. Leach sent out one to Stahl.

Then Boston had an inning. Pat Dougherty, the great batsman, was unable to connect safely with Dr. Phillippi's pills. Pat sent a fly out to Beaumont. Collins singled to right. Sebring making a fine stop of the grounder headed for the crowd. Stahl gave Beaumont a fly close to the ropes and Freeman flied out to Clarke.

It was evident that Boston was bound to hit the ball, and that sooner or later some one of the home team would get in a few of those three-base hits so important in the series.

Wagner was the first man up in the second, and the band played a few bars of "Down Where the Wurzburger Flows." A long fly to Dougherty was the best Hans could offer. Bransfield flied out to Freeman close to a bunch of snap shot instruments on the foul line. Ritchey was fanned.

The band played "Tessie," and the rooters sang a verse with Lieut McGreevy beating time with a megaphone.

Parent and Lachance were disposed of at first. Ferris and Criger followed with singles but Dineen struck out.

In the third, the three Pirates up failed to reach first, Dineen making two assists and Parent one.

For Boston Dougherty was called out on strikes the third ball a high wide drop looked to be out of his reach. This pleased the Pittsburg man in the stand, and he sang out to "keep it up." Collins and Stahl sent out long flies showing that Phillippi was not as troublesome as in the first two games.

In the fourth Pittsburg started the batting with the top of the list. Beaumont hit weakly and was thrown out by Ferris, the latter making a point to play well in and come fast for grounders from Beaumont. Fred Clarke hit close to the foul line, but was called back, and was disposed of on strikes. He threw his bat viciously and said something not taught at Sunday school. Leach drew a pass and started for second. Wagner hitting straight at short. Parent started to cover second, but tried to return and slipped. Ritchey going to third. Then came a case of calling the turn, and Criger won out. Wagner started for second. Criger made a full swing to let the ball go to second and, turning, caught Leach off third for third out. The band played and the whole crowd joined in the applause. Right here is where Boston got into the game. Buck Freeman, the first man up, smashed one over the ropes in left center for three bases. Parent dropped one a few feet from the plate and reached first before the ball. Lachance hit a weak grounder that Bransfield picked up and tossed to Leach, who covered first. Freeman holding third, and Parent slipping down to second. Hobe Ferris was implored to hit her out, and he made good with a ringing single to right center, scoring Freeman and Parent. The band played, the rooters sang, and the crowd from one end of the field to the other applauded the winning hit of the game. Criger put Ferris on second with an out. Dineen made a sharp single to right and Ferris tried to score, but was thrown out by a yard, Sebring handling the ball in fine style.

With two out in the fifth Sebring drove a fierce liner to left. Dougherty slightly misjudged the ball and then saw Sebring walk to third as the ball went past the ropes. Dineen put on extra speed and fanned Phelps.

Boston went out in order. Leach contributing a fast play on Collins' grounder along the line.

Phillippi opened the sixth with a sharp single to left. Then came a lightning play by Criger. Dineen put in his finest work and fanned Beaumont, who first tried to bunt with Collins watching him as cat would watch a mouse. Beaumont chased a slow drop for the third strike. Criger snapped the ball to first and Phillippi was blocked off and touched out by Lachance. This was the time to celebrate. The band played "Tessie" and the rooters sang, the entire crowd joining in the jubilee for it was the winning play and checked a sport by the visitors. Clarke singled only to see Leach fly out to Dougherty.

With two out in this inning George Lachance hit through the ropes in right field for three bases, and jogged home on Ferris' sharp single to center. Criger singled, but was forced by Dineen.

"Hold them, boys," was Capt. Collins' admonition, as he took the field for the seventh. With two men disposed of Ritchey worked in a base on balls. Then Sebring hit to Dineen and was out at first.

One Boston man got to first in this inning on Wagner's wild throw, after which not a man on either side reached first base. Clarke was the first man up in the ninth, and drove a fierce liner to the left that Dougherty pulled in. Leach was an easy out to Buck Freeman. Then came the final play described above, and the victory dance of the Comanches.

Pirates Doomed from Start

The Pittsburg club was doomed as soon as William Dineen threw the first ball across the plate. He had several points the best of Phillippi, and the Boston players were quick to notice the advantage.

Hobe Ferris, who made a poor start in the series, was the bright particular star of the game. He drove in all the runs made by Boston, and covered his position in fine style.

Parent, as usual, was fast, and Lou Criger was at his best. Stahl was fast.

Boston put up a perfect game and went for everything, and Dineen, nor any other pitcher, for that matter, never pitched a better game. Always cool and on the mark, he worked with Criger for every man. It was a rare treat in battery work, and phased the men from Pittsburg, who have for three long years been playing with inferior ball teams when compared with the brilliant aggregation from the Huntington-av grounds.

For the visitors, Tommy Leach put up a fine game. Ritchey was fast and sure, as usual, but the lack of stick work made the visitors look bad. Fast teams must hit to look good, and the Burgers were not hitting the Boston pitchers. They were not the only club this season who failed to connect with the curves of the Boston artists, including Hughes, Winter and Gibson.

All the combination plays were made by Boston, who got a total of 14 bases to six for the visitors. The last victory was decisive enough to force a word of praise from the biggest National league rooter in America for Jimmie Collins' boys. Better still, many loyal National league rooters dropped all feeling in the matter and offered hearty congratulations to the new world's champions.

The players who took part in the last series went through an awful strain, and all were heartily glad when the whole thing was over and they were at liberty to return once more to their homes and families.

Now for a nice rakeoff and a merry goodby.

Echoes of the Game

It would be a pleasant thing to have the same teams meet again next fall.

Over 100,000 persons saw the series of eight games.

Barney Dreyfuss was disappointed, but sent invitations to his old Boston friends to join him at a late lunch last evening at the hotel Vendome.

The Boston players will meet at the American grounds this morning to settle up business and make ready to leave town.

The Pittsburg players will leave for home this morning.

Lieut Rufus D. Fessenden was on hand to clear the field for the march of the royal rooters after the game.

Charley Waldron said he was a big winner on the series.

Barney Dreyfuss backed his boys for about $7000.

Cy Young and Billy Dineen proved to be the greatest pair of pitchers now in the business. Both worked hard and kept in prime condition for the hard work.

There was an outpouring of close followers of the game at the Huntington-av grounds yesterday. Among them was John Merrill, George Richardson, Hugh Duffy, Jimmy Canavan, Fred Doe, John Carney, Tom McDermott, Charley Marston, Ted Daly, William Parsons, William Emerson, Sam Wright, Tom Pettitt, M. J. Kittridge, Pat Moran, Otto Deinninger, Barney Lannon, Paul Radford, Patrick

Hurley, "Gid" Gardiner, Harry Schafer, Dupea Shaw and Senator M. J. Sullivan.

The first "world's series" as it was then called wasn't authorized by any official body. Instead, the series was essentially a private exhibition between the National League champion Pittsburgh Pirates and Boston's Americans. But it captured the imagination of fans who poured into the Huntington Avenue Grounds — and over the fence and onto the field — in record numbers. A best-of-nine affair, Boston fell behind early in the series, dropping two of the first three games under circumstances most observers considered suspicious. But when the series moved to Pittsburgh, Boston's notoriously loyal and equally loud fans, known collectively as the "Royal Rooters," worried the Pirates to distraction with their incessant singing of their theme song, a popular ditty called "Tessie." A couple of sore arms on the Pittsburgh pitching staff didn't hurt either.

Boston came back to win the series in eight games. They were the unchallenged kings of baseball.

THE SERIES THAT ALMOST NEVER GOT PLAYED

from *Sports Illustrated*, October 26, 1968

What is generally conceded to be the first World Series almost never got played. It was saved by a last-minute phone call involving Lou Criger and Cy Young, the most famous battery of their day — and one of the greatest of all time — and Jimmy Collins, the third baseman–manager of the Boston Americans (also known as the Puritans and as the Pilgrims). That call is vividly remembered today by Fred Parent, one of their teammates and, at 92, the last surviving Boston player in that first Series.

The call came through as Criger and Young were waiting at a railroad station near the Americans' Huntington Avenue diamond for a train to take them home to the Midwest. As far as both were concerned, the season of 1903 was all finished and done with. They were packed and ready to go, convinced, like many of their teammates, that their contracts had run out. All they knew about a possible World Series between their team and the Pittsburgh Nationals was what they had read in the Boston papers of September 25, *i.e.,* that it had been called off.

"We didn't have much communication with the management in those days," says Fred Parent.

A lot of things were different in baseball in 1903. Parent remembers that there were no clubhouses for visiting teams, and the players drove from hotels to the fields wearing their uniforms. But when they got there they played real ball. Parent loves to talk about those Boston Americans. There was Pat Dougherty, who hit a couple of home runs in one of the games. "He could hit, run and throw," says

Fred. "I faced him first when he was pitching for Bridgeport in the Eastern League. He could do everything well." And then there was Candy LaChance, who played first and went to church with Parent. "He was a really nice fellow."

Buck Freeman, who had hit 25 home runs in 1899, was the cleanup batter and played right field. "Buck's legs weren't too good. We'd tried him at first base one year, but he was no good on ground balls. He couldn't cover much territory in right." Then there was Lou Criger, the catcher. "He wasn't a great hitter by any means. He'd hit to right field even though he was right-handed. He had a low batting average, but Lou would drive in a lot of runs. And what a catcher. In eight years I never saw him drop a foul ball. Even Ty Cobb had all kinds of trouble running the bases on Lou."

Certainly it was a well-rounded team, this 1903 Boston American aggregation, what with its hitting, fielding, pitching and catching.

Its series with the Nationals, the Boston counterpart in the other league, had been arranged after a long period of interleague warfare, which ended — more or less — when both leagues signed an agreement permitting the owner of the Nationals to bar the American League from Pittsburgh forever. Sometime during the season when it looked as if Pittsburgh would be an easy winner in its league, that same owner, Barney Dreyfuss, approached Milwaukee Lawyer Henry J. Killilea, who owned the American League-leading Bostonians, with the idea of staging a best-out-of-nine-games playoff in September. The deal was made; the dates were set. Then the Boston players revolted, and Killilea announced to the press that the Series was off. The cause of the revolt was a disagreement over the players' split of the gate. Killilea wanted half Boston's share of the receipts; the players wanted more. They read the statement from Jimmy Collins in the September 25 papers that there would be no Series, that Killilea was adamant, and they got ready to leave — and were on the way. But Killilea recanted, and Collins had to round up the Americans. He got in touch with most of them at home and, as Parent says, put in the crucial call to the railroad station after he found out where Criger and Young were. A clubhouse meeting was called for September 26. Killilea finally said he'd take only 25% of the proceeds coming to him (half of the total proceeds) and let the team have 75%. Thus the stage was set for a unique event — a World Series in which the winning-team (Boston) members got less money than members of the losing team. The Boston Americans each received $1,182.17 plus $98 apiece that they raised at a banquet in Boston. But Barney Dreyfuss turned over all his proceeds to his Nationals, and their final shares totaled $1,316.25 each. "Things just weren't worked out very well for the Series," Freddy Parent asserts.

It wasn't just the arrangements for paying the players. The fields they played on were far too small for the crowds they drew. The October 3 game in Boston sold 18,801 admission tickets, and another 20,000 crowded in free. The October 10 game in Pittsburgh drew 17,038 paid. Exposition Park in Pittsburgh normally held about 8,000 maximum. Pictures in the Boston papers show police using rubber hoses and nightsticks to move the fans back. Ropes went up to keep them back, and it was a triple if you hit it into the crowd behind those ropes. In the four games in Pittsburgh 18 triples boomed into the crowds, 13 of them hit by the Bostons. "Sure, if we got the ball we wanted we'd deliberately try to hit it into the crowd behind the ropes," Parent admits. "In Boston the fans broke down the fence. And before it broke down some fans were pulling up others with ropes over that fence for $1 or $2 a head. What a way to run a World Series!"

There were other mixed-up aspects to the contest. The great Honus Wagner, for example, never looked worse. He batted .222, made many errors and got only one hit in his last 14 times at bat. Near the end of the games in Pittsburgh, this famed shortstop was being showered with confetti — and not as a tribute. Parent himself hit 59 points higher, made some great plays and was being cheered in Pittsburgh by the time the Series neared its end there. "Wagner was hurt and wouldn't speak to me on the field or right after the Series," Parent says. "I'm afraid he choked." At the end of it all Boston won five games to three, after trailing three games to one.

How does Parent explain the shift? "We just couldn't get started," he says. "We didn't get the breaks in these first four games. We were hitting the ball hard — and we were a hitting team — but it would go straight to someone, or one of the Pittsburgh players would come up with a sensational catch. Kitty Bransfield caught one I hit, and as

I ran past he himself said he was a lucky s.o.b. [Bransfield was the Pittsburgh first baseman.] After we started getting the breaks we could have beaten them 50 games easy."

What Parent feels was the greatest fielding play of the Series is an example of Pittburgh's early breaks. In the fourth game played at Pittsburgh, Duke Farrell, the Boston team's drunk ("It was hard stuff, you know," Parent says), pinch-hit with three on and with Boston rallying. Even with a hangover Farrell could still hit, and he laced a line drive over Wagner's head. It looked like a sure hit, Parent explains (and he was on third), but Fred Clarke, Pittsburgh's playing manager, came tearing in from left field and made a great, one-handed catch. That saved two runs, and the final score of that fourth game was Pittsburgh 5 and Boston 4. "I have a picture of us on the bench about that time — and you should have seen the long faces," Parent declares.

By the time the Series got going the Pittsburgh pitching staff had been riddled for one reason or another, but the team still had Deacon Phillippe, who won the three games that Pittsburgh took and was dubbed a hero. Parent doesn't recall that Phillippe was so great. "He just had a curve and a changeup, and we always could have hit him with any breaks," he claims. Although Sam Leever, who had won over 20 for Pittsburgh, came up with a lame arm for the Series, he did pitch one complete game and part of an earlier one, but Parent scoffs at that. "Sam was afraid we'd hit the hell out of him," he asserts. "He, too, had nothing but a curve and change-up." Ed Doheny, who had won 16 games for Pittsburgh, went insane near season's end and ended up in an institution.

Parent's own team had at least one pitching problem: Tom Hughes, a 21-game winner, appeared for only one short two-inning stretch in the Series. Bill Dinneen, who was later to become a great umpire, was the Boston hero with three wins, two of them shutouts. And old Cy Young, by then 36, had a couple of wins. What happened to Hughes, who had just as many wins as Dinneen in the regular season? "For some reason," says Parent, "Collins didn't like him by Series time. He must have crossed Jimmy somewhere along the line in the season. Collins was a quiet, nice man, but you couldn't cross him. He started Hughes one day after Tom had spent a night on the town. I think Tom did it because he wasn't being pitched.

Naturally he was whacked and never appeared in the Series again. It was about the end for Tom."

While Parent has some contempt for the way the first modern World Series was run, he has only admiration for the way the game was played then compared with now. "The pitchers were smarter then," he says. "If you got a couple of hits in a row you were bound to be brushed back on the first pitch your next time up. No manager would give signs to the batter. It was up to him. If you didn't do what was right at the plate you heard about it. You gave signals to the base runner. The batter had to think; he just didn't do what the manager ordered."

After that first Series the baseball war broke out again, and there was no World Series in 1904. John J. McGraw, who managed Baltimore, jumped out of the American League in 1902 and joined the New York Giants in the National. John Brush, the Giants' owner, backed up his manager 100%. The Giants won the pennant in 1904 but refused to play the Americans. It took another year for public opinion to bring about the first official World Series between the two leagues in 1905.

But even though the 1904 Series wasn't played, Fred Parent knows how it would have come out. "The Giants would have been duck soup for us," he says. "They were afraid of us. We'd played them in the spring and had really whacked them, both Joe McGinnity and Christy Mathewson. We would have won."

And there is sadness in Parent's memory about the breakup of the 1903–1904 Boston Americans. "General Taylor, the new owner, did it. He was drunk half the time, and when he didn't like a player that was that. He didn't like Jimmy Collins, and he got rid of him. He didn't like Pat Dougherty and sold him to New York. He got rid of Candy LaChance when Candy wouldn't become a switch hitter. General Taylor did give us all more money in 1904. My salary went up from $3,500 to $4,200, but at the end of 1907 he sold me to Charley Comiskey and the White Sox."

That was the end of the first World Championship team.

Shortstop Freddy Parent, a native of Maine, was a keen observer of the Series. One only wishes that sportswriters had thought to interview more participants in the Series before they passed away. Before the first pitch was thrown, the Boston players nearly withdrew from the Series due to their displeasure over the financial arrangements made by owner Henry J. Killilea. At the eleventh hour, however, Killilea mollified his ball club and the Series went on. Pittsburgh owner Barney Dreyfus, however, was more generous to his Pirates than Killilea was to the Americans. Despite losing the Series, the Pirate players actually made more money than the winning Americans.

THE IRISH IN BASEBALL

from *The Boston Post*, March 21, 1904

That Jimmy Collins can do something besides play baseball was strikingly shown St. Patrick's night, when before 500 members of the Macon A.O.H. [Ancient Order of Hibernians] and their friends he responded to the toast, "The Irish in Baseball." Collins held the attention of his auditors from start to finish, and at the conclusion of the banquet, was warmly congratulated by the guests and by the officers of the A.O.H.

Collins' fellow players, who were present in a body, sat spellbound as they listened to their captain dwell on the great ball players of the past and present who came from Irish blood.

Collins said in part:

"Since the first regular game of baseball was played in the Elysian Fields in Hoboken, in the late '40s, ball players of Irish birth or extraction have taken a most important part in the development of the national game. Books could be written of the great ball players with Irish names. I am a ball player, not an after-dinner speaker, although for myself and for the other members of the team I appreciate the kindness of your officers in inviting us to celebrate with you the natal day of Ireland's patron saint.

"In the few minutes allotted me I will try to recall a few of the famous ball players who cherish Ireland as their birthplace or the birthplace of their beloved parents. It is a hard task to remember them all, and I know you will forgive me if I forget some whom you as baseball lovers admired.

"For over 50 years baseball has been America's national game. Baseball requires brains and muscles, and that the Irish are both brainy and muscular can be substantiated by looking over the roster of the 18 major league baseball clubs. In the history of organized ball over 80 per cent, I think, of the great players have been of Irish birth or extraction. This country has its heroes, and baseball heroes hold their place in the minds of millions of baseball lovers."

Mike Kelly First of All

"As my mind runs back it recalls the lamented and immortal Mike Kelly, undoubtedly the greatest player the game has ever known. Kelly took pride in his nationality. With characteristic Irish wit Kelly, great ball player that he was had a heart as big as himself, and few men hold the place he does with those who knew him.

"Between Kelly and the present generation there were too many players of Irish extraction for me to attempt to enumerate them. Tim Keefe, Kid Madden, Martin Bergen, John Ward and Mickey Welch were a few of the old-timers."

Many in Both Big Leagues

"In the makeup of the 16 big teams of today the players of Irish extraction are hard to remember because of their number.

"On our own team, which is fast getting into condition in your beautiful city, are the names of Dougherty, Doran, Farrell, Dineen, Freeman, Stahl, O'Neill and Gibson. On the New York American team are Powell, Keeler and Conroy. The Philadelphia Athletics are managed by Cornelius McGillicuddy, and a few of his players are Dan Murphy, McGeehan and Coakley.

"On Washington last season was the lamented Delehanty, one of the greatest hitters the game has ever known; Drill, the catcher, Moran and Carey."

"On the St. Louis Browns were Jesse Burkett, the great batsman, Emmet Heldrick, Mike Kahoe, Barry McCormick and Dick Padden. The Chicago White Sox are owned by Charles Comiskey and managed by Jimmy Callahan and two of the star pitchers last season were Harry White and Pat Flaherty. Tom Daly played second base and Sullivan and Slattery were two of the Chicago catchers.

On the Detroit team were Wild Bill Donovan, one of the game's premier pitchers, and George Mullin, another star box artist. In the field was Jimmy Barrett and behind the bat was Jim McGuire.

"On the Cleveland team Jack McCarthy, Third Baseman Bradley

and Charley Hickman were a few of the players, and I am told that Napoleon Lajoie, who is conceded to be the greatest player now in the game, has Irish blood in him."

National League Irishmen

"In the National league the percentage of Irish players is as great, if not greater. Boston has its Carney, Cooley, Delehanty, Moran, Needham and Malarkey.

"New York has its McGraw, McGinnity, Bresnahan, Warner and Cronin.

"Philadelphia is managed by Hughey Duffy, who is one of the greatest players the game has ever produced and who today holds the batting record made some years ago. To win games, Duffy has Dooin, Raftery, Douglass and Kid Gleason.

"Brooklyn is directed by Ned Hanlon and has its Flood, Sheckard and Doyle.

"Joseph Kelley is manager of the Cincinnati club, and a few of his players are Bergen, Seymour and Magoon.

"Pittsburg has Bransfield, Kennedy, Leach and Beaumont, and St. Louis has the O'Neill twins and Patsey Donovan."

Irish Magnates

"Just as Irish ball players have contributed their share in placing baseball where it is today, so have men of Irish blood risked their money in promoting the game. Henry Killilea owns the Boston American club, Kilfoyle owns half the Cleveland club, Comiskey owns the Chicago club and Frank Farrell is the principal stockholder in the New York club. The national board of arbitration is made up of Mike Seeton, Judge Kavanaugh, Jim O'Rourke, Tim Murnane and J. H. Farrell.

"I do not claim that all ball players are Irish. Other nationalities have furnished their quota of star ball players. It makes little difference what a ball player is as long as he plays good ball. I know I have forgotten many names and I hope the forgotten ones will appreciate that I did not expect to be called upon to speak. As much as ball players of Irish extraction have done for the game in the past, I look for them to do as much if not more in the future. America needs baseball, and baseball will always, I think, need a few players with the O's and the Mac's."

Manager and third baseman Jimmy Collins was the best player on the new team over its first few seasons. He was also the most popular with fans, due in no small part to his Irish heritage. They identified with the tough, no-nonsense Collins, and the Buffalo, New York, native found that in Boston he was rarely without company, as he constantly received invitations to dinners, testimonials, and other social events.

Even at spring training in Macon, Georgia, fans still sought out Collins's company, and he wisely responded with a knowing nod to his Irish forebears, ensuring that his words would make a hit back in Boston.

FREDERIC P. O'CONNELL

WITH BOSTON'S WORLD'S CHAMPION BALL PLAYERS — WAY DOWN SOUTH

from *The Boston Post*, March 27, 1904

MACON, MARCH 26 — "By all odds the best town for training I know of," is the enthusiastic way in which Jimmy Collins describes Macon, where the Boston worldbeaters are getting into condition for another championship race. Collins voices the sentiments of the entire Boston team, and while some of the boys think the town pretty slow at times, all are delighted with the weather here, the two baseball diamonds and the excellent practice which the Mercer University boys give them each afternoon.

Maconians cannot do too much for the worldbeaters. Last spring the Collins team did their training here, and the natives claim no little share of the credit in Boston defeating the Pittsburgs for the championship of the world. "It was the good start the Bostons got that enabled them to win the pennant, and the good start was made possible because the boys were in the pink of condition," say the natives.

Last season Collins was delighted with Macon as a training camp. This spring he is even more pleased, and as long as he runs the Boston team he will have the team train at Macon.

Since arriving here on March 6 the weather has been perfect. It has been warm enough for the boys to feel like extending themselves without having sore muscles, and it has been just cold enough for the boys to put ginger into their work. It has not rained a single drop except during the night, and then the rain was only heavy enough to keep the dust down and not make the ball park muddy. Nothing has been too good for the world beaters since their arrival here. Their practice each day is watched by admiring hundreds, and their games against Mercer have been liberally attended.

Macon's colored population (and the colored contingent seems larger than the white) simply idolizes the world beaters. When Jack O'Neill ran his famous race against Lee, the champion sprinter of the State, the colored population backed O'Neill to the last cent, and his victory marked an epoch in the colored section of the town. Men, women and children turn out for the practice games. The courtesy of the different golf and country clubs around Macon has been extended to the world beaters, and while baseball takes up most of the time of the Collins team, they appreciate the Southern hospitality.

Slow at night, when compared with a big city like Boston or New York, there is the good side to a slow town. Since coming here there have been but three shows at the opera house and none of the boys have found it possible to spend their money even if they had it — for just now the boys are down to hard pan, salaries not beginning to run until the first of April. Collins has had but a few touches, whereas if the boys were in a big city they would be touching the manager almost every day.

Macon is not a small town by any means even if the theatrical folks call it a "tank" because they play here only one night. There is enough life here to satisfy all, and the boys find lots of pleasure in taking an easy chair in front of the Lanier and watching the Southerners parade up and down each night. The Lanier is located on Mulberry street, in the heart of the downtown district, and the hotel is one of the busiest in the South.

Not a day passes that several Bostonians do not register, and they soon make themselves acquainted with the players, who are all good talkers and who like to meet people from home except the kind of "butters in" who are always asking the players about themselves, how much they hit for last season and how much they are going to hit for during the coming season. If there is anything a ball player dislikes it is being asked questions about himself by a rank outsider.

Typical of a Southern city, Macon has its Confederate soldiers and monuments, its swell residential districts, its darky sections, its market places and its horde of politicians, for everyone here is talking politics at all seasons of the year and elections are held more frequently than they are in the North.

The loud praises of the old Baltimore team, who trained here several seasons ago, caused Collins to try his luck here, and whether it is luck or Collins's excellent good judgment, which has characterized his management of the Boston American team, one thing is certain — no club in either league has been served up better weather than has the world beaters this season.

With Collins and Chick Stahl occupying the room made sacred to Southerners because Jefferson Davis and Sidney Lanier, the poet, once slept in, the team is most comfortably located in the Lanier, one of the leading hotels of Macon, centrally located on the principal street of the town and within a mile of both the Mercer and City parks. Forenoon practice the past few days has been held at the City Park, which covers in all about 100 acres of land with its fair buildings, a mile track, several stables and a ball park, enclosed and separate from the rest of the park. The property of the city, the ball park is let to the Macon team of the South Atlantic league, and the City Council was only too pleased to allow the Boston team the use of it. It has a skin diamond and the ground is fast, in keeping with the fielding put up by the world beaters. Signals are worked here in the forenoon, for outside of a few colored jockeys and horse trainers, no one is allowed in the park. After dinner the Collins team goes to the Mercer College grounds. Like the City Park the Mercer field is a mile distant from the hotel, which is about the right distance to make the boys walk or run. To the Mercer grounds the boys go through the leading business and residential sections, and the daily parade of the world beaters is watched with interest.

Mercer is one of the largest colleges in the South, and while the team is not as fast as the big Northern colleges, the boys are in fine shape, having been outdoors since March 1. They do not nurse their arms when playing against Boston, and at times the world-beaters have their hands full in winning the game. Two of the Mercer pitchers are fast men and use terrific speed and an assortment of curves to help out. Coach Betts of the Mercer team is an old Boston boy, and nothing is too good for the Boston players. Practice each day at Mercer is watched by a large crowd, and the "rooting" of the "darkeys" gives the Collins team no end of pleasure.

Boston has its crazy ball fans, but a couple of hundred darkeys can make more noise in five minutes than 5000 Boston fans can make during a whole game. One of the accompanying pictures shows a bunch of Macon beauties who are present every afternoon to cheer for the Collins team.

Macon has its historic places as well as Boston. Several battles in the Civil war were fought around here, and five miles from the town is an old fort which has been visited by all of the players. Half a mile from the hotel is the Ocmulgee River, where the boys went fishing last Sunday, and the market place on Saturday night is worth going a long ways to see.

Just now the Superior Courts of the county are in session, and the scene is characteristic of the South. Each forenoon can be seen hundreds of men around the courthouse, and wagons and carriages surround it on all sides. Before forenoon practice many of the boys take in the sessions of the court, and the trials of several colored men charged with stealing chickens beats any burlesque show for genuine fun and amusement.

Spring has struck Macon in a delightful manner for the players. The trees are all in blossom, the grass is green and walks out into the surrounding country afford no end of pleasure.

Ante-bellum slaves are as plentiful as flies, and with the promise of a few cents the slaves relate some interesting experiences. Each night in the hotel a band of colored minstrels give a concert, singing plantation songs, and the players join in the chorus. Several of the boys have excellent voices.

All in all the training of the world beaters is attended with a lot of pleasure. Now that the aches and pains are out of their bodies the men are enjoying themselves. They take in everything and are the life of the hotel with their everlasting "kidding." Put a bunch of healthy ball players in a small Southern city and there is sure to be something doing all the time.

Frederic P. O'Connell came from a well-connected Irish family — his brother served as Boston mayor John Fitzgerald's personal secretary. But O'Connell turned his back on politics in favor of baseball. Though younger than most of his peers, O'Connell may well have been the most talented writer and reporter of the bunch. Profiles such as this simply weren't done, but the Post, *Boston's dominant newspaper at the time, gave O'Connell plenty of room to ply his trade, often placing his work outside the sports page where casual fans could be regaled with his tales of inside baseball — including, in this story, the casual racism so prevalent at the time.*

Unfortunately, O'Connell died young. Shortly after reporting on the suicide of manager Chick Stahl in the spring of 1907, O'Connell passed away from pneumonia.

MY GREATEST DAY IN BASEBALL

from *The Chicago Daily News,* 1945

A pitcher's got to be good and he's got to be lucky to get a no-hit game. But to get a perfect game — no run, no hit, no man reach first base — he's got to have everything his way.

I certainly had my share of luck in the twenty-three years I pitched in the two big leagues because I threw three no-hitters and one of them was perfect. You look at the records and you'll find that Larry Corcoran, who pitched for the Chicago Nationals "away back when," was the only other big leaguer ever to get three no-hitters, before me and none of his was perfect.

So it's no job for me to pick out my greatest day in baseball. It was May 5, 1904, when I was pitching for the Boston Red Sox and beat the Philadelphia Athletics without a run, hit, or man reaching first. Of all the 906 games I pitched in the big leagues that one stands clearest in my mind.

The American League was pretty young then, just four seasons old, but it had a lot of good players and good teams. I was with St. Louis in the National when Ban Johnson organized the American League, and I was one of the many players who jumped to the new circuit.

Jimmy Collins, whom I regard as the greatest of all third basemen, was the first manager of the Boston team, and in 1903 we won the pennant and beat Pittsburgh in the first modern World Series.

Before I get into the details of my greatest day, I'd like to tell something about our Red Sox of those days. We had a great team. Besides Collins at third, we had Freddie Parent at short, Hobe Ferris at second, and Candy La Chance on first.

In the outfield were Buck Freeman, who was the Babe Ruth of

that time, Patsy Dougherty, who later played with the White Sox, and Chick Stahl. Bill Dineen was one of our other pitchers, and he'd licked the Pirates three games in the World Series the fall before.

Every great pitcher usually has a great catcher, like Mathewson had Roger Bresnahan and Miner Brown had Johnny Kling. Well, in my time I had two. First, there was Chief Zimmer, when I was with Cleveland in the National League, and then there was Lou Criger, who caught me at Boston and handled my perfect game.

As I said, my greatest game was against the Athletics, who were building up to win the 1905 pennant, and Rube Waddell was their pitcher. And I'd like to say that beating Rube anytime was a big job. I never saw many who were better pitchers.

I was real fast in those days, but what very few batters knew was that I had two curves. One of them sailed in there as hard as my fastball and broke in reverse. It was a narrow curve that broke away from the batter and went in just like a fastball. And the other was a wide break. I never said much about them until after I was through with the game.

There was a big crowd for those times out that day. Maybe 10,000, I guess, for Waddell always was a big attraction.

I don't think I ever had more stuff and I fanned eight, getting Jasper Davis and Monte Cross, the Philly shortstop, twice. But the boys gave me some great support, and when I tell you about it, you'll understand why I say a pitcher's got to be awfully lucky to get a perfect game.

The closest the Athletics came to a hit was in the third, when Monte Cross hit a pop fly that was dropping just back of the infield between first and second. Buck Freeman came tearing in from right like a deer and barely caught the ball.

But Ollie Pickering, who played center field for Mr. Mack, gave me two bad scares. Once he hit a fly back of second that Chick Stahl caught around his knees after a long run from center. The other time Ollie hit a slow roller to short and Parent just got him by a step.

Patsy Dougherty helped me out in the seventh when he crashed into the left field fence to get Danny Hoffman's long foul; and I recall that Criger almost went into the Boston bench to get a foul by Davis.

Most of the other batters were pretty easy, but all told there were ten flies hit, six to the outfield. The infielders had seven assists and I had two, and eighteen of the putouts were divided evenly between Criger and La Chance.

Well, sir, when I had two out in the ninth, and it was Waddell's time to bat, some of the fans began to yell for Connie Mack to send up a pinch hitter. They wanted me to finish what looked like a perfect game against a stronger batter.

But Mr. Mack let Rube take his turn. Rube took a couple of strikes and then hit a fly that Stahl caught going away from the infield.

You can realize how perfect we all were that day when I tell you the game only took one hour and twenty-three minutes.

We got three runs off Waddell, and when the game was finished it looked like all the fans came down on the field and tried to shake my hand. One gray-haired fellow jumped the fence back of third and shoved a five-dollar bill into my hand.

The game was a sensation at the time. It was the first perfect game in twenty-four years, or since 1880, when both John M. Ward and Lee Richmond did the trick. It also was the second no-hitter ever pitched in the American League. Jimmy Callahan of the White Sox pitched the first against Detroit in 1902, but somehow a batter got to first base.

During my twenty-three years in the big leagues I pitched 516 games in the National League and won 289, and then I went into the American League and won 222 there. So all told I worked 906 games and won 511.

By the way, you might be interested to know that in my last big league game I was beaten 1–0 by a kid named Grover Cleveland Alexander.

CY YOUNG'S BASEBALL EPIGRAMS

from *The Boston Post*, May 8, 1904

- I like to win games. It makes me feel good and helps my club.
- My employers pay me a good salary. I always try to earn it by being in shape to do my best.
- I like to strike men out. There's a certain indefinable satisfaction in seeing your batsmen fail to connect with your curves.
- Boston is the best baseball town in the country. The newspapers encourage the game more than in any other city, the crowds are fairer and the "knockers" are scarcer.
- Be in good shape all the time is the best advice I can give to youngsters. Let the drink alone and get your regular sleep.
- Dissipation of any sort will shorten your baseball career.
- Take things comparatively easy during the off-season. Baseball is a winter. Don't try to be as rich as Rockefeller.
- Don't think the club can get along without you. Your place can be filled. Don't get foolish and think you're the whole thing.
- Baseball games are won by playing ball. There is a certain element of luck, to be sure, but don't figure on luck when you set out to pitch or get a hit.
- I try to remember the strong and weak points of the batters who oppose me.
- If a batter likes a high ball I generally try to send one just below the knees.
- Don't abuse the umpire. He is trying to do his best to earn an honest living.

- In thinking you have been robbed by an umpire, remember his judgment is supposed to be as good if not better than yours. He is paid for the job.
- Light farm work in the off-season has helped me. It is healthier than life in a big city.
- Of course I am glad to be a world beater. Who wouldn't?
- Don't let your head turn because the crowd cheers you.
- The "mob" is fickle. Pitch bad ball and they will soon let you know that you are the wrong man in the box.
- I never win games before they are pitched.
- I always begin a game confident of winning. If I thought I was going to lose I'd ask to be excused for the day.
- Don't tell what you're going to do to the other team. The other team might "do" something to you.
- I like the sound of base hits better than I do grand opera if my team is making them.
- Pitchers, like poets, are born and not made.

Cy Young's perfect game, tossed on May 5, 1904, versus Philadelphia, was the first in modern baseball history, a feat that most observers considered a virtual impossibility. Batters strove only to make contact, fielders' gloves were next to nonexistent, and the condition of the infield made bad hops common. Players rarely garnered their own bylines at the time, but Young's achievement was considered so spectacular he was asked to share the secrets of his success.

ARTHUR McPHERSON

BRIGHT RED STOCKINGS FOR PILGRIMS WHILE PLAYING AT HOME NEXT YEAR

Pilgrims Have Asked for Waivers Upon Five
of Their Players — President Taylor Leaves
for the Pacific Coast.

from *The Boston Journal*, December 19, 1907

The Boston Red Sox: That is what Jim McGuire's bunch of lightning calculators on the baseball field will be called next year. Some antiquated fossils may continue to designate them as the Pilgrims, but none of the up-to-date fans will do that, for the order has gone forth that the Boston American team next year will wear red stockings while playing on the home grounds. There will be nothing bashful about that red, either. It will be an aggressive blazing color scheme that will be heard farther than the chortle of the fan when the home team wins out in the fifteenth inning.

A representative of Wright & Ditson closed arrangements yesterday with President Taylor and Treasurer McBreen for the uniforms for next year. The going-away costume will be of gray with red trimmings on coat and shirt and blue stockings. The at home apparel will be white with the exception of the passionate stockings. It was at first proposed that the red stockings be worn on the road, but the officers of the club decided that it would be better to try them on the home populace and among friends at first. If they do not interfere with the fans' vision of the game or do not incite the crowds to riot they may be worn on the road another year.

Before this date, the Red Sox had no formal nickname. Although headline writers and members of the press would occasionally refer to the ballclub as the Pilgrims or Somersets or Collinsmen, the most popular nickname, and the one used by most fans, was simply "the Americans," to differentiate the club from its National League rival, which was still known simply as "the Bostons."

The Red Sox name, which harked back to the original Red Stockings and also echoed the nickname of Chicago's White Sox, wasn't very popular initially. For a brief period of time around 1910, many sportswriters called them the Speed Boys in reference to the number of stolen bases Red Sox runners were accumulating. But brevity eventually won the day; Red Sox, and the even briefer Bosox or simply Sox, was a headline writer's dream.

PAUL H. SHANNON

FENWAY PARK IS FORMALLY OPENED WITH RED SOX WIN

24,000 Boston Fans Go Wild With Delight
When Jake Stahl's Men Bat Out a Victory
Over the Highlanders in Eleventh Inning

from *The Boston Post,* April 21, 1912

Over the winding roads and across the narrow bridge that leads to
Fenway Park, the baseball-hungry fans of Boston threaded their impatient way yesterday noon to get a long awaited glimpse of the stal-
wart crew that big Jake Stahl leads to action.

Into the mammoth stand, out upon the sun-kissed bleachers and
swarming over the field, forming a human fringe to the expansive
playing space where the Red Sox were to make their initial bow
of the 1912 season, the fans of Boston forced their way, until when
the umpire gave the word for play to begin more than 24,000 loyal
Red Sox supporters were waiting to pass judgment upon park and
team.

Fans Like the Park

The mammoth plant, with its commodious fittings, met with distinct approval, and as for the team, well — the cheer that arose when
the great Tris Speaker scorched that single to left in the 11th, sending Steve Yerkes home with the winning run, was a fitting tribute to
the estimation in which Boston holds its Red Sox.

Three hours before, a curious, impatient crowd had gathered
within the big inclosure, hoping for a Red Sox victory and a fourth
straight win from New York. It was well along toward twilight when

that same crowd, no longer a mildly enthusiastic body but a yelling, cheering mob, hurried back to the four corners of Greater Boston to spread the news of an uphill fight, a thrilling finish and a great 11th inning defeat for Wolverton's Highlanders.

It was an old time Red Sox victory. Handicapped at the very start by a temporary weakness in the pitcher's box, and forced to come from behind all the way until Jake Stahl's timely, two-bagger had tied up the contest in the eighth, the Boston team has seldom before given such an exhibition of bulldog tenacity and fight. If ever a team deserved to win the Red Sox did yesterday, and this in spite of errors and loose play that would have put a high school team to blush.

It was well for Jake Stahl's team that it has a pitcher of Charlie Hall's calibre for just such emergencies. It is a fortunate thing, as well, that the Red Sox squad can boast of so many lusty hitters, and that Yerkes and Tris Speaker came through as they did in this nerve-racking, 11-inning fight. For, while the Boston team was threatened with disaster by a seeming collapse in the first few innings of the game, it was the nerve and fight of this great trio that finally enabled the Sox to come up on even terms with their opponents and ultimately win out.

Yerkes' Heavy Hitting

On a soft and slippery field, whose condition might well have excused the commission of even more frequent blunders, the work of these three men shone like beacons. Yerkes, in spite of three errors, for which the soft spots around the second bag were almost wholly to blame, made up for his misdeeds by grand work at the bat. In seven times up he hammered out three singles, a brace of doubles, scored three of the seven runs and helped to drive in two more himself. Speaker drove in Boston's first and last tally, made three hits and was robbed of two more by catches that were little short of miraculous. Hall also had his day.

Buck O'Brien, picked by the majority to find the Highlanders rather easy prey, had to pay the penalty of an eight-day layoff and was found signally wanting. From the very start it was easily to be seen that the Brockton lad possessed little of his usual effectiveness, and when his wildness robbed him of the least pretense to an ability to locate the plate, his quick departure was foreshadowed. Nevertheless, in the hope that Buck might settle down, Manager Stahl kept him on the rubber until the Highlanders had taken his measure for four innings and piled up five big runs.

Red Sox Narrow the Gap

A likely-looking rally in Boston's fourth and the acquisition of three runs that brought the home team up to within a solitary score of the invaders had forced Relief Pitcher Hall into the fray, and right nobly did the Californian acquit himself. From the moment that the "Sea Lion" took his position upon the rubber the game assumed a different aspect, and hope which had been glimmering but feebly broke into quick flame.

In the seven innings that Hall worked but three hits were made off him, and the one run that the Highlanders got was the result of a base on balls and an ill advised throw to second base. At the bat, however, Hall atoned for this one tally that he gave the New Yorkers, scoring one run, and driving out a lusty two-bagger that should have ended the game in the ninth inning. His pitching was a duplication of the fine work that he had performed against New York on the latter's own grounds, and the Californian finished as strongly as he had begun.

The Highlanders, desperately anxious to win this one game in Boston and put an end to their monotonous string of defeats, used up no less than three pitchers, but all to no avail. Against the heavy cannonading of the Red Sox hitters they fell one by one, Vaughan, the redoubtable left hander, being the pitcher who has to stomach the blame for defeat. Caldwell was yanked at the first sign of weakening. Quinn was removed when an incipient rally threatened in the ninth, and finally the bats of Yerkes and Speaker put Vaughan to the bad in the 11th inning.

Fourteen Red Sox Hits

While the Highlanders were scratching out eight scattered singles, the Red Sox were running up a tally of 14 safe drives with a total of 19 bases, and had it not been for the ground rule, which limits hits into the crowd to two bases each, the contest would have been ended without the necessity of playing two extra sessions. Five long two-baggers did the Red Sox make, drives by Hall, Stahl and Speaker counting for two sacks when they might just as easily have gone for three sackers or home runs.

The fielding of neither team was of very high class, but, as explained before, the condition of the diamond was largely accountable. Yerkes had three boots, while Wagner, Stahl, O'Brien and Hall are credited with one each. The New York errors were much fewer, but they were very costly, one of Dolan's bad errors and a passed ball by Charlie Street in the 11th allowing the Sox to score the run that robbed the fast gathering darkness of a chance to call the game with the teams on even terms.

Contrary to expectations, there were none of the usual opening day functions, the two days' postponement called off the parade and flag-raising, and making that far-famed Letter Carriers' band conspicuous by its absence. The only pretension to the opening day frill was the hurling of the ball by Mayor Fitzgerald, but Boston's modest chief executive pulled off this feat so quietly that few excepting those within closest proximity knew that this important duty had been transacted.

First Inning Bad for Boston

The first inning as usual was a bad one for Boston. Zinn, the first man up, drew a pass and Wolter got an infield hit when Buck O'Brien covered the sack on a grounder to Stahl rather lamely, Chase sacrificed, Hartzell singled to left, but Wolter knew the strength of Lewis' arm and but one run came in. Daniels hit to O'Brien. Buck made a good stop and caught Wolter 15 feet from the plate, but he threw low to Nunamaker and Daniels was safe, while Wolter scored. Dolan was hit by the pitcher after Nunamaker had caught Hartzell off second base. Gardner singled and Daniels counted. Street ended the agony by fanning.

In the last half two-baggers by Yerkes and Speaker gave Boston one run.

The third inning was another bad session for O'Brien. Hartzell got his base on Yerkes' fumble and Dolan singled after Daniels fanned. Then came a wild pitch, a pass to Street and a single by Caldwell. This accounted for two runs.

In the fourth O'Brien hit one man and passed two more, but a

lucky wild pitch that struck Gardner's bat resulted in an easy roller
to Stahl and a fortunate escape from runs. This ended O'Brien.

Sox Get After Caldwell

The Sox started after Caldwell in the last half. Gardner began by hitting safely and Lewis drew a pass. Dolan's error filled the bases with
none down. Nunamaker fanned. Henriksen was sent in to hit for
O'Brien and drew a base on balls, forcing Gardner in. Quinn replaced Caldwell at this point. Hooper forced Henriksen and Lewis
counted. Yerkes dropped a single in left and Wagner came across.
Speaker ended the inning with a grounder to Chase.

A pass to Hall, Hooper's sacrifice and Yerkes' fourth safe hit sent
in the tieing run in the sixth. The seventh passed without a score,
but both teams got a man across in the eighth. A pass to Wolter, a
steal and a bad throw to second let Kauff, who had replaced Wolter,
go to third with one down and Chase's single scored him. In Boston's half, two-baggers by Yerkes and Stahl tied the game up again.

The ninth and 10th were critical moments for both sides, sensational catches by Lewis and Daniels cutting off likely scores.
Vaughan replaced Quinn in the ninth, after Hall had doubled with
one out, and this left the Californian languishing upon the sacks.

In the 11th, when it became apparent that this inning would end
matters in case of no decision, Yerkes got a life on Dolan's fumble
and continued on to second when the New Yorker made a bad
throw. A short passed ball let him move on to third, and a wild yell
arose when Speaker drove a scorcher between Dolan and Hartzell
and sent the winning run across.

*The lease arrangement at the Huntington Avenue Grounds proved
costly to the club, as did the cost of insurance following a series of fires
that destroyed many wooden ballparks. After the Red Sox were purchased by the Taylor family, owners of the* Boston Globe, *they decided
to build their own fireproof concrete and steel ballpark next to an old
dump in the Fens, calling the ballpark Fenway Park to make the name
of their real-estate company, Fenway Real Estate, better known.*

*As originally designed, the park was supposed to have a second deck
and was engineered with such a structure in mind. But the notion was
abandoned because of time constraints and never built, although when*

Tom Yawkey renovated the park in 1933–1934, he reportedly had the foundation reinforced in case he ever decided to add the planned-for feature.

After Tim Murnane died, Paul Shannon, who also served as sports editor of the Boston Post, *became the most respected baseball reporter in town. His account of the first official game played at Fenway Park, a 7–6 victory over New York, foreshadowed a pennant and world championship.*

T. H. MURNANE

BOSTON NOW SUPREME IN BASEBALL WORLD

Stahl's Lads Twice Fight Way Out of Seeming
Defeat. Henriksen and Bedient Big Factors
In Triumph Over Giants.

from *The Boston Globe,* October 17, 1912

Words were never invented that could fully describe the outburst of insane enthusiasm that went thundering around Fenway Park yesterday afternoon as Steve Yerkes crossed the rubber with the winning run in the 10th inning.

Men hugged each other, women became hysterical, youths threw their caps in the air, one man in the bleachers fell in a dead faint, strong hearts lost a beat and started off again at double time.

Lose at the Last Trench

John McGraw, the little Napoleon, dashed across the field to offer his congratulations to Manager Jake Stahl. The cheering lasted fully five minutes, while the Boston players, all smiles, modestly retired to their dressing rooms.

The great New York fighting machine had lost at the last ditch, and with heads bowed low the Giants pushed through the crowd, practically unnoticed.

Mathewson Heartbroken

Christy Mathewson, the greatest pitcher of all time, had lost, after pitching a remarkable game. It was no fault of his. It was the one game in his 12 years on the ball field that he had set his heart on winning, for it meant the championship of the world and one more thrill before passing out of the limelight as a remarkable performer.

Mathewson, the baseball genius, was heartbroken and tears rolled down his sun-burned cheeks as he was consoled by his fellow-players.

In its frenzy the crowd could only see the victors, and yet the defeated National League champions were no less worthy of appreciation, considering the game fight they put up from first to last in the most remarkable series of games ever played.

"Red Sox Win!" — What That Means

"The Red Sox win!" was the short but telling sentence that went flashing over the wires to the most remote corners of all America. This meant that the Boston Speed Boys had taken the deciding game for the greatest honors of the sport, and that each Boston player had made his title clear to $4024.68.

It meant that Boston was in possession, once more, of a real champion team, continuing its record of winning when it came down to cases. It meant that the Boston public had liberally supported a great ball team, a team as modest as it is great, and one that has played the game fair from first to last, as true sportsmen, who could stand defeat, but who dearly loved the laurel wreaths of victory.

Teams Never Under Such a Strain

Never before were two teams subjected to such a strain. Players lost control of their nerves, and then came back strong in sheer desperation.

Signals were discovered, even yesterday, but the Red Sox, having new ones, they were being changed to prevent any chance of the McGraw-Robinson combination from passing the news to the batsmen.

Manager McGraw was on the lines every second that his men were at the bat, watching, catlike, the movements of the battery and the movements of the infielders and outfielders.

Mathewson pitched to his field, and with the exception of Snodgrass his men responded superbly.

Bedient Pitches Grand Game

The Red Sox made five errors, but no damage was done as Hugh Bedient tightened up and cut down the next batsmen when trouble threatened.

And what a grand game this young Bedient did pitch. For seven innings he held the Giants to one run. This was developed out of a pass, when, with two down and two strikes on Murray, the real Giant hero of the series, "Red" laced out a fine double, and the visitors were in the lead.

The managers were looking for the first sign of weakness by their pitchers. Marquard and Tesreau of the Giants and Joe Wood and Ray Collins of the Red Sox were kept continually warmed up, and while Bedient could have gone to a finish, he was taken out in the seventh to give young Henriksen a chance to hit, for the Red Sox must tie the score if they hoped to win.

How Henriksen Bounded into Fame

With men at first and second and two down, Henriksen was soon in for two strikes, as "Matty" was working the young man in a most artistic manner. Seeing one coming on the outside corner of the plate, Henriksen chopped it along the ground directly over the third-base bag for a single, and Stahl came in with the tying run.

The scene that followed sent a cold chill along the spines of many a Giant. McGraw's men now realized that the Red Sox were still in the game, bound to fight it out to the bitter end, and now having an even chance for victory.

Olaf Henriksen at once went into the hero class. A little New England League graduate had turned the trick, and the fans were now on edge for rooting as never before for the Speed Boys.

Joe Wood Takes Command

Joe Wood, not in his best form, but with his heart as strong as ever, was now on the job, showing fine speed and good command. The Red Sox had a fine chance to land the game in the ninth, when, with one down, Stahl smashed out a double, only to see Wagner and Cady send up high flies.

When the Giants scored in the 10th, on Murray's double and Merkle's single, it looked bad for the home team, and the crowd settled down to see the game band of Red Sox take a dose of bitter medicine.

Clyde Engle was sent to bat for Wood, who injured his hand in stopping a hot shot from Meyers, the last man up in the 10th. Engle hit a long fly to left center that Snodgrass tore after, muffed and allowed to get away, Engle reaching second to the music of a hundred thousand yells.

Up to Harry Hooper

It was up to Hooper to bunt his man to third. "Matty" was now pitching his most skillful ball, never allowing his shoots to raise above the knee, hoping to force the Boston man to send up a fly.

Hooper tried to sacrifice, and the ball rolled foul. Then he cut loose and smashed the ball to deep left center, where Snodgrass made a great running catch, practically saving the game at this stage.

Engle half-expected Snodgrass to lose the ball, and played too far off second. Had he properly judged the play, he could have reached third after the catch.

Yerkes Draws a Pass

This was heartbreaking, but the home players were now on edge and determined to make "Matty" put them over. Yerkes insisted, and was passed, for Mathewson did not care to groove the ball over for a strike.

It was now up to the Texas cotton planter, Tris Speaker, the hero of a thousand battles. The first ball was sent up for a foul. Merkle should have taken this ball and closed the game with a Giant victory. But he hesitated and allowed Meyers to try for the ball, which dropped less than five yards back of first base.

Speaker's Hit Scores Engle

This disturbed Mathewson. He curved one into Speaker about knee high, and saw it shoot out to right field. Engle, with a fine lead, turned third and beat the ball to the plate by two yards.

Yerkes slipped around to third, and Speaker to second, and the score was tied once more.

Lewis was now up. The Giant infield was playing close in. A long fly to the outfield would land the money. Mathewson was using his headpiece, and kept the ball less than a foot from the ground, hoping to see it raised for a weak infield fly.

But Lewis doped out "Matty's" plans, refused to go after the low ones, and was passed, filling the bases.

Gardner's Fly Wins Game

Gardner realized that he was being worked to hit a very low ball and he allowed two to go by for balls. Then he missed one. "Matty" could not afford to take a chance, for a pass meant forcing in the winning run, and the next ball was over the inside corner, well above the knee.

Gardner had a good toehold and met the ball with a natural sweep, to see it start for Devore in deep right field.

The second the ball was hit a mighty shout went up, for it was plain that Gardner had produced the fly that would send Yerkes over the plate with the winning run.

Hooper's Catch His Best Ever

There was some fine individual fielding, with Hooper, the headliner, Harry making the finest catch of his baseball career. Doyle hit the ball, and Hooper turned and went down to the field on the dead run. Turning completely around as he went close to the short fence, he hooked in the ball with his back to the field, only a few feet from the fence, cutting off a sure home run.

This was in the fifth inning, when the Giants turned in two hits, the first man on trying for second, only to find Cady's throw perfect.

Other Fielding Features

Wood saved a run in the 10th by a remarkable one-handed stop. With a man at second, Meyers hit the ball hard and, to the surprise of all, Wood got it with his bare hand. As a result, however, he was in no shape to continue the box work, had it been necessary.

In the sixth, Jake Stahl made a remarkable long-range pickup of a low throw by Wagner. Wagner put ginger into the home team when he got Devore at first after a great stop well to his right. Yerkes made several clever plays, while Cady's throwing was the finest of the series.

Speaker was a whole show in center, and he and Stahl led the hitting for the Red Sox.

Herzog, Fletcher and Doyle made clever running assists for the Giants, but on the whole, Boston got in the greater number of clever plays.

Only One Stolen Base

Not a Boston man attempted to steal a base. The Giants tried for second, three times and reached there once. Devore was given a clean steal, although Wagner claimed the out. Both pitchers forced the runners to hold close to their bases, the Boston basemen keeping a sharp lookout for the Giant runners when at second, where a stolen base might mean a run.

Boston got men to first in six of the ten innings, while the Giants had men on in every inning. Each team got 14 men to first.

Umpire Rigler made one very bad decision, calling Yerkes out at first in the eighth. The Boston man had the ball clearly beaten. Hall made a protest and was sent to the dugout.

Best Game, Smallest Crowd

The last game was the most interesting of the series, and yet the smallest crowd was out to see the great finish, even with perfect weather and the game of all games staged in prospect.

The players of both teams were "all in" after the game. They had gone through a grueling fight for eight games, working on their nerve, keyed up to the highest pitch, and the players will not be fully normal for many weeks.

In sizing up the teams before the series, I said that they were evenly matched and would probably go to the full limit. This proved to be the right dope, and without a band of music in sight and the crowd small, the Speed Boys came across at the last ditch, as true champions should, caring little for the rooting, for it's the basehit that wins the money.

Great Finish of Great Season

It was a great finish of a great baseball season at the new park. The best people of New England were entertained as never before at a Boston ball field. The American League record for a season in the way of attendance was passed.

Every member of the Boston team did his very best. Not one man faltered, and the wild yarns about the players were manufactured, often for a purpose. Most of these stories developed in the brains of persons closely connected with the New York club — an old trick from that source.

Red Sox Refused to Scare

Some of the Boston players received Black Hand letters for the purpose of shattering their nerves before and during the series. But these did no harm, for a gamer bunch never trod a diamond.

Starting in good shape at Hot Springs, with one purpose in sight, Manager Jake Stahl and his Speed Boys reached the supreme ambition of their lives yesterday when they met the champion Giants at their best and forced Johnnie McGraw and his aggressive boys to lower their colors to the American League Champions.

Once More — Hats Off to Red Sox!

Three hundred baseball writers, from all quarters of this country, Canada and Cuba, gave full reports by wire to their papers, and all had pleasant things to say of their treatment in Boston by Pres James McAleer and his assistant, Herman Nickerson, as well as for Pres Brush of New York and his assistant, John Foster.

For one, I am indeed pleased that the hard grind of a championship season is over, with the Speed Boys the winners, and my heart will go out to as fine a band of ball players as I ever traveled with.

Once more — Hats off to Manager Jake Stahl and his band of history makers, the Boston Red Sox!

The Play in Detail

The first two men up in the first inning were thrown out by Wagner. Snodgrass worked a pass and made second safely when Wagner dropped a perfect throw from Cady. Murray was thrown out by Gardner.

Hooper tried to bunt and rolled one to Merkle. Yerkes struck out. Speaker singled and made two bases on Doyle's muff. Lewis struck out.

In the second Merkle struck out. Herzog sent a long fly to Speaker. Gardner fumbled Meyers' grounder. Fletcher singled to center.

Cady hit the ball to Wagner and Meyers ran for third. Wagner threw to Gardner, who muffed the ball and men were safe at second and third. Mathewson then sent a long fly to Speaker.

Gardner walked. It was "Matty's" first pass of the series. Stahl hit to Doyle for a force out. Wagner singled. Cady sent up a weak fly for Merkle, and Bedient was thrown out by Doyle.

Giants Score in Third

In the third Devore walked on four pitched balls. Doyle hit a grounder that Gardner fumbled long enough to lose the forceout at second, but got his man at first. Snodgrass rolled one to Stahl.

Murray drove a liner that Speaker made a great try for, reaching the ball, but failing to hook it in, Devore scoring the first run, Wagner threw out Merkle.

Hooper and Yerkes were thrown out on weak grounders, and Speaker struck out.

Herzog opened the fourth with a fine double to left. Meyers sacrificed. The infield closed in. Fletcher sent up a fly for Gardner and Mathewson flied to Hooper.

With one down, Gardner drove a low liner that Snodgrass failed to hang on to and Larry tried for third, but was thrown out. Doyle relaying the ball to Herzog for a close play, Stahl then struck out.

Devore opened the 5th with a single off Bedient's shins, but was thrown out trying for second. Hooper made a wonderful catch of Doyle's fly close to the right-field fence. Snodgrass singled. Murray flied to Cady.

Sox Out on Three Pitches

Boston went out on three pitched balls. Wagner putting his fly close to the left-field bleachers, where Murray took the ball.

In the sixth, with two down, Meyers drew a pass, but Fletcher struck out.

Hooper sent up a weak fly for Merkle. Yerkes was trying to back out of the way of the ball when it hit his bat and dropped safely in short center.

Speaker walked, refusing to go after wide ones. Lewis hit into a forceout. "Duffy" started for second and Meyers threw to Mathewson, who sent the ball to Herzog, where Yerkes was caught by a yard.

Boston's chances now looked slim indeed.

Mathewson led off with a single in the seventh, but was forced by Devore. Doyle sent a high one for Wagner. Devore stole second, although it looked as if Wagner had his man blocked off. Snodgrass was thrown out by Gardner.

Boston Ties in Seventh

With one down, Stahl dropped a Texas Leaguer in center. Wagner walked. Cady sent up a weak fly for Fletcher.

Henriksen went to bat for Bedient and doubled over third base, scoring Stahl with the tying run.

Joe Wood came in to pitch for Boston in the eighth. Murray was disposed of by Stahl. Yerkes made a clever assist on Merkle. Herzog singled, but Meyers was thrown out by Yerkes.

Boston went out in order.

Devore got to first on balls, with two down in the ninth, and then Doyle was thrown out by Yerkes.

With one down, Stahl hit to left for two bases. A safe hit would now win the game, but Wagner sent a long fly to Devore, and Cady flied to left.

Won in the 10th

In the 10th, with one down, Murray drove a liner into the bleachers at left center, and took second, on a single by Merkle that Speaker kicked, allowing Merkle to make second.

Herzog was disposed of on strikes, and Wood saved a run by making a great one-handed stop of Meyers's vicious drive.

Engle was sent to bat for Wood, and drove a long fly to left center that was muffed by Snodgrass, Engle taking two bases.

Hooper tried to sacrifice, failed, and then drove the ball to deep center, where Snodgrass pulled it down.

"Matty" worked Yerkes too long and finally passed him. Speaker sent up a foul fly that Merkle failed to go after. Tris then spanked one to right field and Engle ran for home, Devore throwing to the plate. Yerkes made third and Speaker second.

"Matty" worked Lewis to the limit and finally passed him, filling the bases. "Matty" worked hard to get Gardner to hit at very low balls, and with two balls and one strike he put one over that Gardner hit to Devore in deep right field, allowing Yerkes to score the winning run.

The 1912 World Series was an absolute classic, matching the Red Sox and phenom Joe Wood against John McGraw's Giants and legendary pitcher Christy Mathewson. In the final game of the Series, the Giants made a number of errors, including what became known as outfielder Fred Snodgrass's "$30,000 Muff," delivering the world championship to Boston.

T. H. MURNANE

RUTH LEADS RED SOX TO VICTORY

from *The Boston Globe*, July 12, 1914

The Red Sox introduced Mr. Ruth, one of the Baltimore recruits, yesterday to the crowd at Fenway Park and with the assistance of Leonard, the Fresno fruit grower, the young man led the home club over the wire by a score of 4 to 3. There was a fine crowd and they enjoyed the short, snappy contest immensely, as only one hour and 31 minutes were taken up in playing the game.

All eyes were turned on Ruth, the giant left hander, who proved a natural ball player, and went through his act like a veteran of many wars. He has a natural delivery, fine control and a curve ball that bothers the batsman, but has room for improvement and will undoubtedly become a fine pitcher under the care of Manager Carrigan.

He held the Naps to five hits in six innings, with one strikeout, but was hit hard in the seventh, when the visitors tied the score by scoring two earned runs on singles by Kirke and Chapman, a sacrifice and a single by O'Neill. That was the curtain for the Oriole importation, and he looked weak only in comparison with Dutch Leonard, who pitched the last two innings, putting six men out in order, four of them on strikes.

Leonard is really pitching the best ball of any man in the American League and is the one man whom Manager Carrigan can depend to hold a game once won.

Boston scored in the first on a single by Scott and a triple by Gardner. Two runs in the fourth came on a pass, singles by Gardner and Carrigan, and a wild throw by O'Neill.

The Naps scored one in the fourth on a muff by Speaker, a sacrifice and a single by Jackson. The two runs in the seventh tied the score, and with Mitchell pitching high-class ball there was trouble ahead for the home team. Lewis, batting for Ruth, hit a grounder that Kirke made a one-hand stop of and then threw wild, so that Lewis went to second and then to third on Scott's out. Speaker responded with a line drive to center, scoring Lewis with the winning run.

There was some fine fielding by Turner, Graney, Scott, Yerkes, Janvrin and Speaker. The same teams will meet Monday, and by that time the Red Sox players should all line up for a week of good, hard work when called on.

Graney opened the game with a single. Turner was thrown out by Yerkes. Jackson singled to center, and Speaker threw home but Ruth took the ball and threw to Yerkes as Jackson was headed to that base. Jackson turned back and Graney tried for home, but was thrown out by Janvrin. Then Jackson was caught napping at first.

Henricksen struck out. Scott singled and was forced by Speaker. Turner sacrificed and Jackson scored the tying run with a single. Lajoie flied out to center. Kirke singled, Jackson going to third, but was left as the next man went out.

Gardner led off with a single. Janvrin sacrificed to see Rehg thrown out by Turner. Yerkes drew a pass and stole second. O'Neill's wild throw allowed Gardner to score. Carrigan scored Yerkes with a single. Ruth flied out to Jackson.

The visitors went out in order in the fifth, Janvrin making two fine onehand plays. The Red Sox went out in order from the head of the list.

Graney opened the sixth with a single and remained at first, to see the next three men go out on flies, Speaker making a beautiful catch of Lajoie's hard drive. Rehg was thrown out by Turner. Yerkes flied out to left and Carrigan struck out.

Kirke opened the seventh with a single. Chapman singled. Leibold sacrificed and O'Neill smashed a single to left, scoring two runs and tying the score. Mitchell hit to Scott for a double play. Lewis went to bat for Ruth and made two bases as Kirke threw past first, fielding the ball to the pitcher. Henricksen failed in two attempts to sacrifice and then put up a weak fly for Graney. Scott hit into a forceout, but made second on the run out. Speaker drove a sharp single to center, scoring Scott. Speaker was thrown out trying for second.

Leonard came in to pitch the eighth and struck out Graney and Turner and got Jackson at first.

Boston went out in order and the visitors went in for their last chance. Lajoie was thrown out by Leonard. Kirke struck out.

This game marked the first appearance of Babe Ruth in a Boston uniform. Despite his initial success, the club soon sent him down to minor league Providence for more seasoning. It would be another year before he began to take a regular turn in the Boston pitching rotation, where he quickly became one of the best left-handed pitchers in the league.

Not until 1918 did he begin to make his mark as a hitter, getting his chance to play in the outfield when the Red Sox roster was depleted as a result of World War I.

STRIKE! STRIKE! STRIKE!

Being a Veracious and Complete Account
of the Funeral Ceremonies of the Once Great
Game of Baseball and the Once Powerful
National Commission.

from *The Boston American,* September 11, 1918

It is two by the village clock. There are 25,000 fans in the stands at Fenway Park. There are twenty-five players in each dressing room under those stands.

They haven't their uniforms on, those players. They are striking. They have asked the National Commission for more money and they haven't got any reply. Which shows that the Commish is going along in regular style.

It is two-thirty by the village clock. There are twenty-five thousand fans out there waiting just the same. There are the twenty-five players in each dressing room, and there are a score of scribes without. There aren't supposed to be any scribes there, but, you know, they get in, even though the magnates and everybody don't want them.

The players have declared that they will not play unless they get a fair piece of the series' receipts. They have told the world, and everybody knows it, but the Commish.

The Commish had been told — at 1:10 — that there will not be any game. The shock was terrible. The Commish should never be awakened that early.

Byron Bancroft Johnson and Garry Herrmann come into view, just when it is two thirty-five by the village clock. They show the strain of the series, they do. Evidently they have been having some series.

"If they concede anything to those — pups, I'm through with baseball: I'm through, I'm through, I'm through," quoth Byron B., juggling his eyeglasses.

"If anything is to happen it will happen mighty quick," snarled Garry H. in his well-known "you know me" method.

It is two forty by the village clock when Ban and Garry and everybody march into the umpires' room. It is only one forty by Ban's chronometer, but he's on Central time.

The committee of players enters the umpires' room. They duck the gas stoves and the collars and neckties and everything. The players look serious enough, though they have to grin now and then when they look around.

"I went to Washington," sobbed Byron B., "and had the stamp of approval put on this World's series. I made it possible, I did," said Ban, striking his chest and directing his sobby eloquence right at Harry Hooper.

"I made it possible, Harry," he continued, beating the tattoo on his broad chest. "I had the stamp of approval put on the World's Series, Harry. I did it, Harry," striking his chest. "I did it."

"But, Mr. Johnson," broke in H. Hooper.

"I did it, Harry," interjected Ban, feelingly. "I had the stamp of approval put on, Harry. I did it, Harry."

"But," said H. Hooper, "we —"

"I did it, Harry," interposed Ban. "I had the stamp of approval put on, Harry. I did it."

"Let's arbitrary this matter, Mister Johnson," declared Garry Herrmann. Then he launched forth into a brilliant exposition of the history of baseball's governing board.

Expert reporters took notes for a while and then quit, befuddled. The umpires and the clubowners retreated.

"Listen," said H. Hooper, in a lull in the terrible babble, "we'll go out and play." They did, and you couldn't blame them.

"By Jolly," murmured Ban. "I did it; I did it."

I'll tell the world he did.

The 1918 World Series was played in early September of a season cut short by the war. But midway through the Series, the players on both teams learned that baseball's ruling National Commission, led by AL president Ban Johnson, had changed the way Series receipts would be divided, seriously cutting into the expected take of players on each club.

The players demanded a hearing before the commission. When they were put off, they struck before game five, forcing the commission to meet. But as Flatley describes in comic fashion, the players found the members of the commission at the Copley Plaza hotel, reeling drunk and in no condition to negotiate. Disgusted, they chose to play for the sake of the soldiers in the stands, but not before extracting a promise that they would face no retribution for the abortive strike. After the Series, the commission reneged on the deal and refused to award the players their world championship medallions.

PAUL H. SHANNON

RED SOX ARE AGAIN WORLD CHAMPIONS

from *The Boston Post*, September 12, 1918

Again are the Boston Red Sox baseball champions of the world.

At exactly five minutes past three o'clock yesterday afternoon, even before the wires began to tell the country that Barrow's men had delivered the punch that was to win the deciding contest in this great struggle for the supreme title, a carrier pigeon, released from the press stand by exultant soldiers started on its long flight to Camp Devens with the news of the fatal third inning and the downfall of the Chicago Cubs.

For six innings after this the contest endured, but this one eventful frame gave the veteran Whiteman a chance to pen the closing chapter in the championship battle of 1918.

Keeps Slate Clean

Once more a Boston team had arisen in its might and preserved a reputation never smirched in the post-season contests for the big stakes. For the fifth time in seven years Boston's championship prestige had been maintained by a team well worthy of upholding its reputation.

Just one unfortunate play by the National leaguers blasted the Cubs faint hopes of winning and gave George Whiteman easily the star of the entire series, the opportunity of writing his record indelibly in the annals of a bitterly waged struggle. Just one sad muff by a player who had been one of the real bulwarks of the Chicago defence sent that team from Fenway Park defeated after one of the gamest fights that a losing outfit has ever made.

Many will blame Flack for Chicago's downfall, and by the strict rules of scoring he must bear the stigma for the Cubs' defeat, yet the

18,000 fans who witnessed the closing game will be inclined rather to extend praise than blame.

Whiteman the Star

In nearly every run that the Red Sox scored in the six games Whiteman, the little Texas veteran, has figured mightily, and yesterday again his was the bat that sent both of the Boston runs across.

Two bases on balls in the third inning — one to Mays, the other to Shean — had put two men on the sacks, and they were at third and second respectively when Whitey came to bat with two men out. A consultation followed and for a moment it looked as though the Chicago team would pass him and take a chance on the even more dangerous McInnis. Finally the Cub board of strategy decided to make the batter hit.

With one ball and one strike the count, Whitey got hold of a ball that was just on the outside and drove it with the speed of a bullet into right field. Flack, who was playing well out, tore in to catch the liner. He reached it by a desperate sprint, but the ball had been driven with such force that it tore his hands apart and dropped to the ground while Shean followed Mays across the plate. The crestfallen Flack made a futile throw home, but there was no play. The second run had been registered and, as it turned out, the championship had been decided right then and there.

It was said afterward that Flack, in the belief that but one man was out at the time, tried to throw the ball before he caught it in the hope of stopping a man from going home. This was denied by Manager Mitchell, who said after the game that it was an out and out muff, that Flack knew two men had been retired, and the only excuse was that the ball was driven with far greater force than the fielder anticipated. At any rate, Chicago's hopes of wresting the championship from the Boston team died at the same time.

So thus it was the good fortune of the Red Sox left fielder to close his big league career in a blaze of glory, such as he had never dared to hope for since he first entered the majors 11 long years ago. To Whiteman it has been given to star both on the offence and defence as few world's series heroes ever have. He can always look back with pride upon the splendid part he took in bringing the 1918 world's championship home to Boston.

Makes Great Catch

Whiteman's active participation in the struggle did not end with that telling drive in the eighth. In the same frame Barber, leading off as a pinch hitter for the Cubs, made a gallant effort to start what might have proven a dangerous rally but for the enterprise and gameness of the Texan.

Hitting the ball squarely on the trade mark, and lining it into short left field, his chances for starting this round with a two-bagger were good until Whiteman made his marvelous as well as sensational play. Tearing in at breakneck speed, Whiteman made a shoestring catch, grabbing the ball just before it reached the ground, and turning a complete somersault after making the catch. The achievement completely stopped the opposition, and gave the stands a chance to cheer and shriek for three full minutes.

In accomplishing this feat, however, Whiteman hit on his head and badly wrenched the muscles of his neck. Compelled to leave the game a minute later after courageously trying to resume play, he was given a tremendous tribute as he passed into the dugout. After the game, Manager Mitchell, in warmly commending this man's work during all six games, said that the catch was one of the most spectacular he has ever witnessed in a post-season battle.

By the score of 2 to 1 the Red Sox vanquished the Cubs in a twirling duel that was anticipated, when the nominations had Mays opposing Tyler on the rubber. Just as expected Mays proved a baffling proposition for the Cubs, the one run scored off him coming in the only round where the submarine was not completely the master of the situation. As for Lefty Tyler, grandly as he worked, he as well as his manager must realize today that he suffered the fate of the pitcher sent too often to the well.

Fully as effective as Mays, and every whit as efficient as in either of his other appearances against the Red Sox, Tyler paid the penalty for his brief lack of control, as well as for the fatal though excusable error by his unlucky right fielder. All through the series bases on balls have been the cause of serious trouble for the Cub southpaws, and the history of the earlier games in the sextet was repeated yesterday.

Passes Prove Fatal

In his opening essay against the Red Sox, a pass in the fourth inning was the cause of Jim Vaughn's defeat. On Saturday last the run that beat this same twirler was started by a batter being hit. Both the men that scored on Ruth's terrific three-bagger last Monday were sent to first on passes by Tyler, and yesterday again those fatal passes caused, or rather led on to the clever southpaw's undoing.

All along it had been conceded that the Red Sox lacked the punch against left-handers and that these same twirlers of the southpaw variety would be very apt to beat them if they possessed control. But lack of control at critical times shattered the hopes of Mitchell and failed to confirm Mitchell's judgment in vesting his whole reliance on two left-handers while great right-handers like Hendrix and Douglas were compelled to sit upon the bench.

Tyler was in splendid form yesterday but for the third and fourth innings. In each of these frames he issued two bases on balls, and had not Flack muffed Whiteman's drive he might have pitched himself out of the hole as he did in the fourth. Of the six hits made off Tyler only one was a cleancut one; and this, a single by Strunk, was safe just because it bounded between Hollocher and Pick, who both came within an ace of stopping the ball.

Mays, on the other hand, was possessed of far better control than Tyler. He pitched one of his finest games and allowed but three safe hits. But Mays was given superb support — as, indeed, have all the Boston twirlers in a series which was marked by but one Red Sox error in six games.

The work of Whiteman, Scott, Thomas and Hooper went a long way yesterday in adding to Carl's efficiency, while the sharp way in which both he and Schang watched the bases kept the opposition from taking any undue risks.

And Stuffy McInnis

Right here it might be added that McInnis, whose first base play has been the finest ever provided for any world's series struggle, added a great deal to the Red Sox defence by co-operating so splendidly with the battery. In the second inning, for instance, he kept Pick, who was on first, constantly guessing till Mays picked the runner off the bag by an unexpected and lightning throw. Later on the same sort of a play, executed by Schang and McInnis, held the Cubs in check in the only round where there was any real danger of Mays being punished.

Flack, eager to atone for his misdeed of the third, was the first man to bat in the following frame, and he drove a clean single to left. An attempt by Hollocher to drive the ball through McInnis on the hit and run play failed because Stuffy was alive to the situation, made a pretty stop and would have forced Flack at second had not this speedster obtained such a considerable start. Then Mann was clipped in the ankle by one of Mays' fast inshoots and the Cubs had two men on bases for the first time in the game, and as it proved eventually, for the only inning where they were able to get a man past first.

With two runs needed to tie and two men on the sacks, the Red Sox caught the signal for a double steal or the hit and run play repeated, so Mays threw to second a couple of times to hold Hollocher on that bag, seemingly paying no attention to Mann.

Suddenly he turned and streaked the sphere across to first. McInnis was waiting, and before Mann could get back on the bag Stuffy dropped on the runner, held him off till he touched him and got the out decision from Umpire Klom. Mann protested bitterly, but the decision was a just one. Leslie was compelled to return to the bench, and with him went the Cubs' one best chance of tieing up the count.

Helped Mays Out

McInnis' wideawakeness and the keenness of the Boston defence in anticipating some such play by the Chicago base runners undoubtedly helped Mays out of a very serious dilemma and without a doubt prevented a tie score, for Paskert, the next batter, drew a base on balls and had Mann held his position on first base the Cubs would have had the sacks filled and only one out. Flack had stolen third base just after the sudden retirement of Mann and Markle's safe hit consequently scored the only Chicago run of the game. But had the sacks been choked two tallies and a tie score would have been the result and the contest might well have gone into seven games for a decision. After the fourth only one Chicagoan reached first. He was passed, but never saw second.

How the Sox scored their two runs in the third has already been told, but in the fourth Tyler showed how superbly he can twirl when danger threatens and he is at his best. Scott led off in this frame with an infield hit, and Thomas sacrificed. Schang was walked and Mays filled the bases by beating out a perfect bunt. But Hooper couldn't hit the ball out of the diamond, and his weak grounder resulted in an out at the plate for Scott. Shean was unlucky because Deal made a brilliant stop with one hand along the foul line and thereby retired the side without scoring.

In a series that has been utterly bereft of any concerted attack by either side, and which shows the lowest number of runs scored for many years, the fielding has been the one big glittering factor. The showing of Scott, Hollocher, Shean, McInnis, Merkle and Dean has been brilliant. The outfielding of Whiteman and Mann has been exceptionally fine, but the backstop work of the Boston catchers on the defence has outshone that of Killifer, who was supposed to far outclass them.

The victory of the Boston team, undoubtedly expected by the majority of the Cubs, was no signal for any very great demonstration. The Boston players were in a very subdued mood through long consideration of the scanty purse which will reward their achievement. This money they will split at Fenway Park at noon today. The Cubs left the field without any fuss and took occasion before dressing to visit the Red Sox clubhouse and congratulate the new champions.

Need Boston fans be reminded that this is the last time that headline has rung true?

F. C. LANE

THE HERO OF THE SERIES

How Baseball's Greatest Honor Came to Hard-
Working George Whiteman Only after Years
of Undeserved Obscurity in the Minor Leagues

from *Baseball Magazine*, November 1918

The career of George Whiteman is one of those semi-tragedies with which the thorny paths to the Majors are thickly strewn. Here is a player who has proved his capacity to fill a regular berth on a World's Championship Club and yet was doomed, through no fault of his own, to spend all the best years of his playing prime in the humble role of a minor leaguer. And now, when it is too late to do him any good, he wins that highest of honors which Ty Cobb himself has never been able to claim, that of hero of a World's Series. Chance which seems to preside over most baseball affairs, never made a more sudden change than when she raised George Whiteman from bush league obscurity to the dizziest eminence in the whole realm of athletic sport.

Every World's Series has its hero. Whenever the realm of sport hails a new world's champion it wreaths the head of some humble athlete with the laurel crown of momentary fame. Some star of the infield or outfield, or it may be the battery is placed upon a pedestal and the spot light of publicity is played upon him for a day or a month until he, too, passes on to make room for a newer idol. It has always been so in baseball annals and it always will be so. For scarce has the last spectator wended his dejected way through the grandstands deserted aisles when the final game is over before the scribes are hard at work on a eulogy of the newest leader in the sport field, the hero of a championship series.

There was a time when Christy Mathewson usurped the public

notice after one of these classic contests. Upon another occasion Frank Baker captured the coveted laurels. Again it was Eddie Collins, and Duffy Lewis, and Babe Adams. Hank Gowdy who led the player procession "over there" was the hero of the 1914 series and long basked in a blaze of glory. Every season's close has welcomed that new addition to the hall of sport fame, the leading actor in the role of series stars.

Who is the hero of 1918? Opinions might easily differ, for several players did yeoman duty and might offer well-founded claims for recognition. There is Jim Vaughn who toiled with masterly ability through three heart-breaking games only to lose two of them through no fault of his own. There was Pick, the newcomer to the ranks, who batted for .389. There was Mays who won both his games, whose masterly pitching decided the final contest. There was Schang, used largely in the utility role, who smote the ball for the colossal average of .444. And there was Scott, whose all but impossible stops and throws cut down many a Cub basehit, spoiled many a Chicago rally.

But survey the field as you will, give to each performer the favor which is his due. And after all is said and done come back to a little heralded athlete, a man who waited long for his one big chance, George Whiteman. For it was Whiteman more than anyone else, who deserves the title of "hero of the series."

What then did Whiteman do? He played in every game. In twenty times at bat he made five hits for a total of seven bases. He scored two of the nine runs made by the Sox. He drove in three of the remaining tallies, for, although it was Flack's error which contributed to the Cubs' downfall, it was Whiteman's line drive that spilled the beans. The dope further tells us that the Texan reached first base four times in addition to the visits he made to that sure haven after a safe hit. He received two bases on balls, was hit once by a pitched ball and reached the initial corner once on an error. Furthermore, he stole one of the three bases credited to the Sox.

Far from being a mediocre performer in the offense he was a live wire from start to finish. And though his batting average, .250, is not large taken by itself, it looms impressively when compared with the team average of .186. But, while Whiteman's record in the offense was better than that of any other regular performer on the team, it was mainly his work in the field which raised him to the baseball hero class. One unimportant error was chalked against his name. Everywhere else he shone resplendent. Harry Hooper, himself, from whom great deeds in the field are taken as a matter of course, could not have improved upon Whiteman's work in the gardens. For the Red Sox left fielder proved a tower of strength from the first game when he made five putouts to the very last when he cut off a Cub rally by one of the most sensational stops ever made on the diamond.

Several times during the series it devolved upon Whiteman to save the game for the Red Sox. And every time he rose to the occasion. In the fifth game he cut off what looked like a sure Cub rally in the very first inning by a circus catch, and temporarily killed the Cubs' chances by a double play. Later in the game he cut down a Cub runner by a throw to the plate, and had the game depended upon his efforts alone, the series would have ended then and there. Fortune, however, chose to cast a belated smile on the efforts of big Jim Vaughn, and the Cubs won out.

Whiteman played a singularly prominent part in the final and decisive encounter. It was his ringing liner which Flack failed to handle cleanly which sent in the two runs which proved a knock-out blow to Cub hopes. True, the crack wouldn't have scored them if Flack hadn't contributed what the scorer regretfully put down as an error. But the error wouldn't have been made if Whiteman hadn't connected with the ball. And whatever doubt may arise as to the credit due him for driving in those winning runs, there is no doubt whatever that he saved the game in later innings. For the Cubs, battling desperately with their backs against the wall, had already won back one of the lost tallies and were on the war path for more. A vicious Texas leaguer spiralled out toward left field. Whiteman ran far in for the hit. If he missed it it would get away for extra bases. But he did not miss. He made a shoestring catch, though in the effort he had to throw himself off balance. He did not dare to use his arms to attempt to save himself for he wanted to hang on to that ball at all costs. So he merely ducked his head and dived headforemost to the turf. He turned a complete somersault and came up standing with the ball in his hands. But he made the play at the imminent risk of breaking his neck and did in fact, wrench that essential member so that he was forced to retire from the contest. It was a wonderful play.

Few will begrudge Whiteman the honor which he has so richly earned. It has been earned indeed. Here is a veteran player whom unkind fate has exiled for years to a minor role in obscure leagues. Here is a player with the proved ability to play on a great team, the real star of the World's Champions. And yet he went begging for a big league job through all the best years of his career and found his proper place late in life, too late to realize the just reward of his talents. His has been one of the unnumbered tragedies of the bush, the hard working, efficient player who lacked just a little of the requisite luck to force admission into hard, forbidding ranks of the major leagues. He is a striking illustration of that fallacy that big league talent is strictly limited. For consider, here was a man, the star of the series, who would never have found a place on the club had the big leagues not been short handed. There is Hollocher, the season's sensation with the Cubs, who owes his chance to the fact that the Chicago team failed in its ambition to secure Hornsby from the Cardinals. And though veteran scribes predicted that both teams would suffer on account of their substitute players it was those players who responded splendidly to the occasion, who carried their full share of the responsibility, who suffered nothing in comparison with the most famous stars on either club.

I talked with Whiteman immediately after the final game while the stands were still ringing with applause of his sensational work. As we talked members of the passing crowd continually accosted the now famous athlete, whose reputation had grown like a mushroom, in a few days' time. "They all want to talk to me now," said Whiteman, with a trace of wistfulness in his voice. "It came late, but I got my chance at last. I was sure I could made good and I guess I have. Not that the experience was so trying to me at that. I wasn't nervous, I knew what I could do. And I have been on pennant winning teams several times in the minors. But some how or other I never seemed to land in the majors. I was strongly considered many years ago. In fact, I was traded to Boston, this same club, along with Tris Speaker. But I never got a show. Speaker didn't connect at first either, you may remember. But he got his chance and he sure made good. But I never seemed to get a chance, I was allowed to drift back to the minors and though I was signed several seasons later on, and played some fourteen games with a fine batting average, I drifted back just the same. It seemed to be my luck.

"I cannot explain it exactly. I think I have been good enough to play in the majors for some years. But I never seemed to get the publicity that some fellows get. I believe it was that as much as anything. If people don't know about you it's a cinch they won't care a great deal to get you on their club. Some fellows are lucky in this thing. The writers seem to come around them and want to write them up. But they seldom came to me. So I went plodding along year after year, hoping that something would break. I had about given up hope when this chance came and I said to myself, 'It is the last chance you will ever get and it is up to you to make good.' I worked hard all the time. I did my best. I am not sure I could do as well again, but it will always be satisfaction to me to know that I was able to do good work, work that I can be pleased with even if the opportunity did come to me when I had about given up hope. If it hadn't been for this season no one would ever have heard of George Whiteman, I suppose. And there you are. I don't know how many other players there have been in the minors that no one ever heard of either, who might have delivered the goods if they had had a chance. It's a hard game, professional baseball, and no one can tell me that you don't have to have luck as well as ability to rise very far in it.

"But, while I think that I should have had a chance a long time ago, I am satisfied. I have had my day, brief as it is, I am certainly better off than hundreds of other fellows who never had their day at all."

So said George Whiteman, with that earnest sincerity which has marked all his work in his brief major league career, a career which as he said, "came too late."

Born in Peoria, Ill., thirty-three years ago, Whiteman is already a fading veteran, according to all major league standards. Most of his career has been spent in minor leagues with but two brief trials in major league company before war thinned ranks found for him a vacancy on the roster of the Red Sox. Five feet six and one-half inches in height, Whiteman is of stocky build as his weight of 165 pounds will indicate. And his face is burned deeply by the Texan sun, for it is in the big State of the south that he resides during the off season. Not much more can the meagre dope books tell of his exploits for his is a record that has soared like a rocket only after long years of seeming mediocrity. But the public will not care particularly about his former career. The public will prefer to dwell upon the showing of this little known athlete upon the one occasion when his chance came. For his response to that solitary call was grand, magnificent, such as few of the very greatest players ever duplicate. Ty Cobb, great as he is, though he has taken part in no less than three world's series, has never been the star of the event. While humble George Whiteman, who was trailing despondently in the minors, while Cobb was burning up the circuits and the whole sport world was ringing with his exploits, has achieved that rarest of stellar roles, and is the true hero of the 1918 Series.

George Whiteman is perhaps the most unlikely and least known World Series hero of all time. A career minor-leaguer, he was plucked from Toronto by general manager Ed Barrow to fill the breach in Boston's outfield caused by the war, often platooning with Babe Ruth.

He got his big chance in the Series when Chicago manager Fred Mitchell chose to start only left-handed pitchers against the Red Sox, keeping Babe Ruth on the bench. Whiteman was in the middle of almost every Red Sox rally and made a number of remarkable catches, including that tumbling shoestring catch in the eighth inning of the final game to save the contest. He hurt his neck on the play but left the field to a stirring ovation as Ruth trotted in to replace him.

When the Red Sox regulars returned from the service, Whiteman was released and never played another game in the major leagues.

LETTER FROM GEORGE WHITEMAN

Houston, Texas
February 12, 1921.

Mr. Ban B. Johnson,
President American League,
Chicago, Ill.

Dear Sir:

With further reference to my letter of December 3, and your reply of December 8 which has reference to the 1913 Worlds Series Emblem to which I am entitled; I am glad that you yourself, feel that I am entitled to this Emblem, and not having heard from the Commission in regard to this, I am again taking the matter up with you. I certainly regret to have to bother you with this seemingly small matter, but it seems that I have no other re-course, and if there is anything further that you can do, I will certainly appreciate it. In the judgment, the Commission should help the player who has been a credit to the game, when they are in position to do so. In my fourteen years of professional Baseball, this is the first time that I have ever asked for anything, and I feel that I should be given consideration in this instance.

Kindly do whatever you feel justified in doing, advising me at your convenience.

Yours truly
Geo. Whiteman

This letter, found in the files of the Baseball Hall of Fame, was one of many that George Whiteman wrote various baseball officials pleading for his promised world championship medallion, which had been denied to all the Red Sox players because of their strike midway through the World Series (see page 67). He was turned down. In fact, every baseball commissioner from Kenesaw Mountain Landis through Fay Vincent upheld Johnson's decision.

But in 1993, Whiteman finally received his due. After the editor of this book exposed the details of the strike in an article on the subject for New England Sport *magazine, major league baseball was approached and asked to make good on Johnson's promise. This time there was no baseball commissioner, and the request was granted. In a ceremony at Fenway Park on September 5, 1993, a 1918 world championship banner was unfurled, and the descendants of the 1918 Red Sox, including 92-year-old Ethel Koneman, George Whiteman's sister-in-law and closest surviving relative, received the medallions.*

F. C. LANE

THE FIRE BRAND OF THE AMERICAN LEAGUE

How Harry H. Frazee Has Proved Himself
the Live Wire of Major League Baseball

from *Baseball Magazine,* March 1919

Harry H. Frazee is the firebrand of the American League. He violated all the rules of that August circuit when he broke in. He has turned them topsy turvy in his breezy passage through, and his exit from the league at some indefinite date in the future, promises to be a riot. His friends who are many, admire his courage and energy; his enemies who are not few, must at least respect his aggressive fearlessness. For whatever his faults and his foibles, he is that which is dearest of all to the American heart, a sizzling, scintillating, live wire.

You need a lot of adjectives to describe Harry Frazee, and yet if we were specializing on grammatical parts of speech, we should say he is one personified verb. His whole career is incessant activity. Above all things else, he is a man who does things. His restless soul welcomes jobs that other men shrink from. Nay more, if work does not come to him fast enough, he goes forth and brings home whole arms full, fairly exulting in the sheer love of doing things, of going through a mass of matters with a whoop and a hurrah. Helter, skelter he may seem to those who watch him pacing restlessly up and down his office and diving into a whole heap of correspondence for some isolated fact he wants to know. But a man who neglected details and allowed his work to go half done, would never accomplish what Harry Frazee has accomplished. Hence, we deduce the fact that he is merely a lightning worker with a system all his own, in the midst of his apparent lack of system.

A phrenologist would be struck at once by Frazee's personality. His body is short, stocky, heavy set, but very active. His head is enormous, and his energy fairly bubbles over. A big brain and boundless energy, say the skull sharps, are the assured foundations of success. Which doubtless explains why Frazee, at an age when most men are merely beginning their careers, is already a millionaire and has lived through more stirring scenes than most octogenarians ever heard of.

Even his friends would call Frazee an Iconoclast. In his brief career, he has overturned and shattered to pieces more of the cherished images of baseball than any other half dozen owners. The dearest traditions of the game have been dismissed by him with indifference verging on contempt. Frazee takes nothing on faith. The fact that other men have held certain tenets means nothing in his young life. He has to be shown. As an example of his audacious disregard for established custom, when he took charge of the Red Sox, the Western Union Telegraph office sent to him for a number of season passes and two party passes. Frazee ignored the demand. A personal representative of the company finally called upon him and requested the passes. Frazee wanted to know why. "Well," said the representative, "we have always had them." "Is that any reason?" snapped Frazee. "Because, perhaps, my predecessors were crazy, should I be crazy too? Give me some passes to use your wires and some party passes, if there are any such things. You can't do it! Why not? My request is just as sensible as yours. Why should I give away the only thing I have to sell, admission to my ball park!" "But," stammered the representative, "the good will of the Western Union —" "You can't hurt me," retorted Frazee. "If I want to send a message over your wires, I do so. The law compels you to take the message. I pay for the privilege. That is all there is to it. If you or your friends want to visit my ball park, you pay for the privilege. That's all there is to that. Your operatives who are on duty, will be admitted. They are working on the field. But I can see no reason why I should give charity to the Western Union."

The relations between the Press and the owners are unusual. The Press has developed baseball through the enormous volume of free publicity it has given the game. Therefore the Baseball writers expect and even demand certain privileges to which they believe themselves entitled. And the owners, time without mind, have accorded these privileges, if not willingly, at least out of wholesome respect for what the Press could do for them in the columns of their papers. Frazee as a theatrical man is fully alive to the value of publicity; probably appreciates it more than most magnates. But he is too thoroughly business-like and independent to stand for what he considers unfair treatment from anyone.

A certain writer on a Boston paper took occasion to pan the Red Sox and Frazee. Whether his reasons were real or fancied, we won't pretend to say. He took a few pot shots at the new owner in his column, and Frazee paid little attention. But finally he got the Hub President's goat. The next time that writer presented his pass, it was taken up. He bought a ticket, but the ticket was taken up, the money returned to him and admission refused.

The paper of whose staff that writer was a member, remonstrated with Frazee to no avail. They brought pressure to bear upon Ban Johnson. The Czar of the American League suggested that Frazee might arbitrate the matter. Frazee curtly refused. Finally the managing editor of the paper in question decided to fight the matter. He met Frazee and said bluntly:

"You can't afford to antagonize the Boston —" mentioning the name of the paper.

"Who is trying to antagonize them?" retorted Frazee hotly.

"You refuse admission to our representative," said the editor.

"I don't have to admit a man who insults me and my Club," answered Frazee. "If you don't know what he has written, read your own paper. And as for antagonizing the Boston —, I don't allow anyone to run my business. I haven't been to you and asked you to discharge this writer. If he is worth money to you, keep him. That is your outlook. But I will not have him in my park. That is my outlook. And as for your paper, I get decent treatment from the other papers in Boston. The Red Sox are as well known as your sheet. But whether they are or not, I won't have you or anyone else running my business for me."

That ended the argument. But having gained his point, Frazee did relent to the extent that he permitted the writer in question to attend the park during world's series time. He is not vindictive, is Frazee, but he does love to carry his point.

Two of the most difficult of the owner's problems are the free list and treatment of the press. What Frazee thinks of the free list is apparent from his treatment of the Western Union representative. In a few minutes, he overturned a long established custom. His diplomacy, (if we can use that word) toward the press is well illustrated by the other incident. And yet Frazee is by no means unpopular with the writers. In fact most of the boys like his straightforward ways. For Frazee isn't small or petty or mean. He is merely fearless. He will not be imposed upon by anyone. And when a problem confronts him, instead of trying to flank it out of position by smooth diplomacy, he charges audaciously straight on the center and carries all the trenches by the sheer impetuosity of his charge.

But the treatment accorded the free list and the press, are not the only traditions of the American League that Frazee shattered without a moment's hesitation. The big, overmastering tradition of the American League is Ban Johnson. And Frazee showed no greater respect for Ban, than he did for anyone else, an attitude so unheard of in American League traditions, that the whole sport world is still gasping with astonishment at the sheer audacity of the man.

In fact Frazee's whole career has antagonized Johnson. In the first place, he was a theatrical man. Johnson long ago posted the axiom that the theatrical profession and baseball should be kept apart. Nevertheless, Frazee is a member of the merry magnates association. Another unwritten rule of the American League was that no new member should be admitted among the magnates without the co-operation or at least the approval, of the dominant president. But when Lannin sold out to Frazee, he dealt direct with the latter, who paid scant attention to Ban's opinions on the deal. Having broken into the league in direct opposition to the established traditions, Frazee reflecting that he had made a good start, proceeded to clean up. When war brought critical days, and Ban Johnson handled problems in a way which displeased Frazee, he was not at all reticent about mentioning the fact.

Frazee's opinions of Ban are breezy and picturesque. He narrated some of these opinions to the writer on a memorable morning at Fenway Park, shortly after Johnson had proposed that the American League close its schedule on August 20th and immediately wind up its affairs with a world's series.

"I rather like to manage my own business" said Frazee, "but if I can't, I at least want to be consulted. If someone puts a sign on my park, closed for the season, I insist on being one of the innocent bystanders to watch the proceedings. Everybody seems to have a tremendous amount of respect for Mr. Johnson's opinions. I don't deny that he has been very successful. I don't question that he was largely responsible for the building up of the American League. I will admit that he has done a great deal for the game and should be given credit. But all those things happened before I came into the league. Since I became an owner, Mr. Johnson has made blunders. Why shouldn't he be blamed for them? If other men make mistakes, people don't go around on tip toe with their fingers on their mouths. They speak right out and give the offender a good call. I help pay Johnson's salary. Why shouldn't I have a right to criticise his work when I believe he has acted foolishly?"

The great park was deserted. Only a few laborers were working on the right field fence. Perhaps they heard some of Frazee's remarks, for he was facing their direction and as he thought of Johnson's latest misdoings, he poured forth his soul in a flood of eloquence that would have moved a stone image. Lurid adjectives, sizzling nouns, and withering verbs followed one another in rapid succession. But omitting the bursts of rhetoric in which his surcharged soul sought relief, there was nothing that Frazee said on that occasion about Ban Johnson that he hasn't said openly. Many men have criticised Johnson quite as bitterly as Frazee ever did, behind Johnson's back. But Frazee said nothing in private that he hasn't said repeatedly to Johnson's knowledge. There is nothing underhand about Frazee. He is open and fearless in all his acts.

Another time honored tradition of the game goes to smash in Frazee's terse characterization, "Baseball is essentially a show business. Surely it is a sport, but it's an exhibit just the same. If you have any kind of a production, be it a music show or a wrestling bout, or a baseball game that people want to see enough to pay good money for the privilege, then you are in a show business and don't let anyone ever tell you different. Baseball is a fine sport, the best in the world. But Major League baseball is a show business and why shouldn't it be? Is there anything disreputable in the show business? William Jennings Bryan when he was in Wilson's cabinet, went into the show business. True, he was a lecturer, but what is that but the show business? The man had something to say that people wanted to hear. And they paid him well for the privilege. The Major League owner builds a big grand stand at immense cost, hires high priced players to make up a team, and stages baseball games. For this he properly charges admission and the public is glad to have the chance to see high grade games. What is there about all that, that should cause anyone sleepless nights? This talk about commercialism in baseball, makes me tired. Baseball as I have seen it, is a clean business run on strictly honest principles. Naturally it calls for investments and naturally the owner expects to realize something on his investment. Why shouldn't he? Even clergymen get paid for their work; why shouldn't ball players and owners?"

Harry Frazee has had an exciting career since he first saw the light of day at Peoria, Ill., thirty-eight years ago. If anyone was ever born to a profession, Frazee was that man. When he was sixteen years old and still attending high school, he was made assistant business manager of the local opera house. At seventeen, he went on the road as advance agent for a small show. It was a moderate success and the following year he secured a better position with another show at a salary of $40 a week. The next year Frazee got a similar job with a show known as "Mahoney's Wedding." He was paid $45 a week, but he held out for a share of the profits. The owners were already discouraged with the production, didn't believe there were going to be any profits, and readily agreed. Frazee carried the show clear to San Francisco, and it cleaned up of $14,000. At twenty, he was business manager for still another show at a salary of $65 and one-third the profits. That was the last time he ever worked on salary. The following season he went into business for himself, and he has cleaned up a fortune in the most hazardous of professions in the years that followed.

Frazee's first success was with a show in which he was associated with Harry Bay, the great Cleveland outfielder. Bay put $300 into the show, enough to entitle him to a one-fourth interest. Fifteen weeks later Frazee paid Bay $3,500 for his share of the profits. He himself continued with the show for a year and cleaned up $16,000.

With this start, Frazee began to be a producer of more elaborate shows. Some of the best known productions in America were placed before the footlights under his management. "It is a fascinating game, but it is a gamble pure and simple," says Frazee. "I read probably one hundred and fifty plays a year. I should read one a day, but I have other things to do, so I neglect my business to that extent. Needless to say, most of these plays are impossible. A large number that are well written and properly executed, nevertheless won't do. Sometimes a play isn't at all well written but it has a catchy idea which will pay the producer to remodel in proper form. And of the few plays that are cleverly written around a theme of genuine interest, most fail to get across. It seems impossible for anyone, no matter what his experience, to pick a sure winner in a play. Charles Frohman used to contend that if one out of nine of his productions proved successful, he was content. That is a heavy loss. The producer spends a good many thousand dollars on a play and it proves a Flivver. But he keeps right on to the next one and next until he finds a winner. Then he hopes to recoup all his losses and leave a comfortable balance on the right side of the ledger. That is the nature of the business. Most of my tries have been Flivvers. My batting average hasn't been high. But I am satisfied. Here and there a play seems to catch on. What the public wants it will pay for. I go in entirely for light shows, farces and musical comedies. The life of a farce is two years at most where a so-called standard production may last for many seasons. But in a farce you clean up quickly if at all. You put out several companies at once and tour the country thoroughly before the farce gets old and turns mouldy on your hands. I go on the theory that people attend the theatre to be amused. I know that many go for instruction and for them, tragedies and Shakespeare are all well enough. But the rank and file go to the theatre for diversion, and I try to give them what they want. There are enough undertakers' announcements in the papers. Gayety and life are in popular demand.

"The biggest clean-up I ever made was with 'Madam Sherry,' I was only a third owner in that show, but we netted $758,000 on that one production. Another show which I produced 'A Pair of Sixes,' cost me $3,600. It netted me $186,000. Those are the bright spots in the producer's life. They offset the shows that he thought would be winners and go to smash, carrying thousands of dollars into the scrap heap."

As Frazee broadened out into a producer, he began to build theatres of his own. He now has a two-thirds interest in the Cort Theatre in Chicago, and he built and operated the Longacre Theatre in New York, until he sold out his interests last winter. Nor are his interests confined to the theatrical end of the game. He has been a devoted follower of boxing and staged James Corbett in some of his most successful plays. He also took on James Jeffries when he was training to fight Johnson and paid him $3,000 a week for a tour in vaudeville.

"Some of my friends told me this tour would be a failure," says Frazee, "but I cleaned up $58,000 as my share of the profits."

Frazee also took the late Frank Gotch, champion wrestler of the world, on a tour at $1,500 a week and he was financial backer behind the promoters who staged the bout in Havana, where Jess Willard knocked out Jack Johnson.

"I lost most of my prospects on that bout," admits Frazee, "as the moving pictures were refused admittance into the country. But I actually cleaned up $6,000 on the contest, nevertheless."

While Frazee was still at high school, he played third base and managed the baseball team. He was always interested in baseball, in fact knew of the chance to buy the Cubs when Murphy went in as an unknown adventurer and made his fortune. But he was too young and lacked the necessary financial backing to plunge into Major League baseball at the time.

"From the very first," says Frazee, "I determined to buy into Major League baseball if I ever had the opportunity. More than that I revolved in my own mind the best prospects, and decided that the Cubs, the White Sox, the Giants and the Red Sox were the four most desirable clubs in Baseball. I bought the Red Sox in preference to the others, because I had the chance. And at that, the Red Sox are the best supported club in either circuit and one of the best investments.

"Naturally the war has cut into the amusement business of which baseball is a part. But I have been fairly lucky. My first year proved to be profitable and last season, though a tight squeeze, I actually made some money when almost everyone else was losing it. Now that the war is over, I look for smooth sailing everywhere. The public is heartily sick of the four years' strain of the war and glad to return to wholesome and proper amusements such as baseball.

"I have signed up my manager, Mr. Barrow, for another year, and believe he will give me another winning club. My selection of Barrow was a target for some critics who thought I knew little about baseball. But I don't know how John McGraw, Connie Mack or anyone else could improve on Barrow's showing with a pennant and a world's championship on his very first appearance. I first thought of securing Barrow not as manager. I had met him in Mr. Johnson's office and was much impressed with his straightforward business-like way of doing things. The thought had been prominent in my mind for some time that I might go abroad for a season and I wanted to feel that my interests were in the hands of a capable executive. Barrow was my idea of such a man. But the war made a change in those projects, so I approached Barrow with the offer of the management. I told him in brief that I had been thinking of giving him the job. His response was equally brief. He said, "I have been thinking that a manager ought to be able to do something with that club of yours." So we speedily arranged matters to our mutual satisfaction.

"I had just completed my $60,000 deal with Connie Mack. It was a lot of money but we won the pennant. My recent deals will no doubt be much criticised. We gave up Lewis and Leonard and Shore for Caldwell, Love, Gilhooley, Walters and some money. I am not going to say how much money we received.

"My main object in making the trade was to secure a smart catcher. We couldn't get Schalk or O'Neill the two leading backstops in the league. Walters looked good to both Mr. Barrow and myself and we determined to get him. If we had to go high, that is all right enough.

"My latest deal, a three cornered affair with Washington and Detroit, gave us the very man to plug up the only other questionable position on our club, third base. Vitt is a fine third baseman, just the man we needed. And as long as we got him what difference does it make what we paid for him? You can't be a piker in Major League baseball. The most economical way in the long run, is to plunge at the beginning and get it over with."

Frazee has two ambitions. He wants to tour the world with a theatrical troupe and he wants to own a stable of race horses. On the first of these two hobbies, he says:

"I have travelled rather extensively in continental Europe, but I want to go around the world and take my time about it. I want to see

Japan and India and the rest, and I have thought for a long time it would be perfectly feasible to take a theatrical troupe abroad. They wouldn't make any money, but they might pay their way. If I can't do that, I might take the Red Sox. The world's ripe for baseball now. It wouldn't be such a bad stunt.

"I have no interest in race track gambling, but I do love fast horses, and I would like to own some. That is my idea of genuine pleasure — having a stable of fast horses. It may be only a dream, but we all have them."

Frazee plays golf but indifferently and has no interest in any other sport save baseball. Before the armistice was signed, he was considering going abroad in the endeavor to organize amusements for the boys on a big scale. He is quick to see the professional values in things. In a recent talk I had with him, he suddenly blurted, "Do you know I would like to book the Kaiser for twelve weeks in vaudeville. After that I would be willing to retire." "You might have to," I ventured. "Not a bit of it," he snapped, "They might throw things at him the first night or two, but after that they would treat him like a gentleman. It would have all other acts backed off the boards."

"People think Mr. Johnson and I are at swords' points," says Frazee. "We have our differences, but how many associates in business don't have differences? I have disagreed with some of Johnson's ideas and he has disagreed with some of mine. We are even, I think. And it's all a matter of business.

"Someone asked me a short time ago if my club was for sale. What a ridiculous question. Of course it is for sale. So is my hat and my overcoat, and my watch. Anyone who wants them can have them at a price. I will dispose of my holdings in the Red Sox at any time for my price. But I am not anxious to sell. I prefer to continue in charge and to run my business in my own way."

It was Frazee's restless mind that conceived the idea of a one man National Commission with ex-President Taft as that man. He was actively promoting this scheme early last summer, but he finally presented the suggestion to Mr. Taft in company with Mr. Hempstead, owner of the New York Giants. For a time Mr. Taft considered the proposition, but finding that he would become involved in various squabbles in which he would logically have no part, he reluctantly withdrew.

Frazee's plan may have been a visionary one, but it was broad and progressive. The value to baseball from the association of such a man as the ex-president would have been immense. It is too bad that nothing came of it. But none the less to Frazee is due the credit for conceiving a bold original plan which would have been of immense value to the game.

Frazee's opinion of Johnson has been freely and frankly expressed. Johnson's opinion of Frazee can be guessed at from certain acts of the big American League chief. I well recall, in that connection, a remark by Charles Somers when he was owner of the Cleveland club. Said Somers, "Johnson is an Indian. He always remembers a friend, but he never forgets an enemy."

Frazee in his short and tempestuous career as a magnate has cruelly crossed Ban Johnson. He has outraged ruthlessly and mercilessly some of Johnson's most treasured prerogatives. Very likely he has earned the resentment of the circuit president and perhaps has deserved to so earn it.

But with the bright days ahead, it is to be devoutly hoped that Frazee and Johnson may get together as friends. Ban is still the arbiter of the league and the pressure he may eventually be able to bring upon a recalcitrant owner is tremendous. But Frazee is too breezy and picturesque an addition to the Baseball family to be discarded at this untimely date. As he frankly confesses, he has his price, but he has qualities which appeal to the public and it is to be devoutly hoped that his price isn't met. For he is a fearless fighter, bold, daring, and audacious. And those are qualities so American in themselves, that they surely have a place in the great American Game.

PAUL H. SHANNON

NEW YORK CLUB GIVES $125,000 FOR BATTERING BABE – BIGGEST PRICE EVER PAID FOR PLAYER

Huggins Announces That Ruth Has Signed

from *The Boston Post*, January 6, 1920

LOS ANGELES, CAL., JAN. 5 — Miller Huggins, manager of the New York Americans, tonight announced he had signed "Babe" Ruth, champion home run hitter, to play with the Yankees next season. Papers were exchanged here late today, Huggins said. He refused to state what salary Ruth was to receive.

George (Babe) Ruth, greatest home run swatter of all time, will drive out home runs for the Boston Red Sox no more. Yesterday afternoon the home run record king passed into the possession of the New York Yankees, the deal being closed over the telephone by Colonel Huston of the New York club and President Harry Frazee, the Red Sox magnate.

The transfer of Ruth was a cash transaction pure and simple and the price paid for him more than double ever before expended for any one player. Although President Frazee, who gave out the news here last night, refused to name the sum that the New York club paid, it is believed that the Yankees gave up in the neighborhood of $125,000 for him, as almost a year ago Colonel Huston offered an even $100,000 in cold cash.

Yanks Must Worry Now

The deal is now consummated, and no matter what attitude Ruth may assume the Boston club has no further interest in his movements. If he intends to hold out for more money, as advices from the coast have suggested, the New York club will have to settle negotiations with him. In purchasing him Colonels Ruppert and Huston have assumed all responsibility for the future actions of the heavy hitter.

While the news of Babe's sale will probably come as a decided shock to thousands of Boston fans, it will be the big sensation of the baseball world. This sale was by no means unexpected by those familiar with the doings of the Red Sox Club and the attitude that Ruth's recent behavior on the coast had inspired.

In fact, only two weeks ago the Boston Sunday Post gave a very plain as well as exclusive hint to its readers that Ruth was on the baseball market, and that the New York Yankees would probably make an offer for him. Those nearest the Red Sox administration could see the handwriting on the wall when Babe, after leaving the Sox in the lurch at Washington late last September, jumped to the coast and forced the Boston management to endure censure and ridicule for his non-appearance in the lineup.

Trouble Began to Brew

At that time it was felt that relations between the club and the heavy hitter were severely strained, and those who could read between the lines began to understand that Babe instead of proving the imagined bulwark of the Boston team was in reality proving a decided menace to the welfare of the team.

When even Ruth's fellow-players began to complain and show their dissatisfaction over the privileges that Babe took without leave, the management was forced to the conclusion that with Ruth remaining a member of the team harmony in the Red Sox family was impossible.

When Ruth, refusing to abide by the conditions of the three-year contract signed by himself last spring, and in which he practically forced the management to concede him a salary of $10,000 per annum, sent that contract back to the team without word of any kind and then issued his ultimatum to the California writers, stating that he would not play under $20,000. President Frazee decided that the time had come for Ruth to pass on, and in consequence he began to give ear to the plea of the New York management, who have always been eager to get the home-run hitter as a Polo Ground attraction. A week or more ago Colonel Huston and Frazee began to get together on this deal and the terms were completed yesterday.

Fans Will Be Sorry

Many will regret the departure of Ruth, probably the most spectacular player who ever wore a Boston uniform since the days of the lamented Mike Kelly. But the regret at his sale will be considerably tempered by the knowledge that he was posing as a holdout. And the dear public, wearied year after year by the lack of good faith and unwarranted demands of players who had small consideration for word or contract, had rapidly begun to lose patience with the temperamental star.

With Ruth gone from the Boston lineup harmony is sure to be restored, and from promises made by President Frazee the Sox will start South in March with the most powerful lineup it has boasted since the golden days of 1915. For Frazee promises to reinforce the Red Sox defences at their weakest points and use every cent of the money obtained for Babe if necessary in going to the baseball market and securing real stars.

In fact lines have been already laid for the acquisition of two real stars who will more than fill the breach left by Ruth's departure. Two experienced men, one from the Detroit and the other from the St. Louis club, are said to be slated to come to the Red Sox and if necessary a third man for whom a substantial figure has been offered will be brought to the Barrow fold.

Hard to Handle

While without question thousands of fans may seize the sale of Ruth as an opportunity to criticise the Red Sox management for apparent commercialism, the fact remains that Ruth, the biggest box office attraction in the game, and the most spectacular player since the days of Rube Waddell, would never have been permitted to leave Fenway Park had it been possible for the Boston club to handle him. But Ruth's failure to respect the club's training rules, his unwillingness to submit to any form of discipline and the bad example he set for the other men, formed a combination that President Frazee was able no longer to endure.

The climax came when Babe, after threatening first to abandon baseball for the movies, then to take up a prize fighting career, capped it all by stating that he would not play for the Sox again unless his present salary was doubled. This was the straw that broke the camel's back.

In many quarters, however, the sale of Ruth will be looked upon as an undisguised blessing to the club, which had been drifting for the past two seasons into nothing else than a one-man affair. So great was the publicity that Ruth attained by his home run hits, and so completely did his personality overshadow that of other and even steadier players on the club, that most of the interest in the club's welfare was dissipated, and the less conspicuous but far more steady players suffered by the contrast. To such an extent did this arise that dissatisfaction entered finally the ranks where the greatest harmony prevailed and real Red Sox stars began to pine for a change.

May Please Players

It is believed that practically every man on the Boston team will be pleased at Ruth's sale to New York. Popular as Ruth was on account of his big-heartedness, the men nevertheless realized that his faults overshadowed his good qualities. Dependable players, real stars like McInnis, Scott, Schang and Hooper, far harder men than Ruth to replace, were forced to believe that the public had less interest in their work and that the home run hitting of Ruth was the one and only attraction at Fenway Park. In a year where the Red Sox had continued in the pennant fight longer than they did this feeling would certainly have proved fatal.

President Frazee in announcing the sale of his heavy hitting star last night gave out the following statement:

"Ruth had become simply impossible, and the Boston club could no longer put up with his eccentricities. While Ruth without question is the greatest hitter that the game has ever seen, he is likewise one of the most selfish and inconsiderate men that ever wore a baseball uniform, and the baseball public, according to press reports from all over the country, are beginning to wake up to the fact."

Was Big Attraction

"Some people may say perhaps that the Boston club sold Babe Ruth simply because of the tremendous sum of money handed over by the New York club, but let them listen to a few facts and perhaps they will change their mind. Ruth is a wonderful box-office attraction and he drew many thousands of people to see the Sox play all over the circuit. Had he been possessed of the right disposition, had he been willing to take orders and work for the good of the club like the other men on the team I would never have dared let him go, for he has youth and strength, baseball intelligence and was a popular idol. But lately this idol has been shattered in the public estimation because of the way in which he has refused to respect his contract and his given word. But I shall enlighten the public some more.

"Twice within the past two seasons Babe has jumped the club and revolted. He refused to obey orders of the manager and he finally became so arrogant that discipline in his case was ruined.

"He would not pitch, but insisted upon playing in the outfield. He had no regard for the feelings of anyone but himself. He was a bad influence upon other and still younger players on the team.

"He left us in the lurch many times and just because of his abnormal swatting powers and the fact that he had been given such tremendous advertising by the newspapers he obeyed none but his own sweet will. At the end you could not talk to him."

Won Pennants Then

"Three years ago Babe was an ordinary player. The Red Sox won pennants without him. But in the past two years he has come so rapidly to the front that the individuality of every member of the Red Sox club has been swallowed up. Fans, attracted by the fame of his hitting, went out to Fenway Park unmindful of the steady work of McInnis, Hooper, Schang, Scott and others who were playing the same steady and brilliant ball, oftentimes handicapped by injuries that should rightfully have kept them out of the lineup. There was no longer any interest in the pennant race. And these same faithful, loyal players really felt it.

"In spite of the fact that Ruth was drawing far more money than anyone else upon the team, he put us in the hole on more than one occasion last summer. Two or three times when the Red Sox were scheduled to play in certain towns Ruth was given permission to run to another town, where he got four or five hundred dollars for playing, and at the same time the club was paying him for his services. On the windup of the season at Washington Ruth left Saturday night and refused to play Sunday, when we finished. Had he stayed and played for the club that was still paying his salary we might have finished in fifth, instead of in sixth place, as there were two or three occasions where a single hit would have won the game and allowed us fifth place. But Babe ran out on us and deserted his mates.

"He went to the coast after his exhibition or barnstorming trips had netted him in the vicinity of $5000. I don't think it is any exaggeration to state that he drew down fully $15,000 from the game last season. Out there on the coast I could have prevented him playing a single game as his contract signed by him gives me that right. But I allowed him to play, unmolested. Then he sends me back his contract in an envelope without a scrap of writing for explanation. This is just a sample of the way Ruth respects his written word and his obligations.

"Now in regard to Ruth being such a tower of strength. How many games can you point out that he won single-handed and unaided last season? He won some, I will admit, but many a time it has been some other player on the team that contributed the deciding smash. Only Babe's long hit always got the credit. We finished in sixth place in spite of Babe and his 29 home runs. This will bring out, I think, very clearly the fact that one star on a team doesn't make a winning ball club. Cleveland had the great Lajoie for years and couldn't win, Detroit has its Ty Cobb and Boston had its Ruth. A team of players working harmoniously together is always to be preferred to that possessing one star who hugs the limelight to himself.

"And that is what I am after — a team of steady, harmonious players. Harmony had departed when Ruth began to swell and I doubt if we could have kept out of the second division this year with Ruth in the lineup. After all, the baseball fans pay to see games won and championships achieved. They soon tire of circus attractions. And this is just what Ruth had become."

Team Will Run Smooth

"With Ruth out of the lineup, I believe that we will have one of the smoothest and most powerful teams that has represented Boston for years. With an infield that includes McInnis, Foster, Scott, Vitt and McNally, an outfield that will have Hooper, Lamar, two other real stars and perhaps a third, with Schang, Devine and McNeill as catchers, and a sextet of first-string twirlers that includes Bush, Pennock, Harper, Russell, Hoyt and Jones, and a second-string of box men from whom we should get at least two fine twirlers, I don't think the Boston club need worry.

"It is up to somebody else to do the worrying. Ruth is taking on weight tremendously. He doesn't take care to keep himself in shape, and I have passed a big liability on to the New York club. He has a floating cartilage in his knee, and this is an impediment that may make him a cripple at any time and put him out of baseball. Boston fans have seen him afflicted many a time at Fenway Park.

"I have my doubts about Ruth ever eclipsing his home run record. He may raise havoc with those stands in New York, but experienced critics are of the opinion that 1919 was his best year. At any rate, I am well satisfied to let him try his fortune with New York.

"I might say in conclusion that the New York club was the only outfit in baseball that could have bought Ruth. Had they been willing to trade players, I would have preferred the exchange, but to make a trade for Ruth, Huggins would have had to wreck his ball club. They could not afford to give me the men I wanted.

"Ruth's great value did not appeal to all the club owners. I could not get Joe Jackson for him in trade, and I know of at least two other stars that Ruth could not have been traded for. I am willing to accept the verdict of all baseballdom, and I think that fairminded patrons of the sport will agree with me that Ruth could not remain on the Boston team under existing conditions."

Secretary Graver returned to town yesterday together with President Frazee. He stated that full arrangements had been made for the training at Hot Springs, that Whittington Park was to be rebuilt, that the Majestic Hotel would be the headquarters of the team, and that the pitchers would go South a few days in advance of the main body. Joe Bush, whose arm is said to have come back, will go to Hot Springs a week ahead of any of the others.

This classic account of the Ruth sale is notable for several reasons. Significantly, the deal is not denounced too strongly; the Boston press was split on the question of whether the deal was good for the Red Sox. And the story also includes Harry Frazee's definitive statement outlin-

ing his reasons for making the deal. But it is important to note that Shannon was really telling only half the story.

Frazee and AL president Ban Johnson had been feuding for years. Their relationship deteriorated further when Frazee sold pitcher Carl Mays to the Yankees over Johnson's objections — Johnson thought the player should have been suspended for jumping the Red Sox. As a result, the American League split into two factions — the Insurrectos, which included the Red Sox, Yankees, and White Sox — and the Loyal Five, the remaining teams in the league that still supported Johnson.

The Boston press sided with Johnson. Although the war between the Loyal Five and the Insurrectos was the biggest story in baseball at the time and recognized in New York as the determining factor behind the deal, Shannon barely makes mention of it. The deal was certainly not made to finance No, No Nannette; the musical had yet to be written.

PART II

YAWKEY'S WAY

Harry Frazee's sale of the team to a syndicate fronted by Bob Quinn in 1923 precipitated the most dismal decade in Boston baseball history. The Red Sox were awful, and even Fenway Park, barely a decade old, fell into disrepair after a 1926 fire destroyed the left-field bleachers.

That all changed in 1933 when the scion of a Michigan lumbering fortune turned 30 years old, purchased the Red Sox, and announced to other league owners that "the money's on the table." His uncle and adoptive father, Bill Yawkey, had once owned the Tigers and won a pennant. Yawkey wanted to go one up on his uncle and win a world championship. He didn't know how impossible a dream that would be. The Red Sox would never be the same.

A 45-year spending splurge followed as Tom Yawkey pursued his personal chimera, that World Series win. Yawkey rebuilt and renovated Fenway Park and spent millions on players in the middle of the Depression, saying, "I am tired of eating New York's dust."

To the local writers, Yawkey proved problematic. They were initially so awed by his millions and so eager for a winning team that they rarely questioned his motives, and much of the writing during those early years was colored by boosterism and lazy reporting. New York was the media capital of the world, and between the two wars Boston journalism suffered, earning a well-deserved reputation for an insular parochialism.

Yawkey's dream of a world championship would be elusive, as the owner proved the old adage that money can't buy everything. He surrounded himself with cronies and yes men and was slow to adapt to changes both within the game and within American society. He built a team that often featured sluggers but never enough pitching, and his failure to integrate in a timely fashion left his club hamstrung. Although Yawkey's way often produced an entertaining product, it would ultimately be a failure in the only way Red Sox fans really cared about. After the war, a new generation of local writers, sometimes spurred on by writers weighing in from elsewhere, would learn to see that.

Although the Red Sox came close to winning the World Series in 1946, they dropped a playoff game for the American League pennant in 1948, lost another pennant on the final day of the season in 1949, and over the next decade and a half failed to remain competitive. Yawkey's world championship remained more fantasy than reality.

STARCH FOR THE RED SOX

from *Collier's*, August 5, 1933

Old Herb Pennock's fast one had steam along the stitching and his hook was shaving them cleaner than a new razor blade on a January morning.

The Yank defense was clicking when called upon, which wasn't often, while Ruth, Gehrig, Combs and the other truncheoneers parlayed their bingles and blasts in such workmanlike fashion that the lowly Red Sox had just been blanked again — this time, 4 to 0, or 4 to a horse collar, as the ball players say it.

Thus, in routine manner, concluded the first bracket of an early season double header between the league-leading New Yorkers and the tail-ending Bostonians.

If the audience had been watching the venerable Mr. Pennock as he wrapped his pitching arm in the fragrant folds of a sweat shirt, wadded his war-worn glove into a yawning hip pocket and pushed the bill of his cap back sufficiently to wipe the beads of dew from his perspiring brow, they'd have seen him wend his way to a box adjacent to the Red Sox dugout.

They'd have seen him there greeting and being greeted by a pleasant-looking young gentleman in faultless spring tailoring — a young gentleman who speaks in a firm, authoritative manner and whose steel-blue eyes look steadily into his listener's. And if the audience could have listened, this is what it would have heard:

From Pennock: "I don't know how you liked 'em, Mr. Yawkey, but they looked good to me losing. You and Eddie must have done something to 'em. Believe it or not, they looked more like a ball club losing than the A's did winning here earlier in the week."

And from Mr. Yawkey: "Yeah, I thought they looked better myself.

Keep your eye on 'em, Herb. They're going to knock that glove right back down your throat one of these days. But I want to congratulate you on the nice game you pitched. You had us breaking our backs at that roundhouse of yours. But watch us, kid, and don't waste all your sympathy. We're going to go places with this ball club yet."

The "Mr. Yawkey," addressed and addressing, was Thomas Austin Yawkey, brand-new owner of the Red Sox, the baby, by many years, of all the major-league magnates, the wealthy young New Yorker, who inherited the residue of a $50,000,000 estate upon his thirtieth birthday last February 21st, and who, four days later, bought perhaps the most dilapidated piece of diamond merchandise to be found on the major-league shelves.

Tom Yawkey holds no working card in the Major and Minor Prophets' Union No. 1. Nor does he profess any powers of peering into the future. Nevertheless, he delivered himself of a truly startling prediction in that Yankee Stadium conversation with the slightly patronizing Mr. Pennock.

Not two weeks later the young magnate sat in his own park in Boston, along with some thousands of New Englanders, and saw these same Red Sox rend these same cocky Yankees limb from limb in a five-game series! After dropping the first half of a Sunday double header, 7 to 8, the suddenly humming Hose took the next four in a row. By slam-bang scores, too — 11 to 9, 6 to 5, 13 to 5, and 8 to 5.

And the Yanks weren't in a slump. They were doing their stuff. They slammed six homers, which ought to be enough. But the suddenly savage Sox saw all they had and raised. They drove *eight* home runs out of the park. They sprayed triples and doubles all over the premises. They banged out 63 hits for 98 bases, driving all the Yankee pitchers off the hill in steady and almost mathematical rotation. Included in that number was the eminent Mr. Pennock in person. He was rushed in upon three separate occasions in a desperate effort to halt the berserk Bostonese, but he might as well have stayed back at the hotel playing pinochle. Upon all three occasions, of a truth and a verity, he had his glove knocked right back down his throat!

Who is this young Mr. Yawkey? What has he done? What does he plan for his tepid tail-enders? Why, in these times of industrial *sturm und drang* did he feel impelled to swap a bale of hard-to-get dollars for a down-at-the-heels baseball outfit? He's a New Yorker.

Why didn't he buy the Giants? It's an open secret that they can be had. How did he reach his decision, and how does he feel about it now?

I undertook to ask him all these things the other day. He answered fully and freely. Both the manner and the matter of the answers completely obliterated any suspicion that here was just a dizzy playboy suddenly sucked into a questionable investment the grief of which he couldn't realize.

For young Tom Yawkey's eyes are very much open.

Baseball isn't something he met only yesterday.

He was weaned on a bat and he must have cut his teeth upon the stitches of a major-league missile. Other kids read about ball players. Tom Yawkey had 'em for playmates. And some of the most famous that ever walked in spikes, too. Ty Cobb, for instance, and old Wah-Hoo Sam Crawford and most of the rest of the great of baseball's immortal yesterday.

For, you see, his uncle owned the Detroit ball club, and the bond between young Tommy Austin and the childless William Hoover Yawkey was as close as that of any father and favorite son.

William Hoover Yawkey bought the Detroit Tigers back in 1903 — the year his nephew, Tommy Austin, was born.

From Tabbycat to Bengal Tiger

William Hoover Yawkey was one of Michigan's industrial magnates. His father had built a fortune in timber and mining properties. This William Hoover Yawkey enlarged and expanded. William Hoover Yawkey was a baseball enthusiast. It was quite the thing in his day for industrial tycoons to buy ball clubs and run them as hobbies.

When William Hoover Yawkey bought the Tigers, they were almost as hopeless a proposition as the Sox his nephew has purchased. He brought in, to help him, a young man named Frank Navin. They purchased some ball players, which is always a good way to start. They got hold of a promising youngster by the name of Ty Cobb. Then there was another one named Hugh Jennings. A hard-hitting outfielder by the name of Sam Crawford was annexed. Then there were others who came and went — Bobbie Veach, George Moriarty, Donie Bush and some more.

The Detroit club gradually began to react. A flaming spirit re-

placed the old hangdogism. Belligerence came on to replace resignation and, in sum and in brief, Detroit's toothless Tabbycat became
the American League's red-fanged, saber-toothed Bengal.

Who doesn't remember Hughie Jennings' famous and triumphant "Eeee-Yah"? Or the gleaming spikes of the pugnacious Cobb
as he hit the dirt in full flight? Or the booming thud of Sam Crawford's massive mace as he poled that old onion into the high summertime's blue?

Into these scenes and amongst these historical characters wandered little Tommy Austin — now Thomas Austin — Yawkey.

The William Hoover Yawkey estate at Sandwich, across the river
from Detroit, was more like a country club where ball players gathered. It was here that young Tom met and knew all the stars. Ty
Cobb, then at the very peak of his fame, became his pal and his idol.

But baseball, while lots of fun, was merely the spare-time enthusiasm of William Hoover Yawkey. His business interests were many
and mighty and he had serious ambitions for his nephew and heir.
He took the boy into his household at the age of seven and began
selling him the idea of preparing himself to carry on the great estate
in his turn.

When Tom's mother died in 1917, the elder Yawkey legally
adopted him. Young Tom was a student in Irving School, Tarry-
town, New York, when his foster father died March 5, 1919. The Tigers then passed into the possession of Navin, who still owns and
operates the club.

Young Tom went on from Irving to Yale, where he was graduated
from the Sheffield Scientific School in 1925. He specialized in mining, metallurgy and chemistry, much of the Yawkey estate being in
oils, mines and minerals. He had played football, baseball and basketball at Irving and he went out for both football and baseball at
Yale.

He lacked the size and the speed to make Yale's varsity teams —
that was the era of Lovejoy, Luman, Pond, Blair and the rest — but
significant of his stick-to-itiveness is the fact that he battered his
way through to the second team and held his place proudly there
from the season's start to its finish. There was nothing of the prima
donna or the quitter about him. He was popular with his classmates
and well regarded by his instructors as a serious, sane and sincere
young man.

After graduation, he went unobtrusively to work superintending the properties that had now become his responsibility. And he had been reared to regard them as a responsibility — not a privilege.

But the love of baseball still burned in his blood and, more often than he should have — or so he expressed it — he'd steal quietly out of the impressive suite of offices he occupies in one of New York's newer and taller business temples and manage to reach the Yankee Stadium or the Polo Grounds just as the umpire caroled "Play ball."

It was his old idol, Ty Cobb, who inadvertently brought him back to the game as an owner. Cobb, as the baseball world remembers, finally topped off his career with a brief stay in Philadelphia. He was attached for duty and rations to Mr. Cornelius McGillicuddy's celebrated Athletics, although he did little but the heavy standing around. Also attached to the Athletics was little Eddie Collins, the dynamic daddy of all second basemen and hand-picked by Connie Mack to succeed him as manager. Collins' official portfolio was that of coach.

On a visit with Cobb, the old Georgia Peach introduced young Yawkey to Eddie and the two forthwith formed a hard and fast friendship. They had two bonds in common, they discovered: Eddie, like Yawkey, was a graduate of Irving School. And Eddie, like Yawkey, was a fancy wing shot.

Damon and Pythias Play Ball

The Yawkey winter home is South Island Plantation down near Georgetown, South Carolina. The place teems with both upland and migratory game. Tom invited Eddie to come shooting with him. By the time the trip was over, the young millionaire and the infield immortal were a regular Damon and Pythias.

And they've stayed that way. It was Eddie, as a matter of fact, who first brought up the matter of the Red Sox to Yawkey — not as a business proposition, but purely as an idle conversational subject one night when they were chinning about baseball.

That the Boston club was in wretched financial shape was no secret to baseball men. Things had gone steadily from bad to worse ever since Harry Frazee had started to wreck it back in 1920 in order to scotch himself in a sliding theatrical business. When Frazee, a theatrical man, bought the club from Joe Lannin after the 1916 season, it had won two successive world championships. In 1917,

Frazee's first year, it ran a strong race for the pennant, only finally to be nosed out by Chicago, but in 1918 it won the world's title again.

This meant that it was a first-rate ball club, and a going financial concern of the first muddy water.

But Frazee's first love was the theater and things weren't going so well for him there. He had produced "Madame Sherry" and had made a lot of money, but his next several ventures laid eggs.

First he turned over to the Yanks Duffy Lewis, Dutch Leonard and Ernie Shore. Then Carl Mays. Then came the Babe. Then, one by one, Waite Hoyt, Wally Schang, Mike McNally, Everett Scott, Joe Dungan, Joe Bush, Sam Jones, the aforementioned Herb Pennock and Elmer Smith.

He sold the Yanks, in brief, a world championship ball club. And when he was through, he knocked down his franchise, the ball park and such hirelings as he hadn't been able to peddle elsewhere, to a syndicate of sportsmen from Columbus, Ohio, fronted by Bob Quinn, business manager of the St. Louis Browns. The price for this diamond junk was reputed to be $1,500,000. The real estate was supposed to represent the million.

The Red Sox Go to the Cleaners

Since he paid less than a half million for the club in the first place and netted $2,000,000 from "No, No, Nanette" alone, Mr. Frazee did well enough for Mr. Frazee, but he left American League ball in the Hub of the Universe as clean as a chicken picked and singed.

Quinn was never able to get the outfit back on its feet. His funds proved insufficient to swing the task of reconstruction. Further, he had worse luck than the man who worked for his board and then lost his appetite. A fine man personally and one who deserved a better fate, he was at length completely strapped.

Some part of that was what Eddie Collins was telling Tom Yawkey as they sat talking baseball — a favorite subject with both.

Young Yawkey was coming into the major portion of his inheritance in a couple of weeks — upon his thirtieth birthday, but Collins had no way of knowing that.

Suddenly the young man turned squarely upon the famous second baseman and said, "Eddie, why don't we buy it?"

"Why don't we *what?*" asked Mr. Collins.

"Let's go partners," said Yawkey. "I'll buy the club and you run it."

"Whew," whistled Collins reflectively. "Gee, I don't know. . . ."

But they did.

Four days after young Yawkey came into complete control of the millions he had schooled himself carefully to handle, the sports pages rang with the news of the sale. New York reporters, locating the young man in his luxurious office, asked him patronizingly why he hadn't bought the Giants, if he itched to own a ball club.

"Because," he said with that wide, boyish grin that is a very attractive part of him, "I'm an American Leaguer, myself. Me? I wouldn't own a National League ball club!"

"But what do you expect to do with it, now that you have it?" I asked as we talked it over.

"I expect," he replied slowly and evenly, "to get a great kick out of making something out of it."

"Money?"

"Some of that, maybe," he smiled, "but by 'something' I mean a first-class, high-spirited ball club. One that will go in there and make the old college try. One that won't move around with its dauber always down. One that will go in there and scrap.

"At that," he continued, "I wouldn't have bought it if Eddie Collins hadn't agreed to be the top sergeant. Eddie's vice president and general manager, with his own block of stock, you know. I'm going to give the club as much time as I can, but it won't be the major portion of it."

"Doesn't the size of the reconstruction job scare you?"

Wanted: Fire and Loyalty

"On the contrary, it's right where I'm getting my biggest wallop. I don't see how any man can get any real satisfaction out of taking a success and merely running it along. That's like landing a fish that somebody else hooked. The big kick comes from taking something that's down and seeing if you can put it up and across. That's what my daddy did. I want to see if I'm as good a man as he was."

"And with what plans?"

"I don't know that I can tell you all of them. I don't know that I know all of them myself. We've got to get some ball players. We've already bought what we could. We got Rick Ferrell and Lloyd Brown

from St. Louis, Pipgras and Werber from the Yanks, and we've tried
to buy more but the deals fell through. But we'll get more players, as
and if they're needed. Players, however, aren't the principal problem.
After you've got all the players you need, you still haven't got much
unless you can get something into 'em.

"You've got to get some fight, some fire, some eagerness, some
loyalty, some team pride into 'em somehow. Baseball, all of it, needs
a lot more of the old-time religion. It needs a few Cobbs and Everses
and Fletchers in there stealing bases, rattling pitchers and — yes,
even getting tough with the umpires. I don't mean brutishness and
rough-neckism, but plenty of sparkle and snap and the old will to
win.

"I don't mean," he continued, "that modern ball players are sis-
sies. But they're too polite, too matter-of-fact, and most of 'em are
too brittle. At least they think they're too brittle and that amounts to
the same thing. There's too much coming out of the game because
of a strawberry, a skinned knuckle or a pain in the sawdust. Cobb,
and those other fellows who played back there when the game was
good, wouldn't quit. They were in there scrapping through hell or
high water. That's why they were good."

"You say," I interrupted, "'back there when the game was good.'
Do you mean . . ."

"Yes, sir," he fired, "I mean the game was better back there and
that the public liked it better. The old-timers played prettier, more
scientific and more interesting baseball. I don't think there's even an
argument on that score. I'd be the last to discount the box-office
value of Babe Ruth. It's probably true that the game owes him a lasting debt for switching public interest away from the Black Sox scan-
dal with his terrific home runs. But even so, I think he and his
brother sluggers have changed baseball completely and I'm not at all
sure that the change has been for the better.

"They've killed, for one thing, the pretty business of base stealing.
That was a major thrill of the old days. And it was a bigger thrill, if
you ask me, than any ordinary home run.

"But who bothers with any real base stealing today? Somebody
tries it occasionally, but what's the use with every batter coming up
to take a free swing, a swing that likely as not will slam the ball into
the center-field clock? The fine and thrilling stratagems of the old

days have almost all been discarded. Baseball needs to see 'em put back.

"My idea of baseball is to outthink the other fellow, outguess him, run him crazy by crossing him up. I want another Wee Willie Keeler who can 'hit 'em where they ain't.' I want a club that won't depend upon brute strength alone. I want a smart ball club. One that will take chances, that will do the unorthodox. I want somebody to steal bases. I'd even like to see 'em try to steal home. As long as they take chances and keep fighting, I don't care about the rest of it. I want it to give me and the crowd a run for our money. If it does that, and loses, it's all right with me. I'd rather they'd take chances and lose than win with dreary, stereotyped baseball.

"I want a resourceful, balanced ball club, not just some one terrific slugger surrounded by a supporting cast the names of which mean nothing. I want a ball club the crowd will love — every man jack on it. I want to hear those bleachers thunder again the way they used to in the old days. I've always had the impression that the bleacherites are a team's real fans anyhow. Big grandstand crowds come and go. Of course there are loyal and faithful supporters in there under the roof, but baseball's time-honored public sits out on the hard planks in the sun. I want to see it given back the thing it used to love, and that's what I'm going to work toward with whatever speed I can make."

"You don't think, then," said I, thinking of the way the minor leagues have folded, how the kids caddy these days instead of playing One Old Cat, and the rest, "that baseball has slipped beyond redemption with the public?"

"No," said he, "the game hasn't lost anything it can't get back. It's lost some of its appeal, yes, but chiefly for the reasons I've been telling you. I believe it will come back if the old features are put back."

Thirsting for Color

"Look, for instance, how the papers blazed with the accounts of that early season tiff between the Senators and the Yankees. Two players bumped each other at second and got up and slung a few fists. From the way the stories hung on, you'd think a couple of nations had declared war on each other. In the old days they had at least one of those a week, with the fans mixing in gleefully occasionally.

"I don't champion such brawls, but I do champion the spirit that makes such brawls possible. Properly bridled and translated into terms of aggressive team play instead of individual outbreaks, it makes the type of baseball that baseball used to be. Give it back the fight, the skill, the science of yesterday and you'll see in packing 'em in again just as it always used to do."

And our advice is to keep at least one peeper focussed upon these rescued Red Sox and this unusual young gentleman who now is their boss.

He's the almost never encountered phenomenon — a product of the present sold completely on the past. And it's going to be extremely interesting to see, as the box scores parade in block formation after one another, whether this puissant young party succeeds in changing the game or whether, as so often sadly happens, the game changes him!

Cunningham was the first Boston baseball writer in a generation to earn a national reputation, a condition that had as much to do with the desultory play of the Red Sox and the emergence of New York as the nation's media center as it did with the ability of Boston's baseball writers.

Yawkey — and his money — sparked renewed interest in the franchise not only in Boston but nationally. In the middle of the Depression, the nation was wowed by Yawkey's extravagant expenditures on ballplayers. For the first time in years, the Red Sox were seen as a team on the rise and worthy of attention.

BILL CUNNINGHAM

RED SOX OWNERS DISPLAY COURAGE

Faith of Yawkey and Collins in Future Despite
Tales of Woe an Object Lesson for All Industry

from *The Boston Post,* December 13, 1933

News that the Red Sox had turned the biggest baseball deal in years, one that ought to set the No. 1 flag spanking in the breezes, came as no surprise to those who assemble regularly around this town pump, if any, perchance, there be, for it was all duly and accurately (which is something of a record in itself) foretold in this spot quite a number of days ago. The stove leaguers will now do some tall and interesting figuring about possibilities, percentages and probable accomplishments.

But it seems to me that there's a bigger story behind the whole thing than that. That's the story of business courage behind the new Red Sox management. This is all really only a sports venture perhaps, yet sports of this magnitude run into very real business and it seems to me that the story of this business deal might well prove inspirational to other business men.

Here, in brief, despite the times, the doubt, the fears, is a firm that's barging straight ahead as if business were booming. Refusing to listen to the pessimists, the defeatists, the weepers and the general yellow-bellies, this particular business firm is spending something like three-quarters of a million dollars upon the renovation of its ball park and something in the neighborhood of a half million more for some first-class ball players.

Take a walk up around Fenway Park and see what's going on!

Look at the men they have at work, the construction materials they're using.

Figure what a boon that building operation is to at least a segment of the community. If other firms had the courage and the foresight to go ahead in such fashion, the depression would pass into history. The purchase of the ball players doesn't fall into that category because the moneys paid out go to the other ball clubs, or to the banks that hold the destinies of some of the other ball clubs, and that brings up another interesting sidelight.

Have Heard Tales of Woe

Banks do have a say now in the affairs of some of the other units, and that's a sober way of recalling that the baseball business in some centres hasn't been recently profitable. The local gentlemen, rather the gentlemen owning the local Red Sox, have heard just as many scary tales about their business as any other business men have. They have just as many terrified competitors as any merchant or industrialist. There are those, even within the ranks of organized baseball, who fear that the game, as a big money-making proposition, is doomed. They have some statistics, too, to support their contentions. They can show depleted receipts and in many cases vanished profits. They point to the vacant seats at the last World's Series.

They even cite contributing causes, aside from the national hard times — the great growth of golf, the changing habits of youth, the absence of available sandlots, the increasing dearth of good players, and three or four other things.

The Messrs. Yawkey and Collins have heard all that. They are the same sort of tales that have driven timid operators in other lines of business to toss in their hands and turn up their coat collars. They are doubts and fears of the sort typified by the small Southern merchant who was so enthusiastic at first about the NRA [National Recovery Administration].

When the Blue Eagle first bloomed, he had one in every window. He talked of nothing but the NRA and how sold he was on it. In fact, so enthusiastic did he become that his friends were kidding him about it. Two or three months passed and then somebody suddenly noticed that all the Blue Eagles had disappeared from his windows and in the place of each was a picture of Christopher Columbus.

"How come?" asked a friend. "Aren't you still rooting for the NRA?"

"Yeah," said the store keeper, "it's all right. I'm all for it; but somehow I got to thinking that Christopher Columbus was a pretty good symbol of this depression, too."

Same State of Wonderment

"How's that?" asked the friend.

"Well," said the merchant, "when he set out from Spain, he didn't know where he was going. When he got here, he didn't know where he was, and when he got back, he didn't know where the hell he'd been!"

It's a cinch that a lot of business men are in the same state of wonderment, but it's likewise a cinch that they'll never emerge from it unless they set the prow straight ahead and crowd on full sail.

That's what the Red Sockers are doing.

And it's not altogether fair to say that it's easy for them because they have a lot of money. They do have a lot of money. That is, young Mr. Yawkey, who's bank-rolling this particular venture, is the master of a huge and far-flung estate. He has properties consisting of timberlands, minerals and kindred natural deposits. But it takes money, much money, to hold things as big as those together in these times. Wealth such as that is subject to tremendous taxation and when the coming Congress gets through they'll probably be taxed even higher.

It may even be a break to be poor in these times. The wealthy are being whittled down to our size with appalling rapidity, and I, for one, don't like to see it, but regardless of who likes it or doesn't like it, it's happening, and no man of wealth these days can cock 'em back and say, "I'm set," for he isn't and he isn't going to be for some considerable length of time yet to come.

So Yawkey and his fidus Achates, Mr. Edward Trowbridge Collins, aren't tossing that cash around just because they happen to have it. They're spending their money as a business investment. They've refused to be frightened by all the sad tales. They decline to believe either that baseball's dead or that things are going so utterly to the dogs that there won't be an audience in this or in any other town for a worthwhile grade of merchandise placed upon attractive display.

To that end they've measured their dollars and have gone out for the goods.

Object Lesson for all Industry

That's exactly what the President and others trying to save the ship have been urging. It's an object lesson of the sort that all industry needs. So forgetting the matters of strike-outs and three-baggers, how's for a sincere hail to a couple of constructive citizens and a hope that their ball club, and ours, lives up to their hopes.

I said, forgetting the matters of strike-outs and three-baggers, but, after all, who can? Can you picture the interested throng in those new Red Sox pavilions when Lefty Grove first walks up on that hill in there next season, wearing the chaste red and white of the old Carrigan team?

And can't you see these sports pages as spring rolls into summer and the first tang of fall creeps into the air, if those Sockers are up in that first division quarrelling on even terms with the Senators and the Yankees?

Prohibition has gone and the Sox have a ball club.

Truly the millennium has dawned.

Yawkey's free spending made a big splash and impressed sportswriters who were tired of starting every story with a variation of the phrase "Red Sox lose again." Over the first few seasons of his tenure, Yawkey spent nearly $4 million buying the team, rebuilding Fenway Park, and purchasing players. For a time, the Red Sox were even referred to as the Gold Sox.

DANIEL M. DANIEL

YOU CANNOT BUY A PENNANT!

Yawkey Has Learned That Poignantly —
McGraw Only Stressed Truth of
Ancient Baseball Axiom — Lady Luck
Dominant Factor

from *Baseball Magazine,* 1936

They say that money is a marvelous and miraculous commodity. It buys food and houses, ships and herrings, cabbages and kings, poesy and politicians, corned beef and corporations. They say it has the amazing quality of purchasing everything — but happiness. And in baseball, the acme of happiness is a pennant. Of course, a world championship must be included in the thesis. But the pennant must come before the classic achievement.

Men have come and men have gone in the major leagues, since the old National Circuit was organized in 1876. And as they have made their tracks along the highway of Time, and contributed their mites to the pageant of the game, they have contributed as well to the old axiom — You cannot buy a pennant!

Calculating, cool business heads, going into baseball for the mere profit, have invaded its more or less Corinthian precincts with the icy ardour of the man seeking his six per cent or more, the arithmetical depth of the accountant, and attempted to make these faculties thrive for the production of a league title. And they, too, have carried their books and their figures, their percentages and their peeves, from the game with the conviction — You cannot buy a pennant!

There have been men in the big leagues who could not contribute too heavily of funds. They felt that shrewdness and acumen, crafty manipulation and planning, would compensate for financial weakness. But they, too, have discovered that no matter what you may use for money — You cannot buy a pennant!

Others have entered into the pennant plot with the idea that vast and intricate systems, scouting organizations combing the country from coast to coast, expensive ramifications spying out the diamond in the rough, could make for success. They, too, have added to the store of learning that — You cannot buy a pennant!

How, then, are pennants won? Each year finds a championship gained in the National and a title won in the American League. Just what is behind these successes?

To be sure, money counts. But, in the main, it is organization — and Lady Luck.

The first case on record of trying to buy a pennant may be traced back to 1888. Chicago had the greatest battery in the National League — John Clarkson, right hander, and King Kelly, catcher. Boston had languished without a pennant since 1883. Chicago, with Clarkson and Kelly furnishing most of the ammunition, had blasted its way to championships in 1885 and 1886, under the able leadership of Cap Anson. In 1887, Detroit took the pennant.

Boston coveted Clarkson and Kelly. In 1888, it amazed the sports world by purchasing Kelly for the then unheard of sum of $10,000. The deal created as much furore as did the purchase of Babe Ruth by the Yankees from the Red Sox in 1920 for $100,000. Back in 1888, selling players for high prices was not an established activity in baseball.

Even with Kelly, Boston did not win. Then it decided to make another effort to lure the pennant with money. It bought Clarkson for $10,000. And how tongues wagged then! But Clarkson did not turn the trick, either.

In 1888 and 1889, Jim Mutrie won the championship with the Giants in New York. Jim had no cash reserves. He knew ballplayers, he knew where to find them, he could inspire a team, and he intrigued the public. It was Mutrie who gave the Giants their name, which is the most picturesque, the most valued in the major leagues. It was Mutrie who coined the phrase, "We are the people." Boston tried to buy the pennant. New York won it.

Since 1888, clubs have tried time after time to get the pennant with money spent in the purchase of stars in their own league. Let me explain here that when I say you cannot buy a pennant, I mean that you cannot hope to succeed by taking the best players of other teams in your own major league. Buying minor league luminaries who develop comes under the heading of Luck.

In the last three years, baseball has been very much intrigued by the purchasing activities of Tom Yawkey, owner of the Boston Red Sox. For three years Yawkey has been trying to buy the American League pennant, and he still is at it, with no better than fourth place as his measure of success, and his need of satisfaction.

Yawkey still is not satisfied that a pennant cannot be purchased. At this writing he is deep in negotiations which are calculated to bring to the Boston banner stars aplenty, many of them from the Athletics. Men who try to buy pennants may be classified in two categories — those who want the championship for financial gain, and those who seek it for love of baseball, for the gratification of an ambition, without the money motive being too predominant.

The writer lists Yawkey in the second rank. Tom has plenty of the wherewithal. He is not in baseball to live off its profits. He is the true amateur, and wants the satisfaction of being in a World's Series. Naturally, Yawkey does not crave to support a hobby at too great an outlay. He knows that a winner will support itself, and then some. But, truly, Thomas wants that pennant just for itself.

While most Boston writers were blinded by Yawkey's millions and rarely criticized him, the national press wasn't so deferential. The prolific Dan Daniel, who not only wrote a daily column but was a regular contributor to both the Sporting News *and* Baseball Magazine, *took a more critical view of Yawkey's spending spree, which exhibited little forethought. In time, Daniel would be proven correct, at least in regard to Yawkey.*

HAROLD KAESE

WHAT'S THE MATTER WITH THE RED SOX?

from *The Saturday Evening Post*, March 23, 1946

When the Red Sox blow a pennant for Joe Cronin, as they have each of the last eleven seasons, the leashing of dogs on Beacon Hill, the latest book denounced by the Watch and Ward Society, and even the feeding of pigeons in the Public Gardens, at once become minor issues in Boston. At such times, generally the ragweed season, Cronin rivals even James Michael Curley as a controversial figure.

Each spring Cronin is expected to lead the Red Sox to their first pennant since 1918 — a mere matter of twenty-seven years. Each fall Cronin is pictured by his critics as a man who could not win a pennant with an All-Star team. This will be a usual spring. The Red Sox will win the pennant in 1946. What will the fall bring? A championship or more abuse for Cronin?

Boston fans have looked expectantly to the Red Sox ever since Tom Yawkey bought them in 1933, and, waving fists full of thousand-dollar bills like a pushcart vendor displaying choice lettuce, set out briskly to build a champion. The Red Sox have finished second four times for him, never very briskly. Yawkey has spent about three million dollars on baseball. Star players have been bought, others developed. The Red Sox have sired a family of farm clubs. Executives have been hired and fired. Attendances have soared. Still no pennant, a frustration that inspires baseball's most puzzling question: "What's wrong with the Red Sox?"

There are at least 1500 answers to the query, ranging from the shape of the ball park to Boston's famous east wind. But one choir of critics consistently sings, "There is nothing wrong with the Red Sox that a new manager wouldn't cure." The choir even practiced a few sour notes on Dave Ferriss Day last September, when the rookie pitching wonder seriously called Joe Cronin "my good manager."

In an Irish town like Boston, a Cronin is not, of course, bereft of friends. For every jeer he gets a cheer. But one thing is sure: The anti-Cronins have been making more noise lately. Besides his failure to win a pennant, the anti-Cronins accuse Joe of torturing his pitching staffs, ignoring percentages, and letting his players loaf. If he isn't too easy, he's too hard. He's a slave to superstition, he plays favorites, and he doesn't know a ballplayer from a singing Cossack.

The pro-Cronins argue that the Red Sox invariably are overrated, that flighty Boston fans think that any Sox team capable of winning five consecutive games should win the pennant. Cronin has never had talent comparable to that employed by the Yankees. Cronin teams, with their tradition of power, are exciting to watch, as witness the 600,000 customers the seventh-place Red Sox drew in 1945.

At first, after Cronin was bought from Washington for $250,000 in folding money and Lyn Lary in 1934, excuses were readily made for him, and admirers gave him everything from Irish terriers to silver services. He was burdened with temperamental stars. Yawkey coddled favorites with hunting parties to his South Carolina island. General Manager Eddie Collins wigwagged signals from his box on the roof.

Now the alibis are largely forgotten, except by those who love Cronin for his courage, by a few sympathetic analysts, and by some who would blame the Triple Alliance of Yawkey, Collins, and Cronin *in toto*. Some dissidents say that Collins is about as active as a book end, and that Yawkey is a bemused example of inherited wealth. Even the Fenway Park pigeons are feathery bums to the sourest Red Sox critics.

But most Red Sox fans are sorry for Yawkey, and most still have a solemn respect for Collins, the great second baseman whose ears and records have been enshrined in the Hall of Fame at Cooperstown, New York. It is Cronin who meets the onslaught head on, his big chin a breakwater for a tide of complaint. Some Bostonians criticize art, some music, some Harvard, but many just criticize Cronin.

"Cronin was a great player. He's a punk manager."

His critics say it more delicately around Louisburg Square, but that's how it sounds in the bleachers. Many hearts that palpitated to Cronin's marvelous hitting in the pinches have grown cold from the chill of successive pennant reverses.

The tenderest spot in Cronin's managerial anatomy is poor Red

Sox pitching. He is blamed for the failure of promising rookies, the sore arms of Woody Rich and Oscar Judd, the wildness of Jack Wilson and Emmett O'Neill, the delayed opportunities for Charley Wagner and Bill Butland, and even George Woods' monstrous appetite.

Asked why Connie Mack won pennants with stars while Cronin failed, Jimmy Foxx explained in *Yank* in August, 1944, that Cronin did not use good judgment picking spots for his pitchers. He concluded, "One manager knew what he was doing, and the other didn't. Cronin didn't."

Foxx denied the critical remarks, as he had others. But on or off the record, Foxx, dozens of players, managers and experts have accused Cronin of mishandling hurlers. Once blamed for changing pitchers too soon, Cronin is now blamed for not changing them soon enough.

"Don't look now, Joe," shouted an irate fan during an enemy rally; "but you've got a guy all warmed up in the bull pen."

The over-all record of traded pitchers fails to make Cronin out a dunce, but Boston fans raved when Bobo Newsom pitched the Tigers to the 1940 pennant; when Denny Galehouse and Nelson Potter helped pitch the Browns to the 1944 pennant; and when Al Brazle hurled for the Cardinals in the 1943 World Series. All once belonged to the Red Sox.

The Red Sox have nearly matched the Yankees as a run-scoring club, so poor pitching largely explains their failures. The short left-field fence at Fenway Park hurts pitchers — but it is on the road that Red Sox teams collapse. Cronin can defend himself by pointing to the superb pitching Lefty Grove, Wes Ferrell, Tex Hughson, and Dave Ferriss have done for him. He can insist that young Red Sox pitchers have been rushed too fast, like Lee Rogers.

Rogers was a personable young southpaw who lacked aggressiveness. Trying to rouse him, Cronin growled, "Get mad at those hitters, Lee. Throw a few under their chins."

The young pitcher's eyes popped, and he asked, "You mean I should treat them like enemies, Joe?"

Cronin is a man of quick and strong likes and dislikes. Yawkey once commented, "Joe's big trouble is that he makes up his mind too fast on young players and never wants to change it."

The trading of Stan Spence, hard-hitting outfielder, to Washington for John Welaj, still gripes Beantown. When Ben Steiner, rookie second baseman, was abruptly released to Louisville last July, there was some astonishment. Why send Steiner, a regular, and keep Jack Tobin, a bench-warmer? One player said, "Steiner went because he is not a Californian and Tobin is."

Bostonians chide Cronin, who was born in San Francisco just after the great fire of 1906, for favoring Californians and scorning New Englanders. Of course there are few complaints over such Californians as Ted Williams, Bobby Doerr and Dom DiMaggio. Cronin was so aroused by one story of his favoritism that he telephoned the offending newspaper and protested. But when the Red Sox fell to seventh place last August, he quipped, "Well, I guess my Californians don't amount to much."

As a manager, Cronin favors the spectacular. Rather than walk quietly down Pennant Avenue, he must do cartwheels and backflips as he goes. He enjoyed himself when he scooped the press by opening the 1936 season with Werber in right field, and when he started Jim Bagby, a rookie, against the Yankees in the 1938 opener — winning with him. He has used Williams, Foxx and Doc Cramer as relief pitchers. When Dave Ferriss, the ambidextrous rookie, did not pitch a midsummer exhibition game against the Braves left-handed, Cronin probably felt the disappointment of a Barnum unable to exhibit an elephant with three trunks.

Many of Cronin's difficulties trace to an emotional makeup. His parents came from Ireland, and gave their youngest son a rich Celtic personality. Cronin is proud, brave and aggressive, but he is also impetuous, sensitive and unpredictable. He dislikes contradiction. His coaches never argue with him.

"Cronin knows the game cold," said one ex-Boston player. "His big fault is not being able to lift a team out of a slump. Cronin usually is more discouraged than anyone during a losing streak."

Evidence shows that the Red Sox generally are fast starters, poor finishers. Only once under Cronin have they been more successful in the second half. They open each season as the Red Sox, close it as the Red Flops. They have worse slumps than most teams, they crumple on the road.

If this is explained by Cronin's personal discouragement, it is one of sport's grimmest ironies. For Cronin as a player always has been a dauntless fighter, a man who swept over obstacles to make himself a dangerous hitter, and one of modern baseball's finest shortstops. Cronin was supreme when setting the pace for his men. He led the Senators to the 1933 pennant when only 26 years old. He was completely inspired when he led the Red Sox to a five-game sweep in Yankee Stadium in 1938. Cronin leads better by example than by precept.

Cronin is a hard worker, eager to accept responsibility, but it often seems that he wants to play all nine positions at once. In 1936, he even tried to sign players to contracts. Joe used to signal pitches from his shortstop position. He did it while leading the Senators to the pennant. But when Herb Pennock, his Red Sox coach, advised him that his pitchers and catchers were burning up over the slur to their intelligence, he stopped. Traded to Cleveland, Jim Bagby said, "I never was allowed to pitch my own games in Boston." Now Bagby again belongs to the Red Sox and probably he is happy, for Cronin no longer plays shortstop or calls pitches.

"Joe, you're so busy giving signals that half the time you don't see the batter hit the ball," Oscar Melillo, his former second baseman, once told him.

"The Red Sox take too much for granted," said a former player. "They don't hustle like the Yankees. Every Yankee has his job, but with the Red Sox, every decision has to be made by the manager."

Cronin took a beating as a playing manager. Tired out from playing shortstop, worried by pitching problems, beset by criticism, Cronin's nerves frayed during the crucial stages of every race. Only his indomitable will carried him through. Men who lived with him on blistering Western trips when the star-spangled Sox disintegrated, became prejudiced against playing managers. Even the stubborn Cronin one day admitted, "If I ever own a club, I won't have a playing manager."

Cronin the manager is not to be confused with Cronin the player. Even his critics admit his capacity for heroic deeds — his five pinch homers in 1943 to set an American League record; his home run his first time at bat after son Tommy was born in May, 1938; his brawl with Jake Powell and other Yankees with 81,841, fans and his own devoted stars looking on at New York, May 30, 1938. Such feats have put Cronin the player on a pedestal in Boston — there he will remain, whatever his fate as a manager.

In explaining Cronin, not enough attention has been given the record price of $275,000 paid for him by Tom Yawkey. That tag was an anchor around Cronin's neck, a constant reminder that he should be the greatest player of all time. He wasn't. Despite all his ability, he was still just another overpriced player. Only worry over his own value could have caused Cronin's fielding collapse his first two years in Boston. Cronin developed the groundball jitters. The slower the grounder, the worse he kicked it. He resorted to kneeling in front of the ball as an outfielder does — the $275,000 squat. One day the ball hit the other knee and bounced clear out to the right fielder.

"For Pete's sake, Joe," protested Melillo, "if you're going to miss 'em, you might as well stand up and miss 'em like a big-leaguer."

On a Ladies' Day in 1935, Cronin played soccer at shortstop while the women booed him boisterously.

"And this," said Mildred, his kind wife, showing a visitor around their 1936 Brookline residence, "I call Joe's Crying Room. He has used it a lot this summer."

The $275,000 outlay not only affected Cronin but it changed Boston fans. Trained by years of second-division baseball to accept gratefully even the catch of a long fly, they leaped to the conclusion that the pennant was in the mail. When it was not delivered, their disappointment was as bitter as that of a boy who has not received the promised atomic pea-shooter for 1000 cereal labels. It was natural for them to take it out on Cronin.

The price also made Yawkey a target for every predatory general manager with a star to unload. Yawkey went on paying until, with the Cramer-McNair deal in 1936, he had spent a million for players alone. Then he switched to the farm-system idea.

In the course of spending his million, Yawkey landed some remarkable characters. In their thirteen seasons under Yawkey, the Red Sox have had enough temperament for three grand-opera companies, but only Joe Cascarella could sing.

Cronin has managed such beauties as Wesley Cheek Ferrell, the man who stamped a $150 wrist watch into a jumble of disassociated cogwheels, because he lost; Ben Chapman, who confused the outcome of a game with the number of hits the scorer gave him; Lefty

Grove, who tried to eat his glove without mustard because someone made a costly error; Buck Newsom, who sprained an ankle hopping down the dugout steps on one foot because it was lucky; Bill Werber, who slugged Babe Dahlgren for making an error.

Werber, who refuted charges that he was 90 per cent temper and 10 per cent mental by becoming a $25,000-a-year insurance salesman in Washington, originally described Cronin as Yawkey's Five-Year Plan. It was Chapman who said, "The Red Sox take the blame for losing, but Cronin gets the credit for winning."

Wes Ferrell was Cronin's monumental headache. The pitcher's destruction of club property, his thumbing his nose at the customers, and his ranting and raving were bearable, until he started blaming Cronin for his defeats. Ferrell would sit in the clubhouse while Cronin was out practicing, and tell whoever walked in, "If we had a shortstop, we'd win the pennant. Cronin has lost me four games already."

So many players agreed with Wesley that a player rebellion threatened. Through his stooges, Cronin learned what the score was, and he was primed when Ferrell walked off the mound in Yankee Stadium in August, 1936 — walked off the field in the middle of an inning without saying good-by to anyone, even the umpires.

Cronin let him go, to announce after the game that Ferrell was fined $1000 and suspended indefinitely. This was the most summary action ever taken by Cronin against a player, although he has fined Jim Tabor as much as $500. Ferrell was reinstated a few days later and ultimately got his money back, as did Tabor. But Wes never admitted that Cronin was a good shortstop.

Other managers might have led such a blue-ribbon cast to the pennant — say, a ruthless Durocher — but Cronin could not. The other stars were jealous of him, his authority was weakened by his own fielding lapses. He was too kindhearted to be consistently tough.

So Yawkey, Collins and Cronin stopped chasing stars. Werber, Chapman, Ferrell, Newsom, Cramer, McNair — one by one Yawkey's speculations were turned in for less glamorous securities. They failed to bring Boston a pennant, but they brought it everything else. There is this to remember about players not good enough for the Red Sox: eighteen of them have played in the last ten World Series.

When Cronin sent the mercurial Werber to Philadelphia, he was accused of letting his personal feelings interfere with his running of the team. When Jimmy Foxx was sold to the Cubs during the 1942 season, Cronin was accused of protecting his job. Foxx, near the end of his playing career and popular in Boston, had managerial aspirations, but he miscalculated if he thought Yawkey was ready to fire Cronin.

When Louisville was permitted to sell Pee Wee Reese, talented shortstop, to Brooklyn, Cronin was suspected of looking out for his job. The Red Sox bought Louisville for $195,000 in 1938, primarily to get Reese. Billy Evans, director of the Red Sox farm system, promised that Reese would succeed Cronin — an announcement which evidently did neither Reese nor Evans any good. Cronin thumbed down the youngster the first time he saw him play, saying, "He's too small. He'll never be a hitter." The Dodgers bought Reese for $35,000 and four players. Soon after the 1940 season started, Larry MacPhail said, "The Dodgers wouldn't sell Reese for two hundred thousand dollars." Reese helped Brooklyn win the pennant in 1941, a year the Red Sox again finished second.

Despite the growing impatience of the Boston press, Cronin generally has had friendly relations with the baseball writers. He'll suggest stories and pictures, but when it comes to a controversial topic, he is as reticent as Joe McCarthy. As the pennantless years have grown into decades, anti-Cronins have found their jeer leaders in the tabloids.

Baseball writers resented Cronin's handling of Ted Williams, even though he bawled out the moody young slugger, benched him, and once fined him $250 for loafing. Writers who thought themselves insulted by Williams wanted him strung up by the thumbs. Instead, Cronin protected Williams by barring the writers from the Red Sox clubhouse in 1941. Cronin could have been right. Williams hit only .356 for four seasons. Heaven knows what the writers hit in 1941!

In 1943, Cronin let Ken Chase stay in a game until he had given eleven bases on balls in four innings. One writer boldly asked, "Why did you let him take such a beating, Joe?"

"You run that paper you're writing for," snapped the manager. "I'll run the Red Sox."

A few days later Cronin was again friendly with the writers. He explained, "I'm not reading the papers any more."

When the Red Sox scored a moral victory in 1938 by finishing as high as second for the first time in twenty years, Cronin was so elated that he threw a champagne party for press and players. Before it ended, a half dozen fights had been barely prevented. The bill ran to over $1000. But Yawkey, who had enjoyed the hottest arguments, paid half of it. Cronin has not since entertained the press formally.

Cronin's eleven-year record with the Red Sox shows four second places, three fourths, one fifth, one sixth and two sevenths — not viewed as spectacular in a city which has not had a pennant in twenty-seven years. The Red Sox have never come close to winning under the Triple Alliance, their nearest approach being in 1940, when they finished eight games behind Detroit, but only tied for fourth place.

Many serious explanations besides Cronin, Collins and Yawkey have been advanced for Red Sox failures. The most logical is the overwhelming might of the New York Yankees, who have won seven of the last eleven races. Even when the 1942 Red Sox won 93 games — and sixteen American League pennants have been won with 93 or fewer victories — the Red Sox finished nine games behind.

The question is: where were the Red Sox in the four seasons of golden opportunity, 1935, 1940, 1944 and 1945, when the Yankees were resting? Alas, they never finished higher than fourth, causing Cronin to sigh, "It looks as though our players are always either coming or going."

Cronin certainly is not admitting that Red Sox failures are primarily his fault. His defense is based on the failure of Red Sox scouting and farm systems to find and develop pitchers and catchers — departments in which the Red Sox have been weakest. Cronin once said, "Yawkey has had more tough luck than any owner. Just when he had put a winning team together, the Yankees came up with Joe DiMaggio, the best all-round player today."

Asked how he won a pennant in Washington in 1933, Cronin replied, "It was easy. It was a veteran team that only needed to be pepped up. I used to be a tough guy then, not a softy."

Cronin resents being called softhearted, but he is. He has forgiven his players innumerable mistakes on and off the field. He has pitied umpires more than he has abused them. He has won the devotion of such youngsters as Johnny Pesky and Dave Ferriss. Unfortunately,

Cronin's many virtues do not show in the American League standings.

Now that Joe no longer is playing, and cannot divert criticism with a home run in the clutch, the attention of Boston fans is focused more sharply than ever on his managing. He must win the pennant in 1946 or 1947. That the Yankees and Tigers have better postwar teams returning than the Red Sox will not quiet Cronin's critics. Their impatience has reached the point where not even valid excuses will be accepted.

It was Yawkey who discharged Billy Evans over the telephone one night late in the 1941 season, cutting loose the most productive talent finder the Red Sox have ever had. It was Collins who sponsored the purchase of so many lackadaisical players from Connie Mack. But it is Cronin who has held the reins of the Red Sox the last eleven sad seasons.

How has Cronin stayed in the saddle? He has stayed because Yawkey wanted him. Yawkey, like innumerable others, idolized Cronin as a player; Yawkey is stubborn, wealthy and loyal.

Yawkey likes Cronin the man. Of Cronin the manager he said, when signing him to a three-year contract in 1944, "I'm perfectly satisfied with Joe. He can manage the Red Sox as long as he likes." When Cronin was being abused as a shortstop, it was Yawkey who said, "Instead of a better shortstop helping the pitchers, don't you think better pitchers would help the shortstop?"

The only major-league managers who have served as long with their clubs as Cronin has with the Red Sox are Joe McCarthy, Jimmy Dykes and Connie Mack.

It is profitable as well as pleasant to be liked by Tom Yawkey. Cronin has served two five-year terms with the Red Sox, and has two years to go on his third contract. At the end of thirteen years, Cronin will have received about $450,000 in salary. Of his tenure as Red Sox manager, Cronin once told a baseball writer with a chuckle, "It looks as if we are going to grow old together."

When Mickey Cochrane was released as manager of the Detroit Tigers in 1938, having won two pennants in five years, it was thought that the Red Sox would sign him as a catcher.

If Yawkey had a closer friend in baseball than Collins and Cronin, that man was Cochrane. Indeed, it was Cochrane's success in lead-

ing the 1934 Tigers to the pennant that prompted Yawkey to buy
Cronin, a dynamic playing manager cut from the same pattern. If
Yawkey had asked Cochrane to join the Red Sox, Cronin probably
would have offered his resignation. He knew that Cochrane's presence would make his situation intolerable. Yawkey, no doubt sensing
Cronin's position, never offered Cochrane a job.

Yawkey couldn't buy a pennant. He hasn't succeeded in building a
winner through his farm system — although his Louisville team has
been in four Little World Series in seven years, winning two of them.
Now Yawkey is challenging the Yankees on another front. He is paying fantastic bonuses to boy wonders, like $15,000 to Dick Callahan
and $19,000 to Ted del Guercio.

"It's ridiculous, the prices the Red Sox are paying," scream New
York scouts, who used to skim the cream by telling the kids, "Whatever any other club offers, the Yankees will give you five hundred
dollars more."

As Cronin nears the start of his twelfth season as Red Sox manager, the sour dish of past pennant failures has been sweetened by
the successive return from the armed services of such fine players as
Johnny Pesky, Bobby Doerr, Tex Hughson, and Jim Tabor, with Ted
Williams and Dom DiMaggio soon to follow.

Already the first spots of pennant fever have broken out in Boston. Even before spring training, two of the town's better baseball
writers have picked the Red Sox to win the 1946 pennant. By midApril a bonfire of optimism probably will be raging again in old
Boston.

And where will the anti-Cronins be then? They'll be in the underground, confidently awaiting the annual opportunity to turn the
bonfire into a pyre for the game guy with the big chin, Joe Cronin.

*The question first posed by Harold Kaese in 1946 has been asked innumerable times since. How can a team with such obvious talent and
means as the Red Sox continue to fall short of the world championship?
That enigma has inspired many millions of words and exasperated
millions of fans.*

Kaese, who began his sportswriting career with the Boston Transcript *in 1936 before moving to the* Boston Globe, *where he would remain until his retirement in 1974, represented a new breed of baseball* writer. Kaese was one of the first baseball writers to use statistics to support his arguments, giving his reports an air of authority that the work of many of his peers lacked. Kaese was also a meticulous note taker and archivist. Whenever something unusual happened on the field, Kaese knew whether it had happened before and under precisely what circumstances.

HAROLD KAESE

TED'S LONGEST HOMER PIERCES STRAW HAT ON HEAD 450 FEET AWAY

from *The Boston Globe,* June 10, 1946

A singular honor fell to Joseph A. Boucher, a construction engineer from Albany, at yesterday's Red Sox-Tigers double-header. The longest home run ever hit by Ted Williams in Boston bounced squarely off his head in the first inning of the second game.

He had never sat in the Fenway Park bleachers before. There were 7897 fans besides himself perched on the sun-drenched wind-whipped concrete slope. Indeed was the elderly Mr. Boucher honored when crowned by a five-ounce baseball that the game's greatest hitter had socked some 450 feet.

"How far away must one sit to be safe in this park?" asked Ted's target for the day, feeling his pate tenderly.

He was sitting in the 33d row of the bleachers, next to the aisle dividing the first and second sections behind the home bullpen. This was a little more than half way up the slope, and surely out of range of anything less than light artillery, he thought.

"I didn't even get the ball," said Mr. Boucher. "They say it bounced a dozen rows higher, but after it hit my head I was no longer interested."

Sun Was in His Eyes

Asked why he did not defend himself by at least putting up his hands, the engineer replied, "I couldn't see the ball. Nobody could. The sun was right in our eyes. All we could do was duck. I'm glad I didn't stand up."

The ball players were not the only ones who had trouble with the wind and sun. The next time the engineer from Albany sits in the bleachers he probably will move to the top row, don sunglasses, and take a glove out of his back pocket as Williams comes to bat.

He was not seriously hurt, because he was wearing a straw hat, in the crown of which was a soft label that acted as a cushion. The ball struck the very center of the crown — a perfect bullseye. It made a tiny little hole that speaks well for the quality of the headpiece. One of my straw hats, for instance, would have broken up like a mat of shredded wheat struck by a hammer.

Mr. Boucher went to the first-aid room, but after being treated by Dr. Ralph McCarthy and two pretty nurses, he returned to his seat in row 33 and enjoyed the rest of the game.

"I am a great baseball fan and I am a Red Sox rooter. I've worked here since the start of the war," said Mr. Boucher. "This is the first time I've sat in the bleachers. I couldn't get into the grandstand."

He has yet to recover a ball hit into the stands, although a fan all his life. Needless to say, he has never come any closer than he did yesterday.

Museum Is Place for Hat

"What would I have done with it anyhow?" he asked. "Well, maybe I could have sent it home to my grandson. I have a ball someplace that was autographed by the old Dodgers, fellows like Jake Daubert and Chief Myers. I thought maybe I'd give it to the Cooperstown Museum."

He would do better, it was suggested, if he gave his straw hat to the museum. It is quite possible that Williams will never hit a longer home run in Boston. Then the hat would make an impressive showing in a glass case, suitably inscribed: "Hat worn by J. A. Boucher of Albany June 9, 1946, when Ted Williams of Red Sox bounced his longest Boston home run off owner's head. Note aperture."

Williams has hit some tremendous homers at Fenway Park. One off Scarborough last week cleared the 420-foot mark in center field. In his first season he hit one exit-high into the right field bleachers off Red Ruffing. But yesterday's drive, borne on a high wind, was his record. Nobody present will forget it, least of all Joseph A. Boucher, who didn't see it but certainly felt it.

Had Kaese not followed the path of Williams's homer, today there would be no red seat high up in the bleachers marking the place where Joseph Boucher's straw hat met its demise.

AL HIRSHBERG

WON IT THE WAY CRONIN WANTED

Hughson's Three-Hitter and Ted's Homer
Perfect Climax — Yawkey Gives Credit
to Manager

from *The Boston Post,* September 14, 1946

CLEVELAND, SEPT. 13 — In their hotel rooms, in the lobby, on the street at the side entrance, in a barroom across the street, where there was a baseball ticker tape, the Red Sox won their first pennant in 28 years. They won it in street clothes, some with cigars or cigarettes in their mouths, some lying flat on their backs on hotel beds, some with a short glass of beer in their hands.

They start ball games here at 1:30 in the afternoon. The 1–0 Red Sox victory over the Indians at League Park was over at exactly 2:59. One minute later, the Yanks and the Tigers began their ball game in Detroit.

When the boys got back to their hotel here, the Detroit game was in the third inning. Everyone scattered. Secretary Tom Dowd passed the word gingerly to be around in case there was a victory party tonight. Everybody stuck around.

Four of the boys, Hal Wagner, Lee Culberson, Tom McBride and Cat Metkovich, strolled over to the barroom. There, they stood around the ticker, watching the returns come in from Detroit, wondering whether or not they'd have to wait longer for this date with fate which has been eluding them so coyly ever since the Tigers lost a doubleheader to Chicago last Sunday to put the Sox in the position where a single victory, coupled with a Tiger defeat, would clinch the flag.

Clem Dreisewerd fell asleep on the end of a divan in the lobby.

Don Gutteridge went out for a walk with a Cleveland friend. Manager Joe Cronin and Owner Tom Yawkey sat calmly up in Dowd's room waiting for a phone call — any phone call that would tell them the answer, which stood poised on the arm of Harry Gumpert, the Yankee pitcher, in Detroit.

Johnny Pesky sat around in the lobby, smoking a cigar and talking to Mike Ryba, who also had a fat stogie sticking out of his mouth. Bill Zuber walked back and forth, a half-smile on his face. Big Dave Ferriss calmly sat tight, talking when people talked to him, mostly just sitting around, showing no emotion whatever.

When the Yanks went ahead in the seventh on Joe Di Maggio's home run, the boys in the barroom came back across the street and into the hotel to make a report. Culby grabbed a big camera from a photographer and focused it on Dreisewerd, still fast asleep. Charley Wagner came down, dressed very prettily indeed, in something soft and brown, sporting a neat, multicolored cravat and wearing a big smile. Jim Bagby grinned as Max Patkin, the Cleveland comedian who was thrown out of yesterday's game by Umpire Cal Hubbard for making gestures on the coaching line while Bagby was pitching, walked by.

Then the news came. Somebody rushed in and yelled, "Yanks win! 5–4."

For a moment, there was no sound. Then, gravely, hardly smiling the boys in the lobby turned and congratulated each other.

Doesn't Forget Pellagrini

There was no rowdiness, no spontaneous eruption, no exuberance. The Red Sox, most of whom were congregated in the lobby when the news was brought in, looked, talked and acted like the champions they are.

Most of the regulars were still in their rooms. There was no sign of Ted Williams, Bobby Doerr, Rudy York, Dom DiMaggio, Tex Hughson and a few of the others.

Mickey Harris came down and smiled, "this is it." Larry Woodall, Del Baker, and Ryba gathered in a little group near the elevators, grinned in response. Mike said, "Now, I'll say it — we're in."

Cronin, still in Dowd's room, was calm and happy sitting in an armchair behind a table piled high with sustenance, he made the statement he's been waiting to make ever since it was obvious that only a general collapse could keep the Red Sox from winning the pennant.

"It was the way I wanted to win," he said slowly, "Hughson pitching a three-hitter, and Williams hitting a home run. That's the way it should be. I've put Hughson in the toughest spots I could find. I've pitched him on the days after night games, when the whole team was tired and listless. I've pitched him against the best in the league. He's the hardest working, most reliable pitcher in the business.

"What did it do for us? Well, Wagner did a great job for us behind the plate. Now I can rest him a little. Partee filled in nicely when we needed him. York was great all season. I got him because I needed a heavy-hitting first baseman. He's won a lot of ball games for us.

"Doerr and Pesky have been great. That double-play combination has been the backbone of our defense. Johnny's been playing with a bad leg. I'll rest him unless he wants to stay in there. I'll rest Bobby too. He's got a thigh injury from sliding which never will heal until I take him out of there."

He stopped and rolled a cigar around in his hand.

"We've been lucky at third and in right," he went on. "There was always somebody available. Don't forget little Eddie Pellagrini. He was at third during that winning streak early in the season. I've been able to shuffle Culby around, and Russell and Gutteridge and McBride and Moses were a big help.

"DiMaggio is in a class by himself. Hughson calls Dom his best pitch, just as Ferriss calls Pesky and Doerr his best. Dave has been great. He has been fighting that second year jinx and the stigma of just being a good wartime replacement. He's got a heart as strong as his arm. Mickey Harris has pitched some great ball for us. These two games he won in New York, first against Chandler and later against Page, were, I think, the most important victories we won all season. As for Ted Williams — what can I say that hasn't already been said? The guy's in a class by himself."

As he talked, Tom Yawkey stood by, on the fringe of the crowd, trying to stay away from the limelight.

We walked over and asked, "Any comment, Tom?"

"No comment," he grinned. "Ask him. There's the guy who won the pennant for us."

Then the man who spent $4,000,000 and waited 13 years for this day jerked his cigar towards Cronin, turned and walked out of the room.

Just when the Red Sox appeared to have the 1946 pennant sewn up, the team went into a tailspin, as several tons of ice were wasted keeping the champagne cold. Hirshberg, who went on to write a number of successful books on a variety of topics, captured the obvious relief when the Red Sox finally won the pennant. But their late-season struggle did not bode well for a World Series win.

JOE MCKENNEY

SOX LOCKER ROOM RESEMBLES A WAKE

Players Trudge Drearily Down That Last Mile to Clubhouse — All Hold Heads High

from *The Boston Post*, October 16, 1946

ST. LOUIS, OCT. 15 — It was the end of the long trail through gold and glory and it ended up in steam.

Throughout the entire ninth inning the Red Sox were spiking their way through the long last mile that leads past dirty hot dog stands under the grandstand into the visiting team dressing room at Sportsman's Park. At first, as Rip Russell and George Metkovich arrived after their pinch hits that helped tie the game, the spikes clicked a happy tune. Even the echoes of the limping Bobby Doerr's sang that the score had been tied.

Sox Take Refuge

And then, as the inning progressed, ended in defeat and the rest of the Red Sox sought the shelter of the showers, a knell for Boston's world championship hopes wandered through the canyons.

Even the steamy smells of the dressing room seemed a refuge from the disaster that couldn't but did come to pass, and the Red Sox fought their way through cheering Cardinal fans in haste.

Mike Higgins was the first to arrive followed by Ted Williams and Johnny Pesky, each carrying the woes of the whole world in their thorny countenances. Tom McBride, the last out of the lost cause, followed with eyes that were red and tears that were fighting their way through his cynicism.

Joe Cronin detoured to congratulate Eddie Dyer in the Cardinals' room and brought up the rear. He sat by his locker nearest the door, took off his shirt and the wake was begun. People of sufficient importance to be admitted to the barred confines gathered around in a perspiring mob and shook his hand in barren silence but with looks that said, "I'm sorry for your troubles, Joe." Joe just sat there and in a monotone that was second base to a whisper, gave the Cardinal outfield credit for St. Louis' joy.

Cronin Credits Outfield

"Everyone of those outfielders was good," said Cronin. "What catches they made. Slaughter, Moore and Walker. They were a great defensive club. Great.

"Winning the pennant early didn't help us any," Cronin went on in reply to one condolence. And then quickly, "But that's no alibi. We've got no alibis. We couldn't get a hit when we needed it."

The mourner stood up then to trade tribulations with his bosses. Eddie Collins told him, "You're still aces, Joe," and Collins' emotions were visible. Tom Yawkey said not a word, but slapped Cronin on his now bared back and Joe, clutching a towel in his left hand, shook hands with the other and said to Yawkey, "Well, stay with 'em, pardner."

Pesky Accepts Blame

The cortege moved alongside Johnny Pesky, the man who hesitated and lost the ball game. It was difficult to bring up the play in the eighth inning on which Enos Slaughter scored all the way from first base on Harry Walker's hit and a half to centre field. But Pesky brought up the subject himself.

"If I was alert I'd have had him at the plate," said Pesky. "When I finally woke up and saw him running for home, I couldn't have got him with a .22."

In many ways the dressing room was just that in more ways than one, for bandages and liniment flowed with the fullness of the wine of victory in the Cardinal celebration next door. Bobby Doerr had bumped his leg on second base, or Red Schoendienst, he didn't remember which, and pulled a muscle in his left leg in the ninth inning. Doerr emphasized that it was not the same spot he had hurt when he collided with Wally Moses in the seventh. "That was my foot," said Bobby and Moses said he couldn't feel his hurts any more.

DiMaggio Pulls Muscle

Dom DiMaggio pulled a muscle in his left thigh as he rounded first base on his double in the Red Sox big eighth inning and had retired from the game then. Dom exhibited his injury for all to see, and one diehard called it a monument to defeat. "If he'd been in centre field in the ninth, Slaughter would never a dared go home," sang the alibi.

The Red Sox used 17 players in the game, but the entire squad was tired from tension and every player was a wet and weary figure as they lined up before their lockers along the walls of the room. Few talked about the game. Dave Ferriss apologized for his failure by saying, "I didn't have too much stuff. I made them too good," but everyone knew that he had tried his very best. It looked as though Tex Hughson was breaking down in a cry, but Tex wiped his eyes and gulped, "I musta swallowed something down the wrong way." Ted Williams sat in front of his locker, not moving to undress beyond his undershirt, and whispered words to his neighbor, Mickey Harris, which were not meant for anyone else to hear.

Photographers insisted on a few final pictures to show, first, that the Red Sox were down, but, secondly, that they were not out. Williams, moaning low on the hard dressing room bench made a fitting subject for the first sitting. Tom Yawkey threw his arms around Dom DiMaggio and Joe Cronin did the same to Ferriss to illustrate courage in the utmost misery of defeat.

DiMaggio was the first player to leave the locker room, although Mike Higgins was the first one dressed. Mike waited with the look of a veteran who had been through this before, and because he was neither a hero nor a goat of the day, no one sought any of his wisdom. The last to dress and the last to leave was Williams. When the word was passed, "The bus is waiting around and outside the park," Ted still was in his undershirt and hadn't moved toward the shower.

Outside a crowd of St. Louis fans, who had overflowed from the mob in front of the Cardinals' quarters, gathered and shouted derisive remarks at Williams inside. "Where's Williams?" they screamed. "Where's the superman?"

Crowd Heckles Williams

They formed two lines on either side of the Red Sox door, and after the police had made sure none was carrying a rope, they stood aside to let Williams run this hot oven of abuse.

In the dressing room only the steam and a few sportswriters remained. Some wanted to chase Cronin and talk more about the game and the Red Sox, but it was declared more in keeping not to mention the faults of the deceased. "We could ask him who he's gonna pitch in the opener next season," fired one funster as a parting shot.

But nobody laughed. Nobody dared laugh at all.

In a dozen different ways — from Ted Williams's elbow injury in a pre-Series exhibition to Joe Cronin's inexplicable decision to use pitcher Bob Klinger for the first time in two weeks to try to preserve a Boston lead in game seven — the Red Sox squandered their best chance since 1918 to hoist another world championship banner, losing to the Cardinals four games to three. Unfortunately, similar scenes would end many Red Sox seasons. For the record, films of the Series demonstrate that Johnny Pesky should be absolved of responsibility for allowing Slaughter to score. The Cardinals' runner got a great jump, and by the time Pesky received the relay it was too late to cut down Slaughter at home plate.

WESTBROOK PEGLER

U.S. BASEBALL MADNESS PLEASANT TO BEHOLD IN FACE OF WORLD'S WOES

from *The Boston Evening American,* October 5, 1948

In a world of wonderful nonsense, far from the hateful mutterings of Europe and the presidential campaign, about 34,000 Americans spent Monday afternoon in innocent raptures as the Cleveland Indians won the playoff game from the Red Sox for the championship of the American League. Score, 8 to 3.

The first tie in the history of the league was a dramatic triviality of great importance. Yet, when the players had got their pores opened and the events began to unreel, the process was simple and logical and not at all surprising.

Gene Bearden of the Indians pitched his way to a repetition of previous routine victories over the Red Sox and home runs and doubles sailed gracefully hither and yon.

There was a nice scuffle of Cleveland players and cops and a few magnanimous customers as a spontaneous tribute to Mr. Bearden as he started away at the end. He was caught up and carried shoulder high by his colleagues, with even old Deacon Bill McKechnie, the Cleveland coach, hoisting one of his mighty legs in the old varsity style.

And from behind, unseen or unrecognized perhaps by most of the crowd, a man in slacks and a brown leather jacket went hopping after them to catch himself a hold and lend a hand. His chrysanthemum shock of yaller hair bobbed as jaunty as any warrior's plume, and there went a really heroic American, Bill Veeck, managing owner of the Cleveland baseball firm.

Pacific Casualty

Bill lost his right foot and some of the leg in an accident with a cannon close to the end of the war in the Pacific where he fought with the Marines. Occasionally ever since, he has had to go into a hospital and have the stump inched away.

He has nevertheless been a young man of dynamic goodness and mischief, as game as the greatest words for courage, itself, renowned for his ingenuity not only in drawing customers to ball-games by extra-curricular nonsense like the bank night of old in the movies, but in finding good ways to give money away.

They will have told you by now all about the juicy hitting which pleased the eye but seemed to discredit the sort of pitching that was fed the Cleveland club in this climax.

Open and Shut

It was not a tight enough game to be dramatic but the nature of the meeting, the tie, the showdown and the imminence of the World Series starting here, were stimulating to the juvenile American soul.

Baseball writers from all over the map, including men from the high and middling minor leagues, had come to Boston anyway to be here for the opening of the World Series Wednesday between the Braves, and the winner of yesterday's afternoon's proceedings.

By themselves these literati make a houseful and there is always an air to these Fall reunions, of a quaint native American custom. They are coming to be, however, something on the order of the advanced conventions of the G.A.R. [Grand Army of the Republic] in that more and more cups are hoisted to the memory of absent comrades and tossed in with less and less of the old abandon of World Series time.

These conniptions have been going on for half a century and hardly a man is now alive who saw the first one. To come to more intimate times, a man begins to find himself off in corners, fellowshipping with other ancients who have widened and thickened and grayed and showing off to the juniors in fabulous memoirs of escapades in prohibition days.

Few Old Players

The baseball writers last much longer than the combatants and so 25-year men are numerous now whereas the players come and go in a rapid parade and few come to World Series when their careers are done and they are paid off. They are very anonymous in street clothes and they forget between one Fall and the next.

The tension over this enormous little game of ball was sensible even along the line of the New Haven up from New York. The Pullman conductor had mocked the loyalty of a baggageman at Providence and had been challenged to bet $100, of inflation money.

The streets converging on Fenway Park, a name faintly fragrant of the unabashed culture of Boston, were choked with taxis and patrons afoot and through the scene there coursed a familiar, happy American lunacy, beautiful and a trace pathetic.

Teams Tired

As the crowd whistled, roared and babbled, young American soldiers in the air-lift were still hauling freight, pinch by pinch, into Berlin and perhaps a quarter of the available bucks in the crowd and among the players were under a threat of a call to a war.

The two American League teams were tired after a long season of physical and emotional strain, the emotion involved being the laudable bourgeois lust for monetary gain. They had come down to the end absolutely even, as though not a game had been played, and, by a poetic freak which the statisticians will savor in years to come, they had each won eleven in their own schedule of head-on games.

The impending World Series, returned the Braves to the, as it were, annual fall gala autumnal classic of the diamond for the first time since 1914. That was the year when a courtly roughneck from Haddock, Ga., the late George Stallings, rowelled and ired a desultory crew and won his pennant after the Fourth of July which found them last.

He left many robust legends but his greatest cultural contribution to his country was his enrichment of profane repartee in baseball and even well beyond.

Superb Scorn

Mr. Stallings had a gorgeous knack of imagery and metaphor and the pity is that the poetry that he murmured from the bench, so florid and glittering with the sequins of his superb scorn, could not be caught for posterity. And yet, as his contemporaries always remarked with awe, he could bow as deep from the waist and sweep the floor with the brim of his hat in the presence of ladies as pretty as any ham in any honeysuckle show you ever saw.

Although this was a grim round of doings at the Fenway, a game in which a good local ball team came to frustration in the last minute, there was a handsome air of sportsmanship throughout. The retarded mass intellect of Brooklyn which expresses its disappointment in mass muckerism and raucous abuse was forgotten as the Bostons, in their thousands, found it in their code to cheer the team that was giving theirs an awful going over.

In the ninth, as Lou Boudreau, the agile and ornate young manager of the Cleveland club got his fourth hit of the day, being two home runs and two singles, as well as a base on balls, he got a cordial salute, which rolled from wing to wing of the stands and across the bleachers.

One Fight

There was only one fight, a pleasure fracas in the center field bleachers which raged on without interference and seemed to be enlivened by some spontaneous partisanship. It was no case for the cops, however, nor even for the moral force of the United Nations, and, having run its course, subsided, no doubt leaving the world a better place to live in.

The soft Coriconian purr, the Irish accent peculiar to Boston and to no other American city any more, what with the prowess of relentless Americanization, was to be heard as a murmur in the crowd and a vaguely stirring spiritual note to the Celtic nature.

With perhaps some little isolated blocks in Waterbury, Danbury and thereabouts in the Connecticut Valley, Boston is the only American city where the tongue survives as Mr. Dooley spoke it.

And in Boston, it may be observed, the culture and character of the American Irish have come to a proud maturity by contrast with the decline of Harvard's old renown and the growth instead of a wormy continental cynicism.

With the Boston Braves already in the Series as NL champs, Boston was baseball crazy as the Red Sox met the Indians in a one-game playoff — the first in AL history — to decide that league's pennant. As the presence of syndicated columnist Westbrook Pegler demonstrates, the game drew national attention. He made great use of his reportorial eye.

WHAT <u>WAS</u> MATTER WITH OUR RED SOX?

from *The Boston Globe*, October 5, 1948

The best catcher on the Red Sox is not Birdie Tebbetts, but Tom Yawkey. Only Tom catches 'em on the whiskers.

In his 16 years as Red Sox owner, Yawkey has spent around $2,000,000 for players alone. What has he got, beside a lot of thrills and laughs? One pennant.

The Red Sox must have muffed one in '46, when they finished first.

Remember the screams of "Pennant sell-out" last Winter, when Joe Cronin negotiated the St. Louis Purchase?

Dan Topping of the Yankees wanted to pass a law forbidding teams like the Browns from selling pennants to Yankee competitors like the Red Sox.

But Topping was unduly exercising his tonsils. The Red Sox got only the closest second in American League history for the $400,000 they paid for Vern Stephens, Jack Kramer, et al.

A few months from now, when snowdrifts are six feet deep in downtown streets, the Red Sox presumably will walk away with the '49 pennant, spending a small fortune for players who will assure them the flag.

The Red Sox never sit still. They are not content to lose the pennant the same way two years in a row. Last Fall they hired a new manager in Joe McCarthy. This Fall they have already fired Phil Troy and George Toporcer.

It's a cinch Troy and Toporcer did not lose the pennant.

When McCarthy Forgot Harris

It is more reasonable to think the pennant was lost when McCarthy forgot Mickey Harris through most of September than because of anything Troy forgot in his little office.

Or that it was lost when Ted Williams, who had to prove he could hit to left, went for the little fish singles and doubles and wound up with one of his lowest slugging percentages.

Or that it was lost when important relief jobs were entrusted to an elderly gentleman named Earl Caldwell, or when Joe Dobson faded after being struck on the wrist by Feller the last day of July, or when Vern Stephens went into a batting slump after a mighty mid-season splurge, or when the pressure got too tough on the manager on the last Western trip.

However uncertain their pitching the Red Sox had the pennant won until Sept. 21, 12 days before the end of the season. They were alone in first place with five of their remaining nine games scheduled at home.

They could not hold the lead, and while they came back to tie, they lost the flag yesterday to the Indians.

It is futile to point to the woeful start which left the Red Sox 11½ games out of first place May 31. All clubs have their ups and downs. If the Red Sox had not opened so poorly they would have won the pennant easily. Yes, and if the Indians had not staggered in the Summer months, they would have won by 15 games.

The fact is the Red Sox led the league from Aug. 26 until Sept. 26. They lost the pennant the last two weeks of the season.

Beginning of the Downfall

The Red Sox downfall began with a coup by Bill Veeck of Cleveland. He finessed Bob Feller into a night game against the Red Sox in Cleveland Sept. 22, when he made it a charity for the stricken Don Black.

The Red Sox were morally obliged to agree to a night game, and while it cannot be assumed they would have beaten Feller in the daylight, they probably would have been better able to scrutinize the stuff he was throwing.

Dobson muffed two games in the few bitter days when the Sox lost the lead — the one in Cleveland, and the 4–3 decision he lost to Washington the past week. The two games lost in New York found Kinder, Johnson, Parnell and Galehouse all tagged robustly.

But the four fatal defeats were not the entire responsibility of the pitchers, for in three the Red Sox power plant generated only two runs.

Better Team Not Good Enough

Strangely, the Red Sox were better at almost every position this season than they were a year ago, and still were not good enough to win.

Bobby Doerr and Dom DiMaggio played better than in 1947; Williams had a better average and knocked in more runs; Tebbetts was far better; Bill Goodman played first base well, and hit over .300; the St. Louis Purchase was a success: Stephens was a brilliant shortstop and strong, if erratic, hitter; Kramer and Kinder were winners; Hitchcock filled in well when Doerr was hurt.

The only disappointing positions were third base and right field. Pesky fielded third well enough, but partly because of an early season injury, did not come close to getting the 200 hits he must approximate to have a superior year.

In right field Sam Mele was the team's major disappointment, and Sam Spence didn't come up to expectations. Mele just couldn't get started at the plate in his second season.

Chief Blame to Pitchers

All in all, the Red Sox had a powerful, well-balanced lineup and batting order.

This puts chief blame for Red Sox failure on the pitching staff, where it undoubtedly belongs.

The Big Three of 1946 — Ferriss, Hughson, and Harris — won 62 games in the pennant year, slumped to 29 victories last season, and this season won only 14 games.

Harris, man in the shape of a blimp when he reported for Spring training, is the only Red Sox pitcher who has a losing record this season.

Possibly because of McCarthy's ability to pick spots for them, and surely because of the runs given them, all other Sox hurlers were at or above .500.

He did not have the best record, but the best Red Sox hurler, probably, was Mel Parnell, rookie southpaw. He will have the lowest earned-run average of Red Sox starters.

Jack Kramer had the best won-and-lost record, but someone has said it was more inflated than China's currency. The Sox scored an average of eight runs per game for Kramer, whereas they averaged only five runs for Parnell. Yet Kramer pitched some excellent ball, and, with Kinder, proved much more valuable to the Red Sox than did Ed Lopat and Red Embree to the Yankees.

It should be noted Red Sox pitching was generally ineffectual despite the presence of Tebbetts, one of the game's best receivers. A few years ago, poor Red Sox pitching was blamed on Sox catchers — after it was blamed on Cronin — which was a generous if undeserved, alibi for the hurlers.

If the Red Sox had won the pennant, we'd now be reading about how the brainy Tebbetts had finessed Sox pitchers into one victory after another. Good catchers help pitchers, but they don't make them.

This brings us to Joe McCarthy, who returned to manage the Red Sox just in time to lose another close pennant race. He has never won one — a close one, that is.

In a way, McCarthy's failure can be taken as a vindication of Cronin. Yet does anyone believe the Red Sox would have come so close under Cronin? Does anyone believe the Red Sox would have come from 11½ games in arrears to lead the league? Well, maybe so, maybe so.

McCarthy Still Great Manager

McCarthy's gold star is for holding the Red Sox together when it would have been very easy to have given up. His best decisions were to play Goodman at first base, and to keep Stephens at shortstop and move Pesky to third.

Certainly, McCarthy showed enough in his first season here to justify his ranking as a great manager. Like Southworth, he excels as a disciplinarian.

Unlike Southworth, McCarthy sometimes plays hunches instead of percentages. As good as he is, McCarthy is not above criticism. No manager is that good.

Twice in the vital last month of the season he let Caldwell lose big games, once on Joe DiMaggio's grand slam homer here and once in the 17–10 defeat in Chicago. And with a Harris sitting on the bench!

On Aug. 22 Harris defeated Washington on five hits. On Aug. 29, however, he allowed the Browns five runs in the first inning. McCarthy then did not pitch Harris again until Sept. 20, when he hurled a four-hitter at Detroit.

The Case of the Castoffs

Cronin chose to lose the '46 World Series with a cast-off pitcher named Klinger. McCarthy probably lost the '48 pennant race with a cast-off pitcher named Caldwell.

Outlook for '49 is bright, of course. McCarthy will know his players better. Young pitchers like Maurice McDermott and Windy McCall will have flawless control. Tex Hughson says his arm not only will be all right next season, but is all right now. Pesky is familiar with third base. Williams can single, or even double, to left.

Now, if Tom Yawkey will only open his purse and buy a few good ball players.

Kaese revisits his favorite topic and was one of the first local writers to assign blame to the organization.

SOX APOLLO

from *The Boston Record*, June 29, 1955

When he was attending Boston University he was known as the Avenue Apollo and the sobriquet fit him snugly. For Harry Agganis had the physique, the demeanor, the superman qualities which placed him on a little Olympus all his own. He appeared indestructible; he'd pop up unpunished from under a pile of bruisers who had plummeted into him from all directions and shout fresh, crisp signals; he seemed invulnerable.

He appeared immune to pain, plague, pox, virus, and that's why the death of Harry Agganis yesterday pierced the heart of the city; plunged the entire sports world into deep grief. Of late there had been ominous words, rumors about Agganis, confined to the Sancta Maria Hospital in Cambridge. Glum, minatory words like "tuberculosis" and "complications" and "isolation" and "lung infection."

Harry would win over all, just as he had been winning over all through a thrill-filled young life, dedicated to physical education and sports accomplishment. He'd beat any sickness one hand tied behind his back. Intimates assured themselves of this; admirers who had watched him play football and achieve All-Everything and then work his way into the major leagues of baseball didn't see how anything could conquer him. So the untimeliest of untimely deaths yesterday was twice shocking.

Agganis was something to see — and only a few short weeks ago he was on display a few lockers away from Ted Williams' roost — after a shower in the dressing room at Fenway Park.

A Greek God for sure — all thew and sinew and shoulders. Some real Atlases in that particular nudists' colony, toweling and relaxing and cooling out after a ball game. Williams, for one, a hunk of handsome man. And blond Jackie Jensen, golden boy from the Golden State. But if a sculptor walked in and wanted someone to take discus in hand and pose in the classical fashion, most likely the artist would select Agganis for his model.

Hairbreadth Harry, others nicknamed him, because of his many electric sports experiences. For Harry had a habit of narrow escapes on the athletic fields and a knack for coming through in the clutch. The facts of his life were much more like fiction.

It all began in Barry's sandy park in Lynn — this phenomenal rise to Yawkey's green acre in Boston's fashionable Back Bay — which is a football throw from the Agganis home on Waterhill Street. Harry was born there and lived there — in a second-floor flat — with his widowed mother Georgia Agganis who only lately got to going a few times a week to Fenway Park and who had just recently learned to score the game herself.

Given a $35,000 bonus by the Red Sox, Agganis and his mom could have moved to much more luxurious lodgings in a more toney neighborhood but Mrs. Agganis didn't want to leave her always fastidious home and Harry was more than satisfied with his trim little room there, which his adoring mother had "wallpapered" almost completely from floor to ceiling with prints, pictures, cartoons, framed clippings.

Waterhill Street and streets for miles around must have been wretched, utterly forlorn, inconsolable yesterday shortly after noon when the tragic news flashed that the imperishable Agganis had passed on. Georgia Agganis was born in Loggonlike, a suburb of Sparta in Greece, but not even one with Spartan corpuscles could stand up under the weight of this tragedy.

Harry's brothers, Jimmy, Demo, Philip, and Paul, and his sisters, Mrs. Mary Arimo and Mrs. Dema Orphanos, and their many children rushed bewildered, blinded by tears, to the flat upstairs on Waterhill Street to lend courage in this awful crisis, for Harry was the baby and thoroughly adored.

Each of his sisters kept a huge scrapbook on Harry's brilliant deeds even though Harry didn't exactly approve. He'd blush and giggle and find something to do in the kitchen when Georgia Agganis or one of his sisters would produce a scrapbook or a trophy or a memento and happily tell the tale it involved.

A spring ago it happened to this correspondent, sent to Lynn to do a "life story" on Agganis, then hitting .360 for the Red Sox. Sisters and mother obliged with many clippings and anecdotes while Harry slipped away, abashed but agreeing: "If it makes them happy, that's good."

The scrapbooks bulged. Harry gave his worshipping kind plenty to clip and paste.

It began with a few small-fry achievements in Barry Park. Then Harry went to Lynn Classical and for four years was All-Scholastic in football and baseball. In the summertime he shone in Legion baseball. All his encomiums did not derive from sports, however. What is little known is the fact that he had a distinct talent as a dramatist, an actor. He was leading man in the school play, *Peter Pan.* He had many lines to memorize. He learned them fast, a real Barrymore. Two nights the Classical auditorium sold out. Harry was box-office as an emoter, too.

From Classical, Agganis enrolled at Boston U. He had at least 60 offers from other campuses. Some of the letters, which might embarrass athletic directors if published because they are lofty lucrative lures, are pasted in Georgia Agganis' scrapbook. He chose B.U. because he wished to be near home and Mom's fine cooking. "I cook nice Greek dishes," said Mrs. Agganis last spring during the "life story" research, "but you know what. Harry likes my cooking best when it's ravioli or spaghetti."

Grief-fractured, too, must have been Bill Joyce, Harry's coach at Classical who sent him to B.U. richly endowed with athletic and scholastic qualifications. Agganis' father died in 1946 and Joyce helped fill the void, becoming Harry's guardian angel.

Joyce has had many jolts out of sports, both as a participant and a pedagogue, but he still says Agganis gave him the top kick of all when Classical went to Miami for a Christmas Day, 1946, championship game with Granby High of Norfolk, Virginia, with Chuck Stobbs as quarterback. Classical won 21–14 with Harry running the team superbly as all the leading football coaches in the nation, around the South for the approaching Bowl games, looked on.

A left-handed passer, wonderful kicker, runner Agganis led B.U. out of the morass of mediocrity. The finest schoolboy athlete in 25 years around Greater Boston became one of the greatest nationally for four seasons. He made many All-America teams even though Boston U. was accorded grudging recognition. Harry forced them to focus those big prejudiced binoculars on Commonwealth Avenue. He had the radiance of Yucca Flats and the mushroom cloud over the Charles could not be overlooked.

In his senior season, Agganis was forced out of a big game with U. of Maryland because of a severe chest injury. It did not permit further throwing of a football. Maybe Agganis should have been sent to the hospital then, but he refused to leave the scene. He kept warming up with the football on the sidelines the rest of the game, hoping to get back in there, but the wing would not function.

A few weeks later, Agganis returned to his generalship of the Terriers protected by a heavy cast on his chest. Asked recently if the injury might possibly be causing his current illness, Agganis replied: "I don't think so."

Professional football clamored for Agganis who had satisfied the militia with a hitch in the Marines. The Cleveland Browns, with their Otto Graham near the exit, reportedly offered him $100,000 for four seasons.

Here was quick, certain fortune. But Agganis made Nick the Greek (Dandales), the fabulous gambler, look like a nickel-nurser. His heart was set on baseball and the Red Sox, even though the Red Sox starting price was much less and even though he wasn't sure he could make the varsity. Long years on the farm loomed on the horizon. While he was All-Scholastic first baseman at Lynn and a collegiate star when spring football practice would permit him to play baseball at B.U., there was no guarantee he had major-league baseball qualifications.

He could step in and sparkle immediately with the football Browns. The road to Fenway, not made for left-hand hitters, was clearly cobblestoned. Agganis traveled it after only one season of apprenticeship at Louisville where his durability was proved when he played every inning of 154 games and encored with another show of full stamina in the lengthy playoffs.

His coach at B.U., Buff Donelli, forecast Agganis' success. "Practice, study, determination should keep Agganis up there in the majors — and improving," said Buff when asked for a few words on the Avenue Apollo last summer. "He's one kid who's got active not oral determination. He's willing to pay the price."

Actually Agganis hand-fought his way into the majors for his fielding had flaws and his hitting wasn't wonderful. It terrified few big-league hurlers. But Harry persisted, perspired, and he won the first-base job this season and he was hitting .313 despite Fenway's anti-southpaw dimensions, when stricken mortally by double pneumonia.

Remember the first time he went South to frivolous, frolicsome Florida to train with the Red Sox? He was young, he was single, he had a gleaming new automobile. All rookies mix business with pleasure on this peninsular playground. But Harry with great vision and self-discipline left his car and gay clothes and his natural craving at home. "I'm going down there to make the team," he said, taking the train. "An auto down there would only get me in trouble."

Life-story in April, 1954. Death-story in June, 1955. Rough, rough indeed. A guy could bawl over this one.

After starring for Boston University, Harry Agganis turned down an offer to play pro football so that he could play baseball for the Red Sox. He was on the verge of becoming a star when he was suddenly struck down. His death is perhaps the most tragic event in Red Sox history.

PART III

THE TRYOUT

In 1945 Boston city councilman Isadore Muchnick, frustrated by baseball's cowardly insistence on the color line, threatened to block the Red Sox Sunday baseball permit unless the Red Sox held a try-out for African Americans. At length, the Red Sox reluctantly bowed to pressure from Muchnick and the black press. In April 1945 three players from the Negro Leagues — Marvin Williams, Sam Jethroe, and Jackie Robinson — traveled to Boston to put the Red Sox to the test before a small group of club officials and coaches.

As the workout neared its end, a voice from the stands reportedly rang out and demanded, "Get those niggers off the field." The echo of those words still reverberates through Red Sox history. Williams, Jethroe, and Robinson were not surprised when they never heard from the Red Sox again.

The tryout took place below the radar screen of most Boston reporters. *Pittsburgh Courier* sportswriter Wendell Smith helped Muchnick arrange the tryout, and his reports spread the story to the African American community throughout the nation. Doc Kountze, who served as sports editor of Boston's black newspaper, the *Guardian,* and had long lobbied for the breaking of the color line, was one of the few Boston reporters of any color to report on the try-out. In the mainstream press, only Dave Egan and Joe Cashman of the *Record* gave the story significant play. The *Globe,* for instance, carried only a one-paragraph wire service story about the tryout.

Given the Red Sox string of near misses in the decade after World War II and their subsequent demise in the late 1950s and early 1960s, the tryout clearly represents the greatest missed opportunity in the history of the team. One can well imagine what the addition of Jackie Robinson might have meant to a team that already included Ted Williams, Bobby Doerr, Johnny Pesky, and Dom DiMaggio. Similarly, had the Red Sox been the first team to integrate, it is impossible to overstate the possible impact that might have had not only on the Red Sox but on the future of race relations in a city that has struggled with that issue for decades.

WENDELL SMITH

SPORTS SPURTS

from *The Pittsburgh Courier,* April 1945

"Listen, my children, and you shall hear
Of the midnight ride of Paul Revere.
On the eighteenth of April, in '75,
Hardly a man is now alive
Who remembers that famous day and year."

BOSTON, MASS. — This is Boston, cradle of America's democracy, where the tattered and torn liberty-loving "Rebels" of the colonies fought off the Red Coats in "every middlesex, village, and farm."

This is where 170 years ago this week America's first great jockey Paul Revere, came riding down the "stretch" by the light of the moon, crying out, "The British are coming!"

And this is where Crispus Attucks, tall, gaunt and bronze, stood defiantly with a rebellious mob of fearless Americans behind the "Old State House" and challenged the British "blitz" of 1770.

He fell — Crispus Attucks did — when the Red Coats let go with that first thunderous volley of powder, and his blood flowed freely across the cobblestone ground he and his compatriots were defending.

Crispus Attucks was a Negro. He was one of the very first to give his life in the defense of this country . . . and a volunteer blood donor before anyone ever heard of the Red Cross.

Like today, those were historic, significant days. Like today, liberty-loving people were fighting off despots and dictators, intolerance and fascism. And, like today, Americans were fighting desperately for the very life of their land — for the democratic ideals and creeds upon which the structure of this country was founded.

Paul Revere, a white man, rode through the countryside by the light of the moon, crying out his warning of the approaching British. Crispus Attucks, a black man, gallantly defied the Red Coats until his blood flowed freely across the cobblestones behind the Old State House.

History Repeats . . . in Different Setting

And today, history is being repeated. It's the same story, only cast in a different setting . . . against a different foe. White and black Americans are fighting side by side on the Western front. They fight together by the light of the moon, and their blood flows freely across the cobblestones of "every middlesex, village, and farm," in the land of the "Gray Coats" of Germany.

That is history . . . and that is a fact. And, I am here in the cradle of democracy . . . here in staid old Boston, where Revere rode and Attucks died, trying to break down some of the barriers and wipe out some of the intolerance they fought to obliterate more than 170 years ago. I have three of Crispus Attucks' descendants with me. They are Jackie Robinson, Sammy Jethroe and Marvin Williams. All three are baseball players, and they want to play in the major leagues. They — and many others like them — have been barred for years solely and simply because they are Negroes.

We came here to Boston — the cradle of democracy — to see if perchance just a spark of the "Spirit of '76" still flickers in the hearts and minds of the owners of the Boston Red Sox and Boston Braves, the city's two major league teams.

We have been here almost a week now, but all our appeals for fair consideration and an opportunity have been in vain. Neither John Quinn of the Braves, nor Eddie Collins of the Red Sox, have displayed so much as a semblance of that indomitable spirit we had anticipated here in the shadow of Bunker Hill.

They stand before us as uncompromising despots. They loom as modern Red Coats resolved to deny us opportunities which are rightfully ours by virtue of heritage.

"We're Not Giving Up — We're Sticking to Our Guns!"

But we are not giving up! We are Americans, the color of our skins to the contrary . . . and we're going to stick to our guns! We are looked upon as "confounded rebels" who would challenge the divine right of baseball's kings.

Nevertheless, we stay on, playing the fife of Americanism, beating the drum of democracy, and waving our tattered flag of citizenship. We have inherited — even if Mr. Collins and Mr. Quinn have not — that indomitable colonial spirit.

Our fight has not gone unnoticed. We have won compatriots here in Boston who assure us that the "Spirit of '76" still lives. In fact, some of them vow that of a cold, crisp night, when the moon is high, you can hear the steady beat of a horse's hoofs across the countryside, and Revere bleating out his warning to the heroic "Minute Men."

And they tell us, too, that during the lull of most any day you can hear the echo of the British shots that felled the tall, gaunt, bronze body of brave Crispus Attucks.

We haven't heard these mythical vibrations as yet, but we're straining our ears . . . and waiting for Messrs. Collins and Quinn.

"Listen, my children, and you shall hear . . ."

WHAT ABOUT TRIO SEEKING SOX TRYOUT?

from *The Boston Daily Record,* April 16, 1945

Here are two believe-it-or-not items, exclusively for the personal enlightenment of Mr. Edward Trowbridge Collins, general manager of the Boston Red Sox.

He is living in anno domini 1945, and not in the dust-covered year 1865.

He is residing in the city of Boston, Massachusetts, and not in the city of Mobile, Alabama.

To bring him up to the very minute with another item of general knowledge, it is not Abraham Lincoln for whom his flags flutter at half-staff, for he breathed his last on April 15, 1865; it is Franklin Roosevelt for whom the bells toll, almost 80 years later to the day. And both men died for the same high purpose, that other men might be made free.

There! We thought that somebody should help Mr. Collins straighten himself out on these little matters. Privately, we had hoped that somebody else might undertake the pleasant duty, but nobody else seems to want to; therefore we feel obliged to inform you that since Wednesday last three citizens of the United States have been attempting vainly to get a tryout with his ball team.

Most Valuable Player

One of them is named Jackie Robinson, and you will remember him as a halfback of all-American proportions at U.C.L.A. He is 24 years of age, and until he was honorably discharged on a recent date, he was a lieutenant in the United States Army. As a shortstop in a Pasadena amateur league, he received the most valuable player award over a shortstop named Vern Stephens. He is the shortstop of the fabulous Kansas City Monarchs. So there he is — a college man, a professional athlete, a discharged serviceman, an American citizen. He has youth and education and athletic ability and much that would seem to recommend him to any baseball organization that honestly wished to give its patrons the finest possible team.

But Eddie Collins has slammed the door shut and placed his back against it.

Another one of them is named Samuel Jethroe. He is 25 years old, and 4-F in the draft, and as an outfielder for the Cleveland Buckeyes, he led his league in batting last year with an enthusiastic average of .353. Incidentally, he played last winter for San Juan in the Puerto Rico league; on the same team and in the same outfield, by chance, with Luis Olmo of the Brooklyn Dodgers; and in that league, he hit a monumental .372, which was approximately 100 points higher than Olmo of the Dodgers.

But Eddie Collins says nervously to City Councilor Isadore Muchnick that his scouts never have seen him play; that therefore he would not consider looking at him. Once upon a time, he personally looked at a boy named Teddy Williams, and liked very much what he saw; but this, we must presume, is an entirely different matter.

The third of the trio is Marvin Williams. He is 24 years of age, and 4-F in the draft, and as the second baseman for the Philadelphia Stars, he whaled away a year ago for an average of .338 in his particular professional league. And the suggestion could be made, on his behalf, that if he can not make the grade with that classy aggregation of Red Sox we espied the other day, room might be found for him in the shabbiest and lowest league in organized baseball, in order that he might be given the opportunity to work his way up the ladder.

Forgetful Man

But Eddie Collins is forgetful. He forgets that this is not 1865; he forgets that this is not Mobile, Alabama; and he forgets, most of all, that exactly one month ago today he wrote a letter to City Councilor Muchnick. It was full of injured innocence. It flatly denied discrimination against Negro ball players. And just to refresh his memory, it said the following:

"As I wrote to one of your fellow councillors last April, I have been connected with the Red Sox for twelve years and during that time we have never had a single request for a try-out by a colored applicant . . . It is beyond my understanding how anyone can insinuate or believe that 'all ball players, regardless of race, color, or creed, have not been treated in the American way' so far as having an equal opportunity to play for the Red Sox."

That masterpiece of prose was written on March 16, 1945. This — you may see for yourself that we are full of breathless information today — is April 16, 1945. Yet since Wednesday last, these three young men have been unable to obtain an appointment for a try-out with the Red Sox despite the polite persistence of Mr. Muchnick.

"We have never," wrote Collins, "had a single request for a try-out by a colored applicant."

Every other method having failed, these three young men will present themselves at Mr. Collins' front gate this afternoon, to inquire whether or not those words were written in good faith; to ask an opportunity, if not with the Red Sox, then with the worst and the weakest of its farm clubs.

THREE RACE BASEBALL CANDIDATES IMPRESS RED SOX COACH HUGH DUFFY

Robinson, Jethroe, Williams, Sparkle in Fenway Park Major Try-out

from *The Boston Guardian,* April 21, 1945

Coach Hugh Duffy of the Boston Red Sox this week told the Guardian sports editor that he was highly impressed with the trio of colored ball players who performed in a practice try-out at Fenway Park last Monday morning.

Okay with Duffy

Guests of the Sox management, the trio were shortstops Jackie Robinson, 24-year-old Pacific Coast league star from U.C.L.A.; Sammy Jethroe, 25-year-old Cleveland outfielder [and Marvin Williams] from the Philadelphia Stars of the colored National League.

"Good boys . . . hustlers!" enthused the Red Sox veteran team coach, Hugh Duffy, baseball immortal himself, speaking in Tuesday morning interview with the Guardian sports editor who wired him the appreciation of the colored sports public. "We were glad to give them a try-out," said Duffy in reply to another question. "They're the same as anybody else . . . Got a soul same as I have. Deserve the same chance as anybody." And Duffy spoke like he meant it, too, regardless as to whether he represented the views of all other Sox officials or not.

Scored by Egan

The three colored candidates had been waiting in Boston for a try-out since Wednesday of last week, according to Dave Egan of the

Record, who put the blast on general manager Eddie Collins, charging the latter with holding up the baseball campaign here which has been carried mostly by the colored press, the Record and the Globe. Up to this writing, the Guardian sports editor has received no comment from Eddie Collins as to whether the club will sign or farm out the trio for further study, which is the custom with white players who impress the coaches. Two coaches, Duffy and Larry Woodall more or less, put their okay on colored players this week.

Traveling secretary Phil Troy of the Red Sox was the first to inform the Guardian sports editor that the trio were in uniform at Fenway Park last Monday undergoing try-outs. Few daily papers here carried the news and most of them still are keeping quiet. Regardless as to the outcome of this initial trial, Coach Hugh Duffy told me this week that the Red Sox would still be open for colored try-outs and that he welcomed all good boys. Whether the rest of the Sox management will go through with this baseball business — and it is a business — is hard to say at this time, but further developments are expected soon. However, the Boston try-outs appeared more significant than those held with the Brooklyn Dodgers. The player candidates here were all young men in their 20's, they exhibited a speed and hustle that really impressed one of the leading veteran coaches of the big leagues, and they exacted official expressions that were quite favorable in sharp contrast to the sad reaction over in New York.

Robinson, former All-American Uclan halfback, has been a leading Pacific Coast league shortstop and is a recently discharged army veteran holding the rank of lieutenant. Outfielder Jethroe last year bashed the ball for .353 in his own league and .372 in the Puerto Rican winter league. Young Marvin Williams batted .338 for the Philadelphia Stars last season.

What the trio thought about the try-out and what their future will bring is another story. But Coach Hugh Duffy has given me his personal reaction and it seems to be good.

WENDELL SMITH

RED SOX CANDIDATES WAITING TO HEAR FROM MANAGEMENT

Three Players Who Received Try-out with Boston Red Sox Are Awaiting Cronin's Report on Their Performance

from *The Pittsburgh Courier,* April 1945

Three Negro ball players, Jackie Robinson, Marvin Williams and Sam Jethroe, were anxiously waiting this week to hear from the management of the Boston Red Sox concerning the tryouts they had last week under the supervision of Manager Joe Cronin and his aides.

The three players worked out at Fenway Park, home of the American League team, on Monday, April 16, at which time they went through an hour and a half under the supervision of Coaches Hugh Duffy and Larry Woodall. Manager Joe Cronin sat in the stands and watched the three players go through their chores with deep interest. Afterwards he admitted that he was particularly impressed with Robinson, former all-round star at UCLA, and currently playing shortstop for the Kansas City Monarchs of the Negro American League; and also with Williams, second-baseman for the Philadelphia Stars of the Negro National League.

The players were sent to Boston by The Pittsburgh Courier and accompanied by the writer.

Following the workout, Coach Duffy told the three players they could expect to hear from the Boston management probably "within the near future."

As a result, Robinson, Williams and Jethroe anticipate some kind of word from Manager Joe Cronin or General Manager Eddie Collins, who promised Atty. Isadore Muchnick, Boston councilman, early in March, that the Red Sox would willingly give Negro players a tryout. Councilman Muchnick was present when the three Negro stars had their tryout at Fenway Park.

Since the tryouts were held in Boston, Manager Joe Cronin has been hospitalized with a fractured leg. He may not be free to consider the applications of the three players until he is well again. As a result, Robinson, Williams and Jethroe may have to wait longer than they would under ordinary circumstances.

Meantime, the Boston team has found the American League road extremely rocky the first week of the new season. At this writing, the Sox have yet to win a game in six attempts. Robinson, Williams and Jethroe are hoping that Manager Cronin will decide that one or all of them might be of service to him at this time. They feel that they might be able to give the team a lift if given the opportunity, and are waiting for the mailman each and every day.

One of the interesting sidelights of the recent tryout was the renewal of friendship between Jackie Robinson and Jack Tobin, Red Sox second-baseman. Both players hail from the West Coast, and played against each other in collegiate circles. Tobin played for St. Mary's, and Robinson won national fame at UCLA. After the workout, Tobin came into the dressing room and greeted Robinson. After discussing their previous athletic encounters, Tobin said to Jackie: "I certainly wish you the best of luck." He then left to catch a train for New York, where the Sox played the following day.

"He's a fine fellow," Robinson said afterwards, "and he was a darn good athlete at St. Mary's."

The tryouts in Boston caused considerable comment in the daily press, and was handled throughout the country by the Associated Press and United Press. Joe Cashman, well-known writer of the Boston Record, commented as follows:

"Manager Cronin was impressed by Robinson's fielding at shortstop. He's good and fast, fast as well, Jack Robinson."

"General Manager Eddie Collins," Cashman wrote, "took their names, baseball histories and brief biographies to file away among the Red Sox's line of prospects. Robinson, Williams and Jethroe will be welcomed at some future date to test the sod and sight the targets at Yawkey's green pastures. Further observation may result in the Red Sox signing one of the trio and then schooling at one of the Sox farms."

Meantime, the liberal New York Post came out vigorously against "jim-crow baseball."

In an editorial on the subject, the Post said:

"Baseball is not a monopoly of lily-whites or gray-greens. It belongs to all the people. It is the typical American game. And so it is part of the American melting pot. Into this sport have come men like Joe DiMaggio, an Italian; Hank Greenberg, a Jew; Alejandro Carrasquel, a Cuban; Lou Gehrig, a German; Sigmund Jakucki, a Pole, and others.

"'There should be a place ready and waiting in it for the ten per cent of Americans who are Negro."

With the daily press leveling off on the subject of the Negro in major league baseball, thousands of fans throughout the country are hoping that at least one of the major league owners will take an unprecedented step and sign a Negro player.

While Wendell Smith reported the tryout to a national audience through the Pittsburgh Courier, *Boston's conservative daily press corps virtually ignored the watershed event — many even failed to report it at all. Locally, Doc Kountze kept Boston's black population informed in the weekly* Guardian. *But apart from Dave Egan, the mainstream daily press was virtually silent.*

Egan, a graduate of Harvard Law School, was an immense talent whose personal problems, including alcoholism, cut short his career. Although he was later honored by the NAACP for his courage, Egan paid a price for his outspokenness. His reputation suffered, and he was later derided as a protagonist of Ted Williams, due in no small part to the ire his heroic reporting of baseball's racial prejudice caused within Boston's journalistic establishment.

PART IV

TEDDY BALLGAME AND THE KNIGHTS OF THE KEYBOARD

Ted Williams came to Boston as a rookie right fielder in 1939, all arms, legs, and enthusiasm. He was brash and cocky and had the quickest bat in the major leagues. The fans loved him, and Williams would respond to their cheers by waving his cap wildly.

But in 1940 the Red Sox moved in the right-field fence and built bullpens to make it easier for Williams to hit home runs, then moved him to left field to save his eyes from the late-afternoon sun. Sox fans suddenly thought Williams was being coddled, and when his bat cooled in his sophomore season, he heard his first boos. The insecure young star overreacted in a couple of interviews and expressed his displeasure at being in Boston. When the words appeared in print, he overreacted again. He went to war with the press and vowed never to tip his cap again.

Things were never quite the same. Although Williams would go on to be the best hitter in the major leagues over the next two decades, his relationship with both the press and the fans was problematic. Williams, whose eyesight was legendary, didn't confine his viewing to the batter's box. He read every word ever written about him, heard every jeer in the stands, and often blamed others for his own failures. He even blamed writers for things they had nothing to do with, such as his slandering of *Boston Globe* reporter Mel Webb, whom Williams always blamed for leaving him off the ballot in the 1947 MVP vote, which he lost by one point to Joe DiMaggio. But in fact Webb didn't vote for the award in 1947. Williams and the press treated each other warily.

Of course, Boston's ultracompetitive sports columnists didn't help the situation, either. They quickly learned that writing about Ted Williams sold papers. For 20 years, Boston fans could depend on at least one or two columns focusing on Williams virtually every day of the week.

And that was part of the problem. While it was true that at any given time there were usually one or two writers in town drilling Williams, there were also usually five or six others defending him. Writers continually changed their opinion about the mercurial star. And Williams, too often unable to control his behavior or temper his comments, gave them plenty to write about, throwing tantrums on the field, spitting and making obscene gestures at the crowd, and generally acting like a martinet even as he sprayed hits all over Fenway Park. Williams dubbed the press the "Knights of the Keyboard," and from his mouth the word *writer* sounded like an obscenity and was usually paired with an adjective or two that were.

In the end, Williams and many of his fans remembered only those columns that attacked him, conveniently forgetting those that defended him. Yet on balance, given his behavior, it is fair to say that Williams's treatment by the press was more balanced than he believed. The following selections demonstrate the breadth of coverage Williams inspired.

TED WILLIAMS BLASTS BOSTON

from *The Boston American,* August 13, 1940

Young Ted Samuel Williams, adolescent Red Sox outfielder, detests Boston!

Theodore wants to be traded to some other major league town.

Ted-kid loathes Boston newspapermen and blames them for inciting the bleacher "wolves."

He said so, frankly and vociferously, in a sit-down before he flew to rejoin his Sox mates in New York today.

"And you can print the whole rotten mess just as I said it," he challenged, as he draped his long frame over a Fenway box pipe rail.

"I've asked Cronin and Yawkey to trade me away from Boston many times this summer," he said. "I don't like the town, I don't like the people, and the newspapermen have been on my back all year. Why?"

His voice was strident, in the key of exasperation, so that several of the ground crew, stirring the infield turf with rakes, paused and cocked an ear.

"Well, why," I asked Ted, "do you think the newsmen have maliciously picked you out to needle? They've hurrahed for you in print, given you more favorable lineage than any other youngster in twenty years."

"Well I earned it, didn't I?" he growled. "What other rookie ever had a better first-year average? Why shouldn't they give me credit?"

"Fine, Ted," I answered, "the town and the newspapers are for you. And you get paid for it proportionately. Twelve thousand five hundred dollars is a . . ."

"Yes," he snorted, "and they're going to pay me more next year — plenty. And I could name some other ball players who got $12,500 in their second year." He spat disgustedly, repeating, "I earned it," and then with emphasis, "I want to get out of the town and I'm praying that they trade me."

"Well look around," I suggested, "where will you find a better ball town or more tolerant fans?"

"Huh," sniffed Ted, his lean, boyish face curled in a pucker, "I suppose Detroit isn't as good a town. Cleveland, Chicago — they need outfielders. And I'll say this too, if they trade me to one of those burgs I'll hold out until they trade me somewhere else."

"New York?" I asked.

Ted stayed ominously silent. New York clearly was the terminus he wished.

Plainly, too, Ted had been nursing his torrent of spleen. The week that he had spent alone in Boston with his sprained sacrum should have purged any superficial sourness in his system. But obviously this was no mere ball player's grouch, a passing black mood, no temporary curdle in his inner chemistry. He felt what he said with a vast conviction. He didn't like Boston's streets, the way the houses were built, the parks, the people, the riverway. Phooie!

But most of all he didn't like the human crows who perch on the rim of the ball park and write typographical sneers.

"I don't like 'em and I never will," he said.

"We've seen some pretty good ball players come and go in this town . . . ," I began.

"Yeah, and I suppose you're going to say 'a lot better than me,'" he grumbled.

"Yes," I said, "some of them were. Babe Ruth was pretty good, Duffy Lewis, Tris Speaker, Harry Hooper. And all of them had their good days and their bad and took their praise and their criticism with equal good nature. Have you ever thought that maybe you're to blame sometimes?"

Ted cocked a hen's eye, lifting a bitter brow.

"O.K., you tell me?" he invited.

"Well," I said, "you've sat sullen and aloof in the locker rooms and the hotels. Sometimes you've looked lazy and careless on fly balls. Occasionally you've snarled things back at the bleachers. You've taken the attitude, perhaps, that you're bigger than the game. Irritation begets irritation both in the locker room and the field. But

Boston, both the fans and the newsmen, like you in spite of the random hoots and critical remarks. They want you to stay."

"Not me," he reiterated, "I want to be traded."

That the months that intervene to October and the end of the season can effect a reconciliation between Ted and his ingrown gripe is improbable. For the boy, now twenty-two, is impregnated with a wish to get away. In the end the club may, in self-defense, have to trade him — unless the combined papa-talking of Joe Cronin and Tom Yawkey can calm him down.

He has, for one thing, a grand illusion about money and the amount that he should be paid, on the premise that despite his junior years he is the equal of any star, both in action and personality, in the league. What he would demand at the close of this season, in the event that he is not bartered elsewhere, he would not say. But he hinted that the figure would be above $15,000. It wouldn't be "peanuts" he said.

The writer has argued with himself the advisability of printing Ted's verbal frothings or, by silence, allowing Ted and the club to work out their problems inside the family. But the situation is such that inevitably the ulcerous condition will have to be lanced publicly. If not now, then in late September or during the mid-autumn. So, to begin with, I had told Ted:

"Whatever you wish to say that is 'off the record,' I'll keep your confidence." But he had thrown his arms wide, palms outward as though wiping the horizon, and said, "You can print anything, that's how it is and how I feel about it."

"They pay you on your record," he vouchsafed. "The bleachers can boo, the newspapers can sneer, but right out there [he pointed to his outfield acre] is where you get the dough or you don't, and I'm going to get mine."

Young Ted's attitude changed suddenly this summer from the half-artless, calf-like good nature of a year ago. Something had happened to his ego, and his clubhouse attitude toward his mates, the press, and the public, became acid. Yet, as this writer wrote, earlier in the year, the Kid was hitting and hustling, so that his inner nature was between himself, his manager, and his parson just as long as he splashed the outfield and fences with his wooshing drives.

He could wear a nest of robins in his hair, eat schnitzel for breakfast, put his pants on backwards, and blister the whole of the Red Sox fellowship — if he busted up ball games. His private behavior and thoughts were his own business — except where he wants to get away and is saturated with that desire, or where he detests the uniform he wears and abhors the people he represents. That is a public matter.

Between the newsmen and himself there has been an increasing coolness — due to Ted's prolonged funks and his self-segregation. The result has been a mutual avoidance. Still, his treatment by the Boston press has been fair in the opinion of this writer — a preponderance of praise and a minimum of criticism. But such is the youth's super-sensitivity that he forgets the cheers and remembers the blurts.

Five or eight years from now, when mature judgment settles in and his adolescent muscle jerks and junior spasms disappear, he may take moral stock of his past and maybe tsk-tsk himself. For the lad is a high-strung nerve victim who thinks whole headfuls of thoughts at a time in a kind of cerebral chop suey instead of single ideas in a sequence like little pig sausages.

Then, like Foxx and Cronin, he may learn to accept the sour with the sweet — maybe in Boston, maybe in Detroit, or New York. Big money, quick fame, mass adulation, a celebrity at twenty-two, have fogged his perspective.

Austen Lake of the Boston American *was a leading columnist from the 1930s through the 1950s. A talented writer who served as a war correspondent during World War II, Lake knew that when Williams expressed his displeasure about Boston, he had a big story. It alerted everyone to the fact that whenever Ted Williams spoke, it was news. Life in Boston would never be the same for the young star.*

GERRY HERN

TED SETS BACK BASEBALL CLOCK

Actions Recall Rowdyism Prevalent in Early
Days Before Clergy Dared Attend Games

from *The Boston Post*, May 15, 1950

A lady from the north shore called the sports department of this
newspaper yesterday afternoon. She was indignant. She wished to go
on record, she said, as being violently opposed to the persons who
objected to the vulgar gestures made by Ted Williams in a fit of anger at Fenway Park on Thursday. She said she didn't know what gestures Williams had used to suggest what the boohing spectators
could do, but, "if I was booed, I would — well, I too, would thumb
my nose at the crowd. I really would."

The rules of self-imposed journalistic decency prevented newspapers from explaining the degrading gestures Williams made to the
crowd at the Detroit-Red Sox double header. Pictures of the performance he gave were discarded by this newspaper for the sake of children, ladies and normal persons to whom the actions would have
been indecipherable, or revolting. There is no intention here to continue with the sordid details of the acts. Persons who do not understand the gestures are the fortunate ones.

The frightening aspect of the incident is that yesterday, before afternoon newspapers were on the street with indirect apology credited to Williams by the Red Sox front office, Williams himself came
to bat. A few persons booed him. An overwhelming majority applauded hard enough to drown out the boos. Remember, those persons cheering had not seen the apology. It was not printed until
after the game started. At best, it wasn't much of an apology. It
sounded somewhat like a mother dragging a reluctant child to a
neighbor's house and saying, "Johnny is sorry he smashed your win-

dow. Aren't you, Johnny?" The persons applauding didn't care what Williams had done the day before. To them, he is king and therefore can do no wrong.

Apology Was Red Sox Handout

Williams didn't make his official apology in public. He did not read it at a press interview. It was merely a handout from the Red Sox office, neatly typed on official stationery. There was no statement from Tom Yawkey, the owner of the club, and none from the general manager, both of whom witnessed the performance. No mention of a fine, or official club regrets for the affront to the decent persons without whom baseball players would be as inconspicuous as lacross players. The only comment came from a low salaried member of the Washington Senators, who had heard of the incident. He said, "If I had done that in Class D baseball in a coal-mining town with only men in the audience, I would have been ridden out of town on a rail that night."

Years ago, before professional baseball achieved its present popularity, the game gave off a haunting fragrance which didn't help attract paying customers. Crowds were small and players were given to excesses of all kinds. They weren't getting much money and they didn't mind being fired. But, gradually, as time went on, smart business men bought into baseball and they realized something would have to be done to elevate professional baseball and take away from it the aura of hooliganism. Finally, one business manager had an idea. It was a very good one and it didn't cost anything and eventually that one idea helped build the game to its present height.

The idea was simple. All the business manager did was mail season passes to the clergy of the surrounding area. His reasoning was simple. The men of the cloth would, by their presence, elevate the tone of the gathering. They would "dress the house," as the show business expression goes. By just appearing occasionally at professional baseball parks they would indirectly give their approval to the game. Thus was born the "clergy pass" which every professional team in the country issues to certified clergymen of all sects. And, from that day, baseball was sanitary.

The American baseball public is not made up merely of persons who are able to attend major league games, or even minor league games. The baseball public is composed of persons in tiny-forest-ringed huts in remote mountain ranges, men and women in desolate shacks on eroded river banks and the crippled and impoverished who can only read about the games in the daily newspapers.

Game's Big Brass Have Responsibility

The public can be hollered at by the players, just as the players can be hollered at by the public.

The only restraint on either party is the simple rule of decency in speech and gesture that is imposed by the traditions of a civilized people. That rule is not wiped out by the newborn adulation of the professional baseball player. The adulation which currently surges through the public stems frequently from the wild-eyed admiration of female enthusiasts, who have suddenly discovered the game of baseball. If you wonder about it, stand outside the players' parking area on the first base side of Fenway Park after a big game. The "Parking Space Joans" gather there after a game and, jammed up against an iron fence, flutter and sputter for an hour panting for the sight of their favorite uniform-wearers.

The smart baseball players submit to the current panic. They know that after one bad season they won't have to worry about it. There are no frantic lines of autograph hunters in Scranton or San Jose.

Club owners, league presidents and the baseball commissioner have a great responsibility because of the mass approval of the game. They cannot forget that clean actions are more important than clean uniforms. An umpire would chase a player off the field if he showed up in a dirty uniform. A manager would bench a player who insisted on wearing a dirty uniform.

Williams is not the only culprit in the case. He merely exposed the weaknesses in the upper register of the game's officials. The high salaried directors of the game, who are merely trustees for the people, are in the sack with him for remaining silent.

To be fair, Williams brought much of the attention on himself, for he was often unable to suppress his anger and frustration. Although the press would occasionally overlook such outbursts, profane gestures such as those described here were impossible to ignore.

DAVE (THE COLONEL) EGAN

COLONEL SENDS WORD TO WILLIAMS: WHY WAIT TIL '54 END? – QUIT NOW

from *The Boston Daily Record,* April 8, 1954

Perhaps it would be an excellent idea if baseball's terrible-tempered Mr. Bang would retire now, instead of at the end of the season.

I know that by remaining he will make a contribution to Ted Williams, the only person he loves, but it is highly questionable that he will do anything of a sensible and constructive nature in the building of a team for tomorrow. The man, of course, should be lying on a cot, talking things over with a psychiatrist and possibly unraveling his twisted mental processes. He should be pitied, of course, rather than censured, for he's not the only one who lacks a few buttons and marbles, yet on the other hand mere boys like Billy Consolo and Tom Brewer and Ellis Kinder (how in the world did he stick his nose in here?) are entitled to protection against that venom that this misanthropic mauler likes to spread.

His supreme selfishness never was better illustrated than when, for money, he revealed his intention of retiring at the end of the season to the readers of the Saturday Evening Post. Not to Tom Yawkey, who obviously had not paid him enough money and put up with the sufficient number of childish tantrums to command his loyalty. Not to Joe Cronin, his general manager, nor to Lou Boudreau, his field manager, who might like to base their plans not only for this year but also for the years ahead on a knowledge of the intentions of the terrible-tempered Mr. Bang. No, he announced his retirement to the readers of a national magazine for the added dough that was in it, and in so doing, he naturally put his best foot forward as usual.

Spurious Idol Concealed by Press

One of the most embattled planks in my platform for the past fifteen years has been that the Red Sox would be better without Williams than with him, and that, indeed, they never would be a team with the one-for-all-and-all-for-one attitude of a team so long as he was its star. Year after year, when he was in his prime, the Red Sox were favored to win pennants, and year after year, he led them to disgraceful defeat. They became the Red Flops while he was setting individual records in meaningless games and compiling loftier batting averages than Joe DiMaggio and emphasizing the difference between starring in a record book at season's end and starring in the clutch moments when control of the nerves and the Adam's apple was of the essence.

Williams, of course, is a defender of free speech, but more especially when he is doing the speaking. He makes known his feeling not only about the public which, in the last analysis, pays his salary and is entitled to do so either with a cheer or a jeer, but also about newspapermen who, by and large, have concealed from the public the feet of clay and the head of bone of this spurious idol. Hence he should have no objection if I practice a limited amount of free speech and say as a fact that he won many an individual award without ever making an important hit in a crucial game.

In the only World Series in which he ever competed, he made five singles, drove in one useless run, and batted a gulpy .200 in seven games. In the famous playoff game with the Cleveland Indians at Fenway Park, he got a stiff neck watching Lou Boudreau and Ken Keltner hitting homers over the left-field wall. In a two-game series in the Yankee Stadium when the Red Sox needed a single victory to win still another pennant, he fell into another of his timely slumps and watched the defeats from a port of vantage. In the ten vital games that the Red Sox played during his starriest era, ten games which would have meant one championship of the world and two additional championships of the American League, he was afflicted with the dry-throated gulps and then resented it when reporters reported it.

Minds of Bassinet Brigade Face Poisoning

He has been something less than a gilt-edged bargain as a competitor, but I had nurtured the fond hope that (a) possibly the snarling tiger had changed his stripes and (b) possibly his exposure to such outstanding competition as Jimmy Piersall and Sammy White and Jackie Jensen and George Kell and Harry Agganis might give him gumption-by-association. It is apparent, however, that he is the same old Williams, and that he will continue to look out for Williams at the expense of the team. He always, of course, has done better in pre-season than in post-season, and this is not the first time that he has announced his impending retirement, nor will it probably be the last. Nevertheless, I think that the Red Sox would be well served by Williams if he should make his retirement retroactive, and start it at once, for he should not be permitted to poison the minds of the bassinet brigade.

One like him is enough.

Williams angered the Boston press when he told the story of his planned retirement after the 1954 season to New York writer Joe Trimble and sold it to the Saturday Evening Post. *Egan wasn't alone in expressing his displeasure, but his words were often the most memorable.*

BOB HOLBROOK

WILLIAMS HITS HOMER, COVERS MOUTH BEFORE 30,338

Family Night Fans Cheer Every Move of
Sox Star. Start of Game Delayed to Permit
Crowd to Enter

from *The Boston Globe*, August 9, 1954

Rising to the occasion as he often does when the spotlight is on him, Ted Williams last night hit a tremendous homer into the right field pavilion as lead-off batter in the sixth to break a 2–2 tie against the Baltimore Orioles.

The Red Sox won, 7–2.

The 30,338 people who flocked into Fenway Park for family night were treated to a new insight into Williams.

Before Williams disappeared into the depths of the dugout he placed his right hand over his mouth in a mocking gesture which meant he was holding back another "spitting incident."

The slugger was fined $5000 for spitting at the fans during Tuesday's game.

Those in the crowd who could see Williams howled. A lot of them missed the action because of the crowd standing to cheer the long-gaited outfielder as he rounded the bases.

As Ted smacked his homer the crowd went wild.

Fans rose to their feet cheering the big guy as he rounded the bases in his lazy, loping fashion.

He made no gestures. He shook hands briefly with all enroute.

He ambled to the lip of the dugout and clapped his right hand to his mouth as he disappeared from the sight of the crowd.

It was obvious that Williams was laughing to himself.

Williams' defiance of baseball laws, writers and fans worked magic for the turnstiles. That fact was proven when it became necessary to hold up the start of the game in order to accommodate the large crowd pouring into the park.

Most of the fans cheered Williams, even before the homer. Some booed, not many. They cheered Williams to the echo every time he stuck his head out of the dugout prior to the game.

Fans came to the box seat section to yell words of encouragement to the big slugger.

Williams grinned. Williams was affable. But Williams was firm in his stand.

He declared before the game, "I'd do the same thing again if I get mad enough. I was right."

Williams reiterated his claim he would spit when he felt like it — if he could afford a $5000 fine.

Yawkey Here

All the while the family night crowd was blocking Landsdowne st. and Jersey st., the main entrances to the park.

Finally, Red Sox officials decided to hold up the game 10 minutes.

Everybody seemed to be talking about Williams.

Even Red Sox owner Tom Yawkey decided to return hurriedly from New York to see for himself how his problem child was reacting to the fine he personally levied after the spitting incident.

Yawkey would make no comment on Williams. He wouldn't divulge whether he had talked to him or not, today.

"I have said everything I have to say about the incident," he reported through publicist Joe McKenney, "as far as I am concerned it is finished."

Frankly, there hasn't been so much interest at the old ball park since the last Williams uprising.

When Williams made his first appearance before the game, he immediately was surrounded by photographers. He waved them away.

A fan yelled from the stands. "Throw them out, Ted. You're a better man than any of them."

Williams said nothing.

Just prior to infield practice Williams poked his head out of the dugout and the fans cheered.

Billy Loes, Baltimore pitcher, strolled by and said to Williams, "They're cheering me, Ted. Not you."

Extra Police on Hand

Williams' "situation" caused the Red Sox to request police to take added precautions in the left field stands where the slugger's most violent detractors usually are found.

Boston police stationed four officers in the section to prevent any untoward incidents. They had little to worry about, judging from the reception that particular section gave Williams when he trotted out for the start of the game.

Williams' antics caused opposing players to mimic him. Some of the Baltimore players were walking around with their hands over their mouths.

There was a show of good relations between Williams and Manager Mike Higgins before the game.

Williams and Higgins held a short conference during batting practice and Williams had his arm around the skipper's shoulders.

The first time Williams came to bat the crowd gave him a hearty welcome. There was some booing, but hardly as much as there usually is.

As the night started out, Williams seemed to have the crowd pretty much on his side.

In the second inning Williams was cheered for a running catch of a line drive by Tito Francona in left center field.

The left-field crowd gave Williams another warm reception when he went to his position after the homer.

Williams remained calm. He strode to the left-field wall and held a conversation with the wall. Not really, for the unseen scoreboard operator was informing Williams of the progress of other night games.

Williams concluded his night in the eighth inning with a single to center field that put runners on first and third with none out to set the stage for Mickey Vernon's three-run homer.

Williams was facing Don Ferrarese when he started his turn at bat. When he singled he did so against George Zuverink.

Ferrarese walked Billy Klaus and had a two balls and no strikes count on Williams when he was lifted for Zuverink.

Williams was lifted from the game by Manager Mike Higgins and Gene Stephens ran for him. Williams trotted off the field without looking right or left, up or down.

He jumped into the dugout and disappeared as the crowd applauded.

If Austen Lake's 1940 story started the trouble between Williams and the press, Teddy Ballgame's dramatic clapping of his hand over his mouth one game after spitting at the crowd was the moment that turned the tide. Almost overnight, the press became less confrontational toward Williams and Boston fans suddenly seemed to accept Williams, remaining in his corner for the rest of his career.

DAVE (THE COLONEL) EGAN

SLIGHT TO TED DISGRACEFUL

from *The Boston Advertiser,* November 24, 1957

It is a fact known only to a few intimates that I neither fawn upon T. Wms. Esq. nor kiss the ground on which he walks, but it is also a fact, borne out by past performances, that I can stir my bile and hotly resent an injustice to him as indignantly as I do when others are victimized.

When the global war was on and shoe clerks were being handed muskets and taught the intricacies of the hay-foot, straw-foot there was confusion about the draft status of the great man and other newspapers in Boston and elsewhere were demanding editorially that he be mustered into the service. It was not an easy stand to take the passions of the day, but I insisted and kept on insisting that though he had all the duties of the least known of our citizens, he also had all the rights of the most anonymous ones. This view prevailed, and he did not go into the service until his time came.

When a baby was born to the then Mrs. Williams while the husband was fishing in the Everglades, an uproar ensued and an issue was raised but, using uncommon common sense, I whispered that this was a personal matter between Mr. and Mrs. Williams and finally it was so voted. And when the Marines dragooned him into the Korean police action for purposes of publicity alone, I raised the roof with my hollers and earned for myself the hostility of all Marines and ex-Marines in these precincts. So it should come as a surprise to no one at all, and especially to the great loner, if now I resent the choice of Mickey Mantle as the most valuable player in the American League.

Ted Dominated League

The supposedly accredited baseball experts in each city of the league consign the honor to the players of their choice. Joe Cashman, baseball editor of the Sunday Advertiser and Daily Record, voted for Williams, and so, I suspect, did the baseball writer for another paper. The third of our local scribblers voted for Gil McDougald of the Yankees, though I can think of two others who were more deserving of it and neither one of them is Mantle. The first, of course, is Williams, who dominated the entire league for the entire season and personally was responsible for the attendance of more than a million in Boston. The second, naturally, was Roy Sievers of the Senators. And the brutal part of it is that neither of them may ever come close to the Most Valuable Player award without getting it.

Sievers won the home-run and the runs-batted-in laurels with a farcical team that would have killed the ambition of a less determined man. Williams won the batting championship after a head-to-head and chin-to-chin battle in which he completely demolished Mantle and his pretensions. Mantle, for his part, won nothing except a share in a World Series in which he played a minor role, but by the votes of men who pose as experts he was given the Most Valuable Player award and it is such an empty honor that he should cleanse his conscience and refuse to accept it.

I need not review the accomplishments of Williams with a team that was taking to the hills but otherwise going nowhere. He hit three homers in a game, not once but twice. He equaled the records held by the immortal Gehrig and others by mammothing four home-runs in four consecutive times at bat. He reached first base safely seventeen consecutive times. He did all this at what for a baseball player is a ripe old age, and in the bargain the oldest man ever to win the batting crown compiled the highest average since he himself batted .406. He may be and should be the athlete-of-the-year. But he is not the most valuable player in a humpty-dumpty league that by classical standards does not boast a solitary good team. Mantle has won that honor though his performances pale in comparison with those of Williams, and poddin me while I take five minutes out to seethe.

Just Popularity Contest

The personality of Williams, a most unfortunate one, should not have entered into it but I suggest that it did. This was not the exercise of an unprecedented ballot. It was a popularity contest, but stuffed as the ballot box was with anti-Williams votes and indefensible as the result was, I am not sure that Williams was the principal loser. It seems to me that the baseball writers were, for who is going to pay the slightest attention to their pontifical prattle after such a miscarriage of justice as this?

So Boston has been robbed of two awards this year for the exclusive benefit of the Yankees. Williams was counted out of the Most-Valuable player election in one of the most disgraceful hours that the Baseball Writers' Association ever has known, and the Rookie-Of-The-Year award was denied Frank Malzone, of which I must tell you more. Tweedledee Harridge, the presiding officer of the league if you will pardon the exaggeration, first ruled that Malzone was a rookie and eligible for the award. The Yankees, who own Harridge and operate the league, objected. Whereupon Tweedledee humbly and apologetically reversed himself and declared Malzone ineligible, and Tony Kubek of the Yankees was declared the Rookie-Of-The-Year.

I am not in a lonely minority when I insist that the Red Sox of last season, though they did not have much else, had both the Most Valuable Player and the brightest rookie in the league, and that is all I have to say on the subject except for my usual constructive suggestion. Where the Most Valuable Player is concerned, there is no need for the wall of secrecy behind which the writers hide. Let their votes be announced to the public. They call themselves experts. Sometimes, in their more fanciful moments, they also call themselves writers. They have a forum in which they can defend themselves. So let their analytical judgments be announced and let it start right now by a breakdown of the voting by which Mickey Mantle unjustifiably received the Most Valuable Player Award over Ted Williams.

Or would this be too embarrassing to too many?

It is important to note that although Egan is often held up as the prime example of the "unfair" manner in which the Boston press derided Williams, he was at times one of Williams's staunchest defenders.

ED LINN

....

THE KID'S LAST GAME

from *Sport,* February 1961

Wednesday, September 26, was a cold and dreary day in Boston, a curious bit of staging on the part of those gods who always set the scene most carefully for Ted Williams. It was to be the last game Ted would ever play in Boston. Not until the game was over would Williams let it be known that it was the last game he would play anywhere.

Ted came into the locker room at 10:50, very early for him. He was dressed in dark brown slacks, a yellow sport shirt and a light tan pullover sweater, tastily brocaded in the same color. Ted went immediately to his locker, pulled off the sweater, then strolled into the trainer's room.

Despite all the triumphs and the honors, it had been a difficult year for him. As trainer Jack Fadden put it: "It hasn't been a labor of love for Ted this year; it's just been labor." On two separate occasions, he had come very close to giving it all up.

The spring training torture had been made no easier for Ted by manager Billy Jurges. Jurges believed that the only way for a man Ted's age to stay in condition was to reach a peak at the beginning of the season and hold it by playing just as often as possible. "The most we can expect from Williams," Jurges had said, at the time of Ted's signing, "is 100 games. The least is pinch-hitting." Ted played in 113 games.

Throughout the training season, however, Ted seemed to be having trouble with his timing. Recalling his .254 average of the previous season, the experts wrote him off for perhaps the 15th time in his career. But on his first time at bat in the opening game, Ted hit a 500-foot home run, possibly the longest of his career, off Camilo

Pascual, probably the best pitcher in the league. The next day, in the Fenway Park opener, he hit a second homer, this one off Jim Coates. Ted pulled a leg muscle running out that homer, though, and when a man's muscles go while he is doing nothing more than jogging around the bases, the end is clearly in sight.

It took him almost a month to get back in condition, but the mysterious virus infection that hits him annually, a holdover from his service in Korea, laid him low again almost immediately. Since the doctors have never been able to diagnose this chronic illness, the only way they can treat him is to shoot a variety of drugs and antibiotics into him, in the hope that one of them takes hold. Ted, miserable and drugged when he finally got back in uniform, failed in a couple of pinch-hitting attempts and was just about ready to quit. Against the Yankees, Ralph Terry struck him out two straight times. The third time up, the count went to 3-2 when Williams unloaded on a waist-high fastball and sent it into the bullpen in right-center, 400 feet away.

The blast triggered the greatest home-run spurt of Ted's career. Seven days later, he hit his 500th home run. He had started only 15 1960 games and he had hit eight 1960 homers. When he hit his 506th (and 11th of the year), he had homered once in every 6.67 times at bat.

Cold weather always bothered Ted, even in his early years, and so when he strained his shoulder late in August, he was just about ready to announce his retirement again. He had found it difficult to loosen up even in fairly warm weather, and to complicate matters he had found it necessary — back in the middle of 1959 — to cut out the calisthenics routine he had always gone through in the clubhouse. The exercising had left him almost too weary to play ball.

Ted started every game so stiff that he was forced to exaggerate an old passion for swinging at balls only in the strike zone. In his first time at bat, he would look for an inside pitch between the waist and knees, the only pitch he could swing at naturally. In the main, however, Ted was more than willing to take the base on balls his first time up.

He stayed on for two reasons. Mike Higgins, who had replaced Jurges as Sox manager, told him bluntly: "You're paid to play ball, so go out and play." The strength behind those words rested in the fact that both Williams and Higgins knew very well that owner Tom Yawkey would continue to pay Ted whether he played or not.

In addition, the Red Sox had two series remaining with the Yankees and Orioles, who were still locked together in the pennant race. Ted did not think it fair to eliminate himself as a factor in the two-team battle. He announced his retirement just after the Yankees clinched the pennant.

Four days earlier, Ted had been called to a special meeting with Yawkey, Higgins, Dick O'Connell (who was soon to be named business manager) and publicity director Jack Malaney. This was to offer Ted the job of general manager, a position that had been discussed occasionally in the past.

Ted refused to accept the title until he proved he could do the job. He agreed, however, to work in the front office in 1961, assisting Higgins with player personnel, and O'Connell with business matters.

The coverage of Ted's last game was at a minimum. It was thought for a while that *Life* magazine wanted to send a crew down to cover the game, but it developed that they only wanted to arrange for Ted to represent them at the World Series. Dave Garroway's "Today" program tried to set up a telephone interview the morning of the game, but they couldn't get in touch with Ted. The Red Sox, alone among big-league clubs, have offered little help to anyone on the public relations front — and never any help at all where Ted Williams was concerned. Ted didn't live at the Kenmore Hotel with the rest of the unattached players. He lived about 100 yards down Commonwealth Avenue, at the Somerset. All calls and messages for him were diverted to the manager's office.

The ceremonies that were to mark his departure were rather limited, too. The Boston Chamber of Commerce had arranged to present him with a silver bowl, and the mayor's office and governor's office had quickly muscled into the picture. By Wednesday morning, however, the governor's office — which had apparently anticipated something more spectacular — begged off. The governor's spokesman suggested the presentation of a scroll at Ted's hotel, a suggestion which Ted simply ignored.

The only civilian in the clubhouse when Ted entered was the man from *Sport*, and he was talking to Del Baker, who was about to retire, too, after 50 years in the game. Ted looked over, scowled, seemed about to say something, but changed his mind.

Our man was well aware what Ted was about to say. The Red Sox have a long-standing rule — also unique in baseball — that no reporter may enter the dressing room before the game, or for the first 15 minutes after the game. It was a point of honor with Ted to pick out any civilian who wasn't specifically with a ball player and to tell him, as loudly as possible: "You're not supposed to be in here, you know."

Sure enough, when our man started toward Ted's locker in the far corner of the room, Ted pointed a finger at him and shouted: "You're not supposed to be in here, you know."

"The same warm, glad cry of greeting I always get from you," our man said. "It's your last day. Why don't you live a little?"

Ted started toward the trainer's room again, but wheeled around and came back. "You've got a nerve coming here to interview me after the last one you wrote about me!"

Our man wanted to know what was the matter with the last one.

"You called me 'unbearable,' that's what's the matter."

The full quote, it was pointed out, was that he "was sometimes unbearable but never dull," which holds a different connotation entirely.

"You've been after me for 12 years, that flogging magazine," he said, in his typically well-modulated shout. "Twelve years. I missed an appointment for some kind of luncheon. I forgot what happened . . . it doesn't matter anyway . . . but I forgot some appointment 12 years ago and Sport Magazine hasn't let up on me since."

Our man, lamentably eager to disassociate himself from this little magazine, made it clear that while he had done most of Sport's Williams articles in the last few years he was not a member of the staff. "And," our man pointed out, "I have been accused of turning you into a combination of Paul Bunyan and Santa Claus."

"Well, when you get back there tell them what . . ." (he searched for the appropriate word, the *mot juste* as they say in the dugouts) ". . . what *flog-heads* they are. Tell them that for me."

Our man sought to check the correct spelling of the adjectives with him but got back only a scowl. Ted turned around to fish something out of a cloth bag at the side of his locker. "Why don't you just write your story without me?" he said. "What do you have to talk to me for?" And then, in a suddenly weary voice: "What can I tell you now that I haven't told you before?"

"Why don't you let me tell you what the story is supposed to be?" our man said. "Then you can say yes or no." It was an unfortunate way to put the question since it invited the answer it brought.

"I can tell you before you tell me," Ted shouted. "No! No, no, no."

Our man had the impression Williams was trying to tell him something. He was right. "Look," Williams said. "If I tell you I don't want to talk to you, why don't you just take my word for it?"

The clubhouse boy had come over with a glossy photo to be signed, and Ted sat down on his stool, turned his back and signed it.

Although we are reluctant to bring *Sport* into the context of the story itself, Ted's abiding hatred toward us tells much about him and his even longer feud with Boston sportswriters. Twelve years ago, just as Ted said, an article appeared on these pages to which he took violent exception. (The fact that he is so well aware that it *was* 12 years ago suggests that he still has the magazine around somewhere, so that he can fan the flames whenever he feels them dying.) What Ted objected to in that article was an interview with his mother in San Diego. Ted objects to any peering into his private life. When he holes himself up in his hotel, when he sets a barrier around the clubhouse, when he disappears into the Florida Keys at the end of the season, he is deliberately removing himself from a world which he takes to be dangerous and hostile. His constant fighting with the newspapermen who cover him most closely is part of the same pattern. What do newspapermen represent except the people who are supposed to pierce personal barriers? Who investigate, who pry, *who find out?*

Ted's mother has been a Salvation Army worker in San Diego all her life. She is a local character, known — not without affection — as "Salvation May." Ted himself was dedicated to the Salvation Army when he was a baby. His generosity, his unfailing instinct to come to the aid of any underdog, is in direct line with the teachings of the Army, which is quite probably the purest charitable organization in the world. Even as a boy, Ted regularly gave his 30-cent luncheon allowance to classmates he considered more needy than himself, a considerable sacrifice since the Williams family had to struggle to make ends meet.

When Ted signed with San Diego at the age of 17, he was a tall, skinny kid (6-3, 146 pounds). He gave most of his $150-a-month salary toward keeping up the family house and he tried to build up his weight by gorging himself on the road where the club picked up the check. One day Ted was coming into the clubhouse when Bill Lane, the owner of the Padres, motioned him over. In his deep fog-horn voice, Lane said: "Well, kid, you're leading the list. You've got the others beat."

Ted, pleased that his ability was being noted so promptly, smiled and asked: "Yeah, what list?"

"The dining room list," Lane said. "Hasn't anyone told you that your meal allowance is supposed to be five dollars a day?"

Nobody had. "Okay, Bill," Ted said, finally. "Take anything over five dollars off my salary."

Bill did, too.

Even before *Sport* went into details about his background, the Boston press had discovered his weak point and hit him hard and — it must be added — most unfairly. During Ted's second season with the Sox, one reporter had the ill grace to comment, in regard to a purely personal dispute: "But what can you expect of a youth so abnormal that he didn't go home in the off season to see his own mother?"

When Williams' World War II draft status was changed from 1A to 3A after he claimed his mother as a dependent, one Boston paper sent a private investigator to San Diego to check on her standard of living; another paper sent reporters out onto the street to ask casual passers-by to pass judgment on Ted's patriotism.

Reporters were sent galloping out into the street to conduct a public opinion poll once again when Williams was caught fishing in the Everglades while his wife was giving birth to a premature baby.

A press association later sent a story out of San Diego that Ted had sold the furniture out from under his mother — although a simple phone call could have established that it wasn't true. Ted had bought the house and the furniture for his mother. His brother — who had been in frequent trouble with the law — had sold it. The Boston papers picked up that story and gave it a big play, despite the fact that every sports editor in the city had enough background material on Ted's family to know — even without checking — that it couldn't possibly be true. It was, Ted's friends believed, their way of punishing him for not being "co-operative."

Ted had become so accustomed to looking upon any reference to his family as an unfriendly act that when Sport wrote about his mother, he bristled — even though her final quote was: "Don't say anything about Teddy except the highest and the best. He's a wonderful son." And when he searched for some reason why the magazine would do such a thing to him, he pounced upon that broken appointment, which everybody except himself had long forgotten.

After Ted had signed the photograph the day of his last game, he sat on his stool, his right knee jumping nervously, his right hand alternately buttoning and unbuttoning the top button of his sport shirt.

When he stripped down to his shorts, there was no doubt he was 42. The man once called the Splendid Splinter — certainly one of the most atrocious nicknames ever committed upon an immortal — was thick around the middle. A soft roll of loose fat, drooping around the waist, brought on a vivid picture of Archie Moore.

Williams is a tall, handsome man. If they ever make that movie of his life that keeps being rumored around, the guy who plays Bret Maverick would be perfect for the part. But ball players age quickly. Twenty years under the sun had baked Ted's face and left it lined and leathery. Sitting there, Ted Williams had the appearance of an old Marine sergeant who had been to the battles and back.

Sal Maglie, who had the end locker on the other side of the shower-room door, suddenly caught Ted's attention. "You're a National Leaguer, Sal," Ted said, projecting his voice to the room at large. "I got a hundred dollars that the Yankees win the World Series. The Yankees will win it in four or five games."

"I'm an American Leaguer now," Sal said, quietly.

"A hundred dollars," Ted said. "A friendly bet."

"You want a friendly bet? I'll bet you a friendly dollar."

"Fifty dollars," Ted said.

"All right," Sal said. "Fifty dollars." And then, projecting his own voice, he said: "I like the Pirates, anyway."

Williams went back to his mail, as the others dressed and went out onto the field.

At length, Ted picked up his spikes, wandered into the trainer's room again, and lifting himself onto the table, carefully began to put a shine on them. A photographer gave him a ball to sign.

Ted gazed at it with distaste, then looked up at the photographer with loathing. "Are you crazy?" he snapped.

The photographer backed away, pocketed the ball and began to adjust his camera sights on Ted. "You don't belong in here," Ted shouted. And turning to the clubhouse boy, he barked: "Get him out of here."

The locker room had emptied before Ted began to dress. For Ted did not go out to take batting practice or fielding practice. He made every entrance onto the field a dramatic event. He did not leave the locker room for the dugout until 12:55, only 35 minutes before the game was scheduled to start. By then, most of the writers had already gone up to Tom Yawkey's office to hear Jackie Jensen announce that he was returning to baseball.

As Ted came quickly up the stairs and into the dugout, he almost bumped into his close friend and fishing companion, Bud Leavitt, sports editor of the Bangor *Daily News*. "Hi, Bud," Ted said, as if he were surprised Leavitt was there. "You drive up?"

A semi-circle of cameramen closed in on Williams, like a bear trap, on the playing field just up above. Ted hurled a few choice oaths at them, and as an oath-hurler Ted never bats below .400. He guided Leavitt against the side of the dugout, just above the steps, so that he could continue the conversation without providing a shooting angle for the photographers. The photographers continued to shoot him in profile, though, until Ted took Leavitt by the elbow and walked him the length of the dugout. "Let's sit down," he said, as he left, "so we won't be bothered by all these blasted cameramen."

If there had been any doubt back in the locker room that Ted had decided to bow out with typical hardness, it had been completely dispelled by those first few minutes in the dugout. On his last day in Fenway Park, Ted Williams seemed resolved to remain true to his own image of himself, to permit no sentimentality or hint of sentimentality to crack that mirror through which he looks at the world and allows the world to look at him.

And yet, in watching this strange and troubled man — the most remarkable and colorful and full-blooded human being to come upon the athletic scene since Babe Ruth — you had the feeling that he was overplaying his role, that he had struggled through the night against the impulse to make his peace, to express his gratitude, to accept the great affection that the city had been showering upon him for years. In watching him, you had the clear impression that in resisting this desire he was overreacting and becoming more profane, more impossible and — yes — more unbearable than ever.

Inside Ted Williams there has always been a struggle of two opposing forces, almost two different persons. (We are fighting the use of the word schizophrenia). The point we are making is best illustrated through Williams' long refusal to tip his hat in acknowledgment of the cheering crowds. It has always been his contention that the people who cheered him when he hit a home run were the same people who booed him when he struck out — which, incidentally, is probably not true at all. More to our point, Ted has always insisted that although he would rather be cheered than booed, he really didn't care what the fans thought of him, one way or the other.

Obviously, though, if he really didn't care he wouldn't have bothered to make such a show of not caring. He simply would have touched his finger to his cap in that automatic, thoughtless gesture of most players and forgot about it. Ted, in short, has always had it both ways. He gets the cheers and he pretends they mean nothing to him. He is like a rich man's nephew who treats his uncle with disrespect to prove he is not interested in his money, while all the time he is secretly dreaming that the uncle will reward such independence by leaving him most of the fortune.

Ted has it even better than that. The fans of Boston have always wooed him ardently. They always cheered him all the louder in the hope that he would reward them, at last, with that essentially meaningless tip of the hat.

This clash within Williams came to the surface as he sat and talked with Leavitt, alone and undisturbed. For, within a matter of minutes, the lack of attention began to oppress him; his voice began to rise, to pull everybody's attention back to him. The cameramen, getting the message, drifted toward him again, not in a tight pack this time but in a loose and straggling line.

With Ted talking so loudly, it was apparent that he and Leavitt were discussing how to get together, after the World Series, for their annual post-season fishing expedition. The assignment to cover the Series for *Life* had apparently upset their schedule.

"After New York," Ted said, "I'll be going right to Pittsburgh." He expressed his hope that the Yankees would wrap it all up in Yankee Stadium, so that he could join Leavitt in Bangor at the beginning of the following week. "But, dammit," he said, "if the Series goes more than five games, I'll have to go back to Pittsburgh again."

Leavitt reminded Ted of an appearance he had apparently agreed to make in Bangor. "All right," Ted said. "But no speeches or anything."

A young, redheaded woman, in her late twenties, leaned over from her box seat alongside the dugout and asked Ted if he would autograph her scorecard.

"I can't sign it, dear," Ted said. "League rules. Where are you going to be after the game?"

"You told me that once before," she said, unhappily.

"Well, where are you going to be?" Ted shouted, in the impatient way one would shout at an irritating child.

"Right here," she said.

"All right."

"But I waited before and you never came."

He ignored her.

Joe Cronin, president of the American League, came down the dugout aisle, followed by his assistant, Joe McKenney. Through Cronin's office, the local 9:00 news-feature program which follows the "Today" program in Boston had scheduled a filmed interview with Ted. The camera had already been set up on the home-plate side of the dugout, just in front of the box seats. Cronin talked to Ted briefly and went back to reassure the announcer that Ted would be right there. McKenney remained behind to make sure Ted didn't forget. At last Ted jumped up and shouted: "Where is it, Joe, dammit?"

When Ted followed McKenney out, it was the first time he had stuck his head onto the field all day. There were still not too many fans in the stands, although far more than would have been there on any other day to watch a seventh-place team on a cold and threatening Wednesday afternoon. At this first sight of Ted Williams, they let out a mighty roar.

As he waited alongside interviewer Jack Chase, Ted bit his lower lip, and looked blankly into space, both characteristic mannerisms. At a signal from the cameraman, Chase asked Ted how he felt about entering "the last lap."

All at once, Ted was smiling. "I want to tell you, Jack, I honestly feel good about it," he said, speaking in that quick charming way of his. "You can't get blood out of a turnip, you know. I've gone as far as I can and I'm sure I wouldn't want to try it any more."

"Have we gone as far as we can with the Jimmy Fund?" he was asked.

Ted was smiling more broadly. "Oh, no. We could never go far enough with the Jimmy Fund."

Chase reminded Ted that he was scheduled to become a batting coach.

"Can you take a .250 hitter and make a .300 hitter out of him?"

"There has always been a saying in baseball that you can't make a hitter," Ted answered. "But I think you can *improve* a hitter. More than you can improve a fielder. More mistakes are made in hitting than in any other part of the game."

At this point, Williams was literally encircled by photographers, amateur and pro. The pros were taking pictures from the front and from the sides. Behind them, in the stands, dozens of fans had their cameras trained on Ted, too, although they could hardly have been getting anything except the No. 9 on his back.

Ted was asked if he were going to travel around the Red Sox farm system in 1961 to instruct the young hitters.

"All I know is that I'm going to spring training," he said. "Other than that, I don't know anything."

The interview closed with the usual fulsome praise of Williams, the inevitable apotheosis that leaves him with a hangdog, embarrassed look upon his features. "I appreciate the kind words," he said. "It's all been fun. Everything I've done in New England from playing left field and getting booed, to the Jimmy Fund."

The Jimmy Fund is the money-raising arm of the Children's Cancer Hospital in Boston, which has become the world center for research into cancer and for the treatment of its young victims. Ted has been deeply involved with the hospital since its inception in 1947, serving the last four years as general chairman of the fund committee. He is an active chairman, not an honorary one. Scarcely a day goes by, when Ted is in Boston, that he doesn't make one or two stops for the Jimmy Fund somewhere in New England. He went out on the missions even on days when he was too sick to play ball. (This is the same man, let us emphasize, who refuses to attend functions at which he himself is to be honored.) He has personally raised something close to $4,000,000 and has helped to build a modern, model hospital not far from Fenway Park.

But he has done far more than that. From the first, Williams took upon himself the agonizing task of trying to bring some cheer into the lives of these dying children and, perhaps even more difficult, of comforting their parents. He has, in those years, permitted himself to become attached to thousands of these children, knowing full well that they were going to die, one by one. He has become so attached to some of them that he has chartered special planes to bring him to their deathbeds.

Whenever one of these children asks to see him, whatever the time, he comes. His only stipulation is that there must be no publicity, no reporters, no cameramen.

We once suggested to Ted that he must get some basic return from all this work he puts into the Jimmy Fund. Ted considered the matter very carefully before he answered: "Look," he said finally, "it embarrasses me to be praised for anything like this. The embarrassing thing is that I don't feel I've done anything compared to the people at the hospital who are doing the important work. It makes me happy to think I've done a little good; I suppose that's what I get out of it."

"Anyway," he added thoughtfully, "it's only a freak of fate, isn't it, that one of those kids isn't going to grow up to be an athlete and I wasn't the one who had the cancer."

At the finish of the filmed interview he had to push his way through the cameramen between him and the dugout. "Oh ——," he said.

But when one of them asked him to pose with Cronin, Ted switched personalities again and asked, with complete amiability, "Where is he?"

Cronin was in the dugout. Ted met Joe at the bottom of the steps and threw an arm around him. They grinned at each other while the pictures were being taken, talking softly and unintelligibly. After a minute, Ted reached over to the hook just behind him and grabbed his glove. The cameramen were still yelling for another shot as he started up the dugout steps. Joe, grinning broadly, grabbed him by the shoulder and yanked him back down. While Cronin was wrestling Ted around and whacking him on the back, the cameras clicked. "I got to warm up, dammit," Ted was saying. He made a pawing gesture at the cameramen, as if to say, "I'd like to belt you buzzards." This, from all evidence was the picture that went around the country that night, because strangely enough, it looked as if he were waving a kind of sad good-bye.

When he finally broke away and raced up to the field, he called back over his shoulder, "See you later, Joe." The cheers arose from the stands once again.

The Orioles were taking infield practice by then, and the Red Sox were warming up along the sideline. Ted began to play catch with Pumpsie Green. As he did — sure enough — the cameramen lined up just inside the foul line for some more shots, none of which will ever be used. "Why don't you cockroaches get off my back?" Ted said, giving them his No. 1 sneer. "Let me breathe, will you?"

The bell rang before he had a chance to throw two dozen balls. Almost all the players went back to the locker room. Remaining on the bench were only Ted Williams, buttoned up in his jacket, and Vic Wertz. One of the members of the ground crew came over with a picture of Williams. He asked Ted if he would autograph it. "Sure," Ted said. "For you guys, anything."

Vic Wertz was having his picture taken with another crew member. Wertz had his arm around the guy and both of them were laughing. "How about you, Ted?" the cameraman asked. "One with the crewmen?"

Ted posed willingly with the man he had just signed for, with the result that the whole herd of cameramen came charging over again. Ted leaped to his feet. "Twenty-two years of this bull——," he cried.

The redhead was leaning over the low barrier again, but now three other young women were alongside her. One of them seemed to be crying, apparently at the prospect of Ted's retirement. An old photographer, in a long, weatherbeaten coat, asked Ted for a special pose. "Get lost," Ted said. "I've seen enough of you, you old goat."

Curt Gowdy, the Red Sox broadcaster, had come into the dugout to pass on some information about the pre-game ceremonies. Ted shouted, "The devil with all you miserable cameramen." The women continued to stare, in fascination, held either by the thrill of having this last long look at Ted Williams or by the opportunity to learn a few new words.

A Baltimore writer came into the dugout, and Ted settled down beside him. He wanted to know whether the writer could check on the "King of Swat" crown that had been presented to him in his last visit to Baltimore. Ted wasn't sure whether he had taken it back to Boston with him or whether the organization still had it.

"You know," he told the writer, "Brown's a better pitcher now than he's ever been. Oh, he's a great pitcher. Never get a fat pitch from him. When he does, it comes in with something extra on it. Every time a little different. He knows what he's doing."

Ted is a student of such things. He is supposed to be a natural hitter, blessed with a superhuman pair of eyes. We are not about to dispute this. What we want to say is that when Ted first came to the majors, the book on him was that he would chase bad balls. "All young sluggers do," according to Del Baker, who was managing Detroit when Ted came up. "Ted developed a strike zone of his own, though, by the second year."

When Ted took his physical for the Naval reserve in World War II, his eyes tested at 20/10 and were so exceptional in every regard that while he was attending air gunnery school he broke all previous Marine records for hitting the target sleeve. But Ted has a point of his own here: "My eyesight," he says, "is now 20/15. Half the major-leaguers have eyes as good as that. It isn't eyesight that makes a hitter; it's practice. *Con-sci-en-tious* practice. I say that Williams has hit more balls than any guy living, except maybe Ty Cobb. I don't say it to brag; I just state it as a fact. From the time I was 11 years old, I've taken every possible opportunity to swing at a ball. I've swung and I've swung and I've swung."

Ted always studied every little movement a pitcher made. He always remained on the bench before the game to watch them warming up. From his first day to his last, he hustled around to get all possible information on a new pitcher.

It has always been his theory that we are all creatures of habit, himself included. Pitchers, he believes, fall into observable patterns. A certain set of movements foretells a certain pitch. In a particular situation, or on a particular count, they go to a particular pitch. There were certain pitchers, Ted discovered, who would inevitably go to their big pitch, the pitch they wanted him to swing at, on the 2-2 count.

And so Ted would frequently ask a teammate, "What was the pitch he struck you out on?" or "What did he throw you on the 2-2 pitch?"

When a young player confessed he didn't know what the pitch had been, Ted would grow incredulous. "You don't know the pitch he struck you out on? I'm not talking about last week or last month. I'm not even talking about yesterday. Today! Just now! I'm talking about the pitch he struck you out on just now!"

Returning to his seat on the bench, he'd slump back in disgust and mutter: "What a rockhead. The guy's taking the bread and butter out of his mouth and he don't even care how."

In a very short time, the player would have an answer ready for Williams. Ted always got the young hitters thinking about their craft. He always tried to instruct them, to build up their confidence. "When you want to know who the best hitter in the league is," he'd tell the rookies, "just look into the mirror."

Among opposing players, Williams was always immensely popular. Yes, even among opposing pitchers. All pitchers love to say: "Nobody digs in against *me*." Only Ted Williams was given the right to dig in without getting flipped. Around the American League, there seemed to be a general understanding that Williams had too much class to be knocked down.

Waiting in the dugout for the ceremonies to get underway, Ted picked up a bat and wandered up and down the aisle taking vicious practice swings.

The photographers immediately swooped in on him. One nice guy was taking cameras from the people in the stands and getting shots of Ted for them.

As Ted put the bat down, one of them said: "One more shot. Teddy, as a favor."

"I'm all done doing any favors for you guys," Williams said. "I don't have to put up with you anymore, and you don't have to put up with me."

An old woman, leaning over the box seats, was wailing: "Don't leave us, Ted. Don't leave us."

"Oh hell," Ted said, turning away in disgust.

The redhead asked him plaintively: "Why don't you act nice?"

Ted strolled slowly toward her, grinning broadly. "Come on, dear," he drawled, "with that High Street accent you got there."

Turning back, he stopped in front of the man from Sport, pointed over his shoulder at the cameramen and asked: "You getting it all? You getting what you came for?"

"If you can't make it as a batting coach," our man said, "I understand you're going to try it as a cameraman."

"What does Sport Magazine think I'm going to do?" Ted asked. "That's what I want to know. What does Sport Magazine think I'm going to be?"

Speaking for himself, our man told him, he had not the slightest doubt that Ted was going to be the new general manager.

"Sport Magazine," Ted said, making the name sound like an oath. "Always honest. Never prejudiced."

At this point, he was called onto the field. Taking off his jacket, he strode out of the dugout. The cheers that greeted him came from 10,454 throats.

Curt Gowdy, handling the introductions, began: "As we all know, this is the final home game for — in my opinion and most of yours — the greatest hitter who ever lived. Ted Williams."

There was tremendous applause.

"Twenty years ago," Gowdy continued, "a skinny kid from San Diego came to the Red Sox camp . . ."

Ted first came to the Red Sox training camp at Sarasota in the spring of 1938. General manager Eddie Collins, having heard that Ted was a creature of wild and wayward impulse, had instructed second baseman Bobby Doerr to pick him up and deliver him, shining and undamaged.

It was unthinkable, of course, that Ted Williams would make a routine entrance. Just before Doerr was set to leave home, the worst flood of the decade hit California and washed out all the roads and telephone lines. When Williams and Doerr finally arrived in Sarasota, ten days late, there was a fine, almost imperceptible drizzle. Williams, still practically waterlogged from the California floods, held out a palm, looked skyward, shivered and said in a voice that flushed the flamingos from their nests: "So this is Florida, is it? Do they always keep this state under a foot of water?"

Williams suited up for a morning workout out in the field, jawed good-naturedly with the fans and got an unexpected chance to hit when a newsreel company moved in to take some batting-cage shots.

The magic of Ted Williams in a batter's box manifested itself that first day in camp. The tall, thin rookie stepped into the box, set himself in his wide stance, let his bat drop across the far corner of the plate, wiggled his hips and shoulders and jiggled up and down as if he were trying to tamp himself into the box. He moved his bat back and forth a few times, then brought it back into position and twisted his hands in opposite directions as if he were wringing the neck of the bat. He was set for the pitch.

And somehow, as if by some common impulse, all sideline activity stopped that day in 1938. Everybody was watching Ted Williams.

"Controversial, sure," Gowdy said, in bringing his remarks about Ted to a close, "but colorful."

The chairman of the Boston Chamber of Commerce presented Ted a shining, silver Paul Revere bowl "on behalf of the business community of Boston." Ted seemed to force his smile as he accepted it.

A representative of the sports committee of the Chamber of Commerce then presented him with a plaque "on behalf of visits to kids' and veterans' hospitals."

Mayor John Collins, from his wheelchair, announced that "on behalf of all citizens" he was proclaiming this day "Ted Williams Day." The mayor didn't know how right he was.

As Mayor Collins spoke of Ted's virtues ("Nature's best, nature's nobleman"), the muscle of Ted's upper left jaw was jumping, constantly and rhythmically. The mayor's contribution to Ted Williams Day was a $1,000 donation to the Jimmy Fund from some special city fund.

Gowdy brought the proceedings to a close by proclaiming: "Pride is what made him great. He's a champion, a thoroughbred, a champion of sports." Curt then asked for "a round of applause, an ovation for No. 9 on his last game in his Boston." Needless to say, he got it.

Ted waited, pawed at the ground with one foot. Smilingly, he thanked the mayor for the money. "Despite the fact of the disagreeable things that have been said of me — and I can't help thinking about it — by the Knights of the Keyboard out there (he jerked his head toward the press box), baseball has been the most wonderful thing in my life. If I were starting over again and someone asked me where is the one place I would like to play, I would want it to be in Boston, with the greatest owner in baseball and the greatest fans in America. Thank you."

He walked across the infield to the dugout, where the players were standing, applauding along with the fans. Ted winked and went on in.

In the press box, some of the writers were upset by his gratuitous rap at them. "I think it was bush," one of them said. "Whatever he thinks, this wasn't the time to say it."

Others made a joke of it. "Now that he's knighted me," one of them was saying, "I wonder if he's going to address me as Sir."

In the last half of the first inning, Williams stepped in against Steve Barber with Tasby on first and one out. When Barber was born — February 22, 1939 — Ted had already taken the American Association apart, as it has never been taken apart since, by batting .366, hitting 43 home runs and knocking in 142 runs.

Against a lefthander, Williams was standing almost flush along the inside line of the batter's box, his feet wide, his stance slightly closed. He took a curve inside, then a fastball low. The fans began to boo. The third pitch was also low. With a 3-0 count, Ted jumped in front of the plate with the pitch, like a high-school kid looking for a walk. It was ball four, high.

He got to third the easy way. Jim Pagliaroni was hit by a pitch, and everybody moved up on a wild pitch. When Frank Malzone walked, Jack Fisher came in to replace Barber. Lou Clinton greeted Jack with a rising liner to dead center. Jackie Brandt started in, slipped as he tried to reverse himself, but recovered in time to scramble back and make the catch. His throw to the plate was beautiful to behold, a low one-bouncer that came to Gus Triandos chest high. But Ted, sliding hard, was in under the ball easily.

Leading off the third inning against the righthanded Fisher, Ted moved back just a little in the box. Fisher is even younger than Barber, a week younger. When Fisher was being born — March 4, 1939 — Ted was reporting to Sarasota again, widely proclaimed as the super-player of the future, the Red Sox' answer to Joe DiMaggio.

Ted hit Fisher's 1-1 pitch straightaway, high and deep. Brandt had plenty of room to go back and make the catch, but still, as Williams returned to the bench, he got another tremendous hand.

Up in the press box, publicity man Jack Malaney was announcing that uniform No. 9 was being retired "after today's game." This brought on some snide remarks about Ted wearing his undershirt at Yankee Stadium for the final three games of the season. Like Mayor Collins, Malaney was righter than he knew. The uniform was indeed going to be retired after the game.

Williams came to bat again in the fifth inning, with two out and the Sox trailing, 3-2. And this time he unloaded a tremendous drive to right center. As the ball jumped off the bat, the cry, "He did it!" arose from the stands. Right-fielder Al Pilarcik ran back as far as he could, pressed his back against the bullpen fence, well out from the 380-foot sign, and stood there, motionless, his hands at his sides.

Although it was a heavy day, there was absolutely no wind. The flag hung limply from the pole, stirring very occasionally and very faintly.

At the last minute, Pilarcik brought up his hands and caught the ball chest high, close to 400 feet from the plate. A moan of disappointment settled over the field, followed by a rising hum of excited conversation and then, as Ted came back toward the first-base line to get his glove from Pumpsie Green, a standing ovation.

"Damn," Ted said, when he returned to the bench at the end of the inning. "I hit the living hell out of that one. I really stung it. If that one didn't go out, nothing is going out today!"

In the top of the eighth, with the Sox behind 4-2, Mike Fornieles came to the mound for the 70th time of the season, breaking the league record set by another Red Sox relief star, Ellis Kinder. Kinder set this mark in 1953, the year Williams returned from Korea.

As Fornieles was warming up, three teen-agers jumped out of the grandstand and ran toward Ted. They paused only briefly, however, and continued across the field to the waiting arms of the park police.

Ted was scheduled to bat second in the last of the eighth, undoubtedly his last time at bat. The cheering began as soon as Willie

Tasby came out of the dugout and strode to the plate, as if he was anxious to get out of there and make way for the main event. Ted, coming out almost directly behind Tasby, went to the on-deck circle. He was down on one knee and just beginning to swing the heavy, lead-filled practice bat as Tasby hit the first pitch to short for an easy out.

The cheering seemed to come to its peak as Ted stepped into the box and took his stance. Everybody in the park had come to his feet to give Ted a standing ovation.

Umpire Eddie Hurley called time. Fisher stepped off the rubber and Triandos stood erect. Ted remained in the box, waiting, as if he were oblivious to it all. The standing ovation lasted at least two minutes, and even then Fisher threw into the continuing applause. Only as the ball approached the plate did the cheering stop. It came in low, ball one. The spectators remained on their feet, but very suddenly the park had gone very quiet.

If there was pressure on Ted, there was pressure on Fisher, too. The Orioles were practically tied for second place, so he couldn't afford to be charitable. He might have been able to get Ted to go after a bad pitch, and yet he hardly wanted to go down in history as the fresh kid who had walked Ted Williams on his last time at bat in Boston.

The second pitch was neck high, a slider with, it seemed, just a little off it. Ted gave it a tremendous swing, but he was just a little out in front of the ball. The swing itself brought a roar from the fans, though, since it was such a clear announcement that Ted was going for the home run or nothing.

With a 1-1 count, Fisher wanted to throw a fastball, low and away. He got it up too much and in too much, a fastball waist high on the outside corner. From the moment Ted swung, there was not the slightest doubt about it. The ball cut through the heavy air, a high line drive heading straightaway to center field toward the corner of the special bullpen the Red Sox built for Williams back in 1941.

Jackie Brandt went back almost to the barrier, then turned and watched the ball bounce off the canopy above the bullpen bench, skip up against the wire fence which rises in front of the bleachers and bounce back into the bullpen.

It did not seem possible that 10,000 people could make that much noise.

Ted raced around the bases at a pretty good clip. Triandos had started toward the mound with the new ball, and Fisher had come down to meet him. As Ted neared home plate, Triandos turned to face him, a big smile on his face. Ted grinned back.

Ted didn't exactly offer his hand to Pagliaroni after he crossed the plate, but the young catcher reached out anyway and made a grab for it. He seemed to catch Ted around the wrist. Williams ran back into the dugout and ducked through the runway door to get himself a drink of water.

The fans were on their feet again, deafening the air with their cheers. A good four or five minutes passed before anybody worried about getting the game under way again.

When Ted ducked back into the dugout, he put on his jacket and sat down at the very edge of the bench, alongside Mike Higgins and Del Baker. The players, still on their feet anyway, crowded around him, urging him to go out and acknowledge the cheers.

The fans were now chanting. "We want Ted . . . we want Ted . . . we want Ted." Umpire Johnny Rice, at first base, motioned for Ted to come out. Manager Mike Higgins urged him to go on out. Ted just sat there, his head down, a smile of happiness on his face.

"We wanted him to go out," Vic Wertz said later, "because we felt so good for him. And we could see he was thrilled, too. For me, I have to say it's my top thrill in baseball."

But another player said: "I had the impression — maybe I shouldn't say this because it's just an impression — that he got just as much a kick out of refusing to go out and tip his hat to the crowd as he did out of the homer. What I mean is he wanted to go out with the home run, all right, but he also wanted the home run so he could sit there while they yelled for him and tell them all where to go."

Mike Higgins had already told Carroll Hardy to replace Ted in left field. As Clinton came to bat, with two men out, Higgins said: "Williams, left field." Ted grabbed his glove angrily and went to the top step. When Clinton struck out, Ted was the first man out of the dugout. He sprinted out to left field, ignoring the cheers of the fans, who had not expected to see him again. But Higgins had sent Hardy right out behind him. Ted saw Carroll, and ran back in, one final time. The entire audience was on its feet once again, in wild applause.

Since it is doubtful that Higgins felt Williams was in any great need of more applause that day, it is perfectly obvious that he was giving Ted one last chance to think about the tip of the hat or the wave of the hand as he covered the distance between left field and the dugout.

Ted made the trip as always, his head down, his stride unbroken. He stepped on first base as he crossed the line, ducked down into the dugout, growled once at Higgins and headed through the alleyway and into the locker room.

He stopped only to tell an usher standing just inside the dugout: "I guess I forgot to tip my hat."

To the end, the mirror remained intact.

After the game, photographers were permitted to go right into the clubhouse, but writers were held to the 15-minute rule. One writer tried to ride in with the photographers, but Williams leveled that finger at him and said: "You're not supposed to be here."

Somehow or other, the news was let out that Ted would not be going to New York, although there seems to be some doubt as to whether it was Williams or Higgins who made the announcement. The official Boston line is that it had been understood all along that Ted would not be going to New York unless the pennant race was still on. The fact of the matter is that Williams made the decision himself, and he did not make it until after he hit the home run. It would have been foolish to have gone to New York or anywhere else, of course. Anything he did after the Boston finale would have been an anticlimax.

One of the waiting newspapermen, a pessimist by nature, expressed the fear that by the time they were let in, Ted would be dressed and gone.

"Are you kidding?" a member of the anti-Williams clique said. "This is what he lives for. If the game had gone 18 innings, he'd be in there waiting for us."

He was indeed waiting at his locker, with a towel wrapped around his middle. The writers approached him, for the most part, in groups. Generally speaking, the writers who could be called friends reached him first, and to these men Ted was not only amiable but gracious and modest.

Was he going for the home run?

"I was gunning for the big one," he grinned. "I let everything I had go. I really wanted that one."

Did he know it was out as soon as it left his bat?

"I knew I had really given it a ride."

What were his immediate plans?

"I've got some business to clean up here," he said. "Then I'll be covering the World Series for *Life*. After that, I'm going back to Florida to see how much damage the hurricane did to my house."

The other players seemed even more affected by the drama of the farewell homer than Ted. Pete Runnels, practically dispossessed from his locker alongside Ted's by the shifts of reporters, wandered around the room shaking his head in disbelief. "How about that?" he kept repeating. "How about that? How about that?"

As for Ted, he seemed to be in something of a daze. After the first wave of writers had left, he wandered back and forth between his locker and the trainer's room. Back and forth, back and forth. Once, he came back with a bottle of beer, turned it up to his lips and downed it with obvious pleasure. For Ted, this is almost unheard of. He has always been a milk and ice-cream man, and he devours them both in huge quantities. His usual order after a ball game is two quarts of milk.

Williams remained in the locker room, making himself available, until there were no more than a half-dozen other players remaining. Many of the writers did not go over to him at all. From them, there were no questions, no congratulations, no good wishes for the future. For all Ted's color, for all the drama and copy he had supplied over 22 years, they were glad to see him finally retire.

When Ted finally began to get dressed, our man went over and said: "Ted, you must have known when Higgins sent you back out that he was giving you a final chance to think about tipping the hat or making some gesture of farewell. Which meant that Higgins himself would have liked you to do it. While you were running back, didn't you have any feeling that it might be nice to go out with a show of good feeling?"

"I felt nothing," he said.

"No sentimentality? No gratitude? No sadness?"

"I said *nothing*," Ted said. "Nothing, nothing, nothing!"

As our man was toting up the nothings, Ted snarled, "And when you get back there tell them for me that they're full of . . ." There followed a burst of vituperation which we can not even begin to approximate, and then the old, sad plaint about those 12 years of merciless persecution.

Fenway Park has an enclosed parking area so that the players can get to their cars without beating their way through the autograph hunters. When Ted was dressed, though, the clubhouse boy called to the front office in what was apparently a prearranged plan to bring Williams' car around to a bleacher exit.

At 4:40, 45 minutes after the end of the game and a good hour after Ted had left the dugout, he was ready to leave. "Fitzie," he called out, and the clubhouse boy came around to lead the way. The cameramen came around, too.

The locker-room door opens onto a long corridor, which leads to another door which, in turn, opens onto the backwalks and understructure of the park. It is this outer door which is always guarded.

Waiting in the alleyway, just outside the clubhouse door, however, was a redheaded, beatnik-looking man, complete with the regimental beard and the beachcomber pants. He handed Ted a ball and mentioned a name that apparently meant something to him. Ted took the ball and signed it.

"How come you're not able to get in?" he said. "If they let the damn newspapermen in, they ought to let you in." Walking away, trailed by the platoon of cameramen, he called out to the empty air: "If they let the newspapermen in, they should have let him in. If they let the newspapermen in, they should let everybody in."

He walked on through the backways of the park, past the ramps and pillars, at a brisk clip, with Fitzie bustling along quickly to stay up ahead. Alongside of Williams, the cameramen were scrambling to get their positions and snap their pictures. Williams kept his eyes straight ahead, never pausing for one moment. "Hold it for just a minute, Ted," one of them said.

"I've been here for 22 years," Ted said, walking on. "Plenty of time for you to get your shot."

"This is the last time," the cameraman said. "Co-operate just this one last time."

"I've co-operated with you," Ted said. "I've co-operated too much."

Fitzie had the bleacher entrance open, and as Ted passed quickly through, a powder-blue Cadillac pulled up to the curb. A man in shirtsleeves was behind the wheel. He looked like Dick O'Connell, whose appointment as business manager had been announced the previous night.

Fitzie ran ahead to open the far door of the car for Ted. Three young women had been approaching the exit as Ted darted through, and one of them screamed: "It's him!" One of the others just let out a scream, as if Ted had been somebody of real worth, like Elvis or Fabian. The third woman remained mute. Looking at her, you had to wonder whether she would ever speak again.

Fitzie slammed the door, and the car pulled away. "It was him," the first woman screamed. "Was it *really* him? Was it *him*?"

Her knees seemed to give away. Her girl friends had to support her. "I can't catch my breath," she said. "I can hear my heart pounding." And then, in something like terror: "I CAN'T BREATHE."

Attracted by the screams, or by some invisible, inexplicable grapevine, a horde of boys and men came racing up the street. Ted's car turned the corner just across from the bleacher exit, but it was held up momentarily by a red light and a bus. The front line of pursuers had just come abreast of the car when the driver swung around the bus and pulled away.

There are those, however, who never get the word. Down the street, still surrounding the almost empty parking area, were still perhaps 100 loyal fans waiting to say their last farewell to Ted Williams.

In Boston that night, the talk was all of Williams. Only 10,454 were at the scene, but the word all over the city was: "I knew he'd end it with a home run . . ." and "I was going to go to the game, but —"

In future years, we can be sure, the men who saw Ted hit that mighty shot will number into the hundreds of thousands. The wind will grow strong and mean, and the distance will grow longer. Many of the reports of the game, in fact, had the ball going into the center-field bleachers.

The seeds of the legend have already been sown. George Carens, an elderly columnist who is more beloved by Ted than by his colleagues, wrote:

"Ted was calm and gracious as he praised the occupants of the Fenway press penthouse at home plate before the game began. Afterwards he greeted all writers in a comradely way, down through his most persistent critics. In a word, Ted showed he can take it, and whenever the spirit moves him he will fit beautifully into the Fenway PR setup."

Which shows that people hear what they want to hear and see what they want to see.

In New York the next day, Phil Rizzuto informed his television audience that Ted had finally relented and tipped his hat after the home run.

And the *Sporting News* headline on its Boston story was:

SPLINTER TIPS CAP
TO HUB FANS AFTER
FAREWELL HOMER

A New York Sunday paper went so far as to say that Ted had made "a tender and touching farewell speech" from home plate at the end of the game.

All the reports said that Ted had, in effect, called his shot because it was known that he was shooting for a home run. Who wants to bet that, in future years, there will not be a story or two insisting that he *did* point?

The legend will inevitably grow, and in a way it is a shame. A man should be allowed to die the way he lived. He should be allowed to depart as he came. Ted Williams chose his course early, and his course was to turn his face from the world around him. When he walked out of the park, he kept his eyes to the front and he never looked back.

The epitaph for Ted Williams remains unchanged. He was sometimes unbearable but he was never dull. Baseball will not be the same without him. Boston won't be quite the same either. Old Boston is acrawl with greening statues of old heroes and old patriots, but Ted has left a monument of his own — again on his own terms — in the Children's Cancer Hospital.

He left his own monument in the record books too. For two decades he made the Red Sox exciting in the sheer anticipation of his next time at bat.

He opened his last season with perhaps the longest home run of his career and he closed it with perhaps the most dramatic. It was typical and it was right that the Williams Era in Boston should end not with a whimper. It was entirely proper that it should end with a bang.

So, the old order passeth and an era of austerity has settled upon the Red Sox franchise.

And now Boston knows how England felt when it lost India.

Ed Linn followed Ted Williams from afar, writing a series of lengthy profiles on Williams, mostly for Sport *magazine. As such, his views of Williams were somewhat more moderate and considered than those of his Boston-based counterparts. His account of Williams's last game, though less well known than John Updike's signature report, is more straightforward and provides a more comprehensive overview of Williams's personality. Linn later penned a biography of Williams titled* Hitter.

PART V

IMPOSSIBLE DREAMS
AND NIGHTMARES

Entering the 1967 season, no one really cared about the Red Sox. They hadn't contended for a pennant for more than a decade and barely 8,000 fans turned out on Opening Day. Oh, before Ted Williams retired in 1960, fathers had taken their sons and daughters to see him, but usually only once, and after his retirement there were few other reasons to go to Fenway Park. Interest in the franchise was at an all-time low. Even owner Tom Yawkey stayed away. Since local officials had turned down his request for help in building a new ballpark several years before, he'd been a virtual stranger and was reported to be contemplating selling the team.

Then came 1967, when general manager Dick O'Connell put together a team of young, hungry players and installed fiery manager Dick Williams as their leader. They shocked the baseball world. Boston's "Cardiac Kids," led by MVP Carl Yastrzemski and Cy Young Award winner Jim Lonborg, captured the imagination of an entirely new generation of Red Sox fans. The city suddenly began to look at the team through new eyes. In the "Summer of Love," all of a sudden there was nothing New England loved more than the Red Sox. The glow of that season has yet to diminish, and the passion for the team has yet to wane. Nineteen sixty-seven changed *everything*.

The success of the 1967 team also reawakened Boston's slumbering sporting press. The *Boston Globe* and, to a lesser degree, the *Herald* dramatically expanded their baseball coverage, and a new generation of younger, hipper sportswriters such as Leigh Montville and Peter Gammons took over. The counterculture embraced the youthful Red Sox, and the alternative press pushed the envelope even further with a more personal style of reporting.

But the Impossible Dream turned nightmarish as the Red Sox lost not only the 1967 World Series but also the 1975 World Series, the 1978 playoff game against the Yankees, and, worst of all, the 1986 World Series versus the Mets. With a roster of stars that included some of the game's most talented players, such as Jim Rice, Luis Tiant, and Roger Clemens, writers found the Red Sox an ever more compelling subject. But to every Red Sox fan's lasting disappointment, the team's defining character became its seemingly inexhaustible quest to experience ever more excruciating varieties of loss.

HAROLD KAESE

THE IMPOSSIBLE DREAM?
"Cardiac Kids" At It Again

from *The Boston Globe,* July 28, 1967

If the Red Sox can finish the season in the same fantastic manner that they finished Thursday's ball game, they will be in the World Series for sure.

It was such a fantastic game that not only did a home run by Joe Foy in the ninth inning jar Jim McGlothlin off the mound, not only did Tony Conigliaro's homer a moment later tie the score, not only did Carl Yastrzemski save a run in the 10th with a superb catch and save it again by throwing out Don Mincher at the plate, not only did Reggie Smith triple and score the winning run on an error by the third baseman, but Sparky Lyle got a bawling out from his manager after being credited with his first big league victory, 6–5, over the Angels.

The nervy young southpaw, recently recalled from Toronto as a relief pitcher, hurled his scoreless — but nerve-wracking — inning with a sore elbow.

Dick Williams knew nothing about the injury until the game was over and won.

"It's not serious, but I gave him hell when I heard about it," said the manager. "Anybody's hurt, we've got to know about it."

Bitter-Sweet Day for Lyle

To what did Lyle credit his first big league victory?

"Great defense."

What did Yastrzemski enjoy most, his 25th homer of the season, his stunning 10th-inning catch off Bill Skowron, or throwing out Mincher?

Yaz: "The throw. I liked that best. The big thing was coming up with the ball clean. I didn't know if he was going or not. (Mincher ran through Billy Herman's stop sign. He was out by 40 feet.) I just let the ball go. I haven't thrown out many this year. Haven't had many chances."

On the one-handed catch of Skowron's liner, did he think he had a chance?

Yaz: "I played him shallow, figuring if he got under the ball it would be off the fence. My first glance at the ball, I thought, 'No.' My second glance, I thought, 'Yes,' and got ready for the jump, which I didn't need. The ball seemed like it hung up there."

Was Conigliaro looking for the fast ball Bill Kelso threw him on the first pitch?

Conig: "Yes, I was. I figured it would be a fast ball. I knew it was my job to tie it up. I was going for the home run."

Had Joe Foy ever hit a home run before off McGlothlin?

Foy: "Never. I've hit 31 home runs up here, all off different pitchers except two. They were off Brunet. McGlothlin threw me a high fast ball. I think he was getting tired and losing his zip."

When Reggie Smith's triple rolled around the right field corner, was the third base coach, Eddie Popowski, tempted to send him in for a home run inside the park?

Pop: "Not a bit. With nobody out, I wouldn't have sent him unless he could have walked in. Why take a chance?"

Did Smith think he had a chance for a home run?

Smith: "Any chance I had I lost when I had to chop my stride to hit second base. The throw (by Bobby Knoop) would have had me."

Was Smith going in on Adair's squib to third, that bounced weirdly through Paul Schaal?

Pop: "No. He waited and went when the ball got away."

Why were there so many problems at third, where Foy booted three grounders and Schaal one?

Foy: "It's funny out there, the way the ball's skipping off the grass. Something's wrong out there."

With Smith on third and none out, what did Dick Williams and Popowski discuss?

Williams: "He asked if I was thinking about a squeeze and I said no. We thought they'd walk Gibson and Adair to fill the bases, but I can see why they'd rather take their chances on two cold men and not on our first three hitters. Their thinking was right, too, because it took the error to win for us."

How did the Red Sox generally feel about their finest comeback of the season?

Stange: "A story-book finish by the Bosox. I didn't see it, because I was in the trainer's room with my arm in the ice, but I heard it."

Williams: "When we went to bat in the ninth, Sal Maglie said, 'Nobody's leaving the park. Let's win it for them.' And we did. This team may only average 24 years, but they seem to get looser as they go along."

Yaz: "What a great comeback. I never thought we'd win this one, the way McGlothlin was pitching."

Conig: "We waited a little long, till the ninth, but it was just a matter of time. We're going to win it. We showed you something today, didn't we?"

The Red Sox surprised everyone in 1967, but the victory described by Kaese on page one of the Boston Globe *alerted all New England to the fact that this Red Sox team actually had a chance. An unknown and enterprising headline writer was the first to make reference to the club's quest as "The Impossible Dream," the title of a popular song from the musical* Man of La Mancha.

SOX BARELY ESCAPE SCREAMING, STREAMING FANS

from *The Boston Globe*, October 2, 1967

As the ball came down in Rico Petrocelli's glove for the last-and-final out, the town went up in the air like a beautiful balloon. Perhaps it will never come down; Red Sox euphoria is a gas that can keep you higher than helium. Or pot.

For an instant Petrocelli looked at the baseball. Then he began to run as though he were Chiang Kai-shek in Peking because he could hear the shrieking mob behind him.

It was the Red Sox Guard charging across the Fenway playing field Sunday afternoon, and the old ball park suddenly became a newsreel from Hong Kong: the Red Guard storming the British embassy. These were the zealots, thousands of them from the congregation of 35,770 at Fenway Park, which was packed tighter than the Black Hole of Calcutta.

They leaped the fences and streamed onto the field, screaming the Red Sox Guard oath — "We're No. 1!" — and displaying their banners.

They made Mao Tse-tung's gang look like peace marchers, yet this was a frenzy of love, not hate.

Respectable people who had left their homes placidly, if nervously, to attend the pennant-deciding rites indulged in by Our Old Town team had become fanatics celebrating a holy war triumph.

"Is Yaz God?" asked one of the banners.

It was an interesting theological question in the light of the miracles achieved by Carl Yastrzemski. Certainly he and his fellows are the children of the gods in this year of 1967.

Karl Marx, who said religion is the opiate of the people, would have revised himself had he watched the Red Sox unite to throw off their ninth place chains. The Red Sox are the opiate right now, Karl, baby, although you might classify them as a religion.

"Just like '46!" proclaimed another banner. "Next Stop St. Louis!" "Spirit of '67!" "Go Sox!" "Wipe out Cardinals!"

The banners were waving and the mob advanced, and pitcher Jim Lonborg stood on the mound savoring it all, ready to be hailed as a conquering hero.

"Then it became a mania — and I was scared to death," Lonborg recalled. He didn't mind being raised to the sky by admirers — but not by 5000 of them, each wanting a piece of him as a relic of their religious experience. He was sucked into the crowd as though it were a whirlpool, grabbed, mauled, patted, petted, pounded and kissed.

"This made Roxbury look like a picnic," said Patrolman John Ryan, a riot veteran who was one of Lonborg's rescuers. "Jim could have been hurt bad. We barely got him out of there."

Lonborg emerged nearly in tatters. His buttons were gone, and though his uniform shirt was still on his back his undershirt had disappeared. Nevertheless his right arm still dangled from the shoulder and his fingers were intact. He would pitch and win again, although his 5–3 decision over Minnesota seemed enough forever at that moment.

Growing more fervent, the crowd split into platoons. One attacked the scoreboard, ripping down signs and everything else that could be lifted for souvenirs. Others looked elsewhere for loot. The fervor had begun to degenerate into the ugliness of vandalism. And the fever in some had become a mood of recklessness that endangered. Twenty or so kids climbed the screen behind the plate like monkeys. Several nearly fell to the concrete 40 feet below. The screen sagged ominously beneath their weight as the people in the seats below looked up helplessly.

Nobody seemed to want to leave the park. A few firecrackers went off, and horns blew endlessly. On the field, most of the Red Sox

Guard had settled into a milling pattern, wandering about the diamond, dazed at the wonder of it all, ecstatic to be treading the hal-
lowed ground.

Joe Tierney led a group of ushers who stood on the mound, protecting that rise from the human bulldozers. A man named Ray Cope-
land from Wellesley stooped at the edge of the mound, scooped up a
palmful of the dirt and poured it into a small box. "Going to take
this back to England," he said. "I've been working in Boston a year,
become a Red Sox fan, but when I go back, some of the soil of
Fenway goes with me to London."

Kris Becker, a college girl from Worcester, plucked a handful of
grass from along the third baseline. "Not sure what I'll do with it yet.
Maybe frame it," she said.

Only the cops prevented the mob from removing the left field
wall.

Last year on the last day of the season the Red Sox choked; they
won and blew 10th place by a half-game. Sunday it was altogether
something else. "You respond differently when you're in first place
than when you're in ninth," said Yastrzemski.

Lonborg set the faithful to chanting and clapping with his bunt single that opened the sixth. The Red Sox, behind 2–0, devoted 24 minutes to their half of the inning and the Minnesotans began to feel
the mysterious power of Our Old Town Team. They threw to the
wrong base, made wild pitches, an error, and put the ball over the
plate to Yastrzemski. It meant five runs for Boston, the team that is
today's American Dream. The inning ended with John Kiley, the
Fenway organist, playing "The Night They Invented Champagne." It
was a hymn to the day, and to the evening to come when Uncle Tom
Yawkey poured for Our Old Town Team.

They drank champagne the way people drink it when it is free, and
many of them probably have heads resembling the Goodyear blimp
today.

The players will sober up by Wednesday, but it will take the town
much longer to get over its Red Sox high.

And now, on this day of revelation, we know what Billy Joe and his chick were throwing off the Tallahatchie Bridge: World Series tickets printed in Detroit, Minneapolis and Chicago.

In a career that has spanned nearly five decades, Bud Collins, first for the Herald *and then for the* Globe, *has been one of the most colorful and memorable sportswriters in Boston journalism. Before he became better known as a tennis commentator, he often covered the Red Sox, where his inventive reports stand out compared to the blander offerings of his peers.*

JIMMY BRESLIN

....

IT'S A GREAT TOWN FOR BASEBALL

from *The Boston Herald Traveler,* October 2, 1967

The day started with the street in front of the ballpark blocked off and everybody was standing in the street and pushing to get inside and see the Red Sox win the American League pennant. The thieves, which this town always has held in great esteem, were at work in the crowd. They were pushing people off balance and then snatching at their tickets or dipping fingers into pockets where wallets could be. Every now and then a woman would let out a squall, but this was only because some legitimate man was pinching her. A thief doesn't do things like this when he is at work. A thief steals.

In the middle of the crowd there was this old, old man who has been stealing in Boston since he could move his hands. Somebody in the crowd recognized him and called out, "Murphy, be good now, Murphy," and Murphy who wouldn't talk if his coat were on fire, put his head down and burrowed into the crowd and was gone.

Inside the ballpark, the day became a long children's hour. The moment an adult took his seat he became a 12-year-old who chanted, "We want a hit" and who jumped up and waved madly at television cameras and then turned and squealed at the field, where a long-haired 24-year-old named Jim Lonborg pitched and Carl Yastrzemski swung a bat and played left field.

Yastrzemski was up at bat four times and he got four hits. He batted in two runs and scored a run. He messed up a play in left field in the third inning and let a run score. But in the seventh inning he came running hatless across the grass and made a fine catch of a fly ball. In the eighth inning he chased a ball hit by Bob Allison of Minnesota and ran it down in the corner of the field. He picked it up and threw to second as if he had just hit the ball with a bat. Allison threw himself on the dirt like a walrus and tried to row around the Red Sox second baseman. Allison was tagged out. The throw choked off Minnesota's one chance to win. All baseball analysts began to say that Yastrzemski was playing quite well.

One who assured everyone of this was Mr. Morris (Moe) Berg, who was in the standing room behind home plate. Moe Berg is a man who came out of Princeton, speaks eight languages and was a major league catcher who caught Walter Johnson in Washington and Lefty Grove in Boston. Moe then disappeared into the world. He sends postcards from the Sahara and never wears anything but a black tie. "I am in mourning for the world," he explains. After the eighth inning yesterday, Moe assured those near him "despite the diluted quality of baseball talent today, Yastrzemski must be bracketed with anybody who ever was regarded as great at playing this sport."

"You're right, he's great," a guy standing with him said.

Then it was the end of the afternoon and the sky was becoming dark and a cool wind ran through the stands and Rico Petrocelli, the Boston shortstop, was going back after this little pop fly hit by the last Minnesota batter of the game, Richie Rollins. Back went Petrocelli, back with his hands up and his mouth open, and he grabbed the ball and people came running onto the field trying to tackle him and kids started climbing up the netting behind home plate. They were climbing up to the radio and television microphones and there were so many of them that the netting began to buckle and they could have all been killed.

The Boston players came into the dressing room shouting and kissing each other. Petrocelli came in eager-faced, only to run into his brother, who was standing in front of the dressing stall. The brother shook his head. The brother's name is Dave Petrocelli and he comes from Brooklyn and he has been to the race track in his lifetime and he has blown too many photo finishes. He likes victories to be official.

"That's right," Dave said, "please hold all pari-mutuel tickets until the result of the race is official." He tapped the brother on the arm. "Detroit got to lose."

The rest of the players kept screaming. "Let me see the bottom line, Rico," the brother said. "Let me see Detroit lose."

"What's the score?" somebody said.

"Three to two Detroit," a voice called out.

"You see?" Petrocelli's brother said.

There was some movement in the crowd of cameramen and players and they made an aisle for Tom Yawkey, who owns the team. He is much thinner now than he used to be and his face is wrinkled and the skin under his chin shows that he is well in his 60's. He was in a white shirt that was open at the collar and brown slacks that were wrinkled. He fished in his shirt pocket for a filter cigarette. He squinted in the lights and everybody reached for his hand and called him "Mister Yawkey." He is one of the last of the sportsmen. He lost millions while he took batting practice with his team and when he couldn't hit any more he played pepper with them. Two years ago, his lawyers began to scream about how much the Red Sox were costing him. He listened to them and went out to the ballpark.

"Detroit's ahead," somebody said to Yawkey.

"I don't care about that," Yawkey said. "This is all I care about."

"Been a long time, Mr. Yawkey," a player called out.

He smiled. "Yes, it has."

"How much have you gone for since you've had this team?" he was asked.

He shook his head. "Oh, I don't know where that's so important. I don't think figures have any place in a thing like today."

"Is it as expensive as owning race horses?"

"Oh, you can go for a lot more with a baseball team. Yes, you can. You can lose a million in a year easily. You see, the expenses that don't show on the field are so high. The cost of finding the players and developing them. Like Nekola. Where would we be if we didn't have Nekola on a payroll?"

He was talking about a man named Bots Nekola, who is an old pitcher who lives on Long Island and is on the Red Sox payroll as a scout. In 1957, a man named O'Brien, who was a high school teacher in Bridgehampton, L.I., called Nekola up and told him about a pitcher named Carl Yastrzemski. Nekola drove out and watched the high school play. Bridgehampton is a tiny place with potato farms set back from the ocean. There were only 12 boys in the senior class that year and Yastrzemski was the pitcher because nobody else in school could throw. Nekola looked at the boy pitch and shook his head.

"He's no pitcher," Bots said to O'Brien.

"He can hit," O'Brien said.

"I got to see more of him," Nekola said. He did. He saw Yastrzemski play semi-pro on a dimly lit field and in one game the boy came around with these wrists snapping and he hit one into the night. A couple of days later, Bots Nekola was telling Tom Yawkey that the boy was worth $100,000. Yawkey did what he always does. He paid. This time his money got him a great one. Then Nekola went out and found Petrocelli in Brooklyn.

And now yesterday, Yastrzemski stood in his undershirt and so nobody screamed that California was ahead. There was silence and the player cocked his head to listen to the radio.

"Six?" he said. Then he shrieked, "Seven! They're ahead seven to three!"

The players walked around and poured beer on each other and the old sportsman, Tom Yawkey, walked up to each of them and spoke to them and everybody worried about the Detroit score. It was, at the end of this summer that has been so terrible, a very good thing to sit around and worry about just a baseball game in Detroit. A toy world has a lot to offer sometimes.

"Eight!" a player screamed. California had scored another run.

Everybody milled around and the time dissolved in noise and a little after twenty to eight the radio voice was saying ". . . the throw to first . . ." and the players around a television set made so much noise nobody could hear the word double play. The way they jumped up and down told you Detroit had just lost.

Outside, a couple of thousand people stood under the streetlights and chanted "We're number one" and a guy in a blue windbreaker bumped into a guy in a yellow shirt and the one in the yellow shirt bumped back and the blue windbreaker turned around and the two of them had a wonderful fist fight.

The final days of the 1967 season were such a big story that noted New York columnist Jimmy Breslin, then writing for the World Journal Herald, *weighed in with his inimitable view.*

THE IMPOSSIBLE DREAM

from *Boston Magazine*, July 1986

The 1967 regular season was a four-team race going into the final weekend. After losing to the Cleveland Indians 6–0 on Wednesday, we really believed that we were out of it, even though we still had two games to play. Chicago seemed to be in control. They had a doubleheader in Kansas City, and the Athletics were the worst team in the majors. More than that, Chicago had its two best pitchers — Joel Horlen and Gary Peters — scheduled to start. Horlen and Peters were one and two, respectively, in earned-run average, but somehow they both lost. All of a sudden, the pennant was up for grabs.

The Red Sox had been having an unusual season, to say the least. We weren't beating ourselves, as we had in the past. And Carl Yastrzemski — who won both the Triple Crown (he led the league in batting and runs batted in, and tied for home runs) and Most Valuable Player — was an inspiration, as much for his fielding as for his hitting. Dick Williams, the manager, had instilled a strong respect for fundamentals from spring training on, something not all the players warmed to.

Williams was sarcastic, and that quality wore thin on some of the team. In Anaheim earlier that summer, I'd pitched a no-hitter into the eighth against the California Angels, and we led 1–0 into the bottom of the ninth. I gave up a hit, then a walk. A run scored to tie the game, and after an out or two, they had a runner on third. Then I threw a curve into the dirt.

The ball bounced off the catcher, Russ Gibson. Gibby thought the ball was behind him and rushed toward the backstop. Unfortunately it had rolled in the opposite direction. I ran toward the plate, the runner came charging home, and my scoop toss to Gibby was too late. We lost 2–1.

Williams was leaning on the dugout railing as we walked in, the same position from which he'd watched the whole game. He said nothing as I walked by and sat down. Then Rico Petrocelli came over and slapped me on the leg in congratulations.

"Hell of a game, Jim," Petrocelli said.

Williams turned and stared.

"Hell of a game, my ass," he snarled. "Take a look at the scoreboard."

Williams decided to pitch me with two days' rest in the crucial Cleveland game, a decision not as absurd as it might now seem. Winning against Baltimore with a big lead, I was lifted in the sixth inning so I'd be rested for the Indians. At least that was the theory.

My best pitch was a sinker ball, and my stuff didn't have to be overpowering to be effective. As my arm tired, my ball would sink more, and the batters would hit more ground balls — which was what we were looking for. But the sinker wasn't there in that Wednesday loss.

Totally down, I left Fenway Park and walked all the way to Charles River Park where I was sharing an apartment with two friends. For some reason, I stopped in front of a flower shop and stared at the blossoms in the window. Some were fresh, others wilted. They'll recover, I thought. They just need water and a little rest. Everything's going to be all right.

With two games left in the season, on Saturday and Sunday, both against the Minnesota Twins, there was again talk that I might go with two days' rest. But neither Dick Williams nor I gave that idea much consideration. I'd had a soft callus on my thumb for two months, and because I threw my breaking pitch with my thumb tucked underneath the ball, flipping the ball off my thumb on the release, that callus would blister after every game. But with only two days' rest, my effectiveness would have been in doubt, since the blistering generally required three to four days to heal.

Sunday would be my day, and it was up to José Santiago to win on Saturday, which he did. By then there was — how should I put it? —

a special sense of excitement in Boston. My roommates, Dennis Bennett, a reserve infielder, and Neil McNerney, who owned a couple of bars, were well-known party persons. I partied pretty well myself. But I'd been careful about resting before starts, and I knew that resting on that Saturday night might be tough. At least in our apartment.

I knew, too, that I pitched much better on the road than at Fenway. Of my 21 wins, only 6 had been at home. I concentrated better on the road, reading quietly in a hotel room the night before a game rather than hanging out with friends. And my luck with Minnesota had been atrocious: 0-3 for the season, 0-6 lifetime. I knew I had to do *something* different to prepare for Sunday's game.

Ken Harrelson approached me in the trainer's room after Saturday's game and offered me the room at the Sheraton-Boston he'd been living in since coming to the Sox from Cleveland in mid-season. "Jeez, we got to get this guy to bed," the other players were saying, and Harrelson decided to do something about it.

"Why don't you just lock yourself in my hotel room?" he said.

"*That* is a good idea," I said, and took the key.

At Saturday's team meeting before the start of the two-game series, we'd focused on the fact that we couldn't let Harmon Killebrew, the Twins' leading home-run hitter, beat us. That day, Santiago walked him whenever Killebrew could hurt us with one swing. We weren't going to allow him to give the Twins a spiritual lift. And putting him on first wasn't much of a risk; he had bad legs, and even if he got to second, he'd be lucky to score on two hits.

That strategy — and knowing it had worked the day before — gave me confidence on Sunday. Bob Allison, who followed Killebrew, was a hitter I could handle.

Walking from the Sheraton, I got to the clubhouse early, and on impulse I grabbed a pen and wrote the figure *$10,000* inside the palm of my glove. Winning the game, I realized, wouldn't simply mean going to the World Series; it would mean a considerable check, too. If I could remind myself of that before every pitch, I figured my concentration would be better.

Still, the game began as if the Twins had me cursed. They scored two runs, both on errors. I walked Killebrew in the first inning, but Tony Oliva's drive went over Yaz's head. George "Scotty" Scott threw wildly to Gibby at home, and Killebrew scored — after we'd all agreed he couldn't. In the third, the Twins scored again when Yaz let Killebrew's single get by him and roll all the way to the wall.

Dean Chance started for the Twins and I'd hit him well, although he ended up winning 20 games that season. I had a home run against him in Minnesota and always felt comfortable facing him at the plate. His delivery was difficult for most batters. A big man, he'd turn his shoulder and most of his back to the hitter before he'd start to bring his pitching arm forward. To right-handed batters, his pitches seemed to be coming at their bodies before swerving across the plate at the last second.

Going into the sixth, Chance had a shutout, and I began to wonder if we'd ever score. When I came to bat — I'd gotten a single my first time up — I noticed that Cesar Tovar, the Twins' third baseman, was playing deep. I'd bunted a lot during the summer, and Bobby Doerr, our batting coach, had emphasized the importance of a pitcher's being able to do the little things that would keep him in the ball game.

"If you want to be able to win more games," he told me, "you've got to do more than throw the ball over the plate. You've got to be able to bunt, hit, run, and run smartly. If you do, and the manager knows, he won't consider you a liability in the late innings and pinch-hit for you. He'll think of you as part of his attack."

Walking the few feet from the batting circle to home plate, I decided to lay down a bunt. They were riding a crest, Chance was pitching great — coming right at the hitters and not trying to trick anybody — and I thought, Why not try to break the pattern?

I went for the first pitch and made it to first when Chance hesitated coming in and Tovar fumbled the ball. Then the next three hitters — Jerry Adair, Dalton Jones, and Yaz — all stroked first-pitch singles. Now the score was tied 2–2, and Chance seemed to be getting a little shell-shocked. I know I would have been. Ken Harrelson hit a grounder to short, and Zoilo Versailles threw home, where he had no play: 3–2. Chance left the game. Al Worthington, the reliever, threw two wild pitches — I felt a little sorry for him, recalling William's wrath — and it was 4–2. Then Killebrew misplayed Reggie Smith's grounder: 5–2.

The Twins threatened me — us — in the eighth. With two outs (Adair made a great play to double up a base runner and got spiked — seven stitches' worth in the leg), they got a pair of singles. Then Allison hit a liner into the left-field corner, where 9 times out of 10 it would have gone for a double. But Yaz made a terrific play and threw Allison out at second. A run scored, but the rally was over.

I was into a terrific rhythm now. My arm was a little weary, so my fastball was sinking well. The crowd had gotten into the game in the bottom of the sixth, and I could feel waves of adrenaline washing through me. I wasn't crazy or wild, just confident. Like Roger Clemens against the Seattle Mariners, I was just going with it.

A pop fly to Rico ended the game. There's a picture that captures that moment — I guess it was shot from our dugout — of Petrocelli catching the ball, Yaz with his arms in the air, and me jumping off the mound, arms also raised. The perfect expression of happiness: all of us in the air at the same time. Triumphant.

Rico, Mike Andrews, Elston Howard, and Scotty all surrounded me. Then all of a sudden those guys disappeared into the clubhouse. But I was savoring the moment. It was such a special time, and we'd worked so long and hard for it. I was screaming to the holy heavens, "We did it! We did it!"

Next I was surrounded by fans, first a few, then what seemed like hundreds. For a moment, that was fine, too. I was happy. They were happy.

Then I realized I couldn't see anybody I recognized. Not a single person. Parts of my clothing started to get ripped off. And I was being moved in a direction — toward the right-field corner — that I didn't want to go in.

"I don't want to go *that* way," I began to say nervously.

Finally, the security police began to turn the crowd in the other direction. When I got to the dugout, my shoelaces were gone, my belt was gone, my inner jersey was somehow gone, my hat was gone.

But we'd at least tied for the pennant, after finishing a half game out of last place the year before. And a half hour later, the Tigers lost. We were the American League champions.

Nothing would ever equal that climactic moment for me — not pitching in the National League play-off for the Phillies or in the

World Series for Boston. Nothing before and nothing after ever came down to that solitary moment: one day, one game, and in the bottom of the ninth, one pitch.

To be carried off the field by adoring fans is the stuff of fiction. I read Bernard Malamud's *The Natural,* and this was that moment: lights exploding, the tower coming down, the old bat being broken, and the Kid coming to the plate with his homemade bat.

That's what that weekend was all about.

Pitcher Jim Lonborg had a dream season in 1967, culminating in his final-day victory over the Twins. The resulting scene is etched into the minds of Red Sox fans everywhere, for it seemed as if all New England streamed onto the field and carried Lonborg off. "Gentleman Jim" obviously appreciated it — after retiring from baseball he opened a dental practice in suburban Scituate.

YAZ CLUTCH STREAK HAS NO PARALLEL

from *The Boston Globe*, October 2, 1967

Like a rocket that starts from a spark, traces a fiery path into the night until it explodes in a shower of light, the Red Sox have dazzled a nation by winning the American League pennant.

Whoever thought that so modest a vehicle as this team guided by Dick Williams would climb into the baseball sky to deliver streamers of excitement and the incandescent confetti of inspired effort?

"I thought we would finish about 10 games over .500 and in fourth or fifth place," said Tom Yawkey seriously, as his players drenched each other with beer after the climactic 5-to-3 victory over the Minnesota Twins.

But Williams, his manager, quipped, "I said all along we'd finish over .500."

And now for the great anti-climax — the World Series.

No known Red Sox hitter ever had a final two weeks to compare with those that Yaz delivered in the hottest stretch of the American League's hottest pennant race.

The Series can do a lot for Boston, for the Red Sox, for still unidentified heroes who may be lurking in the wings, but what can it do for Jim Lonborg, for Carl Yastrzemski?

Tris Speaker may have done it, or Duffy Lewis, Chick Stahl or some other Red Sox giant of long ago, but Ted Williams didn't, nor Jimmy Foxx, nor Vern Stephens.

As the Sox won eight out of the last 12 games for their eighth pennant, Yaz made 23 hits in 44 times at bat for an average of .523 hit safely in 11 of the games, drove in 16 runs, scored 14 and hit five homers.

In the two all-or-nothing games against the Twins, he made seven hits in eight times up.

If any player in baseball history — Babe Ruth, Rogers Hornsby, Ty Cobb, Lou Gehrig — ever had a two-week clutch production to equal Yastrzemski's, let the historians bring him forth.

Certainly no other Globe writer has done anything comparable on the athletic field, even though Leonard Fowle and John Ahern have won boat races and Bud Collins owns some tennis trophies.

Of Yastrzemski, Dick Williams said, "I never saw a player have a season like it."

And Rico Petrocelli said, "You'll never know how much he meant to us. We just knew he was going to hit."

And Tom Yawkey said, "At no time has this club ever been close to trading Yastrzemski."

In the Red Sox clubhouse, Yastrzemski wept from joy; in the visiting clubhouse, the Twins wept from Yastrzemski.

On Yawkey's 35 Red Sox teams, he has had few inspirational players. Joe Cronin, Ted Williams, Dom DiMaggio. These men wore the capes of baseball greatness — but none approached Yastrzemski for combining the qualities of baseball proficiency and on-the-field leadership. Baseball is a game in which individual players seldom fire up a lot of other players, but Yastrzemski did it this season.

He did it with his arms, legs and sharp eyes, with his desire, with his optimism and determination. And even though a ball rolled through him for an unearned run Sunday, how fitting it was for him to cut down Bob Allison trying to advance the tying run to second on what looked like a double into the left field corner.

The Red Sox put it together this season, which is why they won, but nobody put it together the way Yaz did, and not many in the annals of baseball ever have.

Strategically, the games with the Twins revolved around the fact that the Red Sox pitched around Harmon Killebrew, whereas the Twins did not pitch around Yastrzemski.

Killebrew got three walks and four hits; Yaz got no walks and seven hits. The Red Sox were careful; the Twins took chances. So today the Red Sox are champions of the American League, as they also were in 1903, 1904, 1912, 1915, 1916, 1918 and 1946.

Now they have a chance to even the score with the Cardinals for the only World Series they have ever lost, and while the Cardinals look like the better team on paper, I would no more bet against Yastrzemski, Lonborg and the Red Sox than I would bet against the United States Marines.

Kaese provided the numbers for what every Red Sox fan already knew: no player in a pennant race has ever played better than Carl Yastrzemski in the final weeks of 1967.

ROGER ANGELL

1967: THE FLOWERING AND SUBSEQUENT DEFLOWERING OF NEW ENGLAND

from *The New Yorker*, November 1967

The laurels all are cut, the year draws in the day, and we'll to the Fens no more. A great baseball season — the most intense and absorbing of our times — is over, the St. Louis Cardinals stand as champions of the world, and hundreds of thousands of New Englanders must winter sadly on a feast of memory. The autumn quiet that now afflicts so many of us has almost nothing to do with the Red Sox defeat in the last game of the World Series, for every Boston fan has grown up with that dour Indian-pudding taste in his mouth. New England's loss is not of a game or a Series but of the baseball summer just past — a season that will not come again, not ever quite the same. What will be remembered this winter, I think, is not so much a particular victory (Elston Howard blocking off the last White Sox base runner at the plate one night in Chicago, Carl Yastrzemski's eleventh-inning homer at Yankee Stadium) or a nearly insupportable loss (all those Baltimore games in September) as the shared joy and ridiculous hope of this summer's long adventure. I resisted at first, but it caught me up, and then I was sorry for anyone who was too old or too careful to care. Almost everyone on the seaboard was caught up in the end, it seemed. Forty-four New England radio stations poured out the news from the Fenway, and home-game telecasts by Ken Coleman, Mel Parnell, and Ned Martin made for late bedtimes from eastern Long Island to the Gaspé. Maine lobstermen pulling their traps off Saddleback Ledge called the news of the previous night's game from boat to boat through the foggy dawn air. The moderator of an August town meeting in Andover, Massachu-

setts, interrupted a hot budget debate to cry, "The Sox are leading, 2–1, in the sixth!" Three hikers descending the Brook Trail on
Mount Chocorua, in New Hampshire, caught the afternoon score
from a transistorized ascending climber. Sunday sailors off Manchester Harbor, on Boston's North Shore, hailed a winning rally
with foghorns and salvos of cherry bombs, and then cheered when a
power yacht broke out a large flag emblazoned "THINK PENNANT!"
Late in August, a patient recovering from surgery stood at the window of his room in the New England Baptist Hospital night after
night, watching the lights of Fenway Park across the city and hearing
the sudden double roar of the crowd — first over his radio and then,
in a deep echo, through the warm night air. The sense of belonging
was best in the crowded streets near the ball park before game time.
Up out of the subway on Commonwealth Avenue, up Brookline Avenue and over the expressway bridge, past the Pennant Grille, past
the button hawkers ("GO SOX!") and the ice-cream wagons and
the police horses; carried along in a mass of children and parents, old ladies in straw porkpies, pretty girls with pennants, South
Boston and Dorchester youths in high-school windbreakers, a party
of nuns; then pushed and jammed, laughing at the crush, through
the turnstiles and into the damp gloom under the stands; and out at
last to that first electric glimpse of green outfield and white bases —
this is the way baseball is remembered, and the way it truly was, for
once, in the summer of the Red Sox.

Even a restrained backward look at this season and this Series
must appear hyperbolic; already there is the odd temptation simply
not to believe one's recollection or the record. The Cardinals, sixth-
place finishers last year, lost their best pitcher for half the season
and still won their pennant easily, entirely dominating the other
powerful contenders that had given the National League its recent
reputation for late-season violence. The Red Sox, who finished the
1966 season one-half game out of the cellar, captured the American
League pennant on the last afternoon of the year by winning the
second of two consecutive essential victories over the Twins and
then waiting for the Tigers to lose their last game. The Baltimore
Orioles, who won the 1966 World Series in four straight games, fell
to sixth place this year, while the Red Sox, Twins, Tigers, and White
Sox clawed and clung to each other like drowning swimmers at the

surface of the American League for more than two months, in the closest pennant race in baseball history. The White Sox sank only two days before the end, at a moment when it appeared that they had the best chance to take the flag and the Red Sox the worst. Finally, the World Series, which promised only to be a numb, one-sided anticlimax, went the full seven games, producing some of the best baseball of the year, and was won at last by the better team.

An appreciation of the Cardinals must be postponed in this account until their appearance, in due course, in the World Series. An appreciation of the Red Sox must begin with a look at their prospects last April, which seemed inadequate even to sustain the wild vernal hopes that leap every year, jonquil-like, in the hearts of their followers. The Sox were a young team, probably a better one than their ninth-place finish indicated, but a review of the troops suggested only that hostilities should somehow be postponed. The up-the-middle strength, the traditional spine of a ball team, consisted of an earnest but light-hitting young catcher named Mike Ryan and two rookies — second baseman Mike Andrews and center fielder Reggie Smith. Third baseman Joe Foy and shortstop Rico Petrocelli could hit an occasional fly ball into the Fenway's short left-field screen, but both were subject to fatal spells of introspection when approaching ground balls. The large, slick-fielding George Scott was set at first, but last year, after making the All-Star team with his early slugging, he had apparently determined to hit every subsequent pitch out of the park, and wound up leading the league only in strikeouts. The two other outfielders — Tony Conigliaro in right and Yastrzemski in left — enjoyed star billing, but neither came close to .300 last year. Yaz, who had won the batting title in 1963, finished at .278, with sixteen home runs; he had never hit more than twenty homers in one season. There was, to be sure, a new manager — Dick Williams, up from two successful years with the Toronto farm — but a new manager in Boston has the same approximate hopes for tenure as a titled Balkan bridegroom in a Hollywood marriage. Any manager, however deep-browed, hates to do much thinking in the first two or three innings, and thus must own a pitching staff. The Red Sox had none, having failed in the winter to improve the corps that was the worst in the league last year. Their best starter, the youthful Jim Lonborg, could strike out batters but had proved too gentlemanly in the clutch ever to enjoy a winning season in the majors. There was one strong late reliever, John Wyatt, and some passable middle-innings men, but absolutely no other starters in sight.

Reasonable hope cannot be constructed out of such a sad pile of feathers, but the lifelong Red Sox fan is not a reasonable man. In him is the perpetual memory of a dozen seasons when the best of hopes went for nothing, so why is he not to believe that the worst of prospects may suddenly reward his fealty? If he is middle-aged, he remembers when, in the early nineteen-thirties, the team's owner, Tom Yawkey, acquired the Sox and almost bought a pennant within a few years, at an immense price, with a team built around such stalwarts as Jimmy Foxx, Joe Cronin, Lefty Grove, and a lanky young outfielder named Ted Williams. He remembers the home-grown squad of the mid-nineteen-forties, which included Williams, Dominic DiMaggio, Johnny Pesky, and Bobby Doerr. Those teams were wonderfully talented and exciting, but unfortunately they coexisted with two Yankee teams that were among the best in league history. There is one Boston pennant to treasure, in 1946, but that memory is accompanied by the awful vision of Enos Slaughter, of the Cardinals, racing all the way home from first on a double by Harry Walker and scoring the winning run of the Series while Johnny Pesky hesitated with the relay at short. There was a tie for first with the Indians in 1948, but the starting Red Sox pitcher for the one-game playoff was an aging journeyman named Denny Galehouse, who instantly unjustified the hunch. Since then, the Sox have been more at home in the second division than in the first. There are other interior daguerreotypes to sustain the New Englander — Ted Williams towering over the plate and grinding the bat between his fists before pulling an outside pitch into the bullpen. Dick Radatz fanning the side in relief — but these are matched by darker plates: Williams hitting .200 in that 1946 Series, Williams never hitting much against the Yankees, Walt Dropo and several other immobile croquet wickets letting grounders bounce between their legs at first, a dozen assorted infielders messing up a thousand double plays. I have studied the diehard Boston fan for many summers. I have seen the tiny, mineral-hard gleam of hope in his eye as he pumps gas under the blighted elms of a New Hampshire village or sells a pair of moccasins to a tourist in the balsam-smelling dimness of his Down East store, listening the while to the unceasing ribbon of bad news by radio from Fenway Park. Inside his head, I am sure, there is a perpetual accompanying broadcast of painful and maddening import — a lifetime's amalgam of ill-digested sports headlines, between-innings commercials, and Fenway Park bleacher cries:

"Hi, neighbor, have a Gansett! . . . DOUBLE-X 9 GAMES AHEAD OF BABE'S SWAT PACE . . . Oh, God, *look* — Slaughter's going for home! C'mon, Pesky, throw the ball, throw the *ball!* . . . YAWKEY VOWS PENNANT . . . but the lowly A's, rising for three runs in the eighth, nipped the Hose in the nightcap . . . Hi, neighbor . . . SPLINTER DEFIES SHIFT . . . and now trail the Yankees by two in the all-important lost column . . . 'He's better than his brother Joe — Dominic DiMaggio!' . . . RADATZ IN NINETEENTH RELIEF STINT . . . and if Pesky takes the ball over his *right* shoulder, Enos is dead, I'm telling you . . . GOODMAN NEARS BAT CROWN . . . Fenway scribes stated that Ted's refusal to doff his cap is nothing less than . . . HIGGINS SEES PENNANT WITHIN TWO YEARS . . . and Doc Cramer's shotgun arm *just* fails to cut down Averill at third . . . DID NOT SPIT KID SWEARS . . . the aging shortstop-manager, lately known in the press box as The Ancient Mariner ('who stoppeth one in three') . . . ZARILLA TRADE STRENGTHENS O.F. . . . . 'better than his brother Joe–Dominic DiMaggio!' . . . HIGGINS, REHIRED, VOWS . . . A bright spot in the Bosox seventh-place finish was Pete Runnels' consistent . . . TED FIRST A.L. SLUGGER TO TOP .400 SINCE . . . but Schilling dropped the ball . . . DELICIOUS NARRAGANSETT ALE. SO, *HI,* NEIGHBOR . . . and Keller matched Gordon's awesome poke over the inviting left-field screen with . . . MALZONE TRADE RUMORS DENIED . . . and Slaughter, running all the way, beat the startled Pesky's hurried . . . CRONIN, NEW MGR, VOWS . . . the hotly fought junior-circuit gonfalon . . . FOXX NEARS SWAT MARK . . . as Slaughter crosses the plate . . ."

By Memorial Day, the Red Sox were only a game above the .500 level, but Manager Williams and the front office had seen enough signs of life on the field to decide that their young enlistees would benefit from the assistance of some experienced noncoms. Successive deals in June brought Gary Bell, a strong right-handed starter, from the Indians and infielder Jerry Adair from the White Sox. Later in the summer, Elston Howard was bought from the Yankees to help behind the plate, and then Ken Harrelson, a brash, hot-dog outfielder with the Kansas City Athletics, signed aboard for a large bonus, after having so enraged the owner of the A's, Charles O. Finley, during a squabble that Finley threw him over the side.

Just before the All-Star game, in mid-July, Lonborg ended a five-game losing streak with a 3–0 shutout over the Tigers. Dick Williams said that this game marked Lonborg's arrival as a great pitcher, but it is likely that Lonborg's immense subsequent season was more the result of his decision in spring training to throw an occasional fast ball in the direction of the hitters' chins. "Keep count of how many batters I hit this year," Lonborg whispered to a sportswriter in April. Lonborg also kept count himself, recording the plunkees in ink on the back of his glove, like a fighter pilot pasting confirmed-kill decals on his plane's fuselage. The final bag came to nineteen, with several dozen near-misses, and the message got around the league that Lonborg was no longer a fine, friendly fellow to swing against. He finished the year with twenty-two wins, nine losses, and two hundred and forty-five strikeouts. Meanwhile, pitchers like Bell, Lee Stange, and José Santiago began showing signs of equal obduracy. Petrocelli, Conigliaro, and Yastrzemski were all off to fine seasons, the rookies Andrews and Smith proved to be quick and unflappable, and Dick Williams established his directorship once and for all by benching George Scott during three essential games because he was overweight. Late in July, the Sox won ten straight games, came home from a road trip in second place, and were met at Logan Airport by ten thousand true believers.

I refused to believe what was happening. Unpleasantly cool, I told Boston friends to keep their eyes on the other teams — the White Sox, who were clinging to first place on the strength of nothing but a fine pitching staff and some hilarious needling of the opposition by their manager, Eddie Stanky; the Twins, obviously the class of the league, who were just beginning their move; and the Tigers, who showed signs at last of wanting the pennant they had seemed capable of winning for the past two years. Then, too, I was waiting for the Red Sox bad break — the moment of ill fortune, the undeserved loss, that so often cracks the heart of a young team playing over its head. The break came on August 18th, and was infinitely worse than

I had imagined. A fast ball thrown by the Angels' Jack Hamilton struck Tony Conigliaro on the cheekbone, finishing him for the season. In that instant, the Sox lost their right fielder, a bat that had already delivered twenty home runs and sixty-seven runs batted in, and the only man on the team who could fill the key fourth spot in the batting order. In a few days, I could see, the Red Sox would . . . In the next few days, the Red Sox overcame an 0–8 deficit in one game and won it, 9–8, jumped off on what proved to be a seven-game winning streak, and climbed from fourth place to within one game of the Twins and White Sox, at the top. I gave up; from that week on, I belonged.

Even to neutralists, the last weeks of the American League race must have seemed excessive. On any given evening late in August, knowing the leader often depended on which edition of the papers one happened to buy. In the first week of September, the four teams reshuffled themselves nervously, the Red Sox lost three games without giving up much ground, and on Labor Day at Yankee Stadium Eddie Stanky had to tackle one of his infielders, Pete Ward, to keep him from punching an umpire and thus being ruled off the turf for the rest of the way. On September 7th, there was a four-way tie for first. My baseball nerves had grown too raw to permit me to keep out of it, and a few days later I flew west to see the four top teams in action. When I arrived in Chicago on September 16th, the Twins, Red Sox, and Tigers were still even-up, and the White Sox, who had slipped a trifle, were making up lost ground brilliantly. Two days before, they had beaten the Indians with a tenth-inning grand-slam home run, and the previous night they had won the first of the three-game series with the Twins, which they had to sweep in order to stay alive. That night, even the half-empty bleachers in White Sox Park (racial troubles on Chicago's South Side cut heavily into the White Sox attendance this year) failed to diminish the wonderful baseball tension in the boxy old stadium. With two weeks to go, the season had narrowed down to the point where each pitched ball seemed heavy with omens, and spectators greeted the most routine enemy pop fly with nervous laughter and applause. The Twins' ace, Dean Chance, was seeking his nineteenth win, and after watching him jam the White Sox batters with his jumping fast balls and low curves I concluded that I was in on a mismatch. Looking confident and workmanlike, the Twins loaded the bases in the fifth on a hit batsman, a single, a sacrifice, and an intentional walk. The White Sox pitcher, Tommy John, then leaped anxiously after a hopper by Ted Uhlaender, managing only to deflect it, and threw the ball past first, as two runs scored. A third came in a moment later on a single, and a fourth in the next inning on a home run by Bob Allison, which the Chicago outfielders studied in flight like junior astronomers. In the bottom of the ninth, it was 4–1, Twins, and the crowd managed only a few imploring cheers for their dying banjo hitters. The first Chicago batter, McCraw, singled, and took third on Ron Hansen's single and Oliva's subsequent error in right. Colavito then hit a perfect double-play ball, which Manager Stanky or some other deity caused to bound suddenly over the third baseman's head, scoring a run. Josephson, the catcher, now dropped an unsurprising sacrifice bunt along the third-base line. Chance pounced on it eagerly, dropped it, cuffed it, scuffled with it, and finally merely glared at it as it lay between his feet like a kitten. The score was now 4–2, with none out and the bases full, and wild bird cries rose into the night. Manager Stanky dispatched his third pinch-runner of the inning to first, and Wayne Causey, batting in the pitcher's spot, came to the plate. Manager Cal Ermer of the Twins called in Jim Kaat, who threw a wild pitch, scoring a run and moving up the runners. Causey tied the game with a fly to right. More strategy ensued. Worthington came in to pitch. Smoky Burgess pinch-hit and was intentionally passed, giving way to another pinch-runner. Buford was also walked, to set up the force at all bases, and Pete Ward, the twelfth Chicago player to appear in this one-third of an inning, came to the plate. He had been hitless in his previous twenty-one times at bat, but he lined the 2–2 pitch smartly off Killebrew's glove and trotted to first, clapping his hands over his head all the way, as the scoreboard rocket display went off. Afterward, in the noisy Chicago clubhouse, I saw two Chicago coaches, Kerby Farrell and Marv Grissom, sitting silently side by side in front of their lockers. They had their pants and spikes off, their feet were propped up, and they were comfortably balancing paper cups of beer on their stomachs. Their seamed, down-home country faces were still alight with the game. As I passed, Farrell nodded his head once and said, "Humdinger."

The next day, a summery Sunday afternoon, Stanky got his sweep as Gary Peters shut out the Twins with four hits and won, 4–0. The cheerful, family crowd got as much pleasure from the scoreboard as from the game; it showed the Tigers losing to Washington, and the Red Sox in the process of dropping their third straight to Baltimore. The Tigers now led Chicago by half a game and the Twins and Red Sox by one, and I passed the time during my flight to Detroit that night trying to fathom the recently announced schedule for post-season playoffs that might be needed to determine a winner; it listed eleven different possibilities for the teams and sites involved in two-way, three-way, or four-way playoffs. The World Series might never come.

There was an enormous, noisy crowd the next night for the first of the Tigers' two-game series with Boston, and Tiger Stadium instantly justified its reputation as a hitters' park when the Red Sox jumped off to a three-run lead in the first. But no lead and no pitcher was safe for long on this particular evening; the hits flew through the night air like enraged deerflies, and the infielders seemed to be using their gloves mostly in self-defense. The Tigers tied it in the second with a cluster of hits, including a homer by Norm Cash, but the Red Sox instantly went one up, 4–3, after Ya-strzemski's bulletlike single up the middle nearly nailed the second baseman on the ear. Cash's second homer retied it in the sixth, and then the rackety, exhausting contest seemed settled by Kaline's single and Northrup's double in the eighth, which put the home side in front for the first time. Just before that, though, in the Boston half of the eighth, there had been an extraordinary moment of baseball. With none out and Petrocelli at first and Dalton Jones on third, the Boston catcher, Russ Gibson, hit a sharp grounder to Dick McAuliffe at second. McAuliffe glanced once at third, freezing Jones there. Petrocelli, hoping for a rundown that would permit the run to score, stopped dead on the basepath, and McAuliffe, ball in hand, ran him back toward first, tagged him, and stepped on the bag in time to retire Gibson for an unassisted double play at first base. No one in the park — at least, none of the ballplayers and none of the sportswriters — had ever seen a play like it.

Yastrzemski came up in the ninth with one out and none on. He already had two hits for the night, and was in the homestretch of an extraordinary season at the plate and in the field, which had made him the favorite to win the Most Valuable Player award in his league. Boston sportswriters, however, are famously unimpressionable, especially when the Red Sox are behind. "Go on!" one of them shouted bitterly from the press box at this moment. "Prove you're the M.V.P.! Prove it to *me!* Hit a homer!" Yastrzemski hit a homer. In the tenth, Dalton Jones, a part-time infielder inserted in the Red Sox' lineup that night only because he hits mysteriously well in Tiger Stadium, won it, 6–5, with another homer. There were some seven hundred members of the Polish National Alliance staying at my hotel, and the delegates' celebrations in the lobby that night made it clear that Yaz's homer, his fortieth of the year, had been voted the finest Polish-American Achievement since Cornel Wilde wrote the "Polonaise Militaire."

The next evening's game, mercifully, was a more languid affair, in which the Tigers kept putting men on base and allowing them to die there. In the third, they hit three successive singles without issue. The Sox had managed one scratchy run in the early going, but the Tigers' fine left-hander, Mickey Lolich, was striking out Boston batters in clusters, and he seemed sure of his seventh straight win after Jim Northrup hit a prodigious two-run homer onto the roof, ninety feet above the right-field wall. Detroit loaded the bases in the eighth with none out but again failed to score, and its lead was somehow only 2–1 when Jerry Adair led off the Boston ninth with a single. Lolich, working like a man opening a basket of cobras, walked Yastrzemski, and then George Scott, after botching up two tries at a sacrifice, singled up the middle to tie it. Earl Wilson, the ace of the Detroit staff, came on in relief for the first time in the year, and gave up a sacrifice to Reggie Smith and an intentional pass to Jones. He then threw a wild pitch, and Yastrzemski sailed in from third. Gibson's fly scored Scott, who slid under Kaline's peg in a cloud of dust and unbelieving silence. Boston won the game, 4–2, and I came home with my first solid conviction about the pennant race: The Tigers could not win it.

No one, it appeared, wanted that pennant in the end. The four teams fell toward the wire in a flurry of failures, in one stretch losing ten out of twelve games against weaker clubs. With three days to go, the White Sox needed only wins against the Athletics and Senators to make up their one-game deficit. Chicago, pitching its two aces,

Gary Peters and Joel Horlen, lost both ends of a doubleheader to Kansas City on Wednesday, and then fell out of the race when it lost to the Senators two nights later. That coup de grâce administered by the A's, a last-place club that had lost both its franchise and its manager in recent weeks, was an act of defiant pride that everyone in baseball, with the possible exception of Eddie Stanky, could admire. Three teams, then, for the final weekend. Minnesota, a game up on Boston, could eliminate the Red Sox by winning either of its two games at Fenway Park. The Tigers, facing two doubleheaders at home against the Angels, would gain at least a tie and playoff by sweeping the four games.

There was perhaps less expectancy than gratitude in the enormous crowd that threw itself into Fenway Park that sunny Saturday. The possibility of winning two games from the Twins while the Tigers lost two looked to be beyond even New England hopes, but there was the plain joy of being there and seeing the old, low-roofed, country-style grandstand and the humpbacked bleachers choked with that enormous sitting and standing assemblage of zealots, all there to shout for the team that had given them such a summer. There was a flurry of governors and dignitaries behind the home dugout, and a much more interesting swarm of kids balanced precariously on top of an immense Old Grand Dad billboard across the street behind the left-field fence. That pale-green, too close fence looked dangerous today — a target for the Twins' Harmon Killebrew, who was tied with Yastrzemski for the homerun lead, at forty-three each.

Then the game began, and all the Twins looked dangerous. They scored an instant run off Santiago in the top of the first, and only a line drive out to the third baseman saved further damage. Jim Kaat, the Twins' enormous left-hander, struck out four of the first nine Boston batters, looking as formidable as he did two years ago, when he beat Sandy Koufax in a World Series game. Kaat's last strikeout, however, was an immense misfortune for the Twins, because he pulled a tendon in his pitching arm and was forced to leave the game. The import of this blow, however, was not immediately visible. Kaat's replacement, Jim Perry, went on fanning the home side, while Santiago continued his anxious-making practice of pitching into and barely out of appalling jams.

It was still 1–0, Twins, when Reggie Smith led off the Boston fifth with a double to the left-field wall, and then Dalton Jones, pinch-hitting, was miraculously safe when his grounder to Carew suddenly leaped up and struck the second baseman in the face. Adair tied the game with a soft Texas leaguer. Yastrzemski then sent a low shot that went past the diving Killebrew but was fielded by Carew in short right. Perry, perhaps still brooding about Boston luck, failed to cover first, leaving no one for Carew to throw to, and the Sox led, 2–1. The Twins tied it in the sixth, but Perry vanished, necessarily, for a pinch-hitter, and George Scott bombed reliever Ron Kline's first pitch into the center-field stands. Baseball luck creates intolerable pressure in a close game, and in the seventh the pressure of the luck and the tie destroyed the Twins. Mike Andrews was safe on a topped roller that trickled about twenty feet toward third, and a moment later shortstop Zoilo Versalles dropped Kline's peg in the middle of an easy double play, making all hands safe. All hands then came home on Yastrzemski's homer off Jim Merritt, which landed beyond the bullpen, and the Red Sox players, leading by 6–2, attempted to pound their hero into biscuit dough as he returned to the dugout. The ensuing Fenway din was diminished only faintly when Killebrew hit a two-run homer over the screen in the ninth off Gary Bell, tying Yaz for the title and bringing the game back to 6–4. It ended that way, but I had to wait until almost nine o'clock that night before my hunch about the Tigers was rejustified, via TV, as they lost their second game. Now there was one day left.

There was no reticence in Boston the next day. A woman calling the Ritz-Carlton that morning suddenly found herself in conversation with the hotel telephone operator, who exclaimed, "What if the bases had been loaded when Killebrew hit that ball? My heart can't *stand* it!" Bad nerves took me to Fenway Park early, and on the way I spotted an empty hearse with a fresh "GO, SOX!" sticker on the rear bumper. At the ball park, several hundred reporters could watch Ricky Williams, the manager's ten-year-old son, working out in uniform at first base during batting practice. I took this to be a last, brilliant managerial hunch by his father: Ricky had accompanied the squad during its all-winning road trip in July. "Look at him," Ken Harrelson said admiringly as the boy made a nifty, Gil Hodges pickup. "The kid has all the moves."

The big boys played the game, though — Chance against Lonborg

— and the weight of it kept the crowd silent. The weight of it also seemed too much for the Red Sox. In the top of the first, Killebrew walked and Oliva doubled, and George Scott, relaying, threw the ball over the catcher's head for the first Minnesota run. In the third, there was another walk, and Yastrzemski let Killebrew's single into left field hop between his legs for another error and another run. The Red Sox managed a hit in each of the first four innings but could not advance the runners. Lonborg pitched on grimly, keeping the ball low. The immense crowd was so quiet that one could hear the snarling and baying of the Minnesota bench wolves between every pitch. The scoreboard reported Detroit ahead in its first game.

It was still 2–0 for the outlanders when Lonborg, leading off the sixth, laid down a sudden bunt on the first pitch and hoofed it out. Adair hit the next pitch through second. Dalton Jones fouled off his first attempt at a sacrifice bunt and then, seeing Killebrew and Tovar, the third baseman, charging in like cavalrymen, socked the next pitch past Tovar and into left, to load the bases for Yaz with none out. The screeching in the park was almost insupportable: "*Go! Go! GO!*" Yastrzemski tied the game with a single up the middle. When the count went to three and two on Harrelson, Yaz took off with the pitch, arriving at second just before Harrelson's high chopper got to Versalles behind the bag; utterly unstrung, Versalles threw home, far too late to get anybody. Dean Chance, unstrung, departed. Worthington, unstrung, came in and threw two wild pitches, letting in another run. The fifth scored when Reggie Smith's hot grounder bounced off the unstrung (or perhaps only unhappy) Killebrew's knee.

It was growing dark, but the dangerous season had one or two moments left. Jerry Adair collided with the oncoming Versalles on the basepath in the eighth, but held on to the ball and flipped out of the dust to first for a double play. The Twins, still fighting, followed with two singles. Allison then lined a hit to left; Yastrzemski charged the ball, hesitated only an instant at the sight of the runner racing for home, and then threw brilliantly to second to cut down the flying Allison. You could see it all happening in the same twilight instant — the ball coming in a deadly line, and Allison's desperate, skidding slide, and the tag, and the umpire's arm shooting up, and the game and the season saved. One more inning, and then there was nothing more to be saved except Lonborg, who had to be extricated — sans sweatshirt, buttons, and cap — from the hands of the local citizenry, who evidently wanted to mount him in the State House beside the sacred cod.

The Boston locker room presented a classic autumn scene — shouts, embraces, beer showers, shaving cream in the hair, television lights, statements to the press. ("Never," said Lonborg, "do I remember a more . . . ecstatic and . . . *vigorous* moment.") But then it all sagged and stopped, for this was still only a half triumph. Detroit had won its first game, and now we had to wait for the radio news of the second game to know whether this was the pennant or whether there would be a playoff with the Tigers the next afternoon.

During that long, painful interval in the clubhouse, there was time to look back on Yastrzemski's season. He had won the triple crown — a batting average of .326, a hundred and twenty-one runs batted in, forty-four homers — but this was not all. Other fine hitters, including Frank Robinson last season, had finished with comparable statistics. But no other player in memory had so clearly pushed a team to such a height in the final days of a difficult season. The Allison peg was typical of Yastrzemski's ardent outfield play. In the final two weeks at the plate, Yaz had hammered twenty-three hits in forty-four times at bat, including four doubles and five home runs, and had driven in sixteen runs. In those two games against the Twins, he went seven for eight and hit a game-winning homer. This sort of performance would be hard to countenance in a Ralph Henry Barbour novel, and I found it difficult to make the connection between the epic and the person of the pleasant, twenty-eight-year-old young man of unheroic dimensions who was now explaining to reporters, with articulate dispassion, that his great leap forward this year might have been the result of a small change in batting style — a blocking of the right hip and a slightly more open stance — which was urged on him in spring training by Ted Williams. There was something sad here — perhaps the thought that for Yastrzemski, more than for anyone else, this summer could not come again. He had become a famous star, with all the prizes and ugly burdens we force on the victims of celebrity, and from now on he would be set apart from us and his teammates and the easy time of his youth.

Detroit led for a while in its last game, and then the Angels caught up and went ahead, but the clubhouse maternity ward was an unhappy place. Players in bits and pieces of uniform pretended to play cards, pretended to sleep. Then, at last, it was the ninth inning, with the Angels leading, 8–5, and the Red Sox formed a silent circle all staring up at the radio on the wall. The Tigers put men on base, and I could see the strain of every pitch on the faces around me. Suddenly there was a double-play ball that might end it, and when the announcer said, ". . . over to first, *in* time for the out," every one of the Boston players came off the floor and straight up into the air together, like a ballet troupe. Players and coaches and reporters and relatives and owner Yawkey and manager Williams hugged and shook hands and hugged again, and I saw Ricky Williams trying to push through the mob to get at his father. He was crying. He reached him at last and jumped into his arms and kissed him again and again; he could not stop kissing him. The champagne arrived in a giant barrel of ice, and for an instant I was disappointed with Mr. Yawkey when I saw that it was Great Western. But I had forgotten what pennant champagne is for. In two minutes, the clubhouse looked like a Y.M.C.A. water-polo meet, and it was everybody into the pool.

A professional sport so constructed that four out of ten teams can still be in hot contention in the final three days of a hundred-and-sixty-two-game season would seem to be a paragon of aesthetic and commercial endeavor. It is possible that the only people in North America who do not hold this view of baseball at the moment are the big-league owners who are currently engaged in a scheme to dismantle their Parthenon. As matters now stand, it is almost certain that in 1971, when the current three-year television contracts expire, both leagues will be expanded from ten to twelve clubs and subdivided into six-team regional conferences; each team will continue to play all the other teams in its league (with the added possibility of a few inter-league contests, to whet midsummer appetites), but the standings will determine only conference champions. Two playoffs will then precede the World Series (or "Super Series," perhaps), with the excellent possibility that at least one pre-playoff playoff will be needed to settle one of the four conference races. The fact that the artificially constructed sub-leagues will most surely produce some inferior champions is of no concern to these planners. What they see is more money and more prizes for all — the initial freshet of dollars that accompanies the appearance of each new, weak franchise team in an expanded league, and the guarantee of three autumn extravaganzas instead of one.

The magnet that is about to pull baseball into this tortured shape is television. The immense sports-television business has never been happy with baseball, which so far includes only two high-revenue packages — the All-Star game and the Series — each year. Moreover, the game does not produce tidy, two-hour segments of marketable time; a nationally televised midsummer Saturday game may creep along into the early evening, and it cannot be puffed up by advance billing, since the meaning of its outcome may not become apparent until late in September. This is almost intolerable to the young men in blazers who run sports TV; their dream is fifty weekends of world championships — in football, in baseball, in surfing, in Senior Women's Marbles, in anything — that are *not to be missed* by the weekend watcher. Every real fan senses, of course, that baseball's long, chancy season perfectly matches the slow, tension-building pace of the game on the field. He knows that baseball is so difficult a game that the worst team in any league is almost a match for the best, and thus a long schedule is necessary to determine a true champion. None of this appears to be of much import to the television industry or the baseball owners, who now propose to replace skill and courage by luck and promotion.

My objections, I am certain, will cut no ice with most baseball magnates, whose instant response to criticism of this nature is to smile and say, "Well, I'm in this for the money, of course." Of course. Baseball is a commercial venture, but it is one of such perfect equipoise that millions of us every year can still unembarrassedly surrender ourselves to its unique and absorbing joys. The ability to find beauty and involvement in artificial commercial constructions is essential to most of us in the modern world; it is the life-giving naiveté. But naiveté is not gullibility, and those who alter baseball for their quick and selfish purposes will find, I believe, that they are the owners of teams without a following and of a sport devoid of passion. They will find that they own only a business.

*   *   *

Cardinal fans who have managed to keep their seats through this interminable first feature will probably not be placated by my delayed compliments to their heroes. The Cardinals not only were the best ball club I saw this season but struck me as being in many ways the most admirable team I can remember in recent years. The new champions have considerable long-ball power, but they know the subtleties of opposite-field hitting, base running, and defense that are the delight of the game. Their quickness is stimulating, their batting strength is distributed menacingly throughout the lineup (they won the Series with almost no help from their No. 4 and No. 5 hitters, Cepeda and McCarver, while their seventh-place batter, Javier, batted .360), they are nearly impregnable in up-the-middle defense, and their pitching was strong enough to win them a pennant even though their ace, Bob Gibson, was lost for the second half of the season after his right leg was broken by a line drive. In retrospect, the wonder of the Series is that the Cards did not make it a runaway, as they so often seemed on the point of doing.

Fenway Park was a different kind of place on the first day of the Series. Ceremonies and bunting and boxfuls of professional Series-goers had displaced the anxious watchers of the weekend. Yastrzemski, staring behind the dugout before the game, said, "Where *is* everybody? These aren't the people who were here all summer." The game quickly produced its own anxieties, however, when Lou Brock, the Cardinals' lead-off man, singled in the first and stole second on the next pitch. Though we did not recognize it, this was only a first dose of what was to follow throughout the Series, for Brock was a tiny little time pill that kept going off at intervals during the entire week. He failed to score that time, but he led off the third with another single, zipped along to third on Flood's double, and scored on Maris's infield out. The Cardinals kept threatening to extinguish Santiago, the Red Sox starter, but bad St. Louis luck and good Boston fielding kept it close. Gibson, hardly taking a deep breath between pitches, was simply overpowering, throwing fast balls past the hitters with his sweeping right-handed delivery, which he finishes with a sudden lunge toward first base. He struck out six of the first ten batters to face him and seemed unaffronted when Santiago somehow got his bat in the path of one of his pitches and lofted the ball into the screen in left-center. It was a one-sided but still tied ball game when Brock led off the seventh (he was perpetually leading

off, it seemed) with another single, stole second again, went to third
on an infield out, and scored on Roger Maris's deep bouncer to second. That 2–1 lead was enough for Gibson, who blew the Boston
batters down; he struck out Petrocelli three times, on ten pitches.
The crowd walking out in the soft autumn sunshine seemed utterly
undisappointed. They had seen their Sox in a Series game at last,
and that was enough.

Five members of the Red Sox had signed up to write byline stories
about the Series for the newspapers, and Jim Lonborg, not yet ready
to pitch after his Sunday stint, kept notes for his column as he sat on
the bench during the opener. He must have remembered to look at
those earlier memoranda on his glove, however, for his first pitch of
the second game flew rapidly in the suddenly vacated environs of
Lou Brock's neck. It was Lonborg's only high pitch of the afternoon,
and was fully as effective in its own way as the knee-high curves and
sinking fast balls he threw the rest of the way. None of the Cardinals reached first until Flood walked in the seventh, and by that
time Yastrzemski had stroked a curving drive into the seats just
past the right-field foul pole for one run, and two walks and an
error had brought in another for the Beantowners. There were
marvelous fielding plays by both teams — Brock and Javier for the
Cards, Petrocelli and Adair for the Sox — to keep the game taut, and
then Yaz, who had taken extra batting practice right after the first
game, hit another in the seventh: a three-run job, way, *way* up in the
bleachers. After that, there was nothing to stay for except the excruciating business of Lonborg's possible no-hitter. He was within four
outs of it when Javier doubled, solidly and irretrievably, in the
eighth, to the accompaniment of a 35,188-man groan. (Lonborg
said later that it felt exactly like being in an automobile wreck.)
When Lonborg came in after that inning, the crowd stood and
clapped for a long, respectful two minutes, like the audience at a
Horowitz recital.

Everyone in St. Louis was ready for the third game except the
scoreboard-keeper, who initially had the Cardinals playing Detroit.
More than fifty-four thousand partisans, the biggest sporting crowd
in local history, arrived early at Busch Memorial Stadium, most of
them bearing heraldic devices honoring "El Birdos" — a relentlessly
publicized neologism supposedly coined by Orlando Cepeda.

Home-town pride was also centered on El Ballparko, a steep, elegant gray concrete pile that forms part of the new downtown complex being built around the celebrated Saarinen archway. I admired everything about this open-face mine except its shape, which is circular and thus keeps all upper-deck patrons at a dismaying distance from the infielders within the right angles of the diamond. The game, like its predecessors, went off like a firecracker, with Lou Brock tripling on the first pitch of the home half. After two innings, Gary Bell, the Boston starter, was allowed to sit down, having given up five hits and three runs to the first nine Cardinal batters. That was the ball game, it turned out (the Cards won, 5–2), but there were some memorable diversions along the way. Nelson Briles, the Cards' starter, decked Yastrzemski in the first with a pitch that nailed him on the calf. Lou Brock, having led off the sixth with a single, got himself plunked in the back with a justifiably nervous pick-off throw by pitcher Lee Stange, and chugged along to third, from where he scored on a single by Maris. *L'affaire Yaz* was the subject of extended seminars with the press after the game. St. Louis manager Red Schoendienst stated that inside pitches were part of the game but that his little band of clean-living Americans did not know how to hit batters on purpose. Pitcher Briles stated that the sight of Yastrzemski caused him to squeeze the ball too hard and thus lose control of its direction. (He had improved afterward, not walking a man all day.) Manager Williams pointed out that a pitcher wishing to hit a batter, as against merely startling him, will throw not at his head but behind his knees, which was the address on Briles' special-delivery package. This seemed to close the debate locally, but that night the publisher of the Manchester, New Hampshire, *Union Leader* wrote an editorial demanding that the Cardinals be forced to forfeit the game, "as an indication that the great American sport of baseball will not allow itself to be besmirched by anyone who wants to play dirty ball."

The great American sport survived it all, but it almost expired during the next game, a 6–0 laugher played on a windy, gray winter afternoon. The Cardinals had all their runs after the first three innings, and the only man in the park who found a way to keep warm was Brock, who did it by running bases. He beat out a third-base tap in the first and went on to score, and subsequently doubled off the wall and stole another base. Gibson, the winner, was not as fast as he had been in the opener, but his shutout won even more admiration from the Red Sox batters, who had discovered that he was not merely a thrower but a pitcher.

The Red Sox, now one game away from extinction, looked doomed after that one, but Yastrzemski pointed out to me that most of his teammates, being in their early twenties, had the advantage of not recognizing the current odds against them. "Lonborg goes tomorrow," he said, "and then it's back to Boston, back to the lion's den." Lonborg went indeed, in a marvelously close and absorbing game that I watched mostly through Kleenex, having caught a pip of a cold in the winter exercises of the previous day. Two former Yankees settled it. In the Boston ninth, Elston Howard, who can no longer get his bat around on fast balls, looped a dying single to right to score two runs — a heartwarming and, it turned out, essential piece of luck, because Roger Maris hit a homer in the bottom half, to end Lonborg's string of seventeen scoreless innings. Maris, freed from his recent years of Yankee Stadium opprobrium, was having a brilliant Series.

Laid low by too much baseball and a National League virus, I was unable to make it back to the lion's den, and thus missed the noisiest and most exciting game of the Series. I saw it on television, between sneezes and commercials. This was the game, it will be recalled, in which the Red Sox led by 1–0, trailed by 2–1, rallied to 4–2, were tied at 4–4, and won finally, 8–4, burying the Cardinal relief pitchers with six hits and four runs in the seventh. Brock had a single, a stolen base, and a home run. Yastrzemski had two singles and a left-field homer. Reggie Smith hit a homer; Rico Petrocelli hit *two* homers. This was the first Series game since the Cardinal-Yankee encounters in 1964 in which any team rallied to recapture a lost lead, which may account for the rather stately nature of most of the recent fall classics. My admiration went out not only to the Red Sox, for evening the Series after being two games down, but to Dick Williams, for having the extraordinary foresight to start a young pitcher named Gary Waslewski, who had spent most of the season in the minors, had not started a Boston game since July 29th, and had never completed a game in the major leagues. Waslewski didn't finish this one, either, but he held the Cards off until the sixth, which was enough. Williams' choice, which would have exposed him to venomous second-guessing if it had backfired, is the kind of courageous, intelligent patchworking that held his young, lightly manned team together over such an immense distance. In the opinion of a good many baseball people, his managerial performance this year is the best since Leo Durocher's miracles with the Giants in the early nineteen-fifties.

Nothing could keep me away from the final game of the year, the obligatory scene in which Lonborg, on only two days' rest, would face Gibson at last. Fenway Park, packed to the rafters, seemed so quiet in the early innings that I at first attributed the silence to my stuffed-up ears. It was real, though — the silence of foreboding that descended on all of us when Lou Brock hit a long drive off Lonborg in the first, which Yastrzemski just managed to chase down. Lonborg, when he is strong and his fast ball is dipping, does not give up high-hit balls to enemy batters in the early going. After that, everyone sat there glumly and watched it happen. Maxvill, the unferocious Cardinal shortstop, banged a triple off the wall in the third and then scored, and another run ensued when Lonborg uncorked a wild pitch. In time, it grew merely sad, and almost the only sounds in the park were the cries and horns from Cardinal owner Gussie Busch's box, next to the St. Louis dugout. Lonborg, pushing the ball and trying so hard that at times his cap flew off, gave up a homer to Gibson in the fifth, and then Brock singled, stole second, stole third, and came in on a fly by Maris. A fire broke out in a box-car parked on a railway siding beyond left field, and several dozen sportswriters, looking for their leads, scribbled the note, ". . . as Boston championship hopes went up in smoke." Manager Williams, out of pitchers and ideas, stayed too long with his exhausted hero, and Javier hit a three-run homer in the sixth to finish Lonborg and end the long summer's adventure. The final score was 7–2. Gibson, nearly worn out at the end, held on and finished, winning his fifth successive Series victory (counting two against the Yankees in 1964), and the Cardinals had the championship they deserved. I visited both clubhouses, but I had seen enough champagne and emotion for one year, and I left quickly. Just before I went out to hunt for a cab, though, I ducked up one of the runways for a last look around Fenway Park, and discovered several thousand fans still sitting in the sloping stands around me. They sat there quietly, staring out through the half darkness at the littered, empty field and the big wall and the flagpoles. They were mourning the Red Sox and the end of the great season.

Angell's annual summations of the baseball season for The New Yorker *are now considered classics. This is the one that first got everyone's attention, for the Red Sox and the American League pennant race provided the perfect subject and unmatched drama for Angell's penetrating retelling.*

A POSTCARD FROM MY BROTHER

from *Yankee*, October 1992

We were walking up Brookline Avenue, the gang and I, looking for a not-too-crowded place where we could grab some burgers and beer, where we could trade some lies and talk some baseball.

It was nearing midnight. The tourists and the college boys having gone home, we veteran, not-so-proper Bostonian sportswriters now had the Cask 'N Flagon, across the street from Fenway Park, to ourselves. "Sit wherever you want," said our waitress, not bothering to meet our eyes as she walked by, and we chose a booth along the right-hand wall, past the jukebox.

Nice place, this place. The Cask 'N Flagon has had different names and different owners over the years — its doors opened in 1947, with some misguided optimist calling the place the Pennant Grille — but it's always been a have-one-on-me joint, a Sam Malone kind of bar long before there was a Sam Malone.

Like the old ball yard across the street, it has nooks and crannies. The place is drunk with old baseball pictures of various shapes and sizes, and chance (as in fate, not Dean or Frank) deposited us at a booth that sits beneath a huge reminder of the 1967 season. There, above the booth and under the glass, were the Red Sox, spilling out onto the Fenway turf to celebrate the Impossible Dream. Rico Petrocelli had only moments before wrapped his glove around a soft liner off the bat of one Rich Rollins, and now, in this picture, there was madness on the lawn — happy fans pouring onto the field, arms and legs flying in every direction as they pursued the game's hero, right-hander Jim Lonborg.

Lonborg has his back to the camera, but he is easily identified; he is, after all, the most beloved Number 16 who ever wore a Red Sox uniform, certainly more famous than Emerson Dickman (1938–1941), Harry Dorish (1956), or Bob Zupcic (1991), though not as great a pitcher as Ellis Kinder (1948–1955). That's Ken Harrelson behind Lonborg, jubilant yet determined to escape the mob, and off to the left Carl Yastrzemski can be seen disappearing into the madness. Another player, his cap already liberated by a fan-turned-souvenir-hunter, is reaching in toward Lonborg. It looks very much like Dalton Jones. But it could be Jerry Adair. Hard to tell. There are other players. There is a man wearing what appears to be a five o'clock shadow. There is a Number 31, a coach maybe, using his left hand to hold down his own cap lest it, too, be liberated by a fan. There is a catcher, pulling off his mask as he walks out of the frame. Mike Ryan? Russ Gibson?

We did the burger-and-beer thing with our waitress, but kept talking about that long-ago season, how it truly was an Impossible Dream, how things seemed so much more innocent and jaunty in those days before cable television, mega-contracts, and George Steinbrenner. The Red Sox came from ninth place in 1966 to a pennant in 1967, clinching a tie for first place on the final day of the season when Lonborg beat Dean Chance and the Minnesota Twins. Later in the afternoon, when everybody's radio screamed the news from out west that the California Angels had defeated the Detroit Tigers, the pennant was Boston's. Is that impossible or what? The mob scene on the field, all those zanies celebrating a tie and now hoping for a Detroit loss as they did their dancing, was itself hauled in by some photographer who had his camera aimed at the pitcher's mound.

And then came a memorable World Series against the St. Louis Cardinals. The Cardinals, led by Bob Gibson, took the Series in seven games.

I kept looking, my eyes wandering, my mind wandering. "My brother was at that game," I finally said. "He went with his friend Larry. I wanted to go too, real bad, but my father wouldn't let me. He said the place would be a madhouse if the Sox won, and he didn't want me over there. I was only 11. Paul was 14. So Paul got to go. He and Larry Papalambros. I stayed home."

Again, my eyes and mind wandered. Paul never did let me forget about that day, how he and Larry jumped over the railing after the final out had been made, how they danced on the Fenway lawn and helped celebrate the Impossible Dream. Being part of it all, being part of history. He was there and I was in Cambridge, watching the game on our junky old black-and-white television, and Paul couldn't resist rubbing it in.

There was no real emotion in my voice as I spoke these words. I was just telling a story; we were just a bunch of guys eating hamburgers and drinking beer. There were interruptions; there were other stories. Somebody mentioned that Jerry Remy, who would one day play for the Red Sox, was also on the field that day, just another kid among the masses.

The last time I was alone with Paul was in November of 1987. I would see him several times after that — at Christmas, at our mother's house, at his house — but this was our last night out together, just the two of us. We talked about a lot of things that night, from jobs and family to houses and cars. He had my aunt's old license plate, and I had my aunt's old clock, and I observed that in this respect I had made out better.

We talked about baseball. We talked about his three boys, all of them baseball-fed from birth. I had just returned from covering the World Series in Minnesota, and I had a present for him: one of those Homer Hankies that had been all the rage in the Twin Cities during the series. Paul thanked me, and then, in the same breath, he reminded me that he was on the field the day the Red Sox realized their Impossible Dream. OK?

Three months later, Paul was driving to Springfield for a business meeting. It was one of those freak accidents. An 18-wheeler in the eastbound lane of the Massachusetts Turnpike blew out a tire, and somehow the tire careened across the median into the westbound lane. Paul, 34 years old, too young and too good a man to be in the wrong place at the wrong time, died instantly.

These were the thoughts that raced through my head as the eyes and the mind wandered. Homer Hankies. Basketball games. The Impossible Dream. Paul. And Paul dying. And then I stopped — and pointed at the wall.

For there, in the photo, in this big, framed burst of energy from 1967, was Paul.

He is right there, about ten feet to the right of Jim Lonborg, throwing his right arm over the shoulder of the player with the five o'clock shadow. He is right there, and there next to him is Larry Papalambros, who seems to be looking away, toward the first-base dugout. He is right there, just as he always said he was.

I had been staring at the photo for five minutes before Paul came into view, but now there was no mistaking it. Paul! His entire body is visible. He is smiling, maybe even shouting at the man with the five o'clock shadow. Paul always was a neat, precise dresser, but this moment catches him in disarray: his collar appears to be crooked, and his shirt is untucked in the front, these no doubt being casualties of the leap over the railing. He is excited, happy. And why not? He is there. And he does not have his kid brother tagging along, getting in the way, being a pest.

I would absolutely track down a copy of this photograph, I announced, but our waitress did not know who owned the negative. The manager had only a name, a Dennis Brearley. "He used to be a photographer with one of the papers," the manager said. I checked up on this Dennis Brearley. He had been a newspaper photographer, most recently with the Boston Herald, but now he was a businessman, a collector and seller of old black-and-white photographs. He had collected thousands of old black-and-white negatives that might otherwise have been destroyed years ago, and he turned a passion into a business. When people want photographs of Boston's landmarks, sports heroes, and political rascals, they call Dennis Brearley.

When I told Brearley my name and why I wanted the photo, he laughed softly. He asked me if I owned a framed picture of a 1917 game at Fenway Park. Puzzled, I told him I did own such a picture, that it was hanging in my den. I told him the picture had been a gift from my brother.

"I know," Brearley said. "That picture came from my studio. I knew your brother very well. We were in the same bowling league. I remember when he came in to order that photo. You were moving or something, right?"

I was moving to Seattle. Paul and his wife, Susan, gave me the picture the night before I left. Brearley now made a heroic attempt to find the negative of that 1967 scene from Fenway Park. He pulled out a dozen different frames depicting the postgame madness —

shots of Yastrzemski, shots of Red Sox manager Dick Williams, shots of Petrocelli after he made his historic catch, shots of the crowd — but he could not find the negative I was seeking. It wasn't where it should have been. It was gone. "It's here somewhere," Brearley said. "I'll find it."

Weeks passed. Finally one day there came a telephone call from the soft-spoken Brearley. Remember Dalton Jones? The onetime reserve infielder had seen the same picture several months earlier, in the same bar, at the same booth, and he recognized himself. It was indeed Dalton Jones, not Jerry Adair, who was photographed reaching in to congratulate Jim Lonborg.

Jones had already done the same detective work I would do, leading to Dennis Brearley. A part-time player with a good glove and a .235 average to show for nine seasons in the big leagues, he never did collect much in the way of souvenirs from that historic season, and this picture, he decided, would be his memory of the Impossible Dream. He had a copy made and hung it in his financial planning office in Plymouth. It was during this transaction — Dalton Jones picking up a copy of an old baseball photograph — that the negative somehow found its way into the wrong envelope.

"It took some digging," Dennis Brearley said, "but I finally found the negative. I'll have a print for you by next week."

I met Dalton Jones for lunch. We sat in his office one summer afternoon, and we looked at the one thing we have in common. I pointed out Paul for him. He pointed out Gary Waslewski and George Scott. Number 31, said Jones, is first-base coach Bobby Doerr. And the man with the five o'clock shadow, the man who is about to have my brother's right arm thrown over his shoulder, is Boston's pitching coach, Sal (The Barber) Maglie.

We had a nice lunch, and Dalton Jones promised he'd point out my brother to anyone who asked about the picture. And I promised I'd always point out Dalton Jones to anyone who asked about the copy that now hangs in my den, next to my cherished "Curley for Mayor" poster.

I have long since stopped referring to this as a mere baseball picture. It is a postcard, really, a postcard from my brother. He is telling me things are fine, and he's still rubbing it in about Dad keeping me home that morning in 1967.

Photographs are magic. Paul is forever 14 years old in this frozen moment, forever happy, and the Boston Red Sox are forever the best team in the American League.

Part of what made 1967 so special in New England is that every fan felt personally touched by the team. Cambridge native and Boston Herald *columnist Steve Buckley was just one of thousands of such fans in 1967, and for Buckley, clearly, 1967 remains a season like no other.*

GEORGE KIMBALL

OPENING DAY AT FENWAY

from *The Phoenix,* April 1971

Years ago — only a few years ago, actually, but still years before the miracle year of 1967 and years before it became chic to root for the Red Sox — the centerfield bleachers at Fenway were traditionally the habitat of the most diehard of Sox aficionados. If the bleacherites weren't the most knowledgeable fans, they were close to it, and they were certainly the most faithful. I suspect I was exposed to more genuine baseball lore, more understandings of the subtleties and stratagems of the game, and perhaps most importantly, more sheer love for the sport by sitting exclusively in the bleachers from boyhood through my early twenties than I've encountered in any reserved seat press box since.

This, of course, was back in the days when the Red Sox were drawing so poorly that they had to schedule night games around the Hatch Shell concerts in the summer and when a gate of 20,000 on Opening Day was considered spectacular. But from April through September the coterie in center field retained a fidelity unmatched anywhere else in the American League. And while the businessmen who bought season tickets might sit next to someone in an adjacent box all season long and never exchange six words, there were people out there who'd been friends for twenty-five years yet never seen each other outside Fenway Park.

There were the beaten old men who looked like they'd just panhandled the 50 cent admission price, the retired gentlemen with their transistor radios and the truck drivers who took their shirts off on hot summer days. There were two old ladies from Dorchester, both named Mary, who attended the afternoon games as faithfully as they attended Mass. They left home early in the morning, bringing their Official Big League Scorebook along to Church, and after lunch in Kenmore Square, showed up at the park before batting practice started. They never went to night games, but the Boys from Chelsea did.

The Boys from Chelsea — three of them, Felix, Vinny, and Joe, all cab drivers, I believe, invariably turned up at night, and two or three of their friends often made it — were inveterate gamblers. They came to games weighted down with 50 cent rolls of pennies, and would wager with each other and anyone else on every conceivable facet of the game, from whether the next batter would get a hit (3 to 1 for Mantle or Williams; 6 to 1 for most pitchers) to an error on the next play (usually about 25 to 1, but you could always haggle) to the possibility of Casey Stengel being ejected during the course of the game. (If you got a bet down at the prevailing 7½ to 1 odds on Jackie Jensen hitting into a double play at every available opportunity, you usually made out over the course of a season.)

And there was Fat Howie. Fat Howie was on speaking terms with every centerfielder in the league. He'd sit right next to the rope (the section in straightaway center, directly in the batter's line of vision, *always* used to be roped off; since the space is needed now, the seats are painted green and customers are allowed to sit there, provided they wear dark clothing) and carry on a running dialogue. Howie would lean over the wall between innings and yell out to Bob Allison: *"Hey, Bob, what's happening in Cleveland?"* (The scoreboard on the left field wall can't be seen from the bleachers in center.) And Allison would check the score and holler back: *"4 to 2 Indians, Howie."* Howie was always there, day or night. I don't know what he did for a living; maybe he took his summers off.

And, of course, there was the gang I hung out with in college. We'd usually catch about 20 or 30 games a year, always going in a group of four or five and always with a case of beer. Back then there was no hassle about bringing your own beer into the bleachers; everyone did it, and probably would still be able to except for one particularly raucous occasion in the spring of 1964 when the bleachers were invaded by a few hundred Friday night beer drinkers posing as baseball fans.

Along about the sixth inning they were very drunk and very angry. The Red Sox were being humiliated by the lowly Kansas City

Athletics (commonly referred to at the time as the "Kansas City Fag-gots," since they wore bright gold suits and green trim, long before mod uniforms became fashionable), and someone heaved an empty beer can in the direction of Jose Tartabull, the A's centerfielder. An umpire ran out to retrieve it, and was greeted by a fusillade of beer cans. This brought the park police out on the field, and the shelling exploded for real. One cop was cold-cocked by a beer can — a full one — and the barrage continued for about ten minutes, abating not because the park announcer warned that the umpires were threat-ening to forfeit the game, but only because the assholes ran out of ammunition. After that they started checking you out for beer when you came through the gate, and — at 55 cents a cup — the price of drinking went up considerably in center field.

Besides me, there were 34,516 other paying customers there last week. I hadn't been to an opener at Fenway for seven years, though I caught a couple at Shea Stadium and K.C. Municipal. I looked around for Howie and the two Marys, but I didn't see them. I sus-pect they'd be pretty uncomfortable out there these days anyway; the bleachers last Tuesday were packed with a crowd that would've been indistinguishable from the occupants of the cheap seats at the Fillmore East: freaks sporting Mao buttons, long-haired college kids, high school hippies, and even teeny-boppers, with bells, beads, and blemishes.

Initially, anyway, that was relieving. For several years now I've found myself trembling whenever the National Anthem is played at sporting events, not out of patriotic sentiment but of fear that some flag-crazed lunatic sitting in back of me will be overcome by his emotions and seize the opportunity to bludgeon me from behind with his souvenir Louisville Slugger. Since the first ball on Opening Day was thrown out by a Vietnam veteran, a former POW, the new crowd did thus provide at least a reassuring measure of collective se-curity during the pre-game ceremonies, helping to compensate for the nostalgic loss of old ambience.

On the very first play of the game, Yastrzemski made an incredi-ble diving, sliding catch by the left field line off Horace Clarke's bat, rolled over and held the glove aloft. Now in the old days Jimmy Doyle from East Boston would've been yelling *"Atta boy, Carl Baby"* in his booming foghorn voice, a voice so loud that even in the middle of 35,000 fans Yaz would've heard him. But the ovation from the bleachers was only polite applause by comparison. *"That was a pretty nice catch,"* commented one of the kids behind me.

Ray Culp retired the Yankees 1-2-3 in the first, but despite two hits the Sox' half of the first was scarcely more auspicious. Luis Aparicio led off with a smash over third base, which Jerry Kenney backhanded with a superb stab observed by everyone in Fenway Park except Aparicio and first base coach Don Lenhardt, who waved Luis around toward second — directly into a rundown. Reggie Smith followed with another single but, after Yaz flied out, Reggie, the team's top base thief, was thrown out trying to steal second.

The Yankees went down in order in each of the next two innings. As the Sox trotted off the field after the third, one of the kids behind me turned to his companion and breathlessly uttered: *"He's pitching a no-hitter!"*

Now, according to every sacred tradition of the game's etiquette, this is something which is *never* mentioned aloud — particularly after only three innings have been played. I was on the verge of turning around and instructing him on the point when his friend smugly added: "He's pitching a *perfect game.*"

Fat Howie would have thrown them both over the wall.

I sat seething as the Red Sox went down 1-2-3 again, and then decided that it was time to make a beer run. "My turn," I said, and after entrusting my scorecard to the guy sitting next to me, began making my way down the aisle. I paused at the top of the runway just in time to see Thurman Munson chop a slow-roller to the third-base side of the mound.

A pitcher fleeter afoot would have handled it with ease; Sox pitching coach Harvey Haddix, about 50 now, could *still* have eaten it alive. Culp himself could probably have made the play three times out of four, but as he lumbered off the mound he not only overran the ball but momentarily blocked out Petrocelli racing in from third. Rico barehanded the ball and whipped it to first in one motion, but too late to catch Munson. An infield single; the Yankees had their first hit, and I knew exactly where the blame lay. *"Smartass punks!"* I shook my fist at them as I descended the stairs.

I returned with the beer to find Reggie Smith on second with a double and Yastrzemski coming to bat. Taking my scorecard back, I matter-of-factly threw out *"Here comes the first run of the season!,"* which would've immediately been covered at 7 to 2 by Felix or Vinny. There was no response to the challenge here, though, and naturally Yaz responded with a run-scoring double.

Between innings the guy who'd been keeping my scorecard wanted to know what the funny little illegibly-scrawled notes in the margin were all about. I briefly considered a number of spectacular fabrications, but finally admitted that I wrote for the *Phoenix* and planned to do a story of some sort about Opening Day.

"Oh yeah?" He eyed me strangely. "If you're a sportswriter why the fuck are you sittin' *here,"* he gestured toward the press box, "instead of up there?" The fact of the matter was that the Red Sox had declined to provide the paper with press tickets, but for some reason I mumbled that I liked it better in the bleachers. At one time that would've been true; today it made me twice a liar.

The middle innings were largely uneventful, except for Duane Josephson knocking Kenney squarely on his ass while breaking up a double play, and the fact that somebody nearby produced a hash pipe. Since the hash was still being circulated when the time came, the people next to me remained sitting through the seventh inning stretch, yet another tradition shot to hell. We did come up with another run in the seventh anyway. Following two singles, a sacrifice, and an intentional walk to pinchhitter Joe Lahoud, Culp hit a sure double-play to short, but John Kennedy, running for Lahoud, bowled over Clarke at second, knocking the ball away and allowing the run to score.

New York led off the eighth with their second and third hits. After an error and two putouts, the bases were loaded, two out, when Clarke stroked a base hit to right apparently certain to score two runs, but Josephson perfectly blocked the plate long enough to get Smith's throw to home and somehow the tying run was out at the plate. *"Perfect throw,"* approved one of the morons behind me. It was *not* a perfect throw; it bounced three times and Scott almost cut it off and the runner had it beaten by at least ten feet had Josephson not had his body in the way.

The Sox scored their third run the way they are supposed to be scored: Yaz singled, went to third on a single by Rico, and came home on Scott's sacrifice fly. Unspectacular, but it is the sort of thing that games are won by. Just as I'd called Josephson a "mediocre catcher" in print that morning — he came through with three hits and that key play at the plate that afternoon — I also picked the Sox to finish second behind Baltimore. One game does not a season make, but I'm looking forward to having reason to revise both assessments. I'm also looking for a new place to sit.

The counterculture embraced the Red Sox after 1967. George Kimball, writing for the alternative Phoenix, *was the first Boston writer to reach these new fans, not covering the game as much as he did the entire scene. Kimball went on to join the* Boston Herald, *where he remains as a columnist, focusing on boxing and golf.*

GEORGE FRAZIER

TIBIALIBUS RUBRIS XV, EBORACUM NOVUM V

from *The Boston Globe,* April 7, 1973

Quamquam nos incipimus beguinam rursus eo tempore variatas est. Eo tempore nos incipimus tempestatem globi castrorum quae iam est aequa ante globus iacietur optima omnium tempestatum, postea MCCMXLV, ubi Alexandrus Cartwrightus quem nulla provincia sciet invenit ludum ab inferis. Nondico scilicet modum quo globus castrorum ludetur eo anno (quod nulla tempestas sine Roberto Clemente unquam poterit esse eleganta quam eos quos unxit cum sanctitate et gracia eorum artorum), sed novam observantiam datur conlusoribus ab dominis suis. Gradatim nos videmus finem plantari sodalitatis quae mercenarius globus parvorum castrorum erat postea suum initium.

Naturaliter, non dici magnum non manere quod deberetur facere subsidiaria pars. Ut punica delenda est. Etiam Bowie Kuhn et Joe Cronin tres erunt sed vah quomodo potentes occiderunt. Croninus olim tam adrogans in perversu sui protestatis nunc est solim figura dum Kuhnus factus est res inrisionis! Inter eos quos flagellabat quod ei non dixerunt domine. Parvus tristis Bowieus Kuhnus qui ubi sanctimonie temptavit persuadere duos obstinatos conlusor es yankium delere ea consilia reconstitutere levem curam rei domesticiae, iussitur adsedere et quies esse. Atque iupitere supreme fecit.

Adhuc globus parvorum castrorum semper erat frustum fallaciae — et gratias agero vobis abnerare mihi, primum iacolavum in castram sumteram sed est nullam demonstratidnem ut eus etiam adesset ludus globi. Praeterea dum Cartwrightus aut quisquis suus nomen erat probabaliter inveniverit globum parvorum castrorum quam id scimus hodie, est testimonium ut berberi in septentrionali africanti ludeverint ludum singulariter similiter nostrum quam iam dudum quam vi anni ante christi natalem diem, Hoyti Wilhelmi aut Luis Aparicioni aut soli spinki. Quam pro spinkos geminos commodum mimos habueram premetos tam debebitis cognoscere pro te ipse. Utcumque diversitas magna erat berberi non habuerunt sliderum, vestitus militares hitexetos aut Davidus Eisenhowerus. Sed autem habuerunt graves clavas et comas similes Keni Harrelsonis.

Tum vero sollicitudo est globi castrorum familiae ad contagionem externum ludi ut effeciveret ut MCMIV double died constitutus sit inventorem gibi castrorum acutus motus cum eo tempore esset mortius nimis se defendere. Sed ne capite meum verbum ei. Id suspicite in iucundo libro homo qui globum castrorum invenit ab Haroldus Petersonus, qui novissimus videtus subscribebat testimonium narratum Abnerus Doubledies globum castrorum non invenit. Sic non audiamus huius amplium qua bishopus mimae dixit. Pila et clava ludere miscet aeque ac Latina quae adhuc scripta est.

Demum vero turpiter ad diem pervenimus cum pila ludentes habentur homines, non possidendi omnia quae facta sunt ob quendam sapuentem atque misericordem virum, nominatim. Marvinum Miller, qui omei ex usu nisi Bowie Kuhn de mensa scriptoria in atrium transferenda curam habet, nunc princeps ludi est ubi pilla et clava luditor. Ludus longissime processit, ab annis quibus praestabtissimus Joshua Gibson in societas sepositu et ubi pila una alba est ad assimulationem Johannis Robinson ab aestivis florentis et admirabilis usque ubi condiciones quae ad quandam manum obligant brevissime tollestus.

Itaque, temestate, avidente, aliud tempus in sole et in paridiso Fenviae incipimus, tempus cum spe culusdam splendoris in gramine, paulo mairoris potentiae pilam ferire quamquam in hac curbe acti sumus, quod oportet nostra dulci memoria Theodori Williams, est quoque unum e nostris suavioribus vitiss quod cum Aprilis mensis severissimus in omnibus aliis locis set hic numquam notum est ubi tempus est spem aeternam surgere, cupiditatem recordationes infelices exstingixere radices inertes imbre verno stimulare. Ah, Bostonia, ubi mense Aprili omnium punctionum immitium nostrarum gonfalonarum bullarum obliviscimur! Ah, Lude pila et clava! Ah, Tiant et Fisk et Yaz, quisque cum clangore epico bellatorum ex Iliade. Ad, Eduarde Kasko, quamvis demens sis! Ah, Tibialibus Rubris XV, Eboracum Novum V.

Si quicuriosus scire vult quam ob rem infernam hoc Latine scribitur, sic est quod paucis ante diebus ut ego et Leo Glynn et Dave Miller togati sedebamus, confessus sum mihi unam sententiam vitae esse et primus scriptor actorum diurnorum "designatus clavator" Latine dicam. Et sibi corenas laureas aptantes inquiunt. "Iuvabimus" et Deo gratias ago iuverut neque causam digniorem scio. Scitisne? Itaque vestra labre contrabite et haec mecum iterate "designatus clavator" — quae Latina adaequant quae vos Americani "designated hitter" appellatis.

In case anyone's Latin is rusty, there is a translation of the above foolishness below.

. . . and Now for the Translation

Though we begin the beguine again, this time there's a difference. This time we begin a baseball season that, even before a ball was thrown, was already the best of all seasons since 1845, when the internationally obscure Alexander Cartwright invented the damn game. I'm speaking, of course, not of the way baseball will be played this year (for no season without Roberto Clemente could possibly be as stylish as those he anointed with the purity and grace of his skills), but of the unprecedented respect now paid the players by their employers. Little by little we are witnessing the end of the plantation society that professional baseball has been since its inception.

Not, naturally, that much doesn't remain to be done. The reserve clause, like Carthage, must be destroyed. And Bowie Kuhn and Joe Cronin will make three. But, oh, how the mighty have fallen. Cronin, once so snotty in the abuse of his power, is now but a figurehead, while Kuhn has become an object of derision among those whom he used to lash for failing to say Sir. Poor, pathetic Bowie Kuhn, who, when he sanctimoniously tried to induce two wayward Yankees to cancel their plans to rearrange their light housekeeping, was told to sit down and be quiet. And, by God, he did.

Still, baseball has always been a bit of a fraud — and I'll thank you to Abner me no Doubledays. General Doubleday may have fired the first Union shot on Fort Sumter, but there's no proof that he ever even attended a ball game. What's more, while Cartwright, or whatever his name was, probably invented baseball as we know it today, there is evidence that the Berbers in North Africa played a game remarkably like ours as long ago as 6000 years before the birth of Christ, Hoyt Wilhelm, Luis Aparicio, or a single Spink. As for Spink twins, I just had my pants pressed, so you'll have to find out for yourself. In any event, the big difference was that the Berbers didn't have the slider, bubblegum cards, doubleknit uniforms, or David Eisenhower. They did, however, have heavy bats and hair like Ken Harrelson's.

Indeed, it was the baseball establishment's uneasiness at the game's having any alien taint that caused it in 1904 to appoint Doubleday the inventor of baseball, a shrewd move, since by then he was much too dead to defend himself. But don't take my word for it. Look it up in the fascinating "The Man Who Invented Baseball" by Harold Peterson, who, when last seen, was signing an affidavit stating, "Abner Doubleday didn't invent baseball. Baseball invented Abner Doubleday." So let's hear no more of that, as the bishop said to the actress. But baseball is no more confusing than my Latin up to now.

We have come at scandalously long last to a time when ballplayers are being treated as persons, not properties — and all because of a wise and compassionate man named Marvin Miller, who, for all practical purposes and if Bowie Kuhn doesn't mind having his desk moved out into the hall, is now the head of baseball. The sport has come a long way — all the way from the years when the greatness of Josh Gibson was tucked away in leagues where only the ball was white to the assimilation of Jackie Robinson by the boys of summer and the blooming of the wonderful world of Willies to a point where the abolition of the reserve clause is only a matter of time.

So we've started another season in the sun at Fenway Park — a season, one hopes, of a certain splendor in the grass, of a little more power at the plate. Though we are haunted in this city, and well we should be, by our sweet remembrance of Ted Williams, it is one of our more endearing foibles that, while April may be the cruelest month everywhere else, you'd never know it around here, where it is a time for hope to spring eternal, for desire to blot out bad memories and stir dull roots with spring rain. Ah, Boston, where, in April, we forget all the ruthless prickings of our gonfalon bubbles! Ah, baseball. Ah, Tiant and Fisk and Yaz, each with the epic clang of warriors out of "The Iliad." Ah, Eddie Kasko, madcap though you be. Ah, Red Sox 15, New York 5!

As for anyone nosy enough to inquire why the hell this is in Latin, why the hell this is in Latin is because the other day while Leo Glynn, Dave Miller, and I were sitting around in our togas, I confessed that my one aim in life was to be the first columnist to say "designated hitter" in Latin. And, adjusting their laurel wreaths, they said, "We'll help you," and, thank God, they did, nor can I think of a worthier cause they could contribute to, can you? So please purse your lips and repeat after me — "designatus clavator" — which is Latin for what you Americans call "designated hitter."

Ei quibus scientia Anglicae robigine laesa translationem ineptiavum quas supra scripsi in pagina I invenire possunt.

Legendary columnist George Frazier of the Boston Globe *could be both arch and infuriating, but he was rarely forgettable. Frazier delighted in showing off in his column, often sending readers scurrying to their dictionaries. In this instance, he took it a step further in a front-page column still talked about today for its sheer audacity.*

FISK'S HOME RUN IN 12TH BEATS REDS, 7-6

from *The Boston Globe,* October 22, 1975

And all of a sudden the ball was there, like the Mystic River Bridge, suspended out in the black of the morning.

When it finally crashed off the mesh attached to the left field foul pole, the reaction unfurled one step after another — from Carlton Fisk's convulsive leap to John Kiley's booming of the "Hallelujah Chorus" to the wearing off of the numbness to the outcry that echoed across the cold New England morning.

At 12:34 A.M., in the 12th inning, Fisk's histrionic home run brought a 7–6 end to a game that will be the pride of historians in the year 2525, a game won and lost what seemed like a dozen times, and a game that brings back summertime one more day. For the seventh game of the World Series.

For this game to end so swiftly, so definitely, was the way it had to end. An inning before, a Dwight Evans catch that Sparky Anderson claimed was as great as he's ever seen had been one turn, but in the ninth a George Foster throw ruined a bases-loaded, none-out certain victory for the Red Sox. Which followed a dramatic three-run homer in the eighth by Bernie Carbo as the obituaries had been prepared, which followed the downfall of Luis Tiant after El Tiante had begun, with the help of Fred Lynn's three-run, first-inning homer, as a hero of unmatched emotional majesty.

So Fisk had put the exclamation mark at the end of what he called "the most emotional game I've ever played in." The home run came off Pat Darcy and made a winner of Rick Wise, who had become the record 12th pitcher in this 241-minute war that seemed like four score and seven years.

But the place one must begin is the bottom of the eighth, Cincinnati leading, 6–3, and the end so clear. El Tiante had left in the top of the inning to what apparently was to be the last of his 1975 ovations; he who had become the conquering king had been found to be just a man, and it seemed so certain. Autumn had been postponed for the last time.

Only out came an Implausible Hero, to a two-out, two-on situation against Rawlins J. Eastwick III, and Carbo did what he had done in Cincinnati. Pinch-hitting, he sent a line drive into the center field bleachers, and the chill of lacrymose had become mad, sensuous Fenway again. Followed by the point and counterpoint.

In the ninth, a Denny Doyle walk and Carl Yastrzemski single had put runners at first and third, which sent Eastwick away and brought in lefthander Will McEnaney. Who walked Fisk to load the bases and pitch to Lynn.

Lynn got the ball to the outfield, but only a high, twisting fly ball down the left field line that George Foster grabbed at the line and maybe 80 feet in back of third base. Third base coach Don Zimmer said he told Doyle not to go, but he went anyway, and Foster's throw got to Johnny Bench in time for the double play. As the Red Sox shook their heads, mumbling "bases loaded, nobody out in the ninth," the Reds had their hero in Foster, who had put them ahead in the seventh with a two-run double.

Then in the 11th, the Reds had it taken away from them by Evans. With Ken Griffey at first, one out, Joe Morgan crashed a line drive towards the seats in right. Evans made his racing, web-of-the-glove, staggering catch as he crossed the warning track ("It would have been two rows in" — Reds bullpen catcher Bill Plummer), then as Griffey stopped in disbelief halfway between second and third, Evans spun and fired in. Yastrzemski, who had moved to first for Carbo's entrance to left, retrieved it to the right of the coach's box, looked up, and guess who was standing on first base, waiting for the ball? Rick Burleson. Who had raced over from shortstop. So Dick Drago, who worked three scoreless innings, the Red Sox and a seventh game all had been saved.

When it was over, it was almost incomprehensible that it had begun with Tiant trying to crank out one more miracle. But it had, and for four innings, the evening was all his. They had merchandized "El Tiante" tee shirts on the streets, they hung a banner that read "Loo-Eee For President" and everything the man did, from taking batting practice to walking to the bullpen to warm up to the rumbas and tangos that screwed the Reds into the ground for four innings, brought standing ovations and the carol, "Loo-Eee, Loo-Eee . . ."

El Tiante had a 3–0 lead from the first inning, when Lynn had followed Yastrzemski and Fisk singles by driving a Gary Nolan kumquat into the bleachers over the pitching mound of the Boston bullpen. Nolan did not last long, followed by a succession of seven, but the Billinghams, Carrolls and Borbons had apparently done what they had to do.

And the abracadabra that had blinded the Reds before began to smudge. In the fifth, after Boston had lost two scoring opportunities, Luis walked Designated Bunter Ed Armbrister, and before he could hear his father incant Grande Olde Game No. 56 ("Walks . . ."), Pete Rose singled and Griffey became the first player in three games here to hit The Wall. Not only was it the first time anyone had scored off Tiant in Fenway in 40 innings, but as the ball caromed away to be retrieved by Evans, the park went silent. In his running, leaping try for the ball at the 379-foot mark, Lynn had crashed into the wall and slid down to one knee.

Lynn eventually was able to stay in the game, but by the time the inning was over Bench had become the second to tickle The Wall, with a single, and it was 3–3. Then when Foster sent his drive off the center field fence in the seventh, it was 5–3, and when Tiant was left in to start the eighth, Cesar Geronimo angled a leadoff homer inside the right field foul pole. El Tiante left to his chant and his ovations. And in the press box, Sport Magazine editor Dick Schaap began collecting the ballots that determined which Red got the World Series hero's automobile.

So, if the honey and lemon works on the throat and the Alka-Seltzer does the same for the head, Fenway will not be alone tonight. She has one drama, and it is perhaps sport's classic drama.

Bill Lee and Don Gullett, the Cincinnati Reds and the Boston Red Sox, and a long night's journey into morning, a game suspended in time as Fisk's home run was suspended beyond the skyline, a game that perhaps required the four-day buildup it got.

Summertime has been called back for just one more day — for the seventh game of the World Series.

Peter Gammons, of Groton, Massachusetts, took over as Red Sox beat writer for the Globe *in 1972. His game reports, notable for both their detail and enthusiasm, provided the perfect counterpart to the ups and downs of the Red Sox in the 1970s. Gammons revived and popularized the "Notes" column, which was soon imitated in papers all over the country. Following stints at* Sports Illustrated *and back at the* Globe, *Gammons is now best known as a commentator on ESPN.*

THE BEST GAME EVER!

from *The Boston Globe*, October 22, 1975

Call it off. Call the seventh game off. Let the World Series stand this way, three games for the Cincinnati Reds and three for the Boston Red Sox.

How can there be a topper for what went on last night and early this morning in a ballyard gone mad, madder and maddest while watching, well, the most exciting game of baseball I have ever seen.

But maybe my opinion doesn't count. I've only seen a thousand or so baseball games. Reds manager Sparky Anderson has been to a billion and he said when it was over, "I've never seen a better one."

It was a game with a hundred climaxes. Fred Lynn hit a three-run homer and the Red Sox were cruising. Easy stuff, take Luis Tiant out suggested the sages, and save him for the seventh game.

But then opportunities went sliding down the river — bases left loaded, two men on and no out and no production, things like that, and you could feel it slipping away, into the batbag of the Big Red Machine.

And then the magic began to disappear from Luis Tiant's wand, that seemingly tireless right arm that had been snaking the baseball past the Reds for so many innings.

Snap, crackle and pop and there were the Reds ahead, 5–3, and King Tut's tomb couldn't have been more silent than Fenway Park as Tiant began the eighth.

Why he was allowed to start the inning was a mystery, because it was obvious he had tired badly in the seventh. Maybe Darrell Johnson wanted him to get a final Fenway ovation.

If so, it cost the Red Sox, because Cesar Geronimo hit Tiant's first pitch into the right field stands to make it 6–3.

And in the skyview seats, the sporting bards of America began typing the obituaries, like this:

"Death, as it must to all teams, came to the Boston Red Sox last night at 11:16 p.m. when Rawley Eastwick the 3d . . ."

Or,

"The powerful Cincinnati Reds, stretched to the limit by the tenacious Boston Red Sox, captured their first World Championship since . . ."

Or,

"Time ran out for the marvelous Luis Tiant tonight as . . ."

Ah, yes, there were deadlines to make, so why not get the story started, because Bernie Carbo was at the plate and barely able to get his bat on Eastwick's pitches.

With the count two and two, Carbo was about to let a pitch go past when suddenly he saw the ball dipping into the strike zone. Carbo chopped at it like a man cutting sugar cane, barely fouling it off. The patient was still breathing. But the 35,205 relatives were gathered at the bedside and saw no hope. It was all over, as the saying goes, but the shouting.

Ah, yes, the shouting. The screaming, the dancing, the ab-so-lute bedlam as Carbo hit the next pitch into the center field seats for the game-tying home run.

I sat in on the Bill Mazeroski home run that won the 1960 World Series for the Pirates, and that has always been, for me, No. 1 among great baseball games played under great pressure. Excitement pyramided in that one to where you didn't think there could possibly be any more.

Now, the Mazeroski game is No. 2. Last night was a Picasso of a baseball game, a Beethoven symphony played on a patch of grass in Boston's Back Bay.

Here's the kind of game it was. The Globe's Bud Collins was assigned to do a piece on the game's hero. At the end of the 11th inning, he said, "I've already crossed off 19 heroes. Maybe they should play a tie-breaker, like tennis."

Or listen to Pete Rose, who said to Carlton Fisk in the 10th, "This is some kind of game, isn't it?," and later in the dressing room, "This was the greatest game in World Series history and I'm just proud to have played in it. If this ain't the National Pastime, tell me what is."

Rose videotapes each game so he can sit back and watch them later. He was a loser in this one, but he is the sort of competitor who can admire such things as Dwight Evans's catch off Joe Morgan in the 11th that saved the game.

Sparky Anderson called the catch "the greatest I've ever seen. You won't see them any better."

The drama piled up like cordwood. Lynn's titanic homer, the Reds' comeback, Lynn slumped against the fence after crashing into it trying for Ken Griffey's triple, the Carbo homer, the Reds escaping a bases-loaded none-out situation in the ninth, the Evans catch, and finally, Fisk's game-winning homer.

As Fisk came around the bases, fans poured out onto the field and he had to dodge them on his way home.

"I straight armed somebody and kicked 'em out of the way and touched every little white thing I saw," he said.

At 12:34 it was over, but the people stayed. John Kiley played "Give Me Some Men Who Are Stout-Hearted Men" and the fans sang along. He played the Beer Barrel Polka and Seventy-six Trombones and they sang some more.

Next to me, Peter Gammons began to write.

"What was the final score?" he asked. In such a game, numbers didn't seem to mean much.

The late Ray Fitzgerald's collection, Champions Remembered, *can still be found on bookshelves in many New England homes. This column was the perfect counterpoint to Gammons's game story. Together, and combined with the unforgettable image of Fisk waving his ball fair, they are the reason many people consider this home run as baseball's most unforgettable moment.*

TOM CLARK

TO BILL LEE

from *Fan Poems*, 1976

Spaceman, how was your trip to Peking?
I hear you didn't have such a great time
and you're off to a terrible start
this season
with an earned run average of 12.12 per game
having given up 26 hits and 11 walks
in your first 16 innings
which is a hell of a shame
because when you're not doing well
the reporters don't like to talk to you so much
and when they don't talk to you I don't find out what you say

It could be when you're going this lousy
you don't say much anyway
I wouldn't blame you
but don't worry
the season's still young
I know you're not
I don't mean I know you're not young
I mean I know you're not worrying
because as you've said many times
for example after Tony Perez hit that painful home run off you in the
    Series
you'll still be alive tomorrow
barring a traffic accident
or cardiac arrest

You are of a philosophical cast of mind I know
even though you are a little temperamental those two traits can exist
    side by side
I mean I have seen you stomping around in the dugout
and screaming at umpires as though you wanted to kill them
but I also know you've read a lot of serious books and have many
    interesting thoughts
such as about whether intelligent life exists on other planets
and about Pyramid Power, of which you are a devotee
and about the Bermuda Triangle, which when you told him about it
    Bernie
Carbo thought you were talking about pussy, and told his gorilla so,
and also about ginseng, which you use before you pitch
the way Popeye uses spinach
before he saves Olive Oyl by punching out Bluto, and of which you are
    thus an exponent,
and about Eastern Religions too
after many years of inquiry into which
you've concluded that techniques of wacked-out meditation
can be applied in the practical field
a baseball field say
so that for instance in your best example
a Tibetan priest could make a baseball disappear
and then materialize again down the line in the catcher's mitt

"*There*," you say, describing it,
"is my idea of a relief pitcher"

You're telling the truth, as usual
and as usual all the writers are
cackling like you were doing standup comedy

You're also telling the truth when you say that people don't generally
    realize how hard you really work
How for instance you're always one of the first guys to get out to the
    park
How you help set up the batting cage
How you shag fly balls and run a couple of miles every day

and how you actually work on catching ground balls behind your back
because you have this theory that because of your exaggerated follow-
    through
you have to

Remember the time you tried your theory out on the late Don Hoak?

It was in 1968 at Winston-Salem in the Carolina League
You were a cocky punk just out of USC
You gloved a ball one handed behind your back
That play started a game ending twin killing
and it also made Don Hoak, then your manager
want to kill you
Hoak chased you all the way to the bus screaming his head off
and when you got on
he stayed outside, yelling at you and pounding on the window

This is your life, Bill Lee, was not what he was saying

Don Hoak never understood you, Spaceman
It wasn't in the stars
Don's nose was just too hard, I reckon
He couldn't conceive of people like you and Hans Arp
who hurl the truth into the bourgeois face of language

People like Reggie Smith and Pudge Fisk
will never understand you either
because you tell it like you see it

You told it like you saw it that time with Ellie Rodriguez
and lost a few teeth for it
but what are a few teeth in the face of the truth?
You tell it like you see it in Spaceman Language like your spiritual
    grandfather Picabia
even when it gets you into hot water
like it did last summer when you shot off your mouth
about how you thought Busing was a pretty good idea
and about how you thought the Boston fans

Who disagreed with you were bigots with no guts

Those contentions were sensible enough I grant you
and I happen to agree with them
but then it's easy for me, I don't have to pitch in Boston
and you do and did
and it wasn't easy last summer
for although you were in the midst of a fine season
the populace was growing weary
of your smart remarks, your blooper pitches
and behind the back catches. Tibet
and Pyramid Power never did
interest Sox fans much, so that when
on May 20 you shut out the A's
with a quasi-spectacular one-hitter
no one seemed to notice,
the response was merely polite,
no one seemed to understand how well
you were pitching, how no lefthander
to put on a Red Sox suit
since Mel Parnell
or even just possibly
the legendary Robert Moses "Lefty" Grove
had pitched quite as effectively
and consistently
as you were doing;
it was as though everybody was just waiting for you
to fuck up.
And you kept on
not fucking up.
On July 27 your unique sinker was never better
than in a 1–0 masterpiece over Catfish Hunter,
the breathtaking parabola of your blooper ball
never more tantalizing or bizarrely elongated.
But still you were not approved of
as you would have been had you not been
funny in the head. You began to speak
curiously after victories.

On August 9 you beat the A's again
and afterwards said they looked
"emotionally mediocre, like
Gates Brown sleeping on a rug."
What did you mean by that?
On August 24 you beat the White Sox 6–1
in a downpour at Fenway. It was one
of your greatest days. At one point you fielded
a ground ball behind your back by sticking
your glove up over your left shoulder,
spearing the ball, and from a sitting position
starting a double play that ended up with
you lying flat on your back in front of the mound.
Still, when it was over, you sensed the contempt
of the writers and fans. They loved you
but they did not love you. "When I'm through,"
you said, "I'll end up face down in the Charles
River." Spaceman, why did you say that?

That was your seventeenth victory
the third year in a row you'd won 17 games
and this time it looked like
you had a good shot at 20 or
better. Little did you know you'd go
through the playoffs, the Series, the winter
and the first two months of a new season
still looking for that next victory. Or
did you know, and is
that what you meant about the Charles River?
You had arm trouble, sure. Then Johnson
kept you out of the playoffs even though
you'd beat the A's twice and called them
emotionally mediocre earlier. In the Series
you pitched well in the second game
but Drago lost it in the ninth. After
the infamous Fisk/Armbrister non-obstruction dispute
in Game Three you said that if you'd
got to ump Larry Barnett you'd have "Van

Goghed" him. You meant you'd have chewed
his ear off? Johnson scheduled you
to start Game Six. "It's not often a
mediocre pitcher gets to start in the
sixth game of a World Series," you said.
(You turned out to be right.) When someone
in the gang of writers asked you if this
was the biggest game you'd ever been asked
to pitch, you said, Nope, this is nothing
compared to the 1968 College World Series.
"That was real baseball," you said. "We
weren't playing for the money. We got
Mickey Mouse watches that ran backwards."
And then when someone else asked what you'd
do if you won and forced the Series into
a seventh game, you said you'd declare an
automatic 48 hours of darkness so Tiant
could get another day's rest. "That's what Zeus
did when he raped Europa," you said.
"He asked the sun god, Apollo, to stay
away for a few days."
                    The next
three days, it rained. Apollo, perhaps
hearing your words on a Tibetan wavelength,
split, and not only did Zeus favor you
by washing out the sixth game, which was set
back from Saturday to Tuesday — he ordained
Tiant to pitch it. And you were pissed
off with Zeus and with Darrell Johnson. You sulked.
But when Carbo's pinch homer tied it
in the 8th, I saw you climb up on the rim
of the dugout and wave out toward the left field
wall, where Carbo's ball had gone,
urging your teammates on. Four innings
later, Pudge Fisk's homer over the same wall
won it for Boston, and you danced in the
dugout with the other Sox,
happy as in Frank Lima's perfect phrase

a bunch of fags in Boystown.
                    That left
the seventh game up to you. You pitched
your ass off, serious for once, and took
a 3–0 lead into the 6th, but then Pete Rose
busted up a double play by banging into Burleson
and up came Tony Perez. I know you hate
me to mention what happened next but it's
a part of the story, Spaceman. You tried to
float your blooper pitch past The Dog
for the second time in one night. That was
once too often, like Tony said later.
You thought you could do it;
you were gambling; that's why
they call you Spaceman. They call
Perez The Dog because he persists. "I saw
him all the way," he said later; "I was
ready for it." Boom! The ball
disappeared into the screens. Two runs. An
inning later you came out with a blister
and a one run lead that was gone by
the time you hit the showers. So much for
Tom Yawkey's World Series Dream. You
sat in the locker room with your head down
amidst your sad teammates later. "I just
went out there and did my job," you said,
in your disappointment using the cliché for once.
"I went out there and threw the shit out
of the ball." The blooper ball you threw
Perez? "Hell, I live by that pitch
and I'll die for it," you said half-
tragically. This time nobody laughed.

And then you left for China.

Tom Clark was one of many literary men drawn to baseball in the
1970s; the poet Donald Hall once wrote a book about Pirates pitcher

Dock Ellis, and Clark wrote a memorable book about the Oakland A's titled Champagne and Baloney. *Outspoken Red Sox pitcher Bill Lee was a favorite of younger writers and probably the subject of more stories than any other Red Sox player of his time. But no one captured Lee better than Clark.*

On one Opening Day in the mid-1980s, the editor sat in the bleachers only to find Lee sitting two seats away. I had a copy of the poem with me, which I showed to the Spaceman. "That's a great poem!" he shouted above the crowd.

THE BOSTON MASSACRE

from *Sports Illustrated,* September 18, 1978

The man had on a gray Brooks Brothers suit, which made him look for all the world as if he were Harvard '44, and he was leaning over the railing of the box next to the Red Sox dugout. "Zimmer!" he screamed, but Don Zimmer just stared dead ahead. The score at that point in last Friday night's game was 13–0 in favor of the Yankees and except to change pitchers a few times the Red Sox manager hadn't moved in three hours. He had stared as Mickey Rivers stood on third just two pitches into the game. He had stared as, for the second straight night, a Yankee batter got his third hit before Boston's ninth hitter, Butch Hobson, even got to the plate. He had stared as the Red Sox made seven errors. And now he stared as the man kept screaming his name.

"I've been a Red Sox fan for twenty years," the man hollered. "A diehard Red Sox fan. I've put up with a lot of heartaches. But this time you've really done it. This time my heart's been broken for good." Finally Zimmer looked up, just as security guards hauled the man away.

From Eastport to Block Island, New Englanders were screaming mad. Only a couple of weeks before, the Red Sox had been baseball's one sure thing, but now Fenway Park was like St. Petersburg in the last days of Czar Nicholas. Back in July, when Billy Martin still sat in the Yankee manager's office and New York was in the process of falling fourteen games behind the Sox, Reggie Jackson had said, "Not even Affirmed can catch them." But by late last Sunday afternoon, when the 1978 version of the Boston Massacre concluded with New York's fourth win in a row over the Red Sox, the Yankees had caught them. And the Yanks had gained a tie for first in the American

League East in such awesome fashion — winning sixteen of their last eighteen, including the lopsided victories that comprised the Massacre — that Saturday night a New Yorker named Dick Waterman walked into a Cambridge bar, announced, "For the first time a first-place team has been mathematically eliminated," and held up a sign that read: NY 35-49-4, BOS 5-16-11. Those figures were the combined line score of last weekend's first three games. The disparity between those sets of numbers, as much as the losses themselves, was what so deeply depressed Red Sox fans. "It's 1929 all over again," mourned Robert Crane, treasurer of the Commonwealth of Massachusetts.

The Red Sox and Yankees began their two-city, seven-game, eleven-day showdown in Boston last Thursday — it will continue with three games this weekend in New York — and it quickly became apparent that this confrontation would be quite different from their six-game shoot-out in late June and early July. On that occasion the Red Sox had beaten the Yanks four times and opened up a lead that appeared insurmountable. Back then the Yankees had so few healthy bodies that catcher Thurman Munson was trying to become a right fielder, and one day a minor league pitcher named Paul Semall drove from West Haven, Connecticut, to Boston to throw batting practice. Had the New York brass liked the way he threw, Semall would have stayed with the Yankees and become a starter. By midnight, Semall was driving back to West Haven, and soon thereafter injuries became so rife among New York pitchers that reserve first baseman Jim Spencer was warming up in the bullpen.

Rivers, the center fielder and key to the Yankee offense, had a broken wrist. Both members of the double-play combination, Willie Randolph and Bucky Dent, were injured and out of the lineup. To complete the up-the-middle collapse, Munson was playing — sometimes behind the plate and sometimes in right — with a bad leg, and the pitching staff had been reduced to *Gong Show* contestants. Paul Semall got gonged. Dave Rajsish got gonged. Larry McCall got gonged. Catfish Hunter, Ed Figueroa, Dick Tidrow, Ken Clay, Andy Messersmith, and Don Gullett were all hurt or soon to be injured. Only the brilliant Ron Guidry stayed healthy. Almost singlehandedly he kept the bottom from falling out during July and early August.

Then, as the regulars gradually began getting back into the lineup, the blowup between owner George Steinbrenner and Martin occurred. Martin resigned on July 24, and the next day Bob Lemon, who had recently been canned by the White Sox, took over. "The season starts today," Lemon told the Yankees. "Go have some fun." Considering the disarray in New York during the preceding year and a half, that seemed a bit much to ask. So was catching Boston. No American League team had ever changed managers in midseason and won a championship. "Under Lemon we became a completely different team," says Spencer. "If Martin were still here, we wouldn't be," snaps one player. "We'd have quit. Rivers and Jackson couldn't play for him. But Lemon gave us a fresh spirit. We kept playing. We looked up, and Boston was right in front of us." The fact that a suddenly revived Hunter had won six straight, that Figueroa had regained health and happiness, that Tidrow had again become hale and that rookie right hander Jim Beattie had returned from the minors with his self-confidence restored didn't hurt.

And while the Yankees arrived in Boston 30–13 under Lemon and 35–14 since July 17 — the night they fell fourteen games behind — the Red Sox had been stumbling. They were 25–24 since July 17. Their thirty-nine-year-old leader, Carl Yastrzemski, had suffered back and shoulder ailments in mid-July, and then he pulled ligaments in his right wrist that left him taped up and in and out of the lineup. He had hit three homers in two months. Second baseman Jerry Remy fractured a bone in his left wrist on August 25 and had not appeared in the lineup thereafter.

Catcher Carlton Fisk had been playing with a cracked rib, which he said made him feel as if "someone is sticking a sword in my side" every time he threw. Third baseman Butch Hobson has cartilage and ligament damage in both knees and bone chips in his right elbow. The chips are so painful that one night he had to run off the field during infield practice; his elbow had locked up on him. When New York came to town, he had a major-league–leading thirty-eight errors, most of them the result of bad throws made with his bad arm. Right fielder Dwight Evans had been beaned on August 29 and was experiencing dizziness whenever he ran. Reliever Bill Campbell, who had thirty-one saves and thirteen wins in 1977, had suffered from elbow and shoulder soreness all season.

The injuries tended to dampen Boston's already erratic, one-dimensional offense, which relies too heavily on power hitting even when everyone is healthy. They also ruined the Sox defense, which had been the facet of play most responsible for giving the Red Sox a ten-game lead over their nearest challenger, Milwaukee, on July 8. No wonder the pitching went sour, with Mike Torrez going 4-4 since the All-Star Game, Luis Tiant 3-7 since June 24, and Bill Lee 0-7 since July 15. And as Boston awaited its confrontation with the Yankees, it lost three out of five to Toronto and Oakland and two of three in Baltimore. The Sox' only lift came in Wednesday's 2–0 win over the Orioles. Tiant pitched a two-hitter that night, and Yaz, his wrist looking like a mummy's, hit a two-run homer. It was one of only two hits the Sox got off Dennis Martinez.

As play began Thursday night at Fenway Park, the Red Sox lead had dwindled to four games with twenty-four to play. "We'll be happy with a split," Lemon said. By 9:05 P.M. Friday — during the third inning of Game 2 — Lemon turned to pitching coach-scout Clyde King and said, "Now I'll only be happy with three out of four." Right about then *The Washington Post*'s Tom Boswell was writing his lead: "*Ibid*, for details, see yesterday's paper." The details were downright embarrassing to the Red Sox.

The embarrassments had begun with a Hobson error in the first inning Thursday. Then a Munson single. And a Jackson single. Zap, the Yankees had two unearned runs. After giving up four straight singles to start the second inning, Torrez went to the showers. Munson had three hits — and the Yankees seven runs — before Hobson got his first at bat in the bottom of the third. After the seventh inning, someone in the press box looked up at the New York line on the scoreboard — 2-3-2-5-0-1-0 — and dialed the number. It was disconnected. When the game ended, the Yankees had twenty-one hits and a 15–3 victory.

New York's joy was tempered by two injuries. Hunter left the game with a pulled groin muscle in the fourth, too soon to get the victory, though the Yanks were leading 12–0. "The bullpen phone rang and six of us fought to answer it," said Clay, who won the phone call and the game. Hunter, it turned out, would probably miss only one start. In the sixth inning, Munson was beaned by Dick Drago. Though dizzy, Munson said he would be behind the plate Friday. "He smells blood," Jackson said.

The next night, the Yankees not only drained Boston's blood but also its dignity. Rivers hit rookie right hander Jim Wright's first pitch past first baseman George Scott into right field. On the second pitch, he stole second and cruised on into third as Fisk's throw bounced away from shortstop Rick Burleson. Wright had thrown two pitches, and Rivers was peering at him from third base. Wright went on to get four outs, one more than Torrez had; he was relieved after allowing four runs. His replacement, Tom Burgmeier, immediately gave up a single and walk before surrendering a mighty home run by Jackson.

Beattie, who in his Fenway appearance in June had been knocked out in the third inning and optioned to Tacoma in the sixth, retired eighteen in a row in one stretch, while the Red Sox self-destructed in the field. Evans, who had not dropped a fly in his first five and three-quarters years in the majors, dropped his second one of the week and had to leave the game. "I can't look up or down without getting dizzy," he said. Fisk had two throws bounce away for errors. Rivers hit a routine ground ball to Scott in the third and beat Scott to the bag, making him three-for-three before Hobson ever got up. The game ended with a 13–2 score and seven Red Sox errors.

"I can't believe what I've been seeing," said King, who has watched about forty Red Sox games this season. "I could understand if an expansion team fell apart like that, but Boston's got the best record in baseball. It can't go on." On Saturday afternoon, Guidry took his 20-2 record to the mound. It went on.

This was to be the showdown of the aces. Dennis Eckersley, 16-6, was 9-0 in Fenway and had not been knocked out before the fifth inning all season. He had beaten the Yankees three times in a twelve-day stretch earlier in the year. When he blew a third strike past Jackson to end the bottom of the first, he had done what Torrez and Wright had not been able to do — shut the Yankees out in the first inning.

"It looked like it was going to be a 1–0 game, what with the wind whipping in and Eckersley looking like he'd put us back together," said Zimmer. After Burleson led off Boston's first with a single, Fred Lynn bunted. Guidry, who could have cut down Burleson at second, hesitated and ended up throwing to first. Then Dent bobbled Jim Rice's grounder in the hole for an infield single. Two on. But Guidry busted fastballs in on the hands of Yastrzemski and Fisk, getting them out on a weak grounder and called third strike, respectively. Despite leadoff walks in the next two Boston at bats, the Sox hitters were finished for the day. Rice's grounder would be their second and last hit of the afternoon.

Yastrzemski seemed to lift his catatonic team in the fourth with a twisting, leaping catch on the dead run that he turned into a double play. But three batters later, with two on and two out, all that Yaz and Eckersley had done to heighten Boston's morale unraveled when Lou Piniella sliced a pop fly into the gale in right center.

"It must have blown a hundred feet across, like a Frisbee coming back," says Eckersley. Lynn came in a few steps but he had no chance. Burleson made chase from shortstop, Scott took off from first. The ball was out of reach of both. Rice, who was playing near the warning track in right, could not get there. Frank Duffy, the second baseman, did, but when he turned and looked up into the sun he lost sight of the ball. It landed in front of him. It was 1–0. After an intentional walk to Graig Nettles, Dent dunked a two-strike pitch into left for two more runs. "That broke my back," said Eckersley. By the time the inning had ended, Eckersley was gone. There had been another walk, an error, a wild pitch, and a passed ball. Seven runs had scored. "This is the first time I've seen a first-place team chasing a second-place team," said NBC's Tony Kubek.

Guidry had not only become the second left-hander to pitch a complete game against the Red Sox in Fenway all season, but also was the first lefty to shut them out at home since 1974. "Pitchers are afraid to pitch inside here," he said. "But that's where you've got to."

The victory brought Guidry's record to 21-2, his earned-run average to 1.77, and his strikeouts to 220; it also brought the New York staff's ERA to 2.07 over the last twenty-six games. "They must be cheating," said Lynn. "Those aren't the same Yankees we saw before. I think George Steinbrenner used his clone money. I think those were Yankee clones out there from teams of the past."

"These guys are — I hope you understand how I use the word — nasty," said Jackson. "This is a pro's game, and this team is loaded with professionals. Tough guys. Nasty."

"This is two years in a row we've finished like this, so it must say something about the team's character," Tidrow said. Before Lemon took over, the only times the word "character" was used in the Yankee clubhouse it was invariably followed by the word "assassination."

With the 7–0 loss figured in, the Red Sox had lost eight out of ten. In those games they had committed twenty-four errors good for twenty unearned runs. Twice pop-ups to shallow right had dropped, leading to two losses and ten earned runs.

Tiant had been the only starting pitcher to win. Evans, Scott, Hobson, and Jack Brohamer, who most of the time were the bottom four in the batting order, were twelve for 123 — or .098. "How can a team get thirty-something games over .500 in July and then in September see its pitching, hitting, and fielding all fall apart at the same time?" wondered Fisk.

After being bombarded in the first three games, all that the Red Sox could come up with in their effort to prevent the Yankees from gaining a first-place tie on Sunday was rookie lefthander Bobby Sprowl. In June, while the Sox were beating the Yankees, Sprowl was pitching for the Bristol Red Sox against the West Haven Yankees.

Clearly he was not ready for their New York namesakes. He began by walking Rivers and Willie Randolph, lasted only two-thirds of an inning, and was charged with three runs. The most damaging blow came after Sprowl gave way to reliever Bob Stanley, who promptly yielded a single to Nettles that drove in two runners whom Sprowl had allowed to reach base. The Yankees would build a 6–0 bulge before coasting to an eighteen-hit, 7–4 victory. Suddenly, New York not only had a psychological edge on the Red Sox, but it also had pulled even with them in the standings.

"It's never easy to win a pennant," said Yastrzemski. "We've got three weeks to play. We've got three games in Yankee Stadium next weekend. Anything can happen." He stared into his locker. Anything already had.

GLOOMSVILLE
The Fans Cried As They Left

from *The Boston Herald American,* October 3, 1978

One run. One common, ordinary, measly run. After 162 assorted games and one classic confrontation, the New York Yankees proved to be one common, ordinary, measly, 400-foot run better than the Red Sox yesterday.

But on the wings of Reggie Jackson's eighth inning home run into the center field bleachers, the Yankees and not the Red Sox will sail into the American League playoffs vs. the Royals in Kansas City tonight.

I only hope all five games, combined, are half as good as yesterday's 5–4 Yankee victory, for their third consecutive A.L. East pennant.

Jackson's indisputable clout was not the whole story of this second showdown game in American League history and also the Red Sox' second loss in these races. The Sox, like the rest of New England, will spend the winter wondering what in tarnation is conspiring against them.

The game, in fact, was a microcosm of the season that had produced it. It was, by turns, taut, shocking, frantic and, from the Red Sox viewpoint, ultimately tragic. The Yanks, of course, thought it was gorgeous.

In a way it was, and as such, it served its purpose. It resolved the issue between what Carlton Fisk later told commissioner Bowie Kuhn are "the two best teams in baseball." But I also won't argue that the Yanks are infinitesimally better. They won it cleanly.

Just as they had in early September, they came out of nowhere to ambush the Red Sox, to wipe out what seemed at the time a plush, 2–0 lead with four runs in the seventh. But just when it appeared the Yanks had it clinched at 5–2 in the eighth, the Red Sox mounted a counterattack that fell a mere 90 feet short, as did their season, too.

Rick Burleson was on his mark at third base with two out in the ninth when Carl Yastrzemski sliced a pop foul over his head and into Graig Nettles' eager grasp. Capt. Carl dropped his chin on his chest and walked blindly into the clubhouse, once again the personification of his ball team.

But please don't blather that neither team deserved to lose. That only derides the fact the Red Sox gave it everything they had.

No matter what the outcome, this was a connoisseur's baseball game, one that can be rolled around in the mind and savored all winter. There was nothing whimsical about any of the runs that were scored, including Bucky Dent's three-run homer in the seventh that turned the game inside out.

Bucky Dent had hit only four home runs all season long. But with his team trailing, 2–0, and runners on first and second, one out, the Yankees' shortstop played the game. He choked up on his bat fully six inches and guarded the plate like life itself.

"The only thought in my mind was to put the ball someplace where it could score a run," he said. But when Mike Torrez laid a fast ball across Bucky's waistband, he put it into the left field net while Yaz, his back turned to snag the carom, sagged visibly at the knees.

This proved once again that the Yanks can beat you up and down their lineup, with finesse or muscle or whatever it takes.

In the very same situation in the Red Sox eighth, with two on and the Yanks leading, 5–4, George Scott took a mighty, wild, futile swipe and struck out. Maybe that, and not Jackson's homer, represents the essential difference between these two clubs.

But this was a game that doesn't deserve to be second-guessed, not even Don Zimmer's decision to pinch-hit Bob Bailey for Jack Brohamer with the Yanks ahead, 5–2, and Scott on second in the seventh. Yankee manager Bob Lemon needlessly summoned his right-handed reliever, Rich Gossage, because Bailey simply stood there and admired the final two strikes.

So perhaps it all proved that, just like last year, the Red Sox lack the pitching and the bench to beat the Yankees.

Yet the Sox racked the best pitcher in captivity, Ron Guidry, for six hits and two runs in 6½ innings, starting with Yaz' line-drive homer into the right field corner in the second.

And Torrez, the Yankee expatriate, pitched two-hit, shutout ball for six full innings. Andy Hassler and Dick Drago held the Yankees off while the Sox tore into Gossage for four hits and two runs in the eighth. And the Sox almost cashiered both him and the Yanks until Yaz' pop fly ended it all in the ninth.

The difference between these two teams was so thin, so ephemeral, and yet, so final, that no wonder people cried as they left the park.

Tim Horgan worked for the Boston Herald *from 1947 to 1990. A graduate of Tufts University, he was named Massachusetts Sportswriter of the Year eight times.*

THE CONFESSIONS OF A ROOKIE IN PEARLS

from *Esquire,* July 1980

Don Forst had a problem. A desperate problem, he explained, calling my flat in London from his Boston office. He had just become editor of the *Boston Herald American,* a Hearst rag with only history in its corner. Not only did the paper have to persuade Jordan Marsh it give it some more advertising — something JM and every other Boston retailer and grocer seemed loath to do; editor Forst also had to jazz up the editorial content and get the paper noticed. Although Forst was fresh from the *Los Angeles Herald Examiner,* he understood one fundamental fact of New England life: every time the Red Sox are on the front page, the paper's street sales skyrocket. If, he reasoned, this front-page piece were a regular column written by a woman, the figures might climb higher. And if the woman knew nothing about baseball — well, then, who knew how high they might go?

I knew nothing about baseball. I had never been to a major league game. I had never heard the name Carl Yastrzemski, and I thought The Gerbil was the team mascot. I didn't know that when a player reached home plate safely he had scored a run, not a point. I thought "no pepper" meant that spices were not allowed on the field. And I was convinced that a hit occurred each time the ball made contact with the bat.

I did know there were nine innings in a game. And, though I pretended otherwise at the time, I was well aware that 1979 was the first year women were legally empowered to enter the clubhouses of major league baseball teams. What I did not know — and what Forst had the good sense not to tell me — was that the Boston Red Sox, the most conservative and old-fashioned of all the baseball teams, regarded their shrine at Fenway with about the same degree of levity with which Moslems view the Dome of the Rock.

In March of 1979 I was homesick, and Forst was determined that I should come home and take on the Boston Red Sox. "You're in danger of becoming an expatriate," he told me. All he could offer me was the reassuring news that my column would *not* be about baseball.

I remember his using the word *anthropology* a lot. "Talk to the pitchers about their anxiety attacks, and talk to the wives about their loneliness, and see what the first baseman has to say about his midlife crisis," Forst suggested. "But for God's sake, don't write about the game."

Despite my editor's encouragement, I did not regard six months with the Red Sox entirely as Margaret Mead might have anticipated a season in Samoa, so I undertook some meager preparation:

1. I read baseball magazines: articles pondering such questions as, Do the Red Sox choke? Who throws the toughest curve ball in the majors? Is Steinbrenner really good for baseball? What can the Yanks do for an encore?

2. I looked up *baseball* in my 1953 *World Book*. The first sentence read: "Baseball has been for many years the national game of the United States." I went on to even higher levels of understanding. It had to be significant that Abner Doubleday, credited with inventing the sport, became a general in the Union Army. Later I would learn that, although Doubleday fought for the Union, he didn't invent baseball. I still don't know who did. Here were *World Book*'s reassuring essentials: "The distance between the bases is 90 feet. The distance from the home plate to the pitcher's box is 60 feet, 6 inches. When one team is in the field, the other team is at bat. It is customary to let the visiting team bat first."

3. I read books: *Ball Four, The Superwives, Five Seasons, The Natural.*

4. I played memory games; I tested myself with the roster. Jim Rice, was he number 14? Fisk, nicknamed Pug? Burleson, a third baseman? I forced myself to spell out two dozen times the name Y-a-s-t-r-e-m-s-k-i.

By the time I realized I would never get it right, the plane was landing in Tampa and I was on my way to spring training.

*   *   *

Nothing could have prepared me for the pleasures of my first baseball field, in Chain o' Lakes Park in Winter Haven. Orange trees blooming by the fences. American flags whipping in the warm breeze. Egrets circling in the Florida sky. Sunshine on the back of my neck. The lines of the diamond white, stark, precise.

The first batter I saw was Carl Yastrzemski. A pitcher threw the ball; a guy who looked older than my editor swung and smashed the white sphere toward the trees. What was the big deal?

It looked so easy that I wanted to be in the batting cage doing what he was doing. I knew better than to approach anyone with a face as sour as Yastrzemski's, but Ted Williams was at spring training, and the great thumper liked to work with the minor leaguers on their hitting. Ted Williams!

I made my way to the minor league field and there found not the Gary Cooper of years past but a paunchy middle-aged man in a navy windbreaker and dark slacks. He wore sunglasses and looked as seedy as a third-rate producer.

I knew Williams hated the press. I knew he believed that the "knights of the keyboard," as he called us, had ruined his time in Boston. But I wasn't around then. And all I wanted was a demonstration. Maybe he'd be willing to give me one.

He was too willing. He took me by the waist, pushed a bat into my hands, then wrapped his large arms around mine. "Put your left foot at a ninety-degree angle," he said. "Move your right one around." A small crowd began to gather. I knew Williams wasn't serious in his attempt to teach me the uppercut, but he was really throwing himself into the assignment.

Suddenly he was belligerent: "You know, I don't believe in women in the clubhouse."

"I haven't been in," I said.

"That's good," he said, and hugged me closer.

"Pitch me a ball!" I yelled to one of the minor leaguers.

A ball floated toward me. I swung at it and missed.

"Strike one," said Williams. I could tell he wanted to resume his real work.

"One more."

Another ball. I hit it. My wrists throbbed as the bat made contact. The ball bounced a few dismal feet, then unceremoniously wobbled to a stop.

"Maybe The Eck [Dennis Eckersley] could teach you how to pitch," Williams said.

I had stalled long enough; it was time to break into the clubhouse. Bill Crowley, the Red Sox's cantankerous PR man, had told me I wouldn't be allowed into the inner sanctum unless I had a special letter from my editor — "on letterhead stationery" — saying that my story required that I see the players while they were still dripping wet.

What to do? During the manager's hour after the game, I studied the face of The Gerbil. The Gerbil is manager Don Zimmer's nickname. His cheeks were puffy and his eyes were slits. As Zimmer answered questions about sliders and injuries, he grunted, dunked cheese squares into mustard, popped them into his mouth, and pulled at a Tab. Over and over he repeated the phrase "We'll have to wait till Boston, won't we?" In this small press mess in which somebody had painted the sign LOCKE-OBER SOUTH, there were maybe thirty reporters, twenty-nine of them men. I knew I had to make my debut. I smiled, I knew, a little too sincerely. "How are you going to feel on opening day when you hear the boos?" I asked Zimmer.

Zimmer glared at me. "I'm looking forward to 'em," he said. "Why shouldn't I?" He wasn't kidding.

What kind of man would look forward to getting booed? *Hey, you, fatso Zimmer. Boo!* He was looking forward to that?

Then he turned to me: "Been in the clubhouse yet?"

"No."

"Why not? That other one was here."

That other one was historian Doris Kearns, who had been there several weeks earlier writing an article for *Look*. Kearns had integrated the clubhouse when it was empty. This was not my intent.

"Take me in," I said.

I sailed past Crowley's office, Zimmer guiding the way. We pushed through the screen door. I think I expected the triumphal march from *Aida* to herald my arrival. But instead, something mostly naked and wet grabbed me. Jim Rice, possibly the strongest athlete in the American League. I felt like a voyeur and a fool. He squeezed my arm tight. "Where are you going?" he asked.

"Out," I said.

"Why? Don't you have a boyfriend?"

"Yes," I said.

"What's the difference?" he said.

The entire clubhouse now stared at me. Zimmer grinned maniacally. My heart was pounding. I knew this was the moment I had to establish myself as A Serious Person. A question formed on my lips: *Jim, do you think you're going to get the pitches this year?* And then I realized I'd look like an even bigger fool. Whom was I trying to kid? I wasn't on a deadline. I didn't have to file. I mumbled something to Rice about there not being any difference and stumbled out. One of the fielders yelled after me, "You better not try this in Boston."

I approached Boston with the proper degree of dread. Now there *were* deadlines and filings. Now, for me and the Sox, what went on at Fenway was business. I got used to ducking tape balls aimed at my head. I learned to ignore Jim Rice and George Scott when they staged discussions of black anatomy. I began to see the humor in being screamed at by Vinnie Orlando, the sixty-three-year-old equipment manager, who I thought was "the towel boy."

All that summer I watched them. We had a lot in common. They spoke English. So did I. I tried to understand them by thinking of them as harmless hoodlums in blue caps and red socks. God knows what they thought about me, trotting after them in my high heels and pearls. Armed with a notebook and an obvious ambivalence, I would stumble along behind them. Way behind them.

Hey, look at that woman in pearls. Who is she? Has to be a reporter. Must be one of those new broads in the clubhouse. Oh, yeah, we've heard about *her.* That's the one who doesn't write about the game. That's the one who doesn't know about the game. Who doesn't have a history with it: Who was Billy Cox? Bobby Doerr? The spectator had every right to boo. *Hey, you, reporter, boo.* The spectator had every right to wonder — as did I — what in the world I was doing there.

I knew one thing. If I couldn't talk to them about their RBIs and ERAs, I could chart what I saw. I hoped a written record would someday help me make some sense of it all.

May 5

An early lesson: I'm not the only one who has trouble with these gloomy millionaires. This afternoon I stood by the batting cage with one of the old-time Boston sportswriters, a member in good standing of the polyester-and-plaid brigade. For fourteen years this man has been sending the Sox daily valentines, but, as the players poured off the field, he might as well have been the Invisible Man. I tried not to think my presence had anything to do with it.

"Hey, Butch," he called to Hobson, the third baseman.

"Hey, Jim," he hollered to Rice.

"Hey, Mike," he said, smiling at Torrez, the pitcher.

"Hey, Rick," he called to Burleson.

"Fred, hey," he yelled to Lynn, an outfielder.

"Dewey, hi," he called to Dwight Evans, an outfielder who views the entire population of the planet as an irritation.

"Hey, Jerry," he called to the second baseman.

Surprise. Jerry Remy said hello.

And so did George Scott, The Boomer.

"Huey," I asked when the players were gone, "how long have you been writing about the Sox?"

"Fourteen years."

"Does it bother you that these guys ignore you?"

"You get used to it," he said.

I did not want to get used to it, so I asked Johnny Pesky, a former Red Sox great turned coach, if all writers were treated like the man I had just seen humiliated.

Pesky shook his head sadly. "It's a shame," he said. "They think if they say hello, it's a commitment."

May 14, 16

Schedules, everything is schedules. Baseball is a daily procedure, a tedious daily routine. We have a sixteen-day home stand now — the longest in twenty years — and five teams will be in and out of Fenway Park. Now the up-and-comers, the Orioles, are here. Their manager, Earl Weaver, sits in the dugout looking like baseball's Ozzie Nelson, and he is actually smiling. "How does it feel to be the most popular manager in the American League?" I ask him. Weaver squints into the May sunlight and laughs, he really laughs. "Love me now, baby. Cuz on the first of September, I turn into an asshole."

I have been accepted into the clubhouse, I think, and I might even have made a friend. Maybe. Tonight, in a game against the Orioles, Rick Burleson, a bantamweight shortstop called The Rooster, went nose to nose with an umpire. To make matters worse, Jim Rice, trying to be the peacemaker, stepped into the fray and bumped the ump, who responded by falling to the ground. After the game, while the other sportswriters made for Zimmer — who, with his "I dunno what happened, I only know what the man tells me," was his usual incisive self — I made for Jim Rice because I knew he was the least popular player with the polyester-and-plaid brigade. Anyone they didn't like had to be pretty terrific. Rice was.

He was happy to explain what had happened, for nothing had happened: he was, he said, "just trying to keep The Rooster from making trouble." Big deal. I asked another question, he gave me another answer. An exchange! I felt like an anthropologist breaking an ethnographic code.

Then I went overboard. "Jim, were you *frustrated* by the game?"

Rice stared at me. He said nothing. I panicked. Was it possible that Jim Rice, whose contract guarantees him $6.7 million for five seasons of baseball, did not comprehend the word *frustrated*?

"Yeah," he said at last. "I did feel frustrated. But you can't win all the time."

I, however, felt I might have started a winning streak. And when the sportswriters came over to Rice and so irritated him that he threatened to dump one into the trash can, I was sure of it.

May 20

I figured out something about ballplayers: never talk to them about what they don't talk about among themselves. Don't, for example, ask them about dope, Woody Allen, busing in Boston, or the lobster at Locke-Ober. Stick to Bill Blass suits, how much Friendly ice cream is paying them for endorsements, whether they prefer Nautilus or Universal systems (they prefer Nautilus), and how many inches they've added to their necks. Once in a while you can get them going on Spyro Gyra, a jazz-rock group much favored by the Bosox. They also like manicotti and Löwenbräu.

There is one word I've learned never to use: *psychological*. Ballplayers freak when they hear the prefix *psy*. I've learned to substitute the word *mental*. To a pitcher, I now say, "Do you think you missed the plate by six feet because you were too mental today?" "Yeah," he'll say. "It was a mental thing. I was real mental today."

And I've learned to avoid politics. This week, I tried to break through to Butch Hobson. "Hey, Butch," I asked, "who do you want for President in 1980?"

"Why?" Hobson asked. "Where is Haywood Sullivan going?"

Haywood Sullivan runs the Red Sox.

May 21

It's taken only one month with the Red Sox to make me wish I could get traded to the New York Yankees. Not because they might win the pennant but because they represent the New Baseball: style and money.

Whom do we Bostonians have for team owners? Haywood Sullivan, our former catcher, and Buddy LeRoux, who will be forever remembered as the short Celtics trainer who held Red Auerbach's towel. To acquire the Red Sox, Sullivan and LeRoux mortgaged themselves to the hilt, befriended the widow Yawkey, and allied themselves (in baseball philosophy) with Boston's heartbreaking all-hitting, no-pitching past. A sweet story, to be sure, but it means they can't compete in the free-agent wars with George Steinbrenner — to say nothing of Gene Autry, Brad Corbett, and Ted Turner. You don't have to understand much about baseball to know that without money — or Earl Weaver — the handwriting is on the wall.

Here is how Boston's owners have demonstrated their baseball savvy. Lacking pitchers, they exiled two of the best: Bill Lee went to Montreal and Luis Tiant to the Yankees. As a result, they lost not only two strong arms but two light spirits, too. Yesterday afternoon, Tiant wandered into the Boston clubhouse to visit his old teammates. Frank Duffy, the Boston shortstop, ambled out after a while, still chuckling. "What's happened?" I asked. "Christ," Duffy said. "This is the first time all season I've heard any laughter in that locker room."

May 28

I allowed myself to think there would be life on the road. I had been warned by another writer, "You'll survive if you don't expect a party," but I didn't take his remark to mean that a road trip is a wake with hot dogs. With us, it was.

On the first day, we were attacked by the forty-degree weather of

Toronto. In the 10:00 A.M. chill, I followed the other writers into the clubhouse and attempted to warm my blue fingers on plastic cups of Red Sox coffee. Nothing strange about that. Then Yaz noticed a skirt.

"What the hell are *you* doing in here?" he bellowed. "What do you think this is, a goddamned coffee klatsch? This is our home! Get out! And I'm not saying this just because you're a woman."

Isn't that unbelievable? The man turns forty in August and he's likely to hit 400 homers, yet he still gives new life to Roy Campanella's observation that in all ballplayers "there's a lot of little boy." Well, maybe Yaz is not such a little boy. It occurs to me that in six weeks of writing Red Sox Diary I have never seen the captain without his pants. It occurs to me that the captain has very possibly never been, in his entire life, without his pants.

It also occurs to me that though I have trouble with Yaz, I am having a fine time with Jim Rice, whom everybody else has trouble with. Flying down to Texas, Rice filled the empty seat next to mine and, without saying more than hello, picked up the sports section of the *Toronto Star* and started to read an article about himself. The writer called Rice what everyone calls him — "arrogant," "moody" — and Rice was incensed. "What does this have to do with my *hitting?*" he demanded. "I'm just not getting the pitches."

I decided to play Joyce Brothers. "You shouldn't read that stuff. What anyone thinks of you is unimportant," I said. "You're going to make yourself crazy."

"Hmmph," he said.

I picked up the book section and discovered a glowing review of a novel by someone I don't much care for. That was too much. I gave in to self-pity — what was I doing on a plane with ballplayers who ignored me or yelled at me? — and then I shredded the book section.

"Hey, what's going on?" Rice asked. He looked at me for a long moment.

I decided to tell him. Rice laughed. "I have an idea," he said. "You read the sports section and I'll cover the books."

And then Jim Rice became Joyce Brothers. "You've been getting more and more uptight, just like us," he began. "Well, don't let us do that to you. You just got to relax. The guys'll get used to you.

Well, maybe not Yaz. He doesn't understand what you're doing here. Heck, neither does anyone else. But don't let that get you. Be yourself."

He was warmed up now. "Like, why do you have that skirt on? It makes you look like an *executive*. What happened to those tight jeans you had on at spring training? Those skirts don't fool anybody. Go back to the jeans. You'll be a lot happier."

June 1

All I seem to do this week is stare out the bus window and listen to their baseball babble. The baseball babble I can't make sense of, but I'm learning to make sense of their glumness and their terrible silences, the inevitable road-trip gloom. I long for the Orioles and the Yankees — even the Blue Jays — but I am stuck with my team, the play-dead Sox. I am the rookie, an initiate into the Bosox family — that extended fraternity of New England players and their faithful who wear their psychic scars like so many pilgrims doing time at Lourdes. My editor is not sympathetic. "Kid," he told me today, "I set you up."

June 5

I am learning that Fenway Park is a racist's paradise: blacks neither stray into it nor — with two exceptions — play in it. Last week I took a walk through the stands. Surprise. I spotted a black spectator. One black spectator, wearing a navy blazer. As I got closer, I noticed the blazer sported the Red Sox insignia. He was a Red Sox security man. The next day I asked Haywood Sullivan why blacks don't come to Fenway. "Blacks tend not to spend their sports dollars as spectators," he said.

Has he ever been to a Celtics game at the Boston Garden?

The (black) Coca-Cola vice-president who handles Fenway was more helpful. "Blacks feel like if they come to Fenway, a Southie will throw bottles at them and yell 'nigger' in their direction, just like all over the rest of Boston," he said.

So I showed up early at batting practice to ask The Boomer and Jim Rice — our only blacks on the starting nine — about racism at Fenway. I waited there with Zimmer, Sullivan, and Clif Keane, a crusty radio personality, for the players to come out to the field.

It couldn't have been better if I'd ordered it. As we sat there jabbering, out lumbered The Boomer on his way to the batting cage. "Hey, Boomer, you old bush nigger," yelled Keane. "You gonna get out there and hit some taters?" Believe it or not, Keane's yell was affectionate, and everybody laughed.

Now, that was interesting less for the niggers-taters vocabulary than for the fact that Boomer and Zimmer are on the outs. Boomer had been benched in Texas, and it was clear not only that he was having a mid-life crisis but that he was on his way out. So all Boomer did in the face of this assault was to roll his eyes like Satchmo. I tried to read meaning into that and failed, so later in the dugout I asked him how he felt when he heard that niggers-taters stuff. I was so worked up about the way The Gerbil and Clif Keane had treated Boomer that I didn't notice The Gerbil sitting at the other end of the dugout.

I did hear him yell, though. "You never heard no such thing! Why would you make up such a thing? You never heard no 'old bush nigger,' and you better not write that in the paper. Why would you make up a thing like that?"

Boomer said, "I'm not getting into this one, babe. I'm in enough trouble as it is."

So I was in it alone with the manager. "Don, what did Clif Keane call The Boomer?"

Zimmer paused. Then he said, "He called him 'an old bush.' That's right. 'An old bush' is what the man said."

An old bush? Now there's a well-known epithet.

June 24

An illumination: I've begun to love the Red Sox. Or could it be that I'm just desperate?

I was driving through the Berkshires to get away from the Sox, but my radio was tuned, nonetheless, to the game. My boys were tied with the Blue Jays in the eleventh inning, with Boston at bat. Bob Watson was at the plate.

(A word about Bob Watson, the black first baseman who has just come to the Red Sox. The day before, I noticed that Watson wears not only a rabbit's foot on his belt but also the Hebrew word *chai*, meaning life, on the inevitable gold chain around his neck.

"Where'd you get the necklace, Bob?" I asked him. "My stockbroker gave it to me," he replied.)

In the eleventh inning the rabbit's foot and the *chai* sign did the job, because Watson homered to win the game! The crowd was cheering and, alone in the car, so was I. So was I.

July 10

I am in their bell jar now, completely oblivious to the outside world. Another road trip, another motel, another pool, another stadium, another press box, more anxiety, more peanuts, please, another Tab. And, for traveling companions, the boys in the box.

I had come to terms with their world, and I was even happy — until we got to Anaheim. There, during a game Nolan Ryan was pitching brilliantly, I discovered I could no longer keep my attention on the play. Looking around for someone to talk to, I spotted a familiar-looking man across the press box, separated from us reporters by a grass wall.

"Why, that's Nixon!" I yelled. "Richard Nixon! What's *he* doing here?"

Larry Whiteside, my friend at *The Boston Globe,* didn't even look up from his typewriter. "Calm down, Marie," he said. "It's only a game. There are a hundred and sixty-two of them a year."

July 14, 25

But there is only one All-Star Game. It's all hustle and glitz here, and, more to the point, there's the sense that baseball has another context besides what goes on on the field. There are old-timers and promoters and lawyers and agents; it's the baseball version of Cannes. So relaxed was I in this circus that I strolled up to Rod Carew and asked him to demonstrate his batting style. Carew obliged by grabbing a bat, rolling it down his arm, gently letting it spin across his palm, and clutching it only at the last second. Then he twirled the bat slightly so that the Louisville Slugger seal faced away from him.

In that heady moment, I forgot everything I'd learned about communicating with ballplayers. "Rod, do you do that because you believe that old canard about the bat being weakest where the seal is?"

Carew smiled and said nothing. When I returned to the hotel, however, a phone message awaited me: "Rod Carew phoned. He says he has no idea what a nonedible canard is. Please explain."

Both Yaz and I are celebrating this week. Yaz has his four-hundredth homer to be happy about, and I have fallen in love. I'm not surprised that I've fallen in love with a New Yorker, but I am surprised that he is a former Red Sox bat boy and, at age forty-one, so devoted a lover of the Red Sox that he once spent $10,000 on long-distance charges from Europe to plug into a summer's worth of Red Sox broadcasts.

We became reacquainted at Yankee Stadium on the first night of the archrivals' confrontation. The only thing we ever disagree on is the subject of Yaz. *Naturally.* I had my theories about Yaz's homer. I tried to predict on "mental" grounds when the captain would reach this first milestone of the summer. I tried my theories out. The former bat boy's response was to yell: "How can I love a woman who doesn't understand that when Yaz gets his pitch and he hits the ball in the right way, he'll get his home run, regardless of who's north, south, east, or west?"

September 15

Yaz almost did me in last week. If the four-hundredth homer was tough, his three-thousandth hit was a nightmare. I was spending as much time as possible in New York because the Sox had collapsed. They're playing out the string, and all attention — last week, anyway — was focused on Yaz. The governor was poised to present Yaz his plaque, the banners were waiting to be unfurled, and the T-shirt vendors were hawking their designs up and down Yawkey Way. The problem was the captain. He suffered from batter's block. For the final two games of the six-game series, he was unable to do anything but strike out, pop up, or fly to a waiting glove. Even I felt sorry for Yaz, growing old before our eyes, straining to reach his milestone and be done with this ceremonial change of baseball life. After six terrible days at Fenway — days that were terrible because of the tension and the madhouse in the stands each time he came to bat, and, for me, days of racing for the ten o'clock New York shuttle — the captain finally did it. Off a Yankee rookie. But done, and, if not so finely, at least finally done.

And I am free at last. Now there are only three more American League cities to visit with my team. And three more department stores to visit in those American League cities before batting practice.

September 21

I wish I could say I kissed the boys a loving good-bye. My last moments with them were gloomy, but somehow they were the most profound we'd had. Last Sunday, in Baltimore, we were slaughtered by the Orioles on a beautiful crisp autumn afternoon.

Since the Orioles have proved unbeatable, the slaughter wasn't surprising, but the fine weather didn't help anybody's spirits. To cheer us up, the Red Sox organization took the players and the press to a steak and lobster place for dinner before we took off on our charter plane for Toronto. At dinner, instead of listening to the poly-ester-and-plaid brigade, I sat with the players and joked around with a few of the pitchers and the new second baseman, Ted Size-more. What was even better was that the players were actually in high spirits. Even Fisk was laughing. Happily for everybody's mood, Zimmer and Yaz were nowhere near.

Until we got back on the bus. Our party went merrily on in the back, and Yaz and Zimmer — Silas Marner and Grumpy — huddled together near the front. The kidding began to get louder. Sizemore kidded the pitchers about going back to Triple A ball, and the pitchers gave it to Sizemore about getting traded from the Cubs. They were just letting off steam. Everybody relaxed. It was clear the laughter was a tonic for this bedraggled team. Clear to everybody, that is, except Silas Marner and Grumpy.

Suddenly Yaz was on his feet, bellowing at his teammates, who had just lionized him for his three-thousandth hit. "If you guys could accomplish something, then you would deserve the right to pop off." No simple little "Shhh" or "Pipe down, guys" for the captain.

Here was the season's capper: the perfect demonstration of the terrible theorem that gnaws at the Red Sox. Yaz screamed about accomplishment — his kind of accomplishment, which means being a hero hitter. Yaz is the old school; and until the management thinks about defense and pitching in September, when the long balls fall short, everybody is going to blame everybody else. Yaz will have his hits, plaques, and tantrums, but it's clear the old school can't carry the day.

And for all I care next season, Yaz's tendons can have him benched till fall. I couldn't care less what The Eck will say about Pudge's bad arm. And as far as I'm concerned, Zimmer's pitching rotation can have two men or twelve. But I wonder if they'll be brooding this year and thinking, "If that could happen to us then, what will this summer bring?" I can assure them of one thing: it won't bring me.

Brenner, the first woman to cover the Red Sox on a regular basis, has since gone on to a distinguished career writing for magazines such as The New Yorker. What makes her story compelling is that despite virtually no baseball background, she nevertheless caught the spirit of a Red Sox team, aptly described as consisting of "twenty-five players, twenty-five cabs."

JOHN UPDIKE

RAPT BY THE RADIO
Tuned-in, Turned-on ... Again

from *The Boston Globe*, October 6, 1986

Forty years ago and 400 miles from Boston, I sat in my father's Chevrolet, in the Shillington (Pa.) High School parking lot, and listened to the seventh game of the 1946 World Series, the Red Sox vs. the Cardinals. Eighth inning, score 3–3, Cardinals up, Enos Slaughter on first base, Harry Walker at the plate; there's a hit to center field, Leon Culberson (substituting for the injured Dom DiMaggio) throws to the infield, shortstop Johnny Pesky cuts it off — Slaughter is being waved around third! Pesky hesitates, the throw is late, Slaughter scores!! The Cardinals hold on to win the game and the World Series. I don't know if I cried, sitting alone in that old Chevrolet, but I was only 14 and well might have. Dazed and with something lost forever, I emerged into the golden September afternoon, where my classmates were jostling and yelling, nuzzling their steadies, sneaking smokes and shooting baskets in a blissful animal innocence I could no longer share.

What had led me, who had never been north of Greenwich, Conn., and didn't know Beacon Hill from Bunker Hill or Fenway Park from the Public Garden, to attach my heart to that distant aggregation of men in white knickers? Ted Williams had made a dent in my consciousness before the war, but it was the '46 Sox that made me a passionate fan. What a team that was! — Ted in left, Dom in center, Doerr at second, Pesky at short, Hal Wagner behind the plate, Boo Ferriss and Tex Hughson on the mound and Rudy York at first, having a great season. Though the Cardinals squeaked by them in that Series, they looked sure to cruise to pennants at least until I got out of high school in 1950. But in fact they didn't, coming perilously close in '48 and '49 but not quite having it in the clutch. The postwar pattern of thrills and spills was set, and whenever they came to Philadelphia, there I was, hanging by the radio.

With its nine defensive men widely spaced on the field, baseball is an easier game to visualize than a fast shuffle like basketball and hockey, and until girls and a driver's license got me by the throat, I spent many an idyllic summer day indoors huddled on the family easy chair next to the hoarse little Philco. The announcers' voices in their granular shades of excitement, and the wraparound crowd noise, and the sound in the middle distance of the ball being hit (not to mention the uproarious clatter when a foul ball sailed into the broadcast booth) made a vivid picture in ways superior to what I would see when, once or twice a summer, I was bused the 50 miles to Shibe Park's bleachers. I even kept box scores of my audited games, and listened on the rainout days when the play-by-play of some remote and feeble contest like the Browns against the Senators would be verbalized from a teletype whose chattering could be heard in the lulls. The two Philadelphia teams were pretty feeble themselves, and created the vacuum into which my irrational ardor for the Red Sox had flowed.

My barber was a Yankee fan; that was the other choice in Pennsylvania. As his scissors gnashed around my ears and his hair tonic corroded my scalp, he would patiently again explain why Joe DiMaggio was a *team* player, and why as a team the Yankees would always *win*. But they didn't like Roosevelt or Truman at the barber shop either, and I would rather lose with Boston than win with New York. When my college choices came down to Cornell or Harvard, the decision was obvious. And yet, those four years in Cambridge, it rather rarely seemed to have dawned on me that the Red Sox were only two 10-minute subway rides (or, on a sunny day, a nice walk along the river) away. Living in New York, though, I would risk the subway up to the Bronx and from within the cavernous shadows of the Stadium admired the aging Williams as he matched strokes with Mickey Mantle, who had replaced DiMaggio as the hood ornament of the onrolling Yankees. The Fifties Red Sox didn't leave much of a mark on the record book, but they seem to have inspired a quixotic loyalty in me. While it is not entirely true that I moved from New York to

New England to be closer to the Red Sox, it is not entirely false either. I wanted to keep Ted Williams company while I could.

Lying in back yards or on the beach, driving in the car or squinting into a book, I listened to the games and internalized Curt Gowdy. That ever so soothing and sensible voice, with its guileless hint of Wyoming twang, relayed popups and bloop hits, blowouts and shutouts to my subconscious; phantom heroes like Clyde Vollmer and Ellis Kinder and Walt Dropo and Sammy White flitted across the airwaves, and Jackie Jensen and Jimmy Piersall glimmered in Williams' lengthening shadow. My wife's parents had a retreat on a far hill of Vermont, without electricity or telephone but with plenty of pine cones and bear turds in the woods. We parked our car on the edge of that woods, and there I would go, many an afternoon, to sit in the front seat and tune in the Red Sox. Curt's voice came in strong from (I think) Burlington — so strong that one day the car battery wouldn't turn the starter over, and we were stranded. I must have been the only man in New England who, rather than lose touch with the Red Sox, marooned his family in a forest full of bears.

The older you get, the stranger your earlier selves seem, until you can scarcely remember having made their acquaintance at all. Whatever held me there, rapt by the radio, all those precious hours? Ted, of course, who was always doing something fascinating — getting injured, going off to Korea, vilifying the press, announcing his retirement, hitting .388, hitting Joe Cronin's housekeeper with a tossed bat, spitting at the stands, going fishing when he shouldn't, etc. But the Red Sox around him had a fascination too; generous-spending Tom Yawkey saw to it that there were always some other classy performers, and some hopeful passages in every season. Yet the wheels inevitably came off the cart, or were lubricated too late in the season, and the Red Sox had that ultimate charm, the charm of losers.

All men are mortal, and therefore all men are losers; our profoundest loyalty goes out to the fallible. Chris Evert, for example, did not win our hearts until Navratilova began to push her around, and I know a man who has been a Chicago Cubs fan for 50 years. Are the killer Mets of today nearly as much fun as those hapless teams of post-expansion days, the "Amazing Mets" that New Yorkers, bored by the Yankees, clasped to their ironical hearts? As a boy in Pennsylvania, I felt sorry for Mr. Yawkey, that all his financial goodness couldn't buy a World Series. I felt sorry for Williams, that he didn't go 5 for 5 every day and that spiteful sportswriters kept cheating him of the MVP award. The Red Sox in my immature mind were like the man in the Hollywood movie who, because he's wearing a tuxedo, is bound to slip on a banana peel. They were gallantry and grace without the crassness of victory. I loved them. I might have loved some other team just as well — an infant gosling, if caught at the right moment, will fall in love with a zoologist instead of its mother, and a German, if kicked often enough, will fall in love with a shoe — but the Red Sox were the team I had chosen, and one's choices, once made, generate a self-justifying and self-sustaining inertia. All over the country, millions of fans root and holler for one team against another for no reason except that they have chosen to.

Since Williams retired — dramatically, as usual — in 1960, my Red Sox ardor, with its abuse of car batteries, has cooled. But I have not been unaware, in the quarter-century since, of the pennants of 1967 and '75, and, just as in 1946, the subsequent seventh-game disappointments in the World Series. I remember, in fact, on a late September Sunday of 1967, crouching with some other suburban men, in an interruption of a touch football game, around a little radio on the grass as it told us that the Twins were losing to the Red Sox while the White Sox were beating the Tigers, thus allowing our Yastrzemski-led boys to back into their first pennant in 21 years. And I remember, as well, another September, in 1978, when my wife and I, heading for a Cambridge dinner date, parked along Memorial Drive and listened to the last inning of the Yankees–Red Sox playoff. We heard about the poky Bucky Dent home run, and we heard in living audio the foul Yastrzemski popup. It was Slaughter rounding third all over again.

The memoirs of a Red Sox fan tend to sound sour, a litany of disappointments and mistakes going back to the day when Babe Ruth was traded. But the other side of this tails-up coin is that time and again the team, as its generations of personnel yield one to another, has worked its way to the edge of total victory. Yaz' famous popup, for instance, was preceded by a heroic week of solid victories, forcing the Yankees to a playoff, and in the game itself, we (notice the reflexive-possessive pronoun) had fought back from a 5–2 deficit to

5–4 and the tying run on third. In sports, not only do you win some and lose some but 25 competitors, in a 26-team sport, are going to come in lower than first. What makes Boston — little old Boston up here among the rocky fields and empty mills — think it deserves championship teams all the time? Having the Celtics is miracle enough, perhaps, not to mention a Patriots team that finally won in Miami. The founding Puritans left behind a lingering conviction, I fear, that earthly success reflects divine election, and that this city built upon a hill is anciently entitled to a prime share. Certainly the scorn heaped in the Boston column upon imperfect Red Sox teams approaches the self-righteous — and not just the sports columns, Mike Barnicle.

Now this summer's team, casually relegated by most April prophets to a fourth- or fifth-place finish, has made it to the playoffs. It seems a strange team to us veteran Red Sox watchers — solid, sometimes great, pitching, and fitful, even anemic hitting. Where are the home runs of yesteryear? Wade Boggs singled his way to some batting championships, and now Jim Rice is hitting for average, too. Only Baylor and Armas seem to be swinging from the heels anymore. Heroism has moved from the plate to the pitcher's mound: Clemens so full of the Right Stuff his uniform fairly pops its buttons, and Hurst and Seaver looking just as resolute. Oil Can Boyd emerged from his month in the doghouse with an enhanced charisma; the one thing made clear in this murky episode was how much we need him, his arm and his twitchy self-exhortations and his terrific name. And Sambito and Schiraldi staggered out of nowhere to help Stanley nail the slippery games down. This nervous-making crew, with its gimpy veterans and erratic infield, has shown toughness and courage and internal rapport, and like last year's Patriots did better than anyone dared hope. These Sox were spared that burden of great expectations carried by so many of their noble, star-crossed predecessors; now they have nothing to lose but the marbles. Once again, I'm tuned in.

Updike's "Hub Fans Bid Kid Adieu" is perhaps the best-known piece of writing on the Red Sox. But Updike, as this story written for the Globe *on the precipice of the 1986 postseason demonstrates, was no Red Sox dilettante.*

BUCKNER'S STORY IS PAINFULLY FAMILIAR

from *The Boston Globe*, October 24, 1986

I have carried the Buckner notes in my pocket for five days. Every day I say I will do the Buckner story and every day something or someone intercedes.

I am beginning to feel guilty. I have to do the Buckner story sometime before this World Series ends. "What is this Buckner story?" my boss asks. "What's the Buckner angle?"

"You know, playing in pain," I reply. "I suppose it's been done. I know Vin Scully and Joe Garagiola are talking about the guy every night, making him a portrait in courage. I suppose that's my angle. Though not in so many words."

"Hmmmmm," my boss says, never a good sign. "Got anything else? Hmmmmm."

I know he would like me to pursue some other, fresher angle — something that would stop a few presses — but I like the Buckner angle. The playing with pain stuff. What the heck. Just because some story has been done doesn't mean it can't be done again.

"Does it?" I ask my boss.

"Hmmmm," he replies.

I don't care. I have these Buckner notes that seem different than any of the other Buckner notes I have read. Why shouldn't they be in the paper?

I was part of a small group that caught the Red Sox first baseman on the field the day before the games began at Fenway. When was that? Monday? Monday.

He detailed all the woes he has had with his left foot for a decade and the Achilles tendon problem he was having at the moment. He was pleasant in doing this, even funny. It was as if he were talking about some old clunker of a car that he was driving, pointing out the dings and dongs with a perverse pride.

He said he ices — let's see — both feet, one knee, plus the backs of his quadriceps and hamstrings before and after every game. He said he was icing an aching shoulder earlier in the year. He said he tapes everywhere. He looks like the Invisible Man, out for a walk, the way he has so much tape after most games.

"Someone said you're a believer in some kind of cryogenics," one of the sportswriters asked. "You're one of those guys who is freezing his body until some cure comes along for whatever ails him."

Bill Buckner laughed. That's what I have here. Bill Buckner laughed.

He — let's see — said he knows exactly what he is doing. He is putting strains on a body that he shouldn't, but he is willing to pick up whatever check comes along at a later date. Has this been in the paper? He knows that somewhere down the line, he will have troubles because of what he is doing now.

"I've been taking anti-inflammatory drugs for 10 years now," he said in these notes. "And I know they aren't good for you. I've been taking two pills a day for 10 years. I have shots. I've had all kinds of cortisone shots."

"How many this year?" a reporter asked.

"Nine," Buckner said. "Those are the ones I hate. They inject 'em right into the spot that hurts."

He talked about the X-ray of his ankle. He said that bone virtually was grinding against bone in there. He said there was supposed to be about an eighth of an inch in separation. He said his X-ray mostly showed a line. The future? He said he had read about plastic ankles and ankle fusions. He said he would be having ankle surgery in the offseason for immediate relief, a cleanout of some of the spurs and chips.

"Sandy Koufax retired because he didn't want to go through this kind of stuff," a sportswriter said. "He decided he'd rather have full use of his arm for the rest of his life than play more baseball."

"I understand that," Buckner said. "Johnny Bench retired for the same reason. He wanted to be able to walk and play golf. I don't feel that way. I'd rather do everything I can to play. I think it's worth it."

I have — let's see — some of his memories before he broke the ankle in the first place, about how he was able to run at an athlete's fast speed. He used to run races from class to class at the University of Southern California against classmate Bobby Valentine. Valentine was the state sprint champion of Connecticut and won every race, standing on the steps of the next building, sticking his tongue out at the end. Buckner kept running those races.

"Stubborn," he said. "I'm German. Just part of my character. I've been that way all my life. I wanted to finish first. I was like that in sixth grade, always trying for the top grade. I couldn't stand it when someone else got a better grade than me. I was the same way in sports. Stubborn."

His stubbornness, I guess, is the angle here. The Buckner angle. With every game, he looks as if he's working under tougher circumstances. He is wearing those Lou Groza boots. He has little range, no speed. He runs . . . the way he runs is the theme contest of this World Series. Is it not?

He runs as if he had been shot. He runs as if he is carrying a large piece of sheetrock on his back. He runs as if he is trying to run underneath barbed wire. He runs as if a giant, invisible hand were pushing against him. He runs . . .

"I don't run," Buckner said in these notes. "I wouldn't call what I do 'running.' I'd call it 'moving.' Somewhere between jogging and walking. That's what I do."

I suppose a lot of this has been covered — Vin and Joe certainly have talked about the man — but what am I going to do? I have the notes. They still sound good to me.

"What do you think?" I ask my boss before the fifth game of the World Series begins. "The Buckner angle?"

"Oh, do what you want," he says.

I did.

Leigh Montville's entertaining columns for the Boston Globe *were must reading for Boston sports fans through the 1970s and 1980s. He should have played the lottery after writing this column, which unintentionally provided all the background needed for what would take place only a few hours later, the ball bouncing between Bill Buckner's legs. Like Peter Gammons, Montville later left the* Globe *for* Sports Illustrated. *He is currently at work on a biography of Ted Williams.*

s"PETER GAMMONS

···

GAME 6

from *Sports Illustrated*, April 6, 1987

It was time for a new season, but the question under discussion was from the old: Do you send Don Baylor up to bat for Bill Buckner?

Philadelphia manager John Felske and scout Ray (Snacks) Shore were standing behind a batting cage in Clearwater, Fla., early in spring training, reliving the night of Oct. 25, 1986. "I was sitting there in my den with two outs in the bottom of the tenth," said Felske, "and I turned to my wife and said, 'This is where I want to be someday.'

"Ten minutes later, I said to my wife, 'God, I hope I'm never there.'"

"I'm a John McNamara man," said Shore, who worked closely with McNamara when they were both with the Reds from 1979 to 1982. "But the one thing I'll never understand is letting Buckner hit against [Jesse] Orosco in the eighth."

"That's because you've never been a manager," Felske said. "Buckner had knocked in 102 runs. He helped get them there. A manager has to live with his players. As a manager, I understand. Why does McNamara have to listen to this crap after he took a team that was picked for fifth place all the way to Game 7 of the World Series?"

Felske paused, composing himself. Then, faster than you could say, "Greg Luzinski, 1977," he said, "But I will agree that he's got to get Buckner out of there for defense . . ."

The next morning, in Winter Haven, Fla., the manager in question, John McNamara, greeted the arrival of the full Red Sox squad with a closed-door, stern speech imploring them to forget what happened last October. Said one player afterward, "We became the first team in history to be told before the first workout of the spring not to think or talk about making it to the seventh game of the World Series."

"Last year should be remembered not for one inning or one game," said veteran relief pitcher Joe Sambito, "but what for most of us was the best of times."

The worst of times, of course, came in the bottom of the 10th inning of Game 6 of the World Series, when the Boston Red Sox turned a 5–3, two-out, bases-empty lead into a 6–5 loss to the New York Mets. In order, Gary Carter singled, Kevin Mitchell singled, Ray Knight singled to score Carter and send Mitchell to third, Mitchell scored on a wild pitch as Knight went to second, and Knight scored the winning run when Mookie Wilson's grounder went through Buckner's legs. Though it has been used many times before, the first paragraph of Charles Dickens's *A Tale of Two Cities* truly does describe Game 6: "It was the best of times, it was the worst of times, it was the age of wisdom, it was the age of foolishness, it was the epoch of belief, it was the epoch of incredulity, it was the season of Light, it was the season of Darkness, it was the spring of hope, it was the winter of despair, we had everything before us, we had nothing before us, we were all going direct to Heaven, we were all going direct the other way."

Game 6 has now taken its place with the other great World Series contests: Game 8 in 1912, Game 4 in 1947, Game 7 in 1960 and Game 6 in 1975. But in a way it stands alone as the greatest "bad" game in Series history. The Mets, who in 1986 won more games (116) than all but two teams ever, were facing the Red Sox, who hadn't won a World Series since Babe Ruth pitched for them. For much of the Series, the two teams bumbled around like a couple of September cellar dwellers. And managers McNamara and Davey Johnson, otherwise sound strategists, often seemed to be off in other worlds.

"Answering questions about that game is something I'll always have to deal with," says McNamara. More incredibly, Johnson will always have to answer questions about screwing up a World Series he won. A month after the game, Larry Bowa, a friend who played with and for Johnson, called him and asked, "What in the world were you thinking?"

Regardless of the managing, there was still very little art to this game. Aside from a sinking Marty Barrett liner that Lenny Dykstra stabbed in the first, a long fly by the star-crossed Buckner that Darryl Strawberry ran down on the warning track in the second and Wade Boggs's dive into the stands in the fourth to catch a Keith Hernandez pop-up, there was small cause, defensively, for Vin Scully to raise his voice. The Red Sox' go-ahead run in the seventh inning and the Mets' tying run in the eighth came after wild throws, and the Mets' tying and winning runs in the 10th came on a wild pitch and the croquet shot through Buckner's wicket. The winning pitcher, Rick Aguilera, had a 12.00 ERA for the Series. And when you look at the box score, your eye immediately falls on the line that reads, "Stanley pitched to one batter in the 10th."

"We lost that game," said Barrett, the Sox' second baseman. "They won the seventh game, but we lost on Saturday night." That's why the game's legitimate heroes, players like Wilson and Orosco, seem to have played only supporting roles. And that's why you wonder if Buckner, McNamara, Bob Stanley and Calvin Schiraldi will forever be scarred, like Fred Merkle, Mickey Owen and Ralph Branca before them.

"Shots," Buckner calls media reminders of what happened. Ten days before spring training he told the *Boston Globe*, "I'm not going to talk about what happened anymore." But Buckner did point out that Stanley wasn't covering first when Wilson's grounder went through his legs. For his part, Stanley took some off-season shots at McNamara's decision-making process, and the pitcher's wife, Joan, was quoted as saying that Rich Gedman "blew it" because he had failed to stop Stanley's inside pitch to Wilson. Roger Clemens, the Boston starter, publicly wondered why McNamara took him out of the game with a 3–2 lead after seven innings, and Baylor privately seethed at not being used. "All season long we won as a team, and as soon as we lost, some of the guys started pointing fingers," says Baylor.

And the Mets? "We had accomplished so much and had come from behind in such dramatic fashion in the playoffs that the sixth game just seemed like a good bounce that gave us the chance to win what we believed we should win," says Wilson. But even Hernandez, who went to the manager's office and popped open a beer after he made the second out in the 10th inning, admitted, "I couldn't believe what I was watching on TV." Says Bobby Ojeda, who was traded from the Red Sox to the Mets the winter before, "Even though we knew we deserved it, we know we won because of Stanley's wild pitch and Buckner's error."

Unlike Game 6 of the '75 World Series, which was about as lively as a Lennon Sisters Special until Bernardo Carbo's eighth-inning, three-run home run tied the game for the Red Sox, this game was filled with might-have-beens from the outset. Especially in the first inning. Ojeda was working on three days' rest — a problem because he is an emotional, combative sort whose best pitch, a changeup, is even more of a strain on the arm than a fastball. "I was working on adrenaline," he says. He also did not have his usual control. After the game began, appropriately enough, with a one-hopper by Boggs that slapped off the glove of Knight at third, Ojeda survived two shots to the outfield, the second by Buckner, whose at bat was interrupted by the arrival of a parachutist. Ojeda walked Jim Rice. Dwight Evans then hit a towering drive off the fence in left center, and Boggs scored easily. True, Dykstra did make a fine play on the carom and rifled a quick, accurate throw to cutoff man Rafael Santana, but . . .

How could Rice not have scored from first with two out? "I couldn't believe it," admits Ojeda. Recalls Red Sox third base coach Rene Lachemann, now a coach for Oakland, "I had to watch Dykstra and the relay, and when I turned to pick up Jimmy, he was barely around second." Rice to this day claims, "The ball was hit too hard to score on." But there were two outs. Did he get fooled, assume the ball was out of the park and go into a trot, as he did in the third inning of the seventh game when he hit the ball off the wall and was thrown out at second on what should have been a double? Despite a knee operation in the fall of '85, Rice is not that slow. But the Red Sox run the bases as if they're guiding golf carts around a retirement community, and Rice — of whom Charles Scoggins of the *Lowell Sun* once wrote, "He stops at each base to scrape the gum off his shoes" — is particularly cautious. So four singles, a walk and a double in the first two innings produced only two runs.

Through four innings Clemens had a no-hitter and that 2–0 lead. To his credit, Ojeda battled for his life, and his survival is particularly amazing considering that — as he found out later — the Red

Sox knew practically everything he was throwing at them. "I was tipping my changeup," Ojeda says. "Since I'm primarily a fastball-changeup pitcher, it didn't take much to figure what was coming if it wasn't going to be my changeup."

Clemens, finally recovered from the flu that had so weakened him in the playoffs and the second game of the Series, struck out six Mets the first time through the order and had retired eight straight entering the fifth. Neither Clemens nor any succeeding Boston pitcher noticed the big woman in red behind home plate who was trying to distract him by continually rolling her arms, much like one of Gladys Knight's Pips. Whoever she was, she was persistent, because she kept it up until the baseball went through Buckner's legs.

Despite his impressive numbers, it hadn't been an easy game for Clemens. Carter, Strawberry and Santana had fouled so many pitches that his four innings seemed more like seven; he had already thrown 73 pitches. "I was throwing hard," says Clemens, "but I wasn't putting the ball where I wanted." Clemens walked Strawberry to lead off the fifth, and Strawberry did for the second time in the game what the Red Sox did only once in their 14 postseason contests: He stole second. Knight fouled off three pitches, then Clemens threw a "bad" slider that Knight hit through the middle for an RBI single.

Then came a Wilson at bat that would have nearly as much importance as the one five innings later. After Clemens threw two fastballs past him and the count reached 2 and 2, Mookie fouled off two pitches. Clemens then tried to get a slider in. The slider to Knight had hurt Clemens, but this one hurt him twice as much. Not only was the pitch out over the plate, but Clemens also released it in such a way that it popped a blister that had been developing on his index finger. Wilson pulled a groundball single into right. The ball took a final, fidgety hop in front of Evans and bounced off his chest. Knight, a slow runner who never would have challenged Evans's rifle arm, dashed to third base.

The Mets still trailed 2–1, but they had runners at the corners with none out. Santana, a .218 hitter during the season, was due up, followed by Ojeda. Here came the first of Johnson's second-guessed maneuvers. He had Danny Heep bat for Santana, who had had two hits off Clemens in Game 2. That meant Johnson's only remaining shortstops were Kevin Elster, a nervous rookie with 22 games of big league experience, and Howard Johnson, a utilityman who is considered a defensive liability.

"How could you be pinch-hitting that early?" Bowa asked. "I thought it might be our one shot to get Clemens out of there," Johnson replied.

Johnson was subscribing to the strategy Earl Weaver had taught him: Use your guns whenever you think your time has come, no matter what inning. But as another manager puts it, "He was only going to use Ojeda one more inning, so why not keep Santana in the game and bat for the pitcher?" Heep hit into a double play that tied the score at 2–2, and Ojeda grounded out. He pitched one more inning, keeping the Sox at bay in the sixth.

Clemens's blister prevented him from throwing his slider, and because he didn't have a particularly good curveball in the late season, he decided simply to move his fastball around and change speeds. Wally Backman and Hernandez singled with one out in the sixth, but Clemens struck out Carter with a perfect pitch on the outside corner. He then held his breath as Barrett snapped up Strawberry's sharp grounder.

In the top of the seventh Roger McDowell walked leadoff hitter Barrett. Rather than sacrifice him over — the Red Sox were 1 for 4 trying to bunt in the game — McNamara removed the bunt sign for Buckner and sent Barrett. Buckner grounded out, moving Barrett into scoring position. When Knight fielded Rice's routine grounder and threw the ball over Hernandez's head, Boston had runners at first and third with one out and Evans up. On a 3-and-2 count, McNamara sent Rice. Sure enough, Evans hit a perfect double-play ball to Backman. However, Rice beat Backman's flip to Elster, and though Elster's throw got Evans at first, Barrett had scored to give the Red Sox a 3–2 lead.

The Red Sox had a chance to make it 4–2 when Gedman punched a two-out single through the shortstop hole into left field. With two outs in a big ballpark, and considering Wilson's weak arm, Lachemann naturally waved Rice around third. However, Rice cut the bag like a 16-wheeler turning into a McDonald's, while Wilson charged the ball and released it quickly. The ball arrived in Carter's mitt on a fly, and Rice was out. "How we didn't score and put the game away in the first eight innings is just as much the story as what happened in the 10th," Barrett said later.

Clemens held the lead in the bottom of the seventh, retiring the side on 17 pitches — giving him 135 for the game. But while pitching to Wilson — naturally — he tore the fingernail on his middle finger, and when he got back to the dugout, he was bleeding from two fingers. McNamara and pitching coach Bill Fischer approached him.

"Does it sting?" McNamara asked.

"Sure, it stings," said Clemens.

"I told them I couldn't throw any sliders, but I could get them out with fastballs and forkballs," Clemens now says. "They told me that if the first couple of hitters got on, they might hit for me."

At the postgame press conference, McNamara clearly implied that Clemens asked out of the game because of the blister. "My pitcher told me he couldn't go any further," said McNamara. When George Grande of ESPN later asked Clemens off-camera what McNamara had said, Clemens got upset and started off to confront McNamara.

"Fischer stopped me and told me it was a misunderstanding, that Mac didn't mean it," recalls Clemens. "I wanted to pitch the eighth inning, then turn it over to Calvin with three outs to go."

Despite that minor imbroglio and the other questions that besieged McNamara over the winter, this fact remains: Through seven innings that October night the manager had looked like a genius. By starting Al Nipper in the fourth game, on a night no Boston pitcher could have beaten Ron Darling, McNamara had given his ace — Clemens — a full five days of rest. And Clemens had given the Red Sox the lead with just six outs to go.

In the top of the eighth, Dave Henderson reached base courtesy of the first of two boots by Elster. Spike Owen sacrificed Henderson to second, then McNamara had rookie Mike Greenwell bat for Clemens. Interestingly enough, McNamara's defense for not sending Baylor up to hit for Buckner three batters later was: "We wouldn't pinch-hit with a lead."

Greenwell struck out, and Johnson had McDowell walk Boggs intentionally. But then McDowell also walked Barrett to load the bases. Johnson had little choice but to bring in Orosco, who would retire 16 of the 18 batters he faced in the Series and should have been the MVP instead of Knight. Here is where Johnson committed his primary strategical boo-boo. The pitcher was scheduled to lead off the bottom of the inning, so with his best reliever in the game and the Red Sox one inning away from a world championship, Johnson should have made a double switch in order to keep Orosco in the game for at least the ninth inning. He could have put Lee Mazzilli or Mitchell in left and put Orosco in Wilson's spot, thus letting the new leftfielder lead off the bottom of the eighth. "Davey forgot," says one manager. "This wasn't one of my better games," Johnson admitted later.

It's far too easy to criticize managers, and very often the critics can't see the forest for the trees. While Johnson can sometimes be an unorthodox strategist, he is usually borne out in the long run by his players' performances. But in this case, he did forget. An inning later he would compound the situation by double-switching Strawberry out of the game, which led to Strawberry's pouting, which led to Strawberry's hotdogging it around the bases in Game 7 to show his manager up, which led to Nipper — who gave up the home run — hitting Strawberry in the back in spring training.

So this was the situation: bases loaded, two outs in the eighth and the lefty Orosco on the mound. The scheduled batter was Buckner, who showed great fortitude — some said folly — by playing on his battered legs. But he was also 10 for 55 in postseason play and 1 for 11 with runners in scoring position for the Series. A lefthanded swinger, Buckner had hit .218 in the regular season against lefty pitchers. And Orosco is, in the words of Dodger scout Jerry Stephenson, "the toughest pitcher in the league on lefties," an opinion supported by the fact that lefthanded hitters batted .187 against him during the season.

Clearly, McNamara had a decision to make. He thought about using Baylor, who was on the bench because the Red Sox couldn't use a DH in the National League park. McNamara and Buckner later denied it, but other players sitting on the bench claim the manager approached Buckner to tell him he was taking him out. But before McNamara could say anything, Buckner talked him out of any move. "When Johnson came out of the dugout, Mac started to tell Buck, 'If they go to the lefthander . . . ,'" says one of the players. "Buck argued, 'I can hit the guy.' He said something else and that was that. It wasn't like a bullying thing. It was as if Mac thought to himself and said, 'Hey, the guy's done this much with all those problems . . .'"

"I was in the clubhouse swinging a bat and was never told that I was going to bat," says Baylor. "Although I did hear that [McNamara was talked out of the move] from another player."

McNamara contends that he didn't want to pinch-hit for Buckner with a lead and that previously he replaced Buckner with Dave Stapleton at first only after Buckner had been removed for a pinch runner. But, in fact, Stapleton had gone in for defense in several postseason games. "We didn't hit for Buckner during the season," said McNamara. "Why then?"

But he also didn't have Baylor on the bench all season. While Baylor had batted only .230 against lefthanders, he was a major reason the Red Sox were there. His homer preceding Henderson's in the fifth game of the playoffs against the California Angels was the biggest hit of the season, and he had transformed the "me" mood of the clubhouse to a "we." Baylor certainly believed he should have batted. When a reporter said after the game, "I guess Buckner doesn't get hit for there," Baylor replied, "Why?"

"It's stupid to even debate about my hitting there," insists Buckner. "I hit the ball pretty hard, too." He did, and Dykstra ran it down in left center. It was still 3–2. Orosco was done, and so was Clemens. And Buckner was still in the game to play defense.

For all of Boston's weeping and teeth-gnashing over the 10th, the Red Sox were fortunate to get that far. In the bottom of the eighth, Mazzilli batted for Orosco and pulled Schiraldi's pitch into right for a single. Then the black flies — Dykstra and Wally Backman — went to work. Dykstra laid down a perfect bunt, and Schiraldi picked it up and bounced a throw to second in the dirt. Backman laid one down, too, and Schiraldi fielded it again, cautiously throwing to first for the out. But the tying run was on third and the go-ahead run on second. Schiraldi walked Hernandez intentionally to load the bases.

Schiraldi went to 3 and 0 on Carter, and as the NBC camera homed in on his face, Calvin looked exactly like a 24-year-old rookie who has suddenly realized that half the nation is watching him. "It just so happened that when I screwed up, it was the World Series," he said.

Johnson gave Schiraldi a break. He flashed Carter the green light to swing, and Carter, ever the hero, swung at a waist-high fastball, hitting it hard to Rice in leftfield. Mazzilli scored easily from third, and the game was tied 3–3. With two outs and Dykstra on third, Strawberry flied out to end the inning.

Then Johnson pulled the double-switch, putting Aguilera in Strawberry's spot and keeping Mazzilli in the game in right. Afterward, while the rest of the Mets rejoiced, Strawberry blasted the manager. "I didn't notice him doing anything spectacular," Johnson said.

The Met manager wasn't off the strategic hook yet. The Mets had runners on first and second with no outs in the ninth after Schiraldi walked Knight and Gedman misplayed Wilson's bunt. The next hitter was Elster. "That's a tough place to ask a rookie to get down a bunt against a guy like Schiraldi," explains Johnson. "A .167-hitting backup shortstop had better be able to bunt," says another manager. But Johnson wasn't taking any chances, especially after Elster had already messed up two balls at shortstop. So he sent up Howard Johnson to bunt. HoJo's stab at the first pitch looked like a pelican diving for a fish. "I didn't like the looks of that," says the manager, "so I took off the bunt. I did the same thing with Orosco in the eighth inning of the seventh game; he singled up the middle for the final run and no one said anything." When Johnson tipped strike three into Gedman's glove for the first out, the second-guessers howled. Mazzilli lined out, Dykstra flied out — and it was on to the 10th.

At precisely 11:59 p.m. Henderson, leading off, rifled an Aguilera pitch off the leftfield scoreboard. "Hendu" might have achieved cult status in Boston, what with his home run in the fifth game of the ALCS, and now this one. With two outs Boggs doubled to left center and the redoubtable Barrett singled him home to give the Red Sox a 5–3 lead. All the Red Sox needed were three outs. Schiraldi may be considered a once-around-the-order short reliever, but he had closed out two of the last three playoff wins, as well as the Series opener, and the Red Sox were going to stick with him.

In the Boston clubhouse, the champagne was laid out. Backman flied out to left. The NBC roadies set up the post game riser as Peter Ueberroth, announcer Bob Costas and Red Sox owners Haywood Sullivan and Jean Yawkey began to get in position. The MVP trophy was going to Bruce Hurst. Hernandez lined out to center. As the last newspaper deadlines in the East approached, journalists typed out flash leads. Fred McMane of United Press International was about to send: "Dave Henderson, playing the hero Boston has sought for 68 years, homered in the top of the 10th inning Saturday night to give the Red Sox a 5–3 victory over the New York Mets and their first World Series title since 1918."

Hernandez disgustedly walked back down the runway to the clubhouse and joined Met scout Darrell Johnson — yes, the very same Darrell Johnson who had managed the Red Sox in the '75 World Series — in the manager's office for a beer. Carter drilled a 2–1 fastball into leftfield. Next up, Mitchell. When Hernandez was at the plate, Mitchell was up in the clubhouse; he had taken his uniform pants off and was on the phone making a reservation for his flight home to San Diego. "I didn't think I'd be hitting," he told Dave Anderson of the *New York Times* this spring. "I hadn't hit against a righthanded pitcher all season in that situation. Heep was still on the bench. I figured he'd hit for me, so I went up to the clubhouse." That shows how closely some players follow the game, because Heep had pinch-hit for Santana in the fifth — and was out of the game. When Johnson read Mitchell's quote, he said, "Now I'm even happier about the deal [for Kevin McReynolds]."

Howard Johnson came running into the clubhouse. "Get out there, you're hitting," he hollered at Mitchell. "I hung up the phone, then I slipped my pants back on," said Mitchell, "but I'd taken off everything under them. My jock, my underwear." Mitchell wasn't totally disconcerted. He remembered that when he and Schiraldi had played together in Jackson, Miss., in 1983, the pitcher had told him that if he ever faced him, he would start him out with a fastball inside, then try to get him with a slider away. That's exactly what Schiraldi did, and Mitchell hit the slider for a single to center.

Schiraldi then got two strikes on Knight. "He was so excited," says McNamara, "that he just forgot how to pitch Knight. No big deal. He's human. He was a rookie." McNamara, who managed Knight in Cincinnati, had told his pitchers that when Knight gets behind in the count, he looks for the inside fastball and fights it off, so they should put the ball on the outside corner. But Schiraldi came up and in. Knight fought it off, dumping a quail into right center, and Mitchell raced around to third. McNamara then decided he'd better go to the veteran Stanley, who had struck Wilson out in Game 3.

Stanley, a $1 million-per-year pitcher, had been unhappy about his bullpen role since McNamara had made Schiraldi the closer in early August. He felt the manager had lost nearly as much faith in him as the Fenway Park fans, whom he blamed for his 6.00 ERA at home. This was what Stanley had foreseen in April, when he vowed, "They may boo me now, but they'll love me when I'm standing on the mound when we win the World Series."

Wilson fouled Stanley's first pitch to the screen, took two balls, then fouled another into the dirt to even the count at 2 and 2. For the second time that morning, the Red Sox were one strike away. Met third base coach Bud Harrelson told Mitchell to be ready to go on a wild pitch.

Wilson fouled off the next pitch, and the next one. What happened next is subject to debate. Stanley told friends that Gedman called for a fastball up and in, then set a target down and out. Gedman has refused any comment except to say: "I should have stopped any pitch." An infielder claims that Stanley misread the sign and that Gedman was in position for Stanley's best pitch — a sinker — out over the plate. Instead, the pitch took off, sailing low and inside. Wilson spun out of the way. The weary Gedman, who was so intense in the playoffs that he chipped three teeth by grinding them, couldn't get his glove on the ball. As it squirted to the screen, Mitchell danced across the plate. Knight went to second.

The score was tied, 5–5. For the third time the Mets had come from behind; the Red Sox, it should be noted, did not come from behind in the entire Series. With "eerie efficiency," as Costas describes it, the visiting clubhouse was cleared of the riser, the trophy, the champagne and the Red Sox owners in less than one minute.

Stanley then missed a chance to end the inning without another pitch, which would have left the Mets with a pitching choice of Doug Sisk or Randy Niemann. As Stanley took his stretch, Barrett signaled for a pickoff, sneaked over to second and waited for Stanley to whirl and throw. "We had Knight dead," says Barrett. While Barrett screamed from the second base bag, the oblivious Stanley delivered to Wilson, who fouled the pitch off.

On the 10th pitch of his at bat, Wilson topped a ground ball toward the first base bag. Buckner was playing deep behind the base. He hustled over to the line, but there was no way he could have made the play himself. Stanley was racing to the bag, but to this day Buckner believes Wilson would have beaten Stanley on the play. "I would have been there," insists Stanley. As Buckner reached down to corner the ball, it skittered between his legs. McNamara has a ready answer for those who felt Stapleton would have made the play. "If the question had been range, that would have been justified criticism," McNamara argues. "But the one thing Buckner has is a soft pair of hands. He catches what he gets to."

As the ball trickled onto the outfield grass, Knight raced home with the winning run — and the Mets had miraculously survived. "When you get within one strike and don't win, you don't deserve to win," Red Sox pitcher Tom Seaver said later.

After a day of rain they played Game 7, and at first it seemed that the Red Sox had suffered no ill effects from the disaster. They jumped off to a 3–0 lead over Darling in the second inning on back-to-back homers by Evans and Gedman and a run-scoring single by Boggs. Hurst, meanwhile, was pitching so well that he allowed only a single base runner in the first five innings. But then the Mets tied the score at 3-all on three singles, a walk and a fielder's choice. Schiraldi replaced Hurst in the seventh, and Knight greeted him with a home run to give the Mets a 4–3 lead. Two more runs scored on an RBI single by Santana and a sacrifice fly by Hernandez. Although the Red Sox closed the gap to 6–5 in the eighth, the Mets came right back with two more runs, on Strawberry's in-your-face homer off Nipper and Orosco's fake bunt. Orosco set the Red Sox down in order in the ninth. It was a game that was fairly exciting unto itself, but following Game 6, it was an anticlimax.

McNamara, Buckner, Stanley and Schiraldi will try to put Game 6 back in the closet, but it will be no easy task. McNamara acknowledged that by holding his little spring training meeting.

"The Mets were a great team," Buckner insists, and he is right. "We had a great year. Last March, was there anyone in this country who thought we'd make it to the seventh game of the World Series? Remember the fifth game of the playoffs, Clemens's 24 wins, all the teams that made runs at us during the season. Forget one game."

Forget it? New Englanders haven't let .307 lifetime hitter Johnny Pesky forget he held the ball in the '46 Series — and he wasn't even at fault. Forget it? When the *Today* show observed Fred Merkle Day a while back, it wasn't because "Bonehead" had a good rookie year in 1908. Forget it? At the New York Baseball Writers Dinner last January, Ralph Branca was introduced to Clemens as "the guy who gave up Bobby Thomson's homer." That happened only 36 years ago.

There are just some things you never forget.

BABE RUTH CURSE STRIKES AGAIN

from *The New York Times,* October 26, 1986

Enos Slaughter ran all the way home again last night. Jim Lonborg's arm was still tired on two days' rest. Joe Morgan slapped a hit off Jim Burton. Bucky Dent's fly ball once again soared over the leftfield fence.

All the ghosts and demons and curses of the past 68 years continued to haunt the Boston Red Sox last night as the New York Mets won the seventh game of the World Series, 8–3 — with an a cappella chorus of fans chanting the Boston players' names derisively — to bring more gloom to the New England region, which has not enjoyed a World Series victory since 1918.

"I don't know nothin' about history," John McNamara said on Saturday night after Mookie Wilson's strange little grounder squirmed its way into history. "And I don't want to hear anything about choking or any of that junk."

Of course he doesn't, but there is no denying that the Boston Red Sox have been playing under a cloud ever since their owner, Harry Frazee, sold off Babe Ruth early in 1920, and that cloud settled over them in this Series.

All the leads they had, all the chances, went down the drain, just as they had in 1946 and 1949 and 1967 and 1975 and 1978.

"Good ups, bad downs," sighed Bob Stanley, the relief pitcher who was on the team when Bucky Dent's fly lofted over the wall, and who was on the mound when Buckner couldn't bend for Wilson's wobbler.

These current Red Sox, who will say they have nothing in common with those other teams, took a 2–0 lead in this Series and then a 3–2 lead coming back to Shea. Even when they dissipated three separate leads and lost early Sunday morning, they appeared to catch a break when it rained for nearly 24 hours, postponing the final game.

John McNamara made the right decision in bypassing Oil Can Boyd in favor of Bruce Hurst, who had beaten the Mets twice in the Series, and they even gave Hurst a 3–0 lead into the sixth inning. But this franchise has seen other breaks go down the drain in the past 68 years.

"That's baseball," Hurst said, volunteering that he was using the game's oldest cliché. "I guess that's why they invented three outs per inning. I got a little tired."

It was human and understandable for Hurst to tire, but the opening of the bullpen door will rank with other accidents, calamities, disasters, bad luck, flops and failures in Red Sox history, and nobody even used McNamara's word, "choking."

The Sox had come so close, in seventh games of the World Series in 1946, 1967 and 1975, in the final weekend of the pennant race of 1949 and in the one-game Eastern Division playoff of 1978, that the fans of New England have developed a loser's twitch, an expectation that the worst possible thing might happen.

The fans knew; the talk show hosts knew. Bill Buckner's ruined ligaments were making him the Gabriela Andersen-Schiess of this World Series. (She was the dehydrated, discombobulated runner who staggered to the finish of the 1984 Olympic marathon.)

The fans knew. It had happened so often before. On top of it, the Red Sox used to have a reputation as a country-club team, with great hitters but without the normal barbed humor and collective wisdom that winning teams must have. Who was it who described the Red Sox as 25 men taking 25 different cabs on their way to dinner?

This year they seemed nothing like that. This year they became a team, as soon as George Steinbrenner and his "baseball people" traded Don Baylor to the Red Sox in March. Baylor became the leader the Red Sox never had, forming a kangaroo court, taunting and teasing the players into becoming closer teammates.

But there are a lot of haunted memories in this franchise, which won the first World Series in 1903, and then won it in 1912, 1915, 1916 and 1918, acquiring the child of nature, George Herman Ruth, who became the best left-handed pitcher on the team and potentially the greatest slugger in the game. Yet the owner sold him to the lowly New York Yankees to finance one of his Broadway shows, and for 68 years it has never been the same.

Any Boston fan can fill in the gruesome details, with blunt opinions, how Ted Williams batted only .200 and drove in one run in the 1946 Series, how Johnny Pesky seemed to hold the ball an instant too long as Country Slaughter steamed home from first on Harry Walker's hit. Perhaps the fans of New England would have talked about the brave comeback against California in the fifth game of the league championship, three runs down in the ninth inning, but now they are likely only to remember the two leads in New York, and the disaster coming out of the bullpen.

The ghosts of 1946 and the other disasters have nothing to do with young Calvin Schiraldi, a sensitive-looking college man who earned a job in the Red Sox bullpen this season, but lost the two games in New York, giving up the go-ahead homer to Ray Knight on his fourth pitch last night.

"Responsible? I blew two games," Schiraldi said, graciously willing to face the press afterward. "I was the one who let the runners score. Will I get over it? I guess. At this time, I don't know how."

Schiraldi had not been born in 1946 when Slaughter went into motion. He was not born in 1948 when the Red Sox lost the last two games to the Yankees. He was 5 years old when Lonborg's arm couldn't make it on two days' rest. He was 13 when Darrell Johnson pinch-hit for Jim Willoughby and brought in Jim Burton.

And he was 6 when Mike Torrez threw the home-run pitch to Bucky Dent. He never even dreamed of playing for the Boston Red Sox. He signed, after all, with the New York Mets. But now this young man with the long eyelashes is a Red Sox for the ages, part of the 68 heartbreaking years, and counting.

Is the "curse" a creation of the New York media? Apparently so, for Vecsey's column, written in the wake of game six, is the first appearance in print of any notion of a so-called "curse" surrounding the Red Sox stemming from the sale of Babe Ruth. Although the details of such a notion are spurious, it nevertheless found resonance among Red Sox fans never eager to look at the real causes of their team's trouble. Four years later Dan Shaughnessy expanded on the notion in his best-selling book The Curse of the Bambino.

THE METS TAKE IT, 8–5

... and Boston Is Mudville Once Again

from *The Boston Globe*, October 28, 1986

NEW YORK — The taste is so very bitter. When the Red Sox get to the seventh game of the World Series, the other team uncorks champagne while the Sox uncork wild pitches.

What is it like to live in a city that wins a World Series? Call your out-of-town friends and ask. Generations of Bostonians may never know. The New York Mets beat the Boston Red Sox, 8–5, in the seventh game of the 1986 World Series last night, and Boston is Mudville once again.

Somebody will rise up and say that the Sox did well to get this close. They'll say that if they told you in spring training that the Red Sox would win the American League East and the AL pennant, you'd be delighted.

But you are not delighted. The Red Sox took you to the edge again. They made you fall in love and then they broke your heart. Again.

The Sox had every opportunity to win their first World Series since 1918, but they failed. They found new ways to miss the mark. They penned another macabre chapter in the region's longest-running horror story.

On Saturday, the Red Sox blew a 5–3 lead in the sixth game of the Fall Classic. Three times they were within one strike of their first world championship in 68 years, but men wearing New York Mets uniforms kept crossing the plate and the Sox were 6–5 losers.

The Sox got a blessing from heaven before Game 7. Sunday's rains postponed the finale, and the Red Sox were able to send Met Master Bruce Hurst to the mound one last time.

Game 7 produced one more barrel of pain. Hurst and the Sox came through with one final tease. They took a 3–0 lead in the seventh game of the World Series.

Sound familiar? Veteran Sox watchers fear a 3–0 lead in the seventh game of the Series. It's a haunting number. Eleven years ago, the Red Sox took a 3–0 lead in the seventh game of the '75 Series. Then Bill Lee threw his famous blooper pitch to Tony Perez, and Darrell Johnson and Jim Burton shifted into gear and the Sox were 4–3 losers.

Is there anything else like this? Year after year, one way or another, the Red Sox let you down.

There was plenty of evidence that this team was different. The 1986 Red Sox were a rare blend of veterans and young stars. They spit in the face of the critics and turned back the challenges.

They took over first place in the AL East on May 15 and never looked back. They pulled off a memorable comeback in Anaheim in the fifth game of the AL playoffs.

But there was no glory to pass around in New York when the Red Sox could have delivered the knockout punch.

The Sox took a 3–2 Series lead to the Big Apple. They needed only one victory to stifle the skeptics and bring Boston its overdue championship.

The sadistic Saturday night loss is the one that will stick like a chicken bone in your throat. Champagne was on ice, Hurst had been tabbed for Series MVP and the elusive World Series trophy was making a rare appearance in the Boston clubhouse. Then the Red Sox lost on three hits, a wild pitch and a Little League error — all after two were out.

"We let it get away Saturday night," McNamara admitted late last night. "Saturday night's ballgame was the thing that was tough."

The final torture/tease was saved for the seventh game. Naturally. The Red Sox have been involved in four World Series since 1918 and have lost each in the seventh game.

The early 3–0 lead should have been a tipoff. It was too easy. Hurst took a one-hitter into the sixth, but before you could say, "Enos Slaughter," the Mets had three runs and Hurst was out of the game.

"He lost a little of his location and his velocity," said McNamara. "He just had had it, but we were still in the ballgame when he left."

It was 3–3 when Calvin Schiraldi came on to start the seventh. And then things started happening again. Series MVP Ray Knight led off with a line-drive homer, then Lenny Dykstra singled. Schiraldi uncorked a wild pitch (instead of a champagne bottle) and Dykstra took second. The immortal Rafael Santana singled, scoring Dykstra. That was it for Schiraldi. Joe Sambito, Bob Stanley, Al Nipper and Steve Crawford paraded in from the bullpen before it was over but couldn't do anything to stop the "Let's go, Mets" chant. In the end, Boston's bullpen killed the Sox as much as anything.

Boston rallied for a pair in the eighth — two runs that served to demonstrate character and further tease the loyal legions back in Beantown. New York's lead was trimmed to 6–5 after the top of the eighth.

But Nipper gave it up in the ugly bottom of the inning, yielding a towering homer to Darryl Strawberry on an 0-2 pitch. The Mets scored another run before the inning ended. New York scored all eight of its runs in its final three innings.

The Red Sox went out 1-2-3 in the ninth, ending it when Marty Barrett struck out at 11:26 p.m.

History will show that this was a very successful season for the 1986 Boston Red Sox. They advanced far beyond expectations and provided inordinate thrills and entertainment for seven months.

But they couldn't finish it off, and that is what Boston fans will remember when they think of the '86 Sox.

Ninety-two-year-old Bostonian Dick Casey saw all the Boston Series games when the Red Sox beat the Cubs in 1918. Before Game 6, he told NBC-TV, "I pray to God I don't die until I see another winner. This is my year. I must be gonna die pretty soon."

Not yet, sir. Stick around a while longer.

Dan Shaughnessy, a Boston Globe *columnist and the author of* Curse of the Bambino, *has chronicled the woes of the Red Sox for more than two decades. He is a native of Groton, Massachusetts, and his latest book (with photographer Stan Grossfeld) is* Spring Training.

A BROTHER'S KEEPER

from *Esquire*, March 1989

The sun throws a morning light that covers the Atlantic like a blanket both soft and warm. Out the back window you can see Egg Rock sitting in the middle of the water like a piece of God's sculpture, and beyond that, on Massachusetts' North Shore, Lynn Harbor and Marblehead. Fresh cookies are on the kitchen table. There is the smell of coffee.

And suddenly, from another part of the house, like thunder signaling the coming of a storm and a darkening morning, there is the terrible sound of the coughing.

"That's him," Billy Conigliaro, the middle brother, says at the kitchen table. He stares out at the water and clasps his fingers tightly.

"He can't keep his lungs clear. The threat of pneumonia is something we fight continually."

He gets up from the table. "C'mon," he says. "I'll show you around." We go into the bar area of the beautiful house in Nahant. Here, on the walls, are the plaques and photographs that tell of the brief, shining career of Billy's older brother, Tony Conigliaro. Tony C.

Here is Tony C., young and lean and dark and handsome, with Willie Mays. Here is Tony with his two brothers, Billy and Richie. Tony was in the big leagues by then, with the Red Sox. Billy and Richie were still kids. But they were ballplayers, too. Here is Tony C. in a Red Sox uniform, crossing home plate. He was the youngest American League home-run champ in history. Even after a terrible beaning in 1967 that took a season and two months out of his career and nearly cost him the sight in his left eye, Tony C. had 164 home runs by the time he was twenty-six.

Those of us who grew up in New England in the '60s and loved baseball thought that even with all the bad luck he had seen — two broken arms with the Sox, a fractured wrist, the eye — he still was going to hit six hundred home runs for the Boston Red Sox. That was long before Tony C. and everybody found out he didn't know anything about bad luck, anything at all.

Down the hall from the plaques and the pictures, a woman is chattering on, almost musically, nonstop.

"You just a big phony." She laughs. There is more coughing, a man's coughing. "You wanna go out in the car today? Maybe we'll go to the mall. Dress you right up and take you to the mall."

Billy Conigliaro says, "That's Yvonne Baker. We call her the Big E. She's one of his nurses. We gotta go around the clock with him."

Then from down the hall comes Yvonne Baker, a pretty, wide-faced black woman pushing a wheelchair into the morning.

Seated in the wheelchair, hands forgotten in his lap, wearing a white T-shirt, the pants from a red jogging suit, and white sneakers, no longer the boy from Swampscott who hit those balls over the wall at Fenway, a forty-three-year-old man trapped in his own body since his heart stopped beating in Billy's car for several terrible minutes seven years ago, unable to feed himself or walk without help or say more than a couple of words, too much of his brain lost for good, is Tony Conigliaro. Tony C.

Billy squeezes his brother's hand and kneels in front of him. "Hey, pal," he says. "How're you doin' today?"

"He was a natural home-run hitter," Billy Conigliaro says. Billy's own big-league career, which began with the Red Sox, was cut short by a knee injury. "Tony grew up with one dream: hitting home runs for the Boston Red Sox."

He was doing it by the age of nineteen. He hit twenty-four home runs in 1964, in just 111 games; he had broken his arm in the spring and gotten a late start. In 1965 he hit thirty-two and won the home-run title. By August 1967, more than halfway through the Red Sox's Impossible Dream season, when magic came back into the storied little ball park, Tony had twenty more.

He was twenty-two years and seven months old on the August night at Fenway in '67 when a Jack Hamilton fastball hit him in the temple and shattered his cheekbone. The Red Sox's dream continued, but Tony C.'s abruptly halted.

"He had been in a little slump before that," Billy remembers. "Before the game that night he told me, 'You gotta get up on the plate to hit home runs. I'm gonna stand a little closer and stand in a little longer.'"

He did not play again in 1967. The damage to the retina was worse than the doctors had originally thought. They told Tony C. the headaches would go away eventually, but he would never see well enough to hit a baseball again.

But he came back. He hit twenty homers in 1969 and was Comeback Player of the Year. In 1970 it was as if Tony, still only twenty-five, had never been away. He hit thirty-six home runs and knocked in 116. Billy was a rookie center fielder with the Red Sox that season. Richie was playing a hot shortstop at Swampscott High.

But Tony still had some trouble seeing the ball in the outfield as late afternoon became night. This he confided to coaches late in the season. Billy believes it got Tony traded to the California Angels. "After everything, they decided to get as much for him as they could before the eye went bad," Billy says today. "Nice business, huh?"

The eye did get worse; he hit four home runs for the Angels in 1971 and retired. He made one more comeback with the Red Sox, in 1975. Only the Conigliaro family and the most lunatic of trivia buffs know that he opened that World Series season as the Red Sox's designated hitter, and even hit his last two home runs. But, really, the vision was no better. It was Conigliaro's heart that kept bringing him back.

The Red Sox sent him to the minor leagues. The last time I saw him in a baseball uniform was at McCoy Stadium in Pawtucket, Rhode Island, in his final baseball summer. After he retired for good, he drifted into television work.

"He never once said, 'Why me?'" Billy Conigliaro says. "He never once complained about his luck."

Yvonne Baker, the Big E, helps Tony C. into the red jacket that goes with the red pants. She positions the wheelchair in front of the large Panasonic television screen. Geraldo Rivera's talk show comes on.

Billy returns to the kitchen. He stares through the doorway at his brother, who stares at Geraldo Rivera. "You can't even ask him how's he feeling," Billy says. "He can't respond."

Yvonne Baker goes over to the kitchen counter and makes fresh coffee. In the living room, Tony Conigliaro's head has dropped to his shoulder in front of the screen. He is asleep.

"It's not Tony," Billy says. "If he could fight, he would fight, because he fought his whole life. Tony could overcome anything, if he just had the chance."

On January 9, 1982, Billy was driving Tony to Logan Airport, only fifteen minutes away from their Nahant home. Tony had been home for the Christmas holidays and stayed to audition for a job as the Red Sox's TV analyst on Boston's Channel 38. According to Billy Conigliaro, Tony had been told the night before that the job was his. "He said, 'I'm finally coming home,'" Billy remembers. It was two days after Tony Conigliaro's thirty-seventh birthday. He still looked like a movie star. He was going to be very big on Channel 38.

In a voice made of stone, Billy Conigliaro says, "We were just talking about the new job and how great it was that he was coming home. We were about two miles from the airport when it happened. A girl had called looking for him a few days before, and I said, 'You ever think of who that girl was that called?' And he didn't answer me right away. So I looked over. And his face was twitching. I thought he was fooling, making fun of the girl or something. He was a great mimic. Now I said, 'Tony, what are you doing?' He didn't answer me. Then his head fell to the side, and tears started coming out of his eyes. I thought to myself, Geez, he's passed out. But he was breathing still, so I didn't think he was having a heart attack. I thought about pulling over to the side and calling for help. But Mass General was close-by, so I pushed down on the gas and started goin' about eighty for the emergency entrance. It couldn't have taken me more than five minutes. But it seemed like an hour. By the time we got there, he had no pulse."

Billy Conigliaro stops here, remembering again what he cannot forget. There is just the sound of the television from the other room. Then he tells of the doctors performing the tracheotomy, and getting his heartbeat back, and how he, Billy, had to go fetch his father, Sal, from the Suffolk Downs racetrack nearby. Sal Conigliaro, dead now, had just had a bypass operation himself. Billy Conigliaro got nitroglycerin pills for his father before leaving Mass General and made him take the pills at Suffolk Downs before telling him about Tony.

They drove back to the hospital. Tony Conigliaro was in the coma from which he would not emerge for three weeks. The sudden cardiac pulmonary arrest had cut off oxygen to the brain's cells. The brain damage, of course, was irreversible.

"My brother was dead for five minutes," Billy says. "How was he going to be normal after that?"

In the room where Tony C. does physical therapy, there is an elevated exercise mat as big as a queen-size bed. There is a table, to which he is attached and turned upside down to help his blood circulate. With the help of a walker, his feet being picked up and laid down by the nurses, Tony C. can be taken outside to walk around the swimming pool that overlooks the Atlantic.

"Sometimes," Billy says, "in the summer, I'll come by and they'll have him lying out by the pool and he'll look, in that split second, like . . . Tony."

A few friends still come by to see him. Tony Athanas, who owns the famous Anthony's Pier 4 restaurant in Boston, comes by, and so does Bill Bates, another friend, and Ben Davidson, the former Oakland Raider whom Tony met in California, will call from a trip to Maine and say he is driving down. Baseball teammates like Rico Petrocelli and Mike Andrews used to come by, but not so much lately, as the years move everybody except his family and closest friends away from the Tony Conigliaro everybody remembers.

"You have to prod him," Billy says. "But sometimes if you give him the first name of a teammate, he'll give you the last. You say 'Rico' and he'll say 'Petrocelli.' If somebody he knows comes over, he'll look up and laugh. Or cry. Really not many people come by anymore. It's been so long. I think they feel funny."

Billy Conigliaro shrugs.

"Don't you?" he says.

In the living room, Yvonne Baker talks Tony C. awake and tells him they're going to the mall soon. Above him, over the fireplace, is a portrait, a lovely portrait, of Tony C. swinging a bat, done by his cousin.

"I just keep pushing him," Billy says. "But it's not even like teaching someone how to talk, because he can't retain anything." He walks into the living room and kneels in front of his brother. He says, "Where you going with the Big E? C'mon. Talk to me. You're going for a . . ." Tony C. says, "Ride." With love that the house can barely contain, Billy, his brother, touches him on the cheek.

Teresa Conigliaro, the mother, has come back from morning errands and immediately offers a plate of cookies. She is sixty-eight years old. She lost her husband to his bad heart in 1987. Half an hour with her tells you she has had a certain marvelous strength her whole life. We have been talking at her kitchen table about this passage in the Bible, from First Corinthians, one promising that God will give no person more burden than he or she can bear.

"I used to believe that," she says. "And the part about seek and you shall find, and ask and you shall receive. I've been asking for five years."

She takes a breath and tries building another smile. "There I go. You can't look back. If I did, I'd cry all the time."

The care of Tony C. is expensive, more than $100,000 a year according to Billy. As I write this, the Conigliaro family is still fighting with Equitable about insurance money through the Major League Baseball Players Association. A 1983 benefit at Boston's Symphony Hall, at which Frank Sinatra and Dionne Warwick performed, raised $230,000, but, as Teresa Conigliaro says, "That was a long time ago."

Yvonne Baker comes into the kitchen for another cup of coffee. Tony C. has gone back to sleep. At forty-three, going on forty-four, he has gray hair and is quite skinny; you already see what he will look like at sixty-four.

In the kitchen, I tell the Big E she has a lot of energy. "It doesn't help if I come in every day with a sad face," she says. "All I do then is drag him down."

In the living room she shuts off the television and pokes Tony C. on the shoulder.

"C'mon fella," the Big E says, "we got interesting things to do today."

*   *   *

Billy Conigliaro drives me to where my rented car is parked. We shake hands. I tell him I will pray for his brother.

"We just don't want people to forget," he says. "You know?"

People shouldn't forget. Sometime this season there should be a big night for the Conigliaro family, a big fundraising night, maybe at the All-Star Dinner, something to put on television. The commissioner-elect of baseball, A. Bartlett Giamatti, has been a Red Sox fan his whole life. He should organize it, so that baseball can remember, so everybody can remember, just once more, on a fine summer night, what it was like when Tony C. was young and he was going to hit balls over the wall forever.

Tony Conigliaro, who died in 1990, never had any luck at all, and his saga is one of the saddest in Red Sox history. He still holds a special place in the hearts of many Red Sox fans. Mike Lupica graduated from Boston College and wrote for both the Phoenix *and the* Globe *while still an undergrad. He then moved on to New York, where he became one of the best-known sportswriters in the country. The author of a number of successful books, Lupica is a columnist for the* New York Daily News *and appears regularly on ESPN's* Sports Reporters.

PART VI

LATER INNINGS

In the wake of 1986, the Red Sox were left reeling. The running story of the team became the ever more elusive and remote search for world championship number six.

Tom Yawkey's wife, Jean, had taken over following her husband's death in 1976. Her passing in 1992 left the franchise in the hands of the Yawkey Foundation, headed by John Harrington. The hiring of youthful general manager Dan Duquette in 1994 seemed to herald an end to the dismal record of the Yawkey era, but as the disappointments piled up season after season, it became apparent that it was still business as usual on Yawkey Way and little had changed. Although the addition of Pedro Martinez and Nomar Garciaparra provided memorable individual performances and enabled the Red Sox to remain nominally competitive year after year, the loss of stars such as Roger Clemens and Mo Vaughn to free agency without compensation proved impossible to overcome.

Season after season unfolded in a maddeningly similar fashion. The Red Sox would get off to a quick start, then the Yankees would make a few key midseason trades, and by the time the Red Sox responded, always too late, the pennant was lost. Postseason appearances in 1996 and 1998 were discouragingly brief. While fans poured through the turnstiles in ever-increasing numbers as Fenway

Park became as much a shrine as a ballpark, the climate surrounding the team was increasingly sour.

The Red Sox front office came under increasing scrutiny. The press observers became as exasperated as the fans. Coverage of the team became more critical as the franchise made coming close and falling short a way of life. The Internet made newspapers from throughout the region available to fans and added new voices who worked almost exclusively in the new medium. Today there is more information available about the team than at any other time in Red Sox history.

Finally, in 2001, Harrington made good on his long-standing promise to sell the team. After an excruciating and needlessly extended sales process, the franchise was sold to John Henry and Tom Werner in the spring of 2002 for more than $700 million.

No one thinks that's the end of the story. Impossible Dreams remain unfulfilled, but there's always next year.

CHARLES P. PIERCE

BLOWING 'EM AWAY

from *Esquire*, June 1998

"Jesus, did you see that pitch?" It is a cloudless day in City of Palms Park in Fort Myers, on the west coast of Florida, the sky a brilliant blue that seems to have its origins somewhere between Tierra del Fuego and Avalon. The Baltimore Orioles are taking their third-inning swings against the Boston Red Sox, and the Baltimore hitters are stepping around in the batter's box as though they were ankle-deep in Gaboon vipers. Tony Tarasco is on tiptoe. Roberto Alomar seems to be preparing to execute a grand jeté, and Joe Carter looks ready to run through the entire "New York, New York" number from *On the Town*. On this fine afternoon, under the high winter sun, the Orioles are coming to the plate with happy feet.

On the pitcher's mound, a slight man in a Red Sox uniform steps again toward home plate. Joe Carter, his feet still moving in tiny steps, winds his upper body into an ungainly swing that makes him look as though he were wielding a broadsword with a watermelon stuck to its tip. The pitch is a change-up — the greatest of all pitches — and it seems to stop midnight in order to ponder exactly how much of a cluck it will make out of Carter, who flails at the ball and catches just a sliver of it, nicking only the very top of one of the stitches. It hops delicately back to the pitcher, who tosses Carter out to end the inning. Up in the press box, I rise from my seat and — rhetorically, at least — invoke the opinion of the Savior.

Pedro Martinez is twenty-six years old. He is wiry, 170 pounds stretched over a five-foot-eleven-inch frame. In his five major-league seasons prior to this one, he has won sixty-five games and struck out 970 batters. In 1997, Martinez went 17–8 with the Montreal Expos. His earned-run average was a razorish 1.90, and he put up 305 strikeouts, all of which was good enough for him to win the Cy Young Award as the National League's best pitcher. It was also good enough for the Expos to decide that they couldn't afford to keep him. Which is only the beginning of this modern baseball story.

Last November, Martinez was traded to the Boston Red Sox, who thereupon signed him to a six-year contract that will pay him at least $75 million. (If the Red Sox exercise their option on a seventh season, Martinez could make as much as $92 million over the life of the contract.) He is going to make more money playing baseball than any other man ever has. It is also more than likely that Martinez will not hold that distinction for longer than a year — especially now that prospective free-agent catcher Mike Piazza has Rupert Murdoch as his paymaster in Los Angeles. How you feel about that depends primarily on how you feel about other people's money, about the uncontrolled intersection of sports and commerce, and, ultimately, how you take your modern baseball story — straight up, no chaser or as nostrum, cut pale with indulgent nostalgia.

Ah, baseball, you Field of Dreams. What are we to make of you? There are people who believe that you stand for something ineffable about the American experience, who believe that you are possessed of an inherent geometric perfection, and these are the same people who are afraid that baseball isn't going to last another half hour. And it's the people most convinced of the sport's importance who seem the least convinced of its durability. Baseball seems to have become a rather sterile faith, followed only by babbling acolytes and apocalyptic preachers — a sports equivalent of those television parsons who rail against "anti-Christian" themes on TV shows, despite the fact that we have it from no less an authority than the Founder that the Gates of Hell will not prevail against His church, which ought to make Ellen DeGeneres seem somewhat less of a threat.

Among the boomer set, there's now a yearning for baseball that's not unlike the current fascination with the Rat Pack, the desperate desire to be as cool as Daddy was. Oh, to be cruising the Sands in Vegas with Frank and Dino, laughing at the erudite wit of Joey Bishop, pulling Peter Lawford out of a potted palm, swaggering through the lobby with a broad on one arm and a chick on the other. Man, that was style. Hoo, boy. How's your bird?

That most of what the Rat Pack produced was complete junk — I mean, *Ocean's Eleven*? — seems as conveniently ignored by the modern nostalgists as is the fact that the entire history of baseball is a history of money.

Like other professional sports, baseball did not suddenly become a business when free-agency replaced the reserve clause. It became a business the first time Harry Wright handed one of his Cincinnati Red Stockings a pay check. Baseball's problems, such as they are — noisily indulgent, hopelessly overdramatized, largely fictitious — are not about money. They are about the distribution of money. Baseball's problems are about economics, which is a different matter. Money is as essential a part of this modern baseball story as it has been to every baseball story since Wright brought his ball club out of Cincinnati.

So there on the mound in the sunshine is Pedro Martinez, for now, at least, the richest man in baseball. If you piled up his salary in one-dollar bills, he could hide behind it. Perhaps you'd have to get all the way up to $1,000 bills before you could see the man behind the great pile of money. And there is a charge in his arm that illuminates even the brightest day.

"What do I mean when I say I pitch from my heart?" he says. "It means something inside me — a feeling I get. It's in my blood, my body. It's not the money. The money, it never steps inside the white lines. It's my pride, my name. My family's name. My reputation. That's worth more than the $75 million they're paying me."

Believe him or not?

How do you take your baseball stories? Counterfeit past or verifiable present?

I mean, Jesus, did you see that pitch?

They began coming to the Dominican Republic when he was very young — all the baseball scouts, flocking into the richer half of a poor little island more thickly even than the Marines did in 1965. The scouts drove the rutted roads up into the hills, where the children hit rocks and battered baseballs with whatever stick they could find. A modern baseball story — straight, no chaser — begins in the Dominican, amid the poverty, where the treasure came to be found.

Pedro Martinez had a big brother named Ramon, and the Dodgers liked Ramon so much they signed him to a contract. They took care of all the blood-borne parasites that came from the high country on the little island. They fixed up his teeth, because disease and poverty are also part of a modern baseball story. By 1990, Ramon was pitching in the All-Star Game.

Pedro was playing rookie ball in the Dodgers organization, drawing big crowds because he was Ramon's brother. "People come to see me," he recalls. "They say, 'He's Ramon's brother. He must throw hard, like Ramon does.' I was a little guy. It was hard for me then."

During the games in which he did not pitch, Pedro sat in the stands behind the plate, working on his English by doing play-by-play to himself. "A lot of people ask me, 'Where did you learn to speak English?' No, really, they really ask me that," he says. "I learned it in school in the Dominican. The people who ask me, they don't know that we learn it there." That is also a part of the modern baseball story — cultural dissonance in a fragmenting world, different languages in the clubhouse instead of different accents, Korea and the Dominican as well as Georgia and Alabama. Pedro would sit in the stands by himself — calling the games, practicing his English, speaking to a wider world that he'd not yet joined.

He came up to the big club in 1993, winning ten games for the Dodgers. However, at that point, Los Angeles was enamored of a second baseman in Montreal named Delino DeShields. The Dodgers traded Martinez to the Expos for DeShields, and Martinez came under the tutelage of Montreal manager Felipe Alou, whom he calls "the greatest man I ever met."

Alou is a classic modern baseball story himself, even though he dates back several decades as one of the three famous Alou brothers, the others being Matty and Jesus. Now, though, in Montreal, Alou cobbles together an entertaining team every year under severe economic constraints. The Expos are a "small market" team, a designation that — like most economic terms applied to the monopolistic enterprise of baseball — doesn't mean what it would appear to mean.

For example, the Cleveland Indians were considered a small-market team, until they became successful and got themselves a new stadium in which to play. As soon as a new ballpark is built in Pittsburgh, there will be a lot less talk about that city being a small market. And then there is the curious case of Atlanta, which is regularly referred to as a small-market football town and a medium-market basketball city even as it serves as the quintessential big-market baseball city. When baseball people talk about markets, they really mean profits. A small-market team is simply an unprofitable one. It is about money, the way baseball stories always are.

Martinez prospered in Montreal. He blossomed as a fearsome starting pitcher under Alou and pitching coach Joe Kerrigan. Martinez's great gift is a compact motion out of which is generated speed that almost seems an optical illusion in one so small. (In fact, he is most often compared to Ron Guidry, the slight fireballer who had several great seasons for the Yankees in the late 1970s and early '80s.) His fastball dips and dives and sails. It rarely moves straight. In Montreal, he developed a change-up and a wicked curveball. He learned to be sufficiently confident in all his pitches to use them regardless of the situation. Martinez established such a reputation for fearlessly pitching inside that he came to be known as a headhunter. The entire National League began to get happy feet.

At the same time, Martinez became aware that there would come a time when Montreal no longer could afford to pay him. This is part of the modern baseball story, which, like all baseball stories, is about money and always has been. During the previous five years, the Expos had lost several All Star–caliber players to free agency without receiving anything in return. Alou had been working with mirrors, but even he needed some young talent with which to mold yet another team. Martinez became the most obviously tradable player Montreal had.

"Once you make some money with that team, you know you must depart," explains Martinez. "So I was ready. I said I was taking off the first chance I got. I pitched last year well, so I could be ready for the next team I was playing for." However, he would miss Montreal. His English had improved, and even his French was coming around. "I cannot write it," he says, "but I can get food in a restaurant. I can talk to people."

He also ached over leaving behind Alou. But by 1997, Martinez was the best pitcher in baseball, and Montreal was shopping him because that is the way things work in the modern baseball story.

In Boston, general manager Dan Duquette was looking for a pitcher who could make even that city's notoriously self-lacerating fans forget the fact that he had allowed Roger Clemens to spirit himself away to Toronto, where Clemens won the American League's Cy Young Award at the same time that Martinez was winning the trophy in the National League. (It should be noted that, at the time of Clemens's departure, Red Sox management regularly referred to the perennial cash cow presently mooing under its supervision as a "middle market" team.)

Duquette worked a deal to bring Martinez to Boston for a couple of promising minor leaguers. He then negotiated the contract that is worth $75 million at its base and that could ultimately bring Martinez $92 million. Baseball blinked and then blanched. The road to the $100 million player — a heretofore mythical beast used mainly to terrify the citizenry into building new stadia to keep the beast at bay — plainly had wound into its final turn. At least nobody was calling Boston a middle market anymore.

In the Dominican, Martinez became as much a national phenomenon as Ramon was. He asked the people in Manoguayabo what they most needed. They told him that the local church had burned down, and his hometown needed a replacement. So Pedro Martinez — a thoroughly modern baseball commodity — set about building a church. He bought the lumber and the piping. He hired contractors and electricians. He turned the first shovelful of earth. He paid all the construction costs, because even the building of a church is about money in this modern baseball story. He was the first person to walk, slowly and reverently, down the aisle of the church that he built.

"All that came to my mind was tears," says Pedro Martinez, pitcher of baseballs, builder of churches. He came north, then, to move on through the next part of his modern baseball story.

The New York Yankees did not dance in the batter's box the way the Orioles did. They stood solidly, and they cuffed Martinez all over the ball yard. He gave up five runs in as many innings, and almost every hit was ropelike, except for the one towering home run that settled behind the fence in left field. It is said that this is how he has bad games — that his control is so good that he is always around the plate, and that his rare mistakes are thereby more serious than those of wilder pitchers who are not as good as he is. In any case, mistakes are what spring training always has been for — in all the old baseball stories and in the modern ones as well. Betting on October in May always has been a fool's wager.

"All I ever wanted was to come up for one day," Martinez says later. "All I wanted to do was sit in the dugout for one game in the major leagues, just to say I made it. Throw one pitch. Maybe take one swing. I just wanted to come up for one day, and now I've been here five years." He says that in the voice of a man looking back down a mountain.

There is a charge in his arm on a bright day, enough of a charge to redeem even his sport from its absurd self-delusions over a past that never was anywhere near as glorious as it has been dressed up to be. Hell, if all we had of Sinatra was "Wee Small Hours," wouldn't that have been enough? Did we need the phony macho posturing and the dumb-ass movies and the pretentious courting of the underworld? The music is immediate, and it is of the moment, and it doesn't have to stand for anything else — especially all that alleged "style" that was little more than the right of drunks to dress like funeral directors. Pedro Martinez, a skinny rich man on the mound with a pitch that can make you jump in your seat from two hundred yards away. That's enough, too. His modern baseball story — moved, in almost every moment, by money — is enough, too. It need not be tied into any other time or place than the one in which it exists. Shoeless Joe and the rest of them can stay where they belong, deep in that hell that lies beyond the cornfield.

Charles P. Pierce wrote for both the Phoenix *and the* Herald *before moving on to* Esquire *and* GQ. *He is the author of* Sports Guy *and* Hard to Forget. *He currently makes regular appearances on Bill Littlefield's NPR program,* Only a Game, *and is a staff writer for the* Boston Globe Magazine.

MOLLY O'NEILL

BATTER UP

What Happens When Ted Williams — the Splendid Spatula — Steps Up to the Plate

from *The New York Times Magazine*, May 30, 1999

Four decades and hundreds of miles separate him from the action, but the baseball legend Ted Williams can still feel spring training in the Florida air.

"Your brother's a helluva ballplayer," he bellows as I walk into his Hernando, Fla., kitchen, high on a hill overlooking several hundred acres, a lake and a golf course. As of this particular afternoon, my brother, Paul O'Neill, of the New York Yankees, has gone about 5 for 50 in spring training. At dinner the night before, a dark cloud surrounded him, and the only thing that lifted it was when I shared with him my plan to spend today cooking with his hero, the Splendid Splinter. The Kid. The Man. The Angler. The Cook. The Colonel. The self-described Old No Patience. Teddy Ballgame.

I might not have recognized the 80-year-old Williams from pictures of the outfielder in his prime, but somehow I knew him right away. Like a grizzly bear stumbling from winter's sleep toward a warming sun, Williams perks up as the days lengthen and spring-training games pepper local television. He's vulnerable to seasonal adrenaline surges, the tingle of joy, the terror of short-lived victory. These contradictory emotions leave Williams as they always have — a solitary man, a man's man, a hungry man.

In the world according to Ted Williams, there is no reason to bother hitting a ball, casting a line or cooking a meal if you don't do it right. Life is rife with things you can't control; the real winners pay attention to the sliver of efforts they can control — their timing at the plate, the arc of their bats, the heat of their skillets.

And in a world unaware of — or perhaps, as Williams tends to think, sadistically insensitive to — the high-strung inner workings of a perpetual perfectionist, cooking becomes a singular solace.

"I want ya ta use the fat from that Argentinian bacon, about a tablespoon, and about a tablespoon a butter. O.K. now, a couple a eggs, three, four, don't mangle 'em, real gentle," he hollers toward Robert Hogerheide, a former Navy chef. After the two strokes that hobbled the Hall of Famer and robbed him of much of his legendary vision, Hogerheide became Williams's cook. His job, for the past year, has been to be Ted Williams in the kitchen. Because nobody cooks the way Ted Williams likes except Ted Williams. And Ted Williams likes what Hogerheide cooks.

"I've worked with him," Williams says. "He's coming along."

Growing up in San Diego with a mother who marched with the Salvation Army, a brother who rebelled and a father who eventually left the family, Williams survived mostly on eggs. "My mother wasn't much of a cook," he says. "I'd make eggs for myself; it was the Depression, and eggs were cheap and plentiful, you see. And oranges! I ate tons of oranges when I was a kid. Still do." Scrambling eggs is like hitting a baseball, adds the last man to bat over .400 — the hardest thing in the world to do. A man has to devote every ounce of his concentration to the task if he wants it done right.

Williams's concern for the temperature of the pan is so significant that he seems ready to bolt from the chair in his rambling, 1980's Mediterranean-style kitchen for some hands-on monitoring. Every ounce of his concentration is focused on the eggs.

"You want the pan warm, just warm, NOT HOT, for Chrissake!" he yells. "A little salt and pepper in there, fine, fine. Now you just move 'em around the pan, don't beat 'em up, just move 'em." As Hogerheide gently swishes the eggs in the warm pan, Williams moves his left wrist in a slow, whisking motion. The muscles of his forearm ripple. He sweeps and snaps his wrist, rhythmically, a one-two-three precision.

"That's the secret of Ted Williams's famous relaxed scrambled eggs," he says. The soft mound of eggs, their yellows barely broken, the whites splattered like paint against a sponged wall, looks effortless to make, but like Williams's game or his cooking, they are the result of exhaustive research and excruciating precision.

Hogerheide slides the eggs in front of me.

"What's the best egg you ever ate?" Williams asks.

"Well, maybe in Paris," I stammer.

"NEGATIVE!" cries the honorary United States Marine colonel who flew combat missions in World War II and Korea. "Ted Williams's relaxed scrambled eggs are the best eggs you're ever gonna eat. Eat! That's right. Now tell me. The best, right?"

The eggs were great, and so was the Argentinian bacon. "Imported!" Williams says. "I got oysters flown in from the Chesapeake, crawfish from the bayous, smoked fish from New York City, bacon from Argentina." Sensing that Hogerheide had raised a brow in disbelief, Williams corrected himself. "Actually you can get that bacon at Wal-Mart," he mutters.

It started back in the '40s. It was spring training, and Williams cooked a big meal for all the guys, including Waite Hoyt, the retired pitcher who was down for a visit.

"Now this guy's been around longer and been to better places to eat than you and I," Williams says. But Williams wasn't daunted, not ever. He went shopping for steaks. "So I get some real beauties. And I come home and I make a little fire in the grill and I rub those babies good with salt and pepper and tons of garlic and I make a beautiful salad. But I keep him waiting. I brown those steaks up good; gee, I did a great job. They were terrific steaks. I see he's getting hungry. I take 'em off the heat, let 'em sit and he's getting real eager. Finally, I serve the meat and by that time, I'm telling you, he's hungry, darned near demolished the thing. I say to him, 'You like the alligator?' And he gets sorta pale."

The next day, Williams heard Hoyt describing the flavor of alligator. "Tasted pretty good, but I wouldn't want to make a steady diet of it," he heard him say.

Williams understands the conservative taste of most ballplayers. "When I was younger, I thought you couldn't beat a good steak or chop," he says. "I regret that I haven't eaten platypus or sturgeon. Shark's pretty good, and I love octopus and any kind of sushi, but I coulda been more adventuresome."

If he could live his life over, Williams says he'd want to be Zane

Grey; to his mind, nobody ever had more fun. "Traveling the world," he says, "hunting and fishing, then cooking and eating what he caught."

Williams (or, more often, Hogerheide) makes steaks or chili peppers, or herbs. But what he loves most is the pure flavor of high-quality meat and vegetables and fish.

There's never enough seafood to suit Williams. The only man to have been elected to both the Baseball Hall of Fame and the Freshwater Fishing Hall of Fame, he has fished around the globe for half a century. When his health began to decline and his world began to shrink, he fished near his home for black bass, grouper and pike.

"Every fish, like every pitch, is different," he says. "The recipes can't replace the feel for the thing, the instinct to meet either ingredient or ball with the certainty of a home run."

Williams blames lingering desires for the discontent that has fueled his life. Of course, a fine country ham is a wonderful thing to eat, but Hogerheide's lamb, a perfect fried pike or lemon meringue pie are impassioned desires that never fade away. For Williams, such desires are a mixed blessing; they represent only fleeting tastes of paradise — and, ultimately, the frustration of a man not free to fulfill all his dreams. "Oh," he says softly, gazing out his sliding-glass doors, "on a day like today, I do miss fishing."

In his immaculate kitchen, well-thumbed cookbooks by Elizabeth David and M.F.K. Fisher, James Beard and Julia Child sit neatly arranged on the shelf near his professional-gauge refrigerator. With the smell of garlic and lamb wafting up from his Eureka-brand stove, Ted Williams perches on a chair in the only place where he has always been serene: the kitchen.

But still, a hunger that exceeds all meal allowances is eating away at him.

"Get that brother a yours on the phone!" he yells. "I need ta talk to that kid. Get him on the phone!" When, by some miracle, No. 21 of the Yankees actually answers the telephone in the team's Tampa clubhouse, Williams's voice softens and warms.

"Paul? This is Ted Williams. I been thinkin' 'bout you. You're a helluva ballplayer," he says.

Ted Williams tells my brother that it's easier to hit inside-out and always better to go low-to-high. "But don't let anybody change ya.

Hit the ball hard up the middle. Don't pull it. Wait for your pitch. And remember that the lousier you're hittin', the more you're thinkin' about hittin'. You shouldn't have a worry in the world. I'm tellin' ya right now, you're a helluva player."

Williams signs off. Slowly, he stretches his legs, grimacing. Still, he looks happy and finally — or, at least, for that moment — satisfied.

That afternoon, my brother finds his groove again. He goes three for four. Ted Williams is eating Hogerheide's garlic lamb when Paul smacks his first hit.

"Take that!" bellows the Colonel. "See that?"

Angler's Pike

    1 cup milk
       Dash of Tabasco sauce
    2 fillets of pike (about 2 pounds each), cut in half, widthwise,
       to fit into a skillet
    ½ cup olive oil
    ½ cup unsalted butter (1 stick)
    ½ cup flour
    ½ cup white stone-ground cornmeal
    1 teaspoon kosher salt
    ¼ teaspoon freshly ground black pepper
    ⅛ teaspoon cayenne pepper
       Juice of 1 lemon.

1. Combine the milk and Tabasco in a large shallow bowl, add the pike and set aside, turning once so that each side of the fillet comes in contact with the milk.

2. In a skillet set over medium-high heat, combine the oil and ¼ cup of the butter. While the butter is melting, combine the flour, cornmeal, salt, pepper and cayenne and place on a plate. When the butter and oil are very hot, but not smoking, remove the pike from the milk, gently shaking off as much milk as possible, and dredge each fillet in the flour mixture, shaking off excess.

3. Slide each fillet into the hot oil and cook until golden on the first side, about 4 minutes. Turn and cook for an additional 4 minutes. Remove fillets to a serving plate and remove the pan from the flame. Squeeze the lemon into the pan, add the remaining ¼ cup of

butter, return to heat and swirl the butter sauce over each of the fillets and serve.

Yield: 4 servings.

Hogerheide's Greek Lamb

    1   head unpeeled garlic, separated into cloves
    ¼   cup olive oil
    1   2½- to 3-pound shoulder of lamb, tied
    1   tablespoon kosher salt, plus more to taste
    1½ teaspoons freshly ground black pepper, plus more to taste
    1   bunch fresh thyme
    1   teaspoon white flour
    1   cup red wine
    2   tablespoons veal demi-glace or 4 tablespoons unsalted
        beef broth.

1. Preheat the oven to 400 degrees. Toss the garlic cloves with 1 tablespoon of the oil, wrap in foil and roast for 20 minutes. Remove cloves from foil and cool.

2. Use the remaining olive oil to rub the lamb, seasoning its entire surface with salt and pepper. Place on a rack in a roasting pan. Use a sharp knife to make enough ¼-inch slits on the surface of the lamb to accommodate each garlic clove.

3. When cool enough to handle, press the garlic cloves out of their skin and push each into a slit in the lamb. Push the thyme sprigs under the string tied around the lamb. Roast for 20 minutes. Reduce the oven temperature to 350 degrees, cover the roasting pan with foil and cook for 60 minutes more. Turn off the oven and leave the lamb in the cooling oven for 15 minutes.

4. Remove the lamb to a serving platter. Place the pan with the drippings over medium-high heat on top of the stove. Sprinkle the flour over the drippings and stir. Add the wine and cook, scraping the pan with a spatula until the wine has evaporated, about 3 minutes. Add the demi-glace or beef broth, stir well and cook for 30 seconds more. Remove from heat and season to taste with salt and pepper. Remove the string and thyme from the lamb, slice the lamb and serve drizzled with the sauce.

Yield: 4 to 6 servings.

Technological Banana Cream Pie

FOR THE PIE:
1 cup vanilla-wafer-cookie crumbs
3 tablespoons melted unsalted butter
1¾ cups cold milk
1 3.9-ounce box instant chocolate-pudding mix
4 ripe bananas, peeled and thinly sliced
¼ cup grated desiccated coconut
2 cups heavy cream
½ cup powdered sugar
4 teaspoons vanilla extract

FOR THE CARAMEL SAUCE:
½ cup granulated sugar
½ cup heavy cream
2 tablespoons unsalted butter
¼ teaspoon salt.

1. In a small bowl, combine the cookie crumbs and butter and stir until combined. Grease a 9-inch pie plate and press the crumbs firmly onto the bottom and up the sides of the plate. In another small bowl, combine the milk and pudding mix and whisk for 2 minutes. Pour it into the plate. Top with the bananas and refrigerate.

2. Place the coconut in a small skillet and place over medium heat. Cook, tossing, until the coconut is golden brown, about 3 minutes. Set aside to cool.

3. Combine the cream, sugar and vanilla in a bowl and whip until it forms stiff peaks. Transfer to a pastry bag fitted with a large star tip and pipe the mixture over the bananas in the pie pan. Sprinkle the top with the cooled coconut and refrigerate for at least an hour.

4. To make the caramel sauce, place the sugar in a small, heavy saucepan set over medium heat. When the sugar begins to melt, stir it occasionally with a metal fork until it turns a deep amber color. Immediately remove from the heat and carefully stir in the cream. (The mixture will sputter.) Stir in the butter and salt. Transfer to a bowl and refrigerate until cool. Transfer to a squeeze bottle.

5. To serve, use the squeeze bottle to make swirls or patterns over dessert plates. Top each plate with a slice of the pie and serve.

Yield: 8 servings.

Yes, former New York Times *food columnist Molly O'Neill is former outfielder Paul O'Neill's sister. Her breakfast visit with Ted Williams was one of the last portraits of the aging slugger before he succumbed to the sickness that took his life in 2002. Yet as O'Neill shows, he remained himself, Ted Williams and no one else, to the very end.*

BOB RYAN

··

OBSERVERS STILL AWESTRUCK
Martinez's Sparkling Performance Loses No Luster a Day Later

from *The Boston Globe*, September 12, 1999

PEDRO'S CONQUERED TERRITORY, USA — It is the sober light of the Day After. You are David Cone. You have been quoted as speaking of the Friday night Pedro Martinez performance in apocalyptic terms. You have now had the benefit of a good night's sleep. Like members of Congress, who are permitted to alter remarks to their satisfaction before they are committed to history in the *Congressional Record,* you are now being offered an opportunity to rethink, or, as Roger Clemens would say, to "re-correct" yourself for the official Baseball Record.

That said, David Cone, what is your final and unalterable reflection on Pedro's one-hit, 17-strikeout embarrassment of the Yankees?

"It was the best-pitched game I've ever seen," asserts the great Yankee hurler.

"Excluding my perfect game, of course," jokes Cone.

That, however, proves to be a throwaway line, for Cone really does believe Pedro's masterpiece was a more dominant pitching display than his 27-up, 27-down dispatch of the Montreal Expos on July 18.

"I've never seen anything better," reiterates Cone. "He had three completely dominant pitches: a great fastball, a knee-buckling curve, and a parachute changeup. Other than that, what else do you need?"

To Cone's way of thinking, Pedro's repertoire is nothing less than unfair.

"I saw [Orel] Hershiser's great year in '88, and he basically did it with one pitch, a hard sinker," says Cone. "Nolan Ryan had a fastball and a curve. Mike Scott, when he was at his peak, had a fastball and a splitter. Dwight Gooden was another one with a fastball and a curve. Pedro has three great pitches."

Let's talk context. Roger Clemens fanned 20 Seattle Mariners in late April 1986. The Mariners turned out to be the strike-outingest team anyone had ever seen. Ten years later, Roger Clemens fanned 20 Detroit Tigers in a meaningless late September game while they were en route to establishing a new whiff standard. What Pedro Martinez did the night before last was on an entirely different plateau.

"He did it here, in Yankee Stadium, in a pennant race, when the team really needed a win," reminds Cone, who is always capable of seeing the Big Picture.

Speaking of the Big Picture, the time has come to slot Pedro in the MVP race. The Cy Young race is over, of course. With 21 wins, a 2.20 ERA, and 274 strikeouts, he has nailed down the pitching triple crown with three weeks to go. No, really. He can't lose. He's got five more wins and 104 more strikeouts than anyone. His ERA edge of damn near a full run per nine innings (Cone is second with 3.10) may be the most astonishing lead of all. Throw in his league-leading .207 opponents' batting average and there really is nothing else anyone needs to know. Pedro Martinez will win his second Cy Young Award.

The MVP award is a different matter. Some people — OK, me — are put off by the idea of pitchers winning the MVP. The Cy Young Award should be their ultimate honor. How can you compare the kumquat that is an everyday player with the squash that is a pitcher? Others — OK, most everyone else — say it's not that difficult when you ask yourself the following question: Where would the team be without him?

Let us, as they say, do the math. The Red Sox are plus-20 for the season. Pedro is plus-17. This may not quite be the 1972 Phillies/ Steve Carlton discrepancy (minus-44/plus-17), but it is impressive and meaningful and about as good an argument as any one player in

the American League has when the simple subject under discussion
is his inherent value to his team. I'm still a guy who believes the
MVP should go to the (Everyday) Player of the Year, but I'm not
voting and so I am here to predict that Pedro wins 'em both.

"I'm a pitcher," says Cone, "and I understand the debate. But I
think it's pretty clear. You take Pedro away from Boston, and where
are they? That sounds like an MVP to me."

This all presupposes more superb Pedro outings. Given that he is
4–0 with a 0.58 ERA in his last four starts (not to mention 11 hits allowed in 31 innings), that's practically a given, isn't it? There haven't
been too many dead spots in his spectacular season. And consider
this: With the DL stint, he's actually saved a little wear and tear on
his arm.

"Absolutely," confirms Cone. "I'm down to pitching once a week
now, and I can tell the difference. I feel much fresher."

Cone is 36. Pedro is not yet 28 (Oct. 25). The veteran admits to
being a bit envious of the prime-of-lifer.

"I was kidding him at the All-Star Game," Cone says. "I said, 'Hey,
it's easy being you. Anybody can win when they throw 97. Come
and see me in seven years or so, and let's see if you can win when
you're throwing 83.'"

The problem for hitters, as Cone reminds us, is that Pedro Marti-
nez does a lot more than throw in the mid 90s. Exhibit A was a Ricky
Ledee at-bat in the eighth inning Friday. This time the raconteur is
Dan Duquette.

"He started him off with two changeups on the outside," recalls
the GM. "Then a curveball to go 1-and-2. If you're Ledee, what do
you look for now? Pedro just blows a fastball by him."

Three pitches. A mid-90s fastball. The "knee-buckling curve."
The "parachute changeup." Superb control. Top-drawer competitive
instincts. Off-the-scale baseball intelligence. Only one man on earth
has all this, and it's Pedro Martinez, the best pitcher in baseball.

*Although Bob Ryan is best known for his coverage of the Boston Celtics
in the 1970s and 1980s, he remains an acute observer of the Red
Sox. Though born and raised in the Philadelphia area, Ryan and the*
Boston Globe *have been synonymous for more than 30 years.*

DAN SHAUGHNESSY

TIME HAS COME FOR HIM TO OWN UP

from *The Boston Globe,* November 30, 2001

News item: Groups seeking to buy the Red Sox submitted final bids yesterday. A leading contender is the Tom Werner–Les Otten group, which includes the New York Times Co., parent company of the *Boston Globe.*

The more I think about things, the Red Sox are a really swell organization. I think I've been too harsh on the Sox over the years. Sure, they've been unlucky and mired in a little championship drought, but when you really think about it, they're better than the Yankees.

Did you know the Sox were actually in first place more days than the Yankees last year? It's true. It's just one of many facts I never realized when I was being unfairly critical of the team. It was injuries and bad luck that hurt us, ah, I mean, hurt the Sox last year. And there's no doubt in my mind that had the Sox made it to the World Series, they would have beaten the Diamondbacks. When it comes to lefty starters, I'll take Casey Fossum over Randy Johnson every time.

The Sox are great and we are darn lucky to have them in our midst. What would life be like without the old hometown team? They entertain us for 12 months every year.

We are truly blessed.

Carl Everett? Misunderstood. Carl is a very religious guy and I think we should go easy on him for a while. Let's give him a 10th chance. What matters is what a player does on the field.

Joe Kerrigan? Not the buffoon you think he is. Kerrigan is actually Casey Stengel in the making. Players absolutely love the guy. He's even developed new treatment for pitchers who can't decide between ice bags and heating pads. Like the pitching coach in *Rookie of the Year,* Joe's using hot ice. Best of both worlds.

Also, pay no attention to that fabricated account of Pedro Martinez peeling off his uniform and going home to the Dominican in September. Pedro actually went home as part of a Red Sox recruiting mission on the island. Totally sanctioned by the team.

Doc Pappas? The best. We used to worry about that apparent conflict of interest with him being a limited partner and all, but upon further review, that was no big deal. Reasonable people know professionals can't be compromised by such conflicts. We were silly to even bring it up.

Some folks complain about the Sox having the highest ticket prices in baseball. "Phooey," I say. Fenway Park is a religious shrine and you can't put a price on a spiritual experience. The Sox are a bargain at any price, and fans able to score tickets should feel privileged.

And as much as I love John Harrington and the Yawkey legacy, things are only going to get better under this new ownership group.

Tom Werner did a great job when he owned the Padres. They were championship-caliber almost every year, sort of. Heck, Werner is the genius behind *Roseanne,* one of the brilliant TV programs of any generation. He's got local roots (I think he ate at Durgin Park once), and he's Katie Couric's boyfriend. It'll be great having smilin' Katie in the owner's box.

What is there to say about Les Otten that hasn't already been said? He's a sports marketing maven and ran American Skiing Co. until it crashed because of bad weather up north. He's humble. Best of all, Les is good pals with my man, Dan Duquette. There can be no higher character reference. Any friend of Dan Duquette is a friend of New England sports.

These guys plan to rebuild Fenway at the present site, which any architect or structural engineer will tell you is a great idea. The Fenway Project promises to be the Big Dig of ballpark renovation. Maybe the Sox can play home games in the old Foxboro Stadium while Fenway is being rebuilt.

Curse of the Bambino? Forget about that, too. The Sox have merely been unlucky. I'm going to have the silly *Curse* book taken out of print and write a more upbeat Sox tome: *Rise Up and Fight Again.* Comes from *Canterbury Tales.* Inspiring, don't you think?

From this point forward, Sox publicist Kevin "Dean Wormer"

Shea is my new top source, and the Red Sox Web site will be my well of information. Maybe we'll even print transcripts of Radio Free Duquette.

No more coverage of the Bruins, Celtics, or Patriots for me. I know which is the important team in this town. And from this point forward, all the news that's fit to print about the Red Sox will be found in this column.

Those Sox sure look like world champs in 2002. This is our year. And I mean "our."

SOX ON CUSP OF BEING FREED
"Carpetbaggers" Taking Over

from *The Worcester Telegram & Gazette,* December 22, 2001

Red Sox fans know too sickeningly well about the dangers of celebrating too early.

Although John Harrington appears to have left his fingerprints behind, the Sox are on the verge of being delivered from almost 70 years of incompetent idiot ownership under varying editions of the Yawkey banner.

The people who gave New England baseball fans drunken general managers, bigoted managers and clueless bullies in uniform should soon be gone.

Is this good?

It can't be any worse, at the very least.

The new bosses spoke yesterday about their plans for Fenway Park, but where the Red Sox play in Boston is nowhere near as important as who populates the front office. The first order of business for John Henry's group is to do a cave-by-cave search and fumigate the executive suites along Yawkey Way — get rid of General Manager Dan Duquette and the sycophantic bobble-head dolls he has hired to assure him that his blunders are all good ideas.

And you wondered how Joe Kerrigan got the manager's job, didn't you?

The new owners — assuming that Henry is approved by his close friends throughout baseball, wink-wink — are from out of town, and the word "carpetbagger" has been mentioned more than once.

Where they are from is irrelevant. George Steinbrenner came from Cleveland, after all, and has somehow managed to put together a pretty strong franchise in New York. The last native New Englander to own the Red Sox was John I. Taylor, of the *Boston Globe* Taylors, and that's going on 90 years ago now.

Duquette is the real problem, and he's a native New Englander. That shows how significant a birth certificate is as a qualification for owning, or running, the Boston Red Sox.

No matter what the new owners do, it will take years for fans to notice much difference. The game is still about the players, and one Pedro Martinez is a lot more important than a dozen billionaires when it comes time to check the standings.

In the ownership shuffle after the death of Tom Yawkey in 1976, the Haywood Sullivan–Buddy LeRoux group did not start running the team until 1978. That was, despite the playoff loss to the Yankees, one of the most powerful Sox teams ever.

Sullivan's lack of money didn't start to become a factor until the early '80s, when he let Carlton Fisk go and traded away players such as Fred Lynn and Rick Burleson for cheaper bodies. The franchise didn't recover from that trough until 1986, after Lou Gorman had come in to add some foam to the wave created by Roger Clemens.

The new men in town face two immediate challenges if they are to stay competitive in a division that includes the best franchise in the game, the Yankees.

They have to do something about the ballpark and do something about the farm system.

The ballpark should be easy. Fenway is one of the franchise's greatest assets and need only be modernized a bit, not destroyed. The major difference in revenues between the Sox and the Yankees is not in ticket income, but in local TV money. A new ballpark won't address that issue, and Boston baseball fans have shown they will pay almost any price to watch their team play, no matter how inept it is.

The farm system is in worse shape than the Argentine economy. It will take years to rebuild, and that should be new ownership's first area of concentration. The lack of a decent farm system is why Sox fans have had to suffer through the likes of Rolando Arrojo and Jose Offerman, lo, these many years.

They may be from out of town. They may even be out to lunch.

But the new owners of the Red Sox have two things going for them as they prepare to take control of the franchise:

Their last names are neither Yawkey nor Harrington.

In addition to the Globe *and* Herald, *a number of other newspapers throughout New England cover the Red Sox on a daily basis. Bill Ballou is one of the best and most independent of these reporters. After the utter collapse of the team over the final weeks of the 2001 season, Ballou's relief at the sale of the Red Sox is representative of the way most Red Sox reporters looked at the event.*

TONY MASSAROTTI

DUKE'S LAST HURRAH?

from *The Boston Herald,* December 23, 2001

It was a week that began with the departure of Carl Everett and cul-
minated with the arrival of John Henry, and along the way the Red
Sox underwent a change in philosophies as well as one in ownership. And on Friday, after the new caretakers of the Red Sox held
their inaugural press conference, a crowded room at Fenway Park
cleared out and filled up again, the latter instance to acknowledge
the arrival of a potentially dynamic new leadoff man.

Said Sox vice president of baseball operations Mike Port amid all
the coming and going at the old ballpark: "It's like a split doubleheader here."

This has been quite a recent stretch for the Red Sox and their fans,
from the winter meetings that began in Boston on Dec. 9 to the dramatic events of Friday. What it all has reaffirmed is this is a Red Sox
town first and foremost, no matter what the Patriots are doing. New
ownership partner Tom Werner said he has been "a passionate baseball fan for all my life" when he joined Henry and Larry Lucchino at
the podium on Friday, and if it's passion he wants now, he's come to
the right place.

Of course, optimism typically sprouts at this time of year, the bitterness of a frustrating season past replaced by the hope of one approaching. We are now closer to the start of spring training than we
are to the conclusion of the wretched 2001 season, and if there is
anything that we have learned in Boston it is that people have short
memories. A year ago at this time, the Sox were celebrating the signing of Manny Ramirez to a $160 million contract, only to see that
hope swallowed up in a season filled with bitterness. Now the hopes
are pinned to Johnny Damon and Dustin Hermanson and perhaps

Pokey Reese, the last of whom the Sox are desperately trying to keep and who further changes the dynamic of the club.

From the old to the new, the one thing everyone seems to agree on is that the Red Sox have improved to the point where they are, well, interesting.

"We're pretty far down the road as far as the constitution of the team," said Lucchino, who will oversee the day-to-day operation of the club as president and CEO. "I think this team is better now than it was last year."

Said current general manager Dan Duquette: "Just watching us play last year, it was pretty clear that we needed more team speed."

Duquette is resentful of the recent speculation about his job security, largely because he has spent so much time lately making significant, productive changes. During the winter meetings, more than one loyal aide lauded Duquette for working tirelessly to improve the ballclub, and the first domino fell when Everett was sent to Texas. In the days immediately following, Duquette acquired Hermanson and John Burkett, then traded for Reese. When the Damon signing came together, a hard budget forced the Sox to nontender the second baseman, though Duquette will exhaust all energy to re-sign him.

Should the Sox retain Reese, the team would grow even more intriguing. In Pokey, the Sox would have someone alongside Nomar Garciaparra who could turn a double play, something that really hasn't happened here since 1997 when Jeff Frye was healthy. And with Damon atop the batting order, the Sox would likely have a lineup sequence of Reese (batting ninth), Damon (first), Trot Nixon (second) and Garciaparra (third), all of whom are good baserunners with average to above-average speed.

When was the last time THAT happened at Fenway Park?

So, after a year in which the overpriced, underachieving Red Sox fielded a beer-bellied softball squad ripe with big names, big salaries and bad attitudes, the Sox seem to have been injected with some much-needed energy and youth. Brian Daubach, who will turn 30 in February, could be the oldest member of an infield in which Reese, Garciaparra and third baseman Shea Hillenbrand all possess above-average range. For all of the concerns about Hillenbrand's defense during the first half of last season, most of his problems came on throws. Late in the year, from July 5 through Sept. 4, Hillenbrand played 43 consecutive games without an error, a noteworthy streak at any position.

Offensively, however, the Sox may now be more equipped to (gasp) manufacture runs, something they have not done . . . ever? Apparently lined with undetectable doses of lead, the Sox uniform weighed down even the fleetest runners in past years. Deposed lead-off man Jose Offerman came to Boston off a 45-steal season in 1998 and has since swiped all of 23 bases (five last season) during his three years with the Sox. As a result, Offerman is now Mike Lansing, a backup with a $6.5 million salary, and it is his contract as much as anyone else's that forced the Sox' hand on Reese.

While Duquette refused to say he regretted signing Offerman to a four-year, $26 million contract before the 1999 season, he did say this: "We already have a $6.5 million second baseman in Offerman, so that's the reality we have to deal with . . . My concern about Jose is that in the last couple of years he hasn't had his speed."

Damon, meanwhile, will play center field and bump Trot Nixon back to right, a decision that benefits the Sox in a pair of areas. Despite manager Joe Kerrigan's ideas of keeping Nixon in center, Duquette was quick to point out that Damon has better range and Nixon a better arm. "The good news for our pitching staff," said Duquette, "is that both of those guys can really run down the ball."

Ah yes, the pitching staff. Duquette proved right on Hideo Nomo, offering the right-hander a three-year, $21 million deal that the pitcher turned down before accepting a two-year, $13 million package from the Los Angeles Dodgers. (That's less, right?) The Sox' offer to Nomo included $1 million of deferred money in each of the three seasons, something the pitcher was unwilling to accept. So now Nomo gets $6.5 million from the Dodgers, which nearly makes him this winter's answer to Jody Reed.

To his credit, Duquette lined up his options well during this offseason, especially given the fact he had several needs to fill. Until the Sox surprisingly non-tendered Reese, Duquette added three starting pitchers (OK, maybe two if you don't count Darren Oliver) as well as a leadoff man and a second baseman. He also disposed of the problematic Everett without taking on a significant financial burden, not to be overlooked given the fact the new owners do not appear to be as aggressive financially as their predecessor.

In the end what Duquette has done here is make some rather

shrewd moves, though that is not completely a surprise. The Duquette Era has not been nearly the disaster that many are now making it out to be, primarily because the Sox thrice advanced to the postseason during his tenure. Duquette brought Pedro Martinez and Garciaparra to Boston, and made the trade that delivered Derek Lowe and Jason Varitek for Heathcliff Slocumb. He took a chance on Tim Wakefield. He signed Rich Garces. He even plucked someone like Daubach, whose production numbers over his first three seasons have been frighteningly consistent. Look 'em up.

The biggest indictment against Duquette, of course, has been the deterioration of the Red Sox' farm system, a fact that contributed mightily to the team's problems a year ago. Part of the reason the Red Sox were forced to spend $110 million on their payroll last season is because they had no better, more reasonably-priced options in their minor-league system. And while some may question giving a four-year contract to someone like Damon, who had all of 14 RBI after the All-Star break last season, the simple fact is there isn't anyone on the horizon from the minor leagues that could supplant Damon in the near future.

And the Sox were forced to spend again, which is something the new owners clearly want to address.

"The Boston Red Sox certainly have the revenues to compete with anyone and revenue drives payroll," Henry said on Friday. "But even with a large payroll, you have to maximize the effect of every dollar and you have to have a strong farm system. One of our first orders of the day is to put emphasis on the player development system."

Eight years ago, of course, Duquette said precisely the same thing.

But then, the beauty of baseball in Boston is that there is always something to talk about.

Massarotti's Sunday column for the Boston Herald, "Covering the Bases," has become indispensable, and he appears frequently on local television and radio. Massarotti was a particularly acute observer of controversial general manager Dan Duquette, who, along with manager Joe Kerrigan, would be let go by the team during spring training in 2002 as the new regime sought to break with the past.

LOOKING FOR TED WILLIAMS

from *Boston Baseball*, July 2002

I heard a rumor, but I don't believe it for a minute. Ted Williams isn't dead.

Close your eyes for a minute and look. Do you see it? All green and gorgeous? Ted's house — Fenway Park. Mid-summer, in the sunshine. Ted Williams isn't dead. He's everywhere here.

I'll show you. See up there, way, way, way up in right field? See the red seat? Ted's still there — section 42, row 37, seat 21 — 502 feet from home plate. In 1946 he hit a home run that landed there. Well, sort of. It put a hole in the straw hat of an engineer from Albany.

Now look up a little farther. The Jimmy Fund sign. No one's ever done more for the Jimmy Fund than Ted. Even when Ted was getting booed and fighting with the press and complaining about everything, that all stopped when it came time to go to a hospital and see a sick kid. See, when Ted was a kid and his mother spent all her time with the Salvation Army and his dad was away even more, Ted just about had to raise his little brother, Danny, all by himself. Then Ted ran away to play baseball and Danny got in trouble and then got cancer and died. Ted never said "no" to the Jimmy Fund.

Now look over to your right, on the façade of the roof. 9–4–1–8–42. The way it was before they changed it. The way it should be now.

Everybody knows number 9. That's Ted. First, as ever.

He's right next to number 4, Joe Cronin, Ted's first manager. Ted drove Cronin and everyone else crazy in his first spring training. He never shut up and he never stopped thinking about hitting. But he was too young. When Cronin sent him down to the minors and a few vets gave Ted the business on his way out the door, Ted vowed he'd come back and make more than all of them put together. He was right, and he did.

Then there's number 1, Bobby Doerr, who played with Ted in the Pacific Coast League, the only guy on the team who could calm Ted down. When Ted talks about "my guys," he means Doerr, Dom DiMaggio, and Johnny Pesky. His guys.

And number 8, Yaz, Ted's successor out in left field. During Yastrzemski's first camp with the Sox Ted gave Yaz a long complicated lecture about hitting. When Ted finished and walked away, Yaz turned to a reporter, almost shaking, and admitted, "I can't understand half of what he says . . . He scares me." And then there's number 42, Jackie, who should've played with Ted and would've if the men who ran the Red Sox had been half as smart as Ted was. You know what Ted said when he was inducted into the Hall of Fame in 1966, don't you? He said, "Baseball gives every American boy a chance to excel. Not just to be as good as somebody else, but to be better. This is the nature of man and the name of the game. I hope some day Satchel Paige and Josh Gibson will be voted into the Hall of Fame as symbols of the great Negro players who are not here only because they weren't given the chance."

That's right, that's what he said. Ted Williams was the first guy, the *very first guy*, to bring this up. And this was in 1966, when it wasn't cool or p.c. to talk about such things, but he did anyway because that's the way Ted was. He just thought it was right and he said it. Five years later the Hall of Fame took Ted's advice.

Now look down a little lower. That's right, look at the bullpens, where a lot of pitchers got a lot of extra work because of Ted. Tom Yawkey had them built in the winter after Ted's rookie year so he could hit more home runs. Didn't work, at least in 1940, when Ted tried too hard and didn't hit a single home run there. The press called it Williamsburg, but the name never really took. It made the fans mad, if you can believe it. They thought Ted was getting special treatment. They were right of course. Ted's always been special.

See the awning above the bench where the Red Sox pitchers sit? Out toward center field? Yeah. That's where Ted's last home run, number 521, the one that made John Updike famous, landed. Smacked it off Baltimore's Jack Fisher in the eighth inning on September 28, 1960. Ted didn't stop at home, didn't tip his cap, just crossed home plate and ran into the dugout and sat there by himself.

Notice how big right field is? The biggest in baseball. That's where Ted played his rookie year, 1939, all arms and legs and enthusiasm. Between pitches, he'd stand out there and practice his swing. When the fans cheered him, he'd pluck his hat off his head by that little button and wave it like mad. Oh god, the fans. They loved him at first, and truth to be told, Ted loved them. That's why he got so damn mad later, when he got booed. You have to care about something to get angry about it, and Ted cared.

Now look out to left field. That's where they moved Ted in 1940, to save his eyes. It worked, and Ted learned to play the wall when it was part tin, part wood, part concrete, when it had dead spots like the parquet floor at the Boston Garden and the scoreboard was bigger and had National League scores, too. Ted played the wall well. This was before it was called the Green Monster. This was when it was covered with ads for Gem Blades and Calvert Gin.

Oh, but the fans in left. With the wall catching the sound behind him, Ted could hear everything they said. And the fans were so close, they could see Ted's ears turn red. The thing's they'd say — God, he'd get mad! But you know what? That's what drove him, that's what got him going. The things they said and stuff those writers, the Knights of the Keyboard, the stuff they wrote. Every word just made him madder. And then Ted would pick up the bat, he'd pick up the bat and walk to home plate and dig in and look out to the pitcher, *another guy* trying to make him look bad, and Ted would dig in, and then, and then . . .

You can't help but look to home. That's where Ted really lived, in that little 4x6 box on the first base side of home plate, focused on that invisible rectangle exactly seventeen inches wide above home plate from his knee to his shoulder, and the square inch or so on his bat where he tried to hit the ball every time. Remember the picture in Ted's book, *The Science of Hitting*, with all the different colored baseballs in the strike zone with Ted's batting average on them when he swung at those pitches? When I first read that book when I was a kid, I thought Ted actually saw all those colored baseballs coming at him, and that he picked out the one with the highest number to hit, and that's why he was so good. Maybe he did see them.

Because no one else in baseball history ever spent more time at bat, saw more pitches, cursed more or swung more than Ted Williams. Forget about his off-the-chart 20/10 eyesight or the one-in-a-million reflexes. Ted Williams was about practice. Said so himself. Listen: "There's never been a kid who hit more baseballs than Ted Williams."

Think about that for a minute, because Ted might be right. When he was a kid, a little kid, he spent hours and hours at the playground, swinging a bat. And he never stopped, not really. I think that anytime Ted was doing anything else he loved, like fishing or flying, he was, in a way, still just swinging the bat, concentrating, looking for a strike, tuning out the world and focusing on only one thing, the only thing that mattered, what he was trying to do right now.

That's the first, best, and only lesson of hitting right there. Hell, it's the only lesson of doing anything.

Can you see him? Can you see him swing?

Ted Williams isn't dead. Close your eyes, and there he is again, bigger than life.

Number 9. Swinging. Kissing it goodbye and walking down the street.

The greatest hitter who ever lived.

For the past 13 years, publisher Mike Rutstein's independent magazine Boston Baseball *has been a thorn in the side of the Red Sox, proving more popular and provocative than their authorized publication. This selection appeared in a special edition shortly after Ted Williams's death.*

CREDITS AND PERMISSIONS

INDEX